W9-AFA-738

B. Affinity Identities;
iii. International

ARE YOU TWO . . . TOGETHER?

ARE YOU TWO... TOGETHER?

A Gay and Lesbian Travel Guide to Europe

Lindsy Van Gelder
& Pamela Robin Brandt

RANDOM HOUSE   NEW YORK

Library of Congress Cataloging-in-Publication Data
Van Gelder, Lindsy.
Are you two . . . together?/Lindsy Van Gelder and Pamela Robin Brandt.
p.   cm.
ISBN 0-679-73599-2
1. Europe—Description and travel—1971–   —Guide-books.   2. Gays—Travel—Europe
—Guide-books.   I. Brandt, Pamela Robin.   II. Title.
D909.V284 1991   914'.04559'08664—DC20   90-53479

Manufactured in the United States of America

24689753

FIRST EDITION

Book Design by Carole Lowenstein

To Our Parents:

Doris Marshall Brandt
Mel Brandt
Marilynn Chamberlain Evans
Les Evans

Allons! the road is before us!
It is safe—I have tried it—my own feet have tried it well—be not detain'd!
. . . Camerado, I give you my hand!
I give you my love more precious than money,
I give you myself before preaching or law;
Will you give me yourself? will you come travel with me?
Shall we stick by each other as long as we live?

    —*Walt Whitman, "Song of the Open Road," from* Leaves of Grass

    Follow the yellow brick road.

      —The Munchkins

ACKNOWLEDGMENTS

Because this book would never have happened without her matchmaking, we first thank Gloria Steinem for fixing us up, as it were, with Random House—and also for the book's title.

Despite our *extreme* bitterness that they remained skinny and fabulous-looking while we ate our way around Europe, we'd like to thank our editor Susan Kamil and our agent Kathy Robbins, both of whom never stopped believing in this book's potential even during our periods of artsy-fartsy grouchiness. We also thank Karen Rinaldi, Carole Lowenstein, and Mitchell Ivers from Random House, as well as Elizabeth Mackey from The Robbins Office, for Taking Care of Business so we could just travel, write, and do all the other fun stuff.

Without our hawk-eyed copy editor, Jolanta Benal, we would have called nipple clamps "clips," hopelessly muddled our report on international hanky codes, and committed numerous other P.I. faux pas.

In Europe, numerous folks helped us to discover the best gay life in their various locales. A complete list of these Fairy Godmothers and Godfathers would require a supplementary book. For service above and beyond, however, we thank Marian Lens, Hugo Vloeberghs, Ann David, Claudia Weinzierl, Bizoux De Clerq, Chris Tillieu, and Christine Moens in Belgium; Catherine Gonnard, Catherine Durand, the late Joseph Doucé, and Daniel Placenti in France; C. Hughes in Wales; Peter Glencross, Ginger daSilva, and Mike Wells in the Netherlands; Giovanni dall'Orto in Italy; Hanne Christiansen and Lisbeth Jørgensen in Denmark; Peter Hedenstrom, Piet van der Waals, and Kerstin Handau in Berlin; and former International Lesbian and Gay Association information secretary David Murphy.

Additionally, many American friends, gay and straight, provided moral and professional support, especially Jane Alpert, Mary Kay Blakely, Sherryl

Connelly, Ed Cripps, Joe Tom Easley, Peter Freiberg, Nancy Haberman, Sharon Kahn, Deborah Kane, Judy Wenning, Perry Deane Young, the Third Thursday Writers Group, and the Garden Party. We owe ya one, kids.

Finally, thanks to WordPerfect Corporation for its Macintosh–to–IBM PC file exchange.

CONTENTS

INTRODUCTION

The real reason we wrote this book is that we wanted to read it.

Ever since we became a couple, in 1978, we've taken to the road together whenever we've had the chance. Nor are we alone. One recent survey by a gay-oriented marketing company showed that gay people are seven times more likely to be signed up for frequent-flier benefit programs than the population at large. Business is booming for gay inns, travel agencies, and specialized tours.

Perhaps gay men and lesbians are natural travelers, because we're more likely to be what the demographers call DINKs (Dual Income, No Kids), or because too many of us still need R and R away from the literal straight-jacket of the workaday closet . . . or simply because the outsider perspective of the traveler is a second skin for us. Most of us have that twitchy sixth sense known as gay-dar. It makes us quick studies at reading between cultural lines—and old hands at anticipating new pleasures around every corner.

As much as the two of us love to travel, we've been frustrated by the scarcity of gay travel writing. There are plenty of gay guidebooks out there; but too often they've seemed to us to be poorly researched (i.e., relying on secondhand and severely aged information from nonprofessional volunteer correspondents), single-mindedly focused on bars and cruising, and/or unvaryingly complimentary toward establishments that just happen to be advertisers. Even the best ones we've seen have consisted almost entirely of listings, with no travel *writing*. Where was the information about gay culture and gay history? Where were our Jan Morrises, our Bruce Chatwins, our M.F.K. Fishers?

One place they're usually not is the straight travel press, where articles about even flamingly queer places may hint at our presence with only a coded reference to "bohemians" or "artists." ("Hey, Mom and Dad, I'm bohemian"?) With a few commendable exceptions such as the backpacker-oriented *Let's Go* and *Real Guide* series, which occasionally mention a gay bar or disco, the mainstream guidebooks also often pretend we don't exist. Unless, of course, you count the guides that sometimes cite us as swishy, resort-ruining fellow travelers to avoid.

We hope we've written something to fill this gap. The book you're reading is the very first gay travel guide to be brought out by a major American publishing house.

We've picked fourteen destinations of special interest to gay men and lesbians: primarily major gay capitals and resorts, like Amsterdam and Sitges, but also sites with gay historical roots, such as King Ludwig's castles in Bavaria and the home of the "Ladies of Llangollen" in north Wales. Since our expense account regrettably didn't last forever, we had to miss Hamburg, Antwerp, Ibiza, and several other places with lively gay scenes. We also left out some locales we and most other tourists love, like Rome and the Swiss Alps, that simply don't have much gay life.

Our essays about these fourteen destinations are designed to be savored not just by Europe-bound gay people, but by armchair travelers of any orientation who are curious to see how gay men and lesbians, past and present, fit into the map of Europe. For those of you who do intend to get up off your futons and go, each chapter is followed by a Practical Information section in which we list selected hotels, both gay and straight-but-guaranteed-gay-friendly, as well as restaurants, discos, bars, and other enterprises popular with gay locals and travelers, plus general information about what to do and how to get around.

According to conventional wisdom, our book might be taken more seriously by the critics (and would no doubt have a longer shelf life) if we restricted ourselves to the established boundaries of the travel-writing genre —i.e., if we stuck to the essays and skipped the "service-oriented" information entirely. (Perhaps you've noticed that Jan Morris doesn't tell you where to go dancing?) Classy coffee table–type ladies that we are, we nonetheless couldn't imagine whetting the wanderlust of our gay brothers and sisters, and then abandoning you all to the whims of homophobic innkeepers. We like to think of this book as a whole new genre of travel writing, period . . . a category we can best describe by imagining that Paul Theroux and Arthur Frommer could have a baby together, and that the kid would grow up to write gay guidebooks.

On the other hand, we make no pretense of being either comprehensive or objective in our recommendations; quite unapologetically, these are highly selective and subjective. We found 'em and we like 'em. If your tastes in gay international establishments run to atmospheric rather than generic, to friendly fun rather than cool cruising, they'll be your kind of places, too.

We've tried to be scrupulously accurate, even though that isn't as easy as it sounds. (Hey, Flash, you think *your* beer-soaked handwriting would be all that easy to decipher after a night of meticulous research in the hottest gay bars in Berlin?) But be forewarned: Gay clubs in Europe go in and out of style, and in and out of business, just as fast as they do in Boston, Toronto, or L.A. We'll never forget the time we followed a guidebook's tip to what was supposed to be a fabulous lesbian bistro on the French Riviera. Instead we hit a heterosexual wedding party, all dolled up in their Sunday best and a bit surprised to spot us in our spandex. With that in mind, we've tried, wherever possible, to point you toward sources where you can find the most up-to-date information when you blow into a new place—usually a gay center, bookstore, local guidebook, or newspaper.

Although our primary emphasis is on couples, we hope many of our suggestions will be useful to singles. This is also emphatically a book for both men and women. As a point of information, we often use the adjective "gay" (as opposed to the clunkier "gay male and lesbian") to refer to both genders, but after a couple of experiences of our own at "gay" places which turned out not to welcome gay *women,* we don't assume that other people necessarily intend the term to be inclusive. If anything, "gay" is more likely to mean "male" in Europe than in North America. Most of the gay establishments we've listed are at least officially open to both genders, even if they're largely frequented by one or the other. When they're not, we say so.

We also occasionally employ terms like "queer" and "dyke." Although we appreciate that some of you might wince at being described as anything but "gay and lesbian" where straight folks can overhear, a lot of us often do use the less politically correct words among friends. They appear in this book in the same *entre nous* spirit of affectionate irony. We're old enough to remember when "gay" was an insult. It's our hope that eventually *no* description of sexual orientation will carry an automatic sting.

A question we've often been asked by well-meaning straight people in the course of our research is why gay readers require a special guide at all. Why, if we're fighting to establish ourselves as part of the larger culture, don't we simply use the guidebooks that everybody else reads? The short answer is that we do—and this book isn't intended to be a substitute for something that tells you the opening and closing times of the Louvre, much less the history of Renaissance sculpture. But gay men and lesbians also need information that the average straight tourist never has to think about.

For starters, there's the specter of homophobia: the ever-present possibility that we won't be welcome, and may even encounter overt harassment, *especially* if we relax and enjoy ourselves . . . which is, after all, one of the reasons people go on vacation in the first place. Anticipating hassles can be particularly nerve-racking in a foreign country, where it's often hard to distinguish among xenophobia, homophobia, a simple language barrier, and relatively nonhostile unfamiliarity with gays.

Beyond the survival basics, we need to know where to find each other —including those of us who aren't necessarily on the prowl for a trick or a lover. Surely one of the joys of foreign travel is the recognition of part of oneself in a stranger, whether it's someone you just met in a train compartment or someone in a portrait painted centuries ago. And surely, if there's a universal human experience, it's love. Tourists who barely speak each other's languages whip out their wallets and show each other family snapshots. Visitors from every corner of the globe flock to the balcony where Romeo supposedly wooed Juliet, the fountain where Petrarch composed odes to Laura, the graves of Héloïse and Abelard, and the palaces of Louis XVI and Marie Antoinette.

Unfortunately, those of us who might find more inspiration in the stomping grounds of Hadrian and Antinoüs or Gertrude and Alice won't get much help from the typical chamber of commerce. All the world may love a lover, but when you and *your* lover are all dressed up for a romantic evening on the town, the maitre d' at Chez Hetero may well peer *behind* you in search of the expected opposite-gender double-date mates, and finally ask, with mingled surprise and distaste, "Are you two . . . *together*?"

We hope our book will give aid and comfort to those of you who, like us, don't want to choose between spending their entire vacations in the gay ghetto or else sleeping in twin beds and never holding hands at dinner.

But we think you'll also discover, as we have, that being a friend of Dorothy's—or one of her *amies* or *amigos*—is a terrific way to see Europe.

Most tourists never get to meet anyone but desk clerks, cab drivers, and waiters. Gay travelers have a resource other visitors don't: a built-in international community of our own. Long before 1992, gay Europeans were sharing a culture, which is your culture, too. Walk into a gay bar or center in any country, and you stand a good chance of walking out with new friends who've been moved by Walt Whitman, Natalie Barney, Harvey Fierstein, David Leavitt, Edmund White, Alison Bechdel, Armistead Maupin, Keith Haring, and Rita Mae Brown, as well as Cocteau, Gide, Wilde, Woolf, Isherwood, García Lorca, Sappho, Rosa Bonheur, Marguerite Yourcenar, Gerard Reve, Anna Blaman, Magnus Hirschfeld, Jimmy Somerville, and Tom of Finland; who march in Gay Pride parades at the end of June (but who are inspired as well by Paris in the teens, Berlin in the twenties, and Greece in the fifth century); who worry, just as you do, about coming out, parents, children, AIDS, politics, lovers, ex-lovers—all the usual suspects . . . and who also know how to have a good time.

You may be a foreigner, but you won't be a stranger.

ARE YOU TWO . . . TOGETHER?

GAY EUROPE

The Basics

$\mathcal{O}$n January 15, 1990—Martin Luther King, Jr.'s birthday, as fate would have it—two gay men were refused a double room at a hotel in Gerona, an old cathedral town not far from Barcelona. Instead of slinking off miserably to the boudoir equivalent of the back of the bus, they called in FAGC, the Catalan gay liberation organization. In an inspired protest, FAGC installed an ornate, hand-carved, king-sized bed in the street outside the hotel, where two men cuddled and frolicked between the sheets for the assembled crowds of onlookers, reporters, and photographers.

May it go down in gay history as the bedspring squeak heard 'round the world.

We've never been denied a room outright, in Europe or anywhere else. For that matter, we've gone whole vacations with nothing more traumatic than a few raised eyebrows. But we certainly know gay male and lesbian couples who *have* been treated like Space Invaders. Just the prospect is usually enough to make us approach the mildest-mannered desk clerk with our hearts slightly in our throats.

If you're taking your first trip to Europe, or your first trip as part of a gay couple, you might want to know that the ease of getting a double bed varies from country to country and according to the fanciness of the hotel. In rural France, it's sometimes hard *not* to get one, especially in the smaller, cheaper hotels. In theory, complete closet cases could probably ask for a twin, or simply for *une chambre,* and then sportingly accept a double. Small hotels all over Europe also often have "family" rooms with a double bed and one or more singles. You're charged according to how many beds you use. If the two of you pile into the double, the management may conveniently assume you're just trying to save money, especially if you're backpackers.

On the other hand, forget Germany and Austria: About the best you can do in most hotels, regardless of your sexual preference, is a double-*sized* bed with two mattresses—and a snuggle-inhibiting crack in the middle. *If* you're lucky. We once had one with an iron bar down the center.

If you're adamantly toting your closet along with the rest of your luggage and you want to play it absolutely safe, you'll have to ask for rooms with Ozzie-and-Harriet twin beds, mess one up for the benefit of the maid, and squeeze into the other with your sweetie, probably throwing your back out in the process. U.S.-style individual-entrance motels—where you can do an end run around the front desk so they'll never know there are two people in that one-bed room—are a rarity. So are big chain hotels featuring your basic American-style rooms with two king-sized beds. Not that we'd recommend a clean-clone chain joint anyway. If what turns you on is a hotel that looks like it could be in either Paris, Texas, or Paris, France, send us your tickets to Europe toot sweet and we'll reserve *you* a room at Newark Airport. Totally apart from our comfort as gay travelers, we tend to prefer small, charming, moderately priced hotels, and that taste is reflected in the Practical Information listings in this book.

The best alternatives we've found involve the old fait accompli. Method A, the simplest: Make your reservations for double-bedded accommodations before you leave home. Method B, a variation on the same ploy: One of you books the room while the other waits at the railroad station or in the car with the luggage. Arrange all the details and get the key. When you return with a husband instead of a wife, or vice versa, just head directly for your room and hope for the best.

In either scenario, you might get some perplexed grilling about whether you really wanted a double-bed room, or "matrimonial chamber," as it's comically known in most of the Romance languages. But don't throw in the guest towel and automatically assume that the probing is hostile. Especially in efficient countries like Switzerland, the asker may only be trying to do a good job.

Even in situations involving iffier motivations, what almost always works is a positive-thinking approach that takes full advantage of the affable yet rock-solid stupidity for which we Americans are so deservedly famous. Just nod at the clerk's query and smile earnestly, as if you're negotiating nothing more controversial than whether you prefer tea or coffee with your breakfast. Odds are at this point that even if the hotel thinks you're scum, they'll realize it's more trouble to hassle you than to accommodate you. Especially if you've already plunked down a deposit. A Bavarian innkeeper once solemnly explained to us that the kind of room we had booked was only for a *Herr und Frau*. *"Ja, ja,"* we beamed. We did get the room.

Alas, no method is foolproof, as a lesbian friend of ours discovered one night in Nice. When the patroness realized that our friend had reappeared with another woman post-registration, she took it as a personal affront. Within earshot of several other guests, she screamed that they wouldn't get away with bringing this sort of filth onto *her* premises. Then she grabbed the key out of their hands.

It was late, and the women were getting up early the next morning to catch a plane. They had already tried several other hotels without finding a vacant room. Their car was safely parked and they'd lugged all their bags into the lobby. As shaken as they were by the whole scene, the couple stood their ground, repeating that the nature of their relationship was none of the hotel's business. This just sent the patroness into new fits of frenzy. Finally another employee arranged a "compromise," whereby the lesbians were permitted to stay in the hotel, but only in a room with respectable twin beds. Naturally, they pushed the beds together, and left them there. But the memory made them feel bad for months after—not exactly one for the "What We Did on Our Vacation" scrapbook.

Even when the management does deign to take your cootie-covered money *and* actually provide you with your furniture of choice, you still may have to tough out their disapproval. On one occasion in the Gascony region of southwestern France, the desk clerk tried with much fanfare to book us into *two* rooms, *each* with a double bed. We thought she simply didn't get it, but we later overheard her and another hotel staffer complaining about *"les lesbiennes."* As a parting gesture the next morning, we turned on a pay shower with the wrench in our trusty Swiss Army knife, which, being good little *lesbiennes*, we carry at all times. Stooping to their level was doubtless not the ideal solution. But we're certain it will comfort us in our old age.

Hotels are the worst land mines, but by no means the only ones. We have two gay male friends who had the wind punched out of their vacation-bound sails when a flight attendant asked them to stop holding hands. It seems they were "offending" a fellow passenger. (We'd bet our in-flight headsets that if this turkey had been offended by someone's race or religion, *he* would have been the one who was told to stuff it.)

For lesbians, public displays of affection are less inflammatory, but there's the extra added attraction, especially outside the northern European capitals, of constantly being perceived by straight men as women out "alone." The expression "lesbian invisibility" took on new meaning for us in Prague, where Lindsy tried her hardest to flaunt her homosexuality at an especially crude bartender who had waylaid her on the way to the john. Since she didn't know how to say "You ain't just barking up the wrong tree, asshole, you're in the wrong forest" in Czech, she tossed out the words for "lesbian" and "gay" in English, French, Italian, and German. Nothing penetrated. Pam, who had been waiting outside, later wondered: "Why the hell didn't you just tell him, *like Martina?*"

Then there was the time a very young waiter at a restaurant on the French Riviera danced attendance on Pam all through dinner. Finally, he asked in halting English if he could show her the lights of Cap Ferrat later that night. Like the nice person she actually isn't, but tries to be in situations involving possible conflicting cultural values, she attempted to slough him off with excuses about being busy. The fellow persisted, offering elaborate, well-meaning tips on how she could rearrange her schedule. It was all getting more complicated, rather than less, and we realized that honesty was the only expedient policy.

"I know you mean to be helpful, but it isn't only that we are busy," Pam at last gently explained. "We are also together, a couple, for many years. I have men as friends, but I do not go out with men, or with anyone but Lindsy."

He looked at us blankly. We tried it again, in French.

He sputtered that never, in his entire life, had he heard of such a bizarre thing.

Monsieur Le Garçon stalked off to the kitchen, where we heard him in animated consultation with his confrères. Before long the entire kitchen staff was hanging out the door staring at us. Our waiter spent the rest of the meal harrumphing about the room in an embarrassed sulk. Meanwhile, the other staff members could barely contain their hilarity; as the night wore on, new waves of guffaws kept wafting out of the kitchen. From what we could tell, they did, at least, seem to regard *him* as the major joke-butt jerk in the incident. The owner of the restaurant, a woman, even made a point of presenting us with a bouquet of flowers. We never figured out whether they understood that we really were lesbians, or whether they thought we'd come up with an infernally clever way to put down an unwanted suitor.

———

In this book, we've listed not only gay hotels, but straight hotels that have all been put through a regimen we've come to call the Drill. Basically the Drill goes like this: "Knock, knock. Hi! We're two lesbians from America and we're writing a guide for gay people." Here we produce dazzling smiles and Random House letterhead. "We think your hotel is charming, and if you can assure us that you welcome our readers, we'll be glad to look at a few of your rooms and consider listing you in our book."

The end result is that *all* straight and/or mixed hotels recommended herein have assured us, in person or in writing or both, that gay travelers are as welcome as straight ones.

We would have preferred kidney stones to the first couple of times we did the Drill. We expected to be pummeled by brooms, if not actually barbecued at the stake, like the good old days. But by the end of several trips to Europe in the course of researching this guide, we got so we could probably come out in our sleep.

Some of the hoteliers who didn't want their establishments listed were hopeless homophobes, pure and simple. But the news isn't all bad. It became clear, after we got ticked off and probed a few objecting proprietors, that what some of them wanted to avoid wasn't gay people in general, but the let's-walk-around-the-halls-naked-and-pee-with-the-bathroom-door-open crowd. (To be fair about such stereotyping, we were repeatedly told by *gay* innkeepers that this type is exactly what a listing in the cruising-oriented gay male guides often attracts.) "We discriminate against badly educated gay men and lesbians who make noise at night, drink too much, and play loud music," one Italian innkeeper wrote us. They discriminate against straights with the same traits. The rest of us are welcome at any time.

It also became obvious to us that what many hotels really wanted to avoid was young *straight* men, unaccompanied by women. In one of those rare cases where gross stereotypes work *for* a minority group, some hoteliers tended to perceive pairs of straight guys as potential all-night partiers and property-damagers. Gay male couples, on the contrary, were often characterized as "neat," "clean," and "real gentlemen." If you guys try to pass in their hotels, you might get bad attitude for all the wrong reasons.

A policy of honesty can work for women, too. In Mykonos, we were Drilling away at a friendly straight female official in the tourist office when an obvious dyke couple walked in and asked vaguely what there was to do in town. The official smiled, admitted there weren't whole lots of sights, and recommended a trip to Delos, the nearby antiquities-center island. The couple shuffled around, and said, yeah, they knew about that, but . . . weren't there . . . *other* . . . things to do? Looking puzzled, the official told them there was a monastery or two. On and on it went, the women finally leaving, disgruntled—just because they couldn't bring themselves to ask, "Hey, where are all the gay bars this island is so famous for?" We did ask, and left with a map on which the official had not only hand-Xed every gay hangout she knew, but rated them for us.

Once, in a small town in Belgium, we ended up having a long talk over coffee late one morning with our kind, lovely straight landlady. She told us she had left her husband for another man several years before. Because she lived in a very repressive Catholic milieu, she was branded by many of the townspeople as an adulteress and had lost custody of her children. She missed them terribly. It was clear to us that she didn't share this heartbreaking story with most people, let alone her guests. "I knew that you, too, were in a special situation," she confided, "and that you would therefore possibly understand."

Moral of all these sagas: It's tedious to come out, but sometimes it's well worth it.

Our funniest international un-closeting occurred the last time we flew into London's Gatwick Airport and ran smack into a labor slowdown by the immigration staff. Instead of simply stamping people's passports, the authorities were conducting in-depth interviews with each and every incoming jet-lagged passenger. Babies howled, tempers flared. In front of us some Swiss people who had a nonrefundable ticket on a connecting flight to Scotland went un-Swissly berserk and tried to jump the line. By the time we reached the front of the line—excuse us, the queue—we'd been waiting for more than two hours, and we were pretty pissed off ourselves.

"I see you're a journalist," said the man in uniform, settling down for a long chat. "My, that must be terribly interesting work! Tell me: Do you work for one paper, or are you a free-lance?"

"At the moment," Lindsy replied, "I'm here to research a lesbian and gay guide to Europe."

His eyes went dead.

Pam was having a similar encounter at the next booth, and we were both waved through instantly. We were struck by a mad desire to pass a note, or hold up a sign, to the sweating, cursing throngs behind us: "Wanna speed things up? Tell 'em you're a pervert!"

When most people think of "adventure travel," they're referring to schlepping up high mountains and down raging rivers. For gay people, of course, even well-trodden paths can be goose-pimply adventure travel, fraught with possible perils. But with the right approach—one that shuns the passive old-style tourist "show me" circuit and its corollary attitudes—a gay European tour can also be adventure travel in the most thrilling and fulfilling sense: an *active* journey into uncharted territory where you'll discover entirely new things about places modern and ancient, people present and past, and your own relationship to it all. Here are some guideposts.

Get out of the cities, at least a little. Gay men and lesbians tend to be an urban people, and your first inclination may be to stick to the big cities. Amsterdam, Paris, Prague, Venice, Rome, Edinburgh, Barcelona, Berlin, et al. are indeed faaaaabulous. But trust us: You also want to see *Europe,* the place in the fairy tales. This picturesque prewar, pre-McDonald's Europe of Hansel-and-Gretel (or Hansel-and-Hansel, or Gretel-and-Gretel) gingerbread houses, spooky Gothic towers, and thatch-roofed, rose-covered cottages is definitely more accessible outside the capitals.

Try at the very least to take some day trips into the boonies. Better yet, if you're not a hardened nightlife bunny, consider staying for part of your trip in the country, even when you're near a city, and take a day-trip *in.* The regions around Brussels, Munich, Frankfurt, Geneva, Zurich, Nice, Lisbon, and Naples are a lot more time-trippingly evocative than the cities themselves. After all, you can go to a disco at home. How often can you watch the moon rise over a medieval village?

There are no guarantees that you won't encounter homophobes in the hinterlands, but with the possible exception of Great Britain—and, tragically, post-Wall Berlin—American-style gay-bashing is practically nonexistent. Violence in general is simply not the problem in Europe that it's become in the United States—off the soccer field, anyway.

Compared to North America, Europe is easy to move around in. We're manic fans of European trains, which in most countries are fast and luxurious and take you almost anywhere, day or night. They also help you avoid European drivers, who in our experience are fast, incompetent, and suffering from advanced testosterone poisoning. Trains are vastly cheaper than planes, and they're a great place to meet people. For Americans, Canadians, and other non-Europeans we especially recommend the Eurailpass (or the cheaper rail passes offered by individual countries). Even in the unlikely—in our experience, unprecedented—event that it ends up costing you slightly more than buying your tickets one by one, a Eurailpass is still worth it for the luxurious freedom to hop on a train without time and language hassles at crowded ticket windows. One of the best deals on the pass is an off-season rate for two people traveling together, who need not be a "family."

In addition to the smaller towns and resorts described in this book, the lavender pins stuck in the map of Europe include the English resorts of Blackpool, Bournemouth, and Torquay; Riccione on the Italian Adriatic coast and Taormina in Sicily; Ibiza and the Canary Islands in Spain; the university town of Utrecht in the Netherlands; the smallish city of Aarhus in western Denmark; Cannes on the French Riviera and Biarritz on the Atlantic coast; the Yugoslav island of Rab; the Hanseatic town of Lübeck in West Germany and the island of Sylt off the German coast near the Danish border; and plenty of other places we're dying to visit and report on—next time.

As for foreseeing the next wave of great gay gallivants (future views coming naturally to us lesbians, astrology being in our genes and all), we've noticed that a couple of Lisbon bars are now advertising in the international gay press. Portugal has all the typical earmarkings for "next hot gay beach resort": great weather, food, architecture, scenery, and prices, plus friendly people. Portugal is also the most racially diverse country of all the old European colonial powers, which is probably a good omen for sexual minorities. Even better, it's managed the integration of Asian, African, and South American people without the nasty racism that's marred British, Belgian, and French political life in recent years.

There are newly prominent lesbian and gay groups all over Eastern Europe: one in Budapest, several in Yugoslavia, over fifty in East Germany, and a group in Prague that will reportedly even arrange accommodations for gay travelers. These places, we predict, will be the most intriguing new gay vacation destinations in the 1990s.

But we also want to urge you to consider getting beyond Gay Geography altogether. For hardball barflies, rural Switzerland has virtually zero major-league queer attractions, but it's one of the most breathtaking places in the known universe. It's also one of the most underrated places on the map in terms of gay-friendliness. The standard big rap against the people is that they "only want your money," but in several trips, we've never had a moment's discomfort there, even in towns that looked disconcertingly like Heidi might toddle down the street any minute, cowbells clanking. If gay money is just as good as anybody else's, we consider that a plus.

We've also had good luck with nongay areas that already have a multicultural mix, like the Basque country in France, and places that have had the opportunity, over the last two thousand years or so, to *gradually* get used to hikers, pilgrims, and other "different" types of transients passing through. In the tiny and decidedly ungay town of Cauterets in the French Pyrénées, near Lourdes, we decided one night to go to dinner at a lovely, romantic restaurant. The patron took one look at us, beamed, and ushered us to the best table in the house: a little den, behind a beaded curtain, decorated in a style that would make the Empress Josephine's boudoir look like a Girl Scout pup tent. We got no gay vibes whatsoever from the guy; no sleazy-straight-voyeur vibes, either. As far as we could tell, he was simply treating us as a real couple, as two people who were obviously "together"—as human beings. *Quelle surprise!*

Use your tongue. It's true that English is widely spoken in urban Europe, particularly by younger people. But don't count on it. We strongly feel that everyone—but especially gay people, who have everything to gain by differentiating ourselves from Mr. and Mrs. Plaid Polyester from Peoria —should in any case make a pass at speaking the local language. In fact, (here we pull out the authorial whips, the cuffs, the tit clamps) if we could *force* you to take a single bit of advice, this would be it.

Obviously you're not expected to speak every European language, or to be utterly dazzling in *any* language. But you certainly *can* learn how to say "please," "thank you," "hello," "good-bye," "excuse me," and "Where's the john?" everywhere. Virtually all Europeans have at least a second language. If you can get by in any major European tongue, especially French or German, you'll double your chances of being understood. You'll also infinitely multiply your chances of making friends—or at least, of making a good impression.

Between us, we have good French, okay Italian, and enough German and Spanish to manage the essentials. If we're in a place where we either don't speak the language at all, or can't cope well enough to negotiate a particular transaction, we'll start a conversation with "Do you speak English, *ou parlez-vous français?*" and then work our way down the ladder of our linguistic skills. We've spoken French with Flemish Belgians, East Germans, Spaniards and Portuguese; Italian with German Swiss; German with Czechs. When we do speak English, we try to obey the Golden Rule and slow down to pen-of-my-uncle level, *sans* slang. (Which is hard, since to the American ear, colloquial language sounds less formal and therefore "friendlier.")

Next to giving up that other overrated American institution, the private bathroom, it's also possible that nothing will save you more money than speaking the native tongue, since you aren't limited to the more expensive hotels that cater to the American tourist and/or international business trade.

A foreign language gives you access to local gay publications and bulletin boards. It helps you feel more in control if you run into problems. Last but not least, it saves you from ordering horse-nostril sandwiches by mistake. If you have never traveled abroad, you have no idea how useful it will be to you, as it has been to us on countless occasions as a half-vegetarian couple, to know how to say, in German, "Please, no tiny pieces of smoked pig's feet in the tuna-fish salad." (Really.)

We can't tell you how many times we've cringed listening to our fellow anglophones (a) speaking ever louder English in the belief that somehow that will help, and (b) reacting as if someone's just peed on their passports when they're still not understood. If you use your high school Spanish to ask a Berliner if he or she speaks English or *español,* you'll at least establish yourself as someone who doesn't assume that the world revolves around English-speakers. Otherwise, you're setting yourself up for this joke, told to one of us by a Frenchman:

Q: What do you call someone who speaks two languages?
A: Bilingual.
Q: What about someone who speaks three languages?
A: Trilingual.
Q: And what do you call someone who speaks only one language?
A: American!

Cultivate a sense of history. "It is not enough for a landscape to be interesting in itself," Stendhal wrote. "Eventually there must be a moral and historic interest."

If there's another cliché about Americans aside from our sterling language skills, it's that we see Europe like babies being wheeled past the entire continent in giant prams: We *ooh* and *ah* at what we see, but since we don't have a clue as to context, it doesn't make any sense. That's a large part of what makes us tourists instead of travelers.

The standard guidebooks, as well as history and art-history texts, play a part in developing this context (and we've learned, incidentally, to bring our own; the tourist info booklets available in English at most of Europe's historical sites are far too shallow to be anything but deadly boring even to nongay sensibilities). But the guides invariably leave the usual major gap. They will acquaint you, for example, with a wealth of art-and-architecture details about Frederick the Great's Sans Souci palace in Potsdam, right down to what part of which room the Caravaggio painting occupies; delineate Frederick's brilliant military strategies so minutely that you could win the 1740–1748 War of the Austrian Succession yourself, if they ever put it in reruns; and inform you of Voltaire's longtime residence at Sans Souci. Wouldn't it put a deliciously different cast on your visit, though, to know that Frederick's pink-and-white rococo pleasure palace was an all-boy preserve strictly off limits to women, including his own wife, whom he only visited a few weeks a year, at Christmas; or that Voltaire had described palace life as "Sparta in the morning, Athens in the afternoon," and Frederick himself as "a likeable whore"? And how *about* that cutie, Caravaggio?

After a week or so of intense history minus Us, it's hard for any gay traveler away from his or her home support system to avoid a dislocated sense of being a figment of one's own imagination. This is hardly fair, considering that a grocery list of the great gay royals alone includes Alexander the Great and Hadrian, from the ancient world; William II, William III of Orange, Edward II, James I, Richard the Lionheart, and possibly Queen Anne, from England; Henri III and Louis XIII, from France, as well as an awful lot of the court of Louis XIV; Queen Christina and Gustavus V of Sweden; Ludwig II and Frederick, of Germany, plus most of the trusted intimates of Kaiser Wilhelm III . . . and at least one or two folks whose buns are on thrones today.

Beyond the serious psychological and sociological implications of our need for role models and all that, we've found that prying open historical closets satisfies exactly the same shallow yet irresistible gossip need as does speculation about living celebrities. And since, unlike, say, certain closeted folk-rock superstars, William II of England (1057–1100) can't sue us for libel, we'll be delighted, whenever appropriate throughout this book, to dish you *all* the dirt we've been able to dig up. (That includes our suggested readings in the Practical Information section, for terrific trash as well as cultured and refined stuff.)

Travel Light. If you travel a lot, you already know this. Otherwise, as fetching as we're certain you look in every single one of your little color-coordinated outfits, packing for every possible social and/or climatic contingency is a literal drag. If in doubt, leave it out. (And we'll say it again: If you want to look really fabulous in Europe, a multilingual phrasebook is your best accessory.)

We're also passionate believers in carrying our luggage on our backs. We think women and gay men look and feel better if they aren't perceived as helpless, which is exactly what you are if you need Sherpas to tote your ninety pounds of Mandarina Duck every time you move an inch. In deference to piss-elegant tastes, we recommend internal-frame backpacks that turn into presentable suitcases with a few deft zipper moves.

(But speaking of piss and elegance . . . if you want to know one of the few items we consider absolutely essential to bring on any trip, you gals-on-the-go in the audience should be sure to check out the Practical Information section for our Belgium chapter.)

Don't pay the "gay tax." Some gay-owned hotels and restaurants are so head-and-shoulders above every other place in town that we'd urge you to patronize them even if you weren't gay. But there are also a dreary number of tacky, overpriced homo havens whose only claim to fame is that they won't spit on you. Do you really want to go all the way to Europe to stay, or even just have a twelve-dollar tap beer, at the Auberge Sleaze-ball?

We managed to hit two gay losers in a row while doing research for this book in rural Great Britain. The first was a place that had advertised itself as a gay bed and breakfast, but turned out to be the nondescript suburban home of a closeted middle-aged couple we'll call Nigel and Clive. We never met Clive, and Nigel didn't see much of him either. In fact, the reason Nigel had begun taking in overnight guests was that Clive had a "lad" on the side. Nigel wanted to cheer himself up by "meeting people"—even though, he confessed to us, he thought most gay men were bitchy back-stabbers and most lesbians were argumentative and nasty.

Not surprisingly, Nigel had very few gay friends with whom he could discuss his troubles. But he did have us, and presumably any other stray queers who straggled into his "guest house." Whenever we were around, he'd try to corner us and dissect, in excruciating detail, all of the terrible things that Clive had done to him over the last twenty years. We felt sorry for Nigel, but nurturing his broken heart wasn't exactly the reason we'd crossed the Atlantic, either.

Still, Nigel was a whole lot more palatable than the next genial host, whose ad in a London gay paper had cheerily noted: "Women especially welcome—ask for Gary and Susan." We figured that G & S might be straight, but that was no problem; maybe one of them had a lesbian sister or something. The important thing was that gay women were valued clients. We were thus a bit taken aback when our knock was answered by a fellow whose scowling face resembled Walt Disney's Grumpy. We asked if we could talk to Gary or Susan.

"Who wants to know?" he demanded.

Grumpy stomped off, cursing under his breath, as Snow White fluttered in. She introduced herself as Susan. She appeared to be either a transvestite or an awfully recent transsexual whose makeover still needed a bit of work. No problem: TVs and TSs are as fine with us as our imagined liberal-straight hosts would have been. What wasn't so fine was that Susan had apparently decided that the key to being a "real" woman was to adopt every simpering, submissive mannerism that the rest of us have been trying to unload for decades. She, at least, was civil, and apologized for the surly fellow, who was indeed Gary. Apparently we—rude ball-busters that we are—had interrupted his dinner. "He's my husband," she sighed in a girl-to-girl stage whisper, rolling her eyes at the man of the house. "And that means he's the boss."

The rooms were cheesy, too. Luckily, there were "vacancy" signs galore in cheaper, cuter guest houses down the road.

Even where the establishment itself is perfectly presentable (and here we mean bars and clubs as well as hotels), the neighborhood may not be. In some European cities, the gay district is the sex district, and the likes of us are only tolerated in that context. You know the rationale: "Hey, let it all hang out—gays, kiddie pornographers, guys who rape cocker spaniels, what's the difference?" This association is far more common in our own country. But one does find it abroad, too, thanks to the universal willingness of gay people to pay through the nose for crumbs just to be with our own. In Zurich, the "gay" hotel we'd heard about proved to be part of a complex that included a ground-floor hetero strip joint. The hotel entryway even featured a photo display of the show's strenuously silicone-enhanced stars, topless. Queens shrieked outside our window all night long, punctuated by the drums from the strip routines.

This kind of olde worlde atmosphere we could have had for the price of a subway token, in Times Square.

Know what your rights are. With a few exceptions, like England's notorious Clause 28, European laws are far more progay than their American counterparts. In 1990, Ireland became the last major European country to abolish its antisodomy statute. The law had earlier been officially censured by the European Court at Strasbourg, the judicial arm of the Common Market countries.

While we in the United States have been losing battles to Moral Majority types, most of our Western European brothers and sisters have been ironing out such relative fine points as adjusting the laws of consent to be the same for gay and straight teenagers. Some countries, like France and Denmark, even have national human rights laws that protect gay people. Nor is there any legal discrimination against HIV+ tourists in Western Europe.

But there are still some legal hurdles for gay American travelers, most of them a consequence of the fact that you and your lover aren't a "family." For example, you're not allowed to go through United States customs as a unit, even if your finances and your suitcase contents are inextricably mingled. On principle, we always try to enter as a family. It even worked, once. But we don't recommend this ploy for those of you who are in a hurry to get home.

Many "family" vacation schemes and price breaks are currently being challenged. In 1989, a suit brought by Lambda Legal Defense Fund forced TWA to change its policy of refusing to let frequent fliers take "unrelated" people on free trips. In 1990, the same airline was involved in the case of a gay man who had a ticket which was nonrefundable except in cases where cancellation was the result of illness or a family emergency. The man's live-in lover had a heart attack the day he was scheduled to travel, but when it came time to claim the refund, TWA refused to consider the lover an "immediate family member." A suit by National Gay Rights Advocates changed their minds. As we go to press, Continental Airlines is involved in a dispute over whether it can require travelers who take advantage of certain vacation packages to have the same last name. Policies on gay issues vary from airline to airline; investigate before you buy.

Something we wouldn't dream of leaving home without is a copy of a notarized power-of-attorney document. Although this piece of paper doesn't have the authority of a marriage license or a "blood" family relationship, it specifically authorizes us to visit each other in hospital intensive-care wards, and to make legal and medical decisions for each other.

One of the most anxiety-producing moments of our traveling life occurred a few years ago when France was still requiring visas of American citizens. We make a point of never checking "single" on any document that asks our marital status, since we're *not* single. At the very least, we make a little box that says "other," and sometimes we're much more explicit. (Hey, they asked, right?) Thus far, we've had no bad reactions from health insurance carriers, credit card companies, or anyone else. But in the case of the French visa application, we were not so dumb as to imagine that we weren't asking for trouble. Possibly expensive trouble, since our nonrefundable airline tickets had already been purchased.

At the French consulate, we nervously got on a long line to hand in our visa applications, and were told to wait until our forms were processed. We were called back within minutes, before any of the people who had been in the line ahead of us.

Uh oh. Major roadblock ahead. Deep doo-doo. Possibly, even, an international incident. We summoned our courage for the fray.

Instead, an extremely cute Frenchman with an earring and a shit-eating grin handed us our processed visas and wished us a wonderful trip.

We really *are* everywhere.

PRACTICAL INFORMATION

GENERAL INFORMATION SOURCES

Between 1992's unification of the European Community countries and the Eastern European situation, all sorts of legal and cultural changes affecting gay people are likely in the near future. Who will know all about whatever happens is the **International Lesbian and Gay Association** (ILGA Information Secretariat, rue Marche au Charbon 81, 1000 Bruxelles 1, Belgium; tel. 502 2471. ILGA Women's Secretariat, Groep 7152, c/o Grada Schadee, Postbus 1352, 5004 BJ Tilburg, The Netherlands). As well as being an information resource, this organization also has a rotating annual world conference drawing gay men and women from all over—and we hear it's a great place to meet people. They also hold numerous smaller regional conferences, like one for Europe and one for Eastern and southeastern Europe, and will send you info on registration as well as conference housing. Another terrific resource for up-to-date gay organization names and addresses for all eastern European nations is **HOSI** (Homosexuelle Initiative Wien, Novaragasse 40, A-1020 Vienna, Austria, tel. 26 66 04), a long-established organization associated with the ILGA.

Since policies on AIDS testing abroad change rapidly, HIV+ tourists may wish to call the **U.S. State Department's Bureau of Consular Affairs** (202-647-1488) for the most recent info on various countries' requirements.

This book concentrates on western Europe. But with the easing of repressive border regulations (combined with already low prices and built-in exotic fascination) looking to make eastern European vacations the hottest trend since sun-dried blackened redfish, we figured some of you would find the following addresses of gay organizations useful, although quite obviously, they do not constitute a comprehensive list of all eastern European gay resources. Contact the ILGA or HOSI for the latest on countries not listed below.

In the case of addresses in care of private individuals, be discreet when addressing envelopes.

(Former) East Germany

AG "Rosalinde" am Jugendklub "Phönix," Im Haus der Volkskunst, Wilhelm-Liebknecht-Platz 21, Leipzig 7033. **Freundeskreis "Rosa Archiv,"** Waldstr. 44, Leipzig 7019. **"HIL,"** B-Göring-Straße 152, Leipzig 7030. **"Lesbengruppe,"** Ulrike Thomas, PSF 1438, Leipzig 7013.

AK Homosexualität (Lesbengruppe), c/o Karin Dauenheimer, PSF 4, Dresden

8021. "Gerede," **Jugendklubhaus "M. A. Nexö,"** Alaunstraße, 36–40, Dresden-Neustadt 8060.

For contacts in what was formerly East Berlin, see "Practical Information, Berlin."

Hungary

Homeros Lambda, c/o Peter Amtrus, Menesi Ut. 17/B/I/7, Budapest, Hungary, or P.O. Box 22, H-1387 Budapest, Hungary. But with this group splitting due to political differences, you might have more luck contacting the gay underground monthly paper published by one of the splinter groups: **Mas-ok,** Budapest 13, Pf. 26, 1253 Hungary.

Czechoslovakia

Lambda Czechoslovakia, c/o J. M. Lany, PoD Kotla'rkou 14, 15000 Praha 5, Smichov, Czechoslovakia; or post. pr. 6, CS-150 06 Praha 56, Košíře, Czechoslovakia. (Reportedly able to help arrange lodgings).

Yugoslavia

Magnus Gay Club and/or **Lezbizka Sekcija,** c/o SKUC, Kersnikova 4, YU-61000 Ljubljana.

GAY TRAVEL AGENCIES /
ADVENTURE TRAVEL COMPANIES

This book is geared to gay traveling couples who are doing it for themselves. In our own travels, we have never used a travel agent, even a gay one, to make our arrangements. As you know, we lesbians are notorious for lengthy anticipation in our love lives, and personally, we find months of mooning over brochures and train schedules fun, too.

There are a couple of instances, however, in which even a basic do-it-yourselfer might need a good gay agent, or want to hook up with a good gay tour—a particularly welcome option for halves of former couples who have just become uncoupled. Unfortunately, the quality of gay travel companies varies just as much as straight ones. So we're listing only a few of the most outstanding.

One instance in which you might want a gay travel agent is in the fast-growing area of adventure travel—meaning action-oriented group tours. Most of these, needless to say, are to remote areas of the world not covered by this book. However, a few companies also run some perfectly wonderful European hiking and biking trips.

A terrific adventure travel company for women is **Woodswomen** (25 West Diamond Lake Road, Minneapolis, MN 55419; tel. 612-822-3809). You might assume from the name that this company is all woodsy backpacking, whitewater plunging, heavy-duty mountaineering, and so on. Not so: Woodswomen also runs a terrific two-week biking exploration in France's Brittany region (absolutely the best way to see this area, as the terrain is easy and trains are limited), and a Swiss Alps trip that combines trail hiking with gondola and cog-railway rides, a bus ride to the birthplace of Santa Claus—and even shopping! Highly recommended.

The **Pacific Harbor Travel** agency (519 Seabright Ave., Suite 201, Santa Cruz, CA 95062; tel. 408-425-5020 or 800-435-9463; 800-541-9463 in California) can book you on the above Woodswomen Brittany trip—or a France–Swiss Alps jaunt or Innsbruck ski trip, among others. In fact, dedicated and responsible agent/owner Marie Henley keeps her eye on the whole adventure travel field for likely tours. She also puts out a newsletter, *Women's Adventure Travel News,* that includes not only listings of her own agency's trips, but all sorts of other travel tips, like mentions of women's guesthouses here and there, medical emergency info, or hints on dealing with airline overbookings. This agency will do for you as much as you want, but lets you make your own arrangements when you'd prefer: much help, no pressure.

For gay men, **Adventure Bound Expeditions** (711 Walnut St., Carriage House, Boulder, CO 80302; tel 303-449-0990) first offered a European adventure in 1990: a vehicle-supported three-country classic alpine walking and camping trip in the spectacular Mont Blanc–Chamonix Valley area of France, Switzerland, and Italy. Tour coordinator Cathy Frank and director David Johnson anticipate other gay European trips in the future.

In addition, some gay hotels—mainly apartment-hotel complexes in European gay-popular beach resort areas (like Ibiza, Sitges, the Canary Islands, or Mykonos), and mainly men-only—book exclusively through gay travel agencies, who generally combine these accommodations with airfare in a package deal. The two biggest that handle this sort of thing are **Mantours** (Motzstraße 70, D-1000 Berlin, Germany; tel. 030 213 8090] and **Uranian Travel** (c/o Infocus Leisure Services Ltd, Infocus House, 111 Kew Road, Richmond, Surrey TW9 2PN; tel. 01 332 1221; telex: 263842 INFOCS G). Colin Wolfe at Uranian, incidentally, assures us that although holidays are geared toward gay men, "lesbians are warmly welcomed at most places"—even if we're likely to be in the minority.

For travelers interested in staying in a private gay home for a day or two, a Dutch operation called **Gay Lesbian Travel List** (GLTL, P.O. Box 5132, 2701 GC Zoetermeer, The Netherlands) has a "homohost" program for all Europe.

Finally, it is often possible to get better airfare deals to resorts like the above by taking a bargain charter to Europe and then arranging the rest of your trip from there. A good international gay agency that specializes in flights for very low prices is **Ticket Kontor** (Reisebüro Brettner & Schau, Feldstraße 37, 2000 Hamburg 6; tel. 040 430 1076; telex: 2 12046). If you've taken advantage of the often low flight fares to London, talk to Martin Rissler at **Key Tours**, 1 Kensington Mall, London W8 4EB.

WHAT TO READ: GENERAL EUROPEAN GAY

Christianity, Social Tolerance and Homosexuality: Gay People in Western Europe from the Beginning of the Christian Era to the Fourteenth Century, by John Boswell (University of Chicago Press). The Yale scholar proves, with a flood of footnotes but an engaging style, that we have *always* been everywhere.

The Pursuit of Sodomy: Male Homosexuality in Renaissance and Enlightenment Europe, edited by Kent Gerard and Gert Hekma (Harrington Park Press). Articles from all over; aside from Boswell, probably the single most comprehensive general gay male European history text.

Immodest Acts: The Life of a Lesbian Nun in Renaissance Italy, by Judith C. Brown (Oxford University Press). One of the earliest documented cases of a European dyke. In what has to be the Renaissance precursor of the line "How 'bout a backrub?," our heroine manages to have sex with her beloved by being seized with the spirit of an angel (male, naturally).

Second ILGA Pink Book: A Global View of Lesbian and Gay Liberation and Oppression. A report, in English, from the International Lesbian and Gay Association. Primarily available in Europe, at gay bookstores. Everything about our legal status worldwide.

Hidden from History: Reclaiming the Gay and Lesbian Past, edited by Martin Bauml Duberman, Martha Vicinus, and George Chauncey, Jr. (NAL). A huge collection of well-researched and well-written essays from many of our most respected gay historians—James Steakley, Jeffrey Weeks, James Saslow, Shari Benstock, and more. Not just European gay history.

Not a Passing Phase: Reclaiming Lesbians in History 1840–1985, by the Lesbian History Group (Women's Press). Essays about British lesbians and lesbian should-have-beens. The chapter on Charlotte Brontë is especially good.

Gay Men and Women Who Enriched the World, by Thomas Cowan (Mulvey Brown). Forty brief, but very informative and amusingly written bios of outstandingly creative sisters and brothers through the ages. These particular forty gay people were picked just because the author loves them, and the text reads like a labor of love.

Homosexuals in History, by A. L. Rowse (Dorset). Arranged by theme rather than by person—"Eminent Victorians," "Russia and Some Russians," "French Poets and Novelists." Gay male heroes only.

WHAT TO READ: OTHER GAY GUIDES

Because the listings in our book are highly selective, opinionated, even attitudinous—quite deliberately limited, in other words, rather than comprehensive—we consider other existing gay guidebooks complementary to rather than competitive with ours.

That's in principle. In actual fact, we don't think many of the other gay guides are very good.

One that is, however, is *INN Places,* from Ferrari Publications, Inc. (P.O. Box 37887, Phoenix, AZ 85069; tel. 602-863-2408), a quality operation that also puts out the reliable *Places of Interest* series. While formerly concentrating on America, all these guides now have European sections that, for sheer volume of *accurate* (as accurate as any annual guide's could be) names and addresses, blows the competition out of the water. *Inn Places* is our fave only because the most detailed descriptions are of accommodations—which is, in our opinion, as it should be, since unlike bars and restaurants, hotels are something travelers often have to evaluate sight unseen in order to make advance reservations. However, in all the above books Marianne Ferrari also lists names and addresses of scads of bars; and makes a pass at indicating, as most guides don't, whether "gay" means men, women, or both. *Places of Interest* also has some nice extras like capsule descriptions of tours and cruises. If we could only buy one other all-Europe book aside from our own, either *INN Places* or *Places of Interest* would definitely be it.

That said, our preferred general approach to supplementary bar, hotel, and restaurant information is to refer readers to periodicals, which, because of publishing schedules, will naturally be more up-to-date than any book could possibly be. Most recommendations are for local newspapers and magazines, and will be found in the individual destination chapters.

However, there are a couple of all-around European resources of this sort you might find useful. **Special up-to-date gay info portfolios for a number of European destinations** (including London, Paris, Antwerp, Brussels, Hamburg, Cologne, Berlin, and assorted places in Austria, Italy, and Scandinavia) can be obtained from **Peter Glencross,** a meticulously accurate researcher who has long published the *Top Guide to Amsterdam*. And for women, the summer edition of Amsterdam's *Ma'dam* magazine contains holiday addresses all over Europe, as well as listing European travel agencies that organize tours for lesbians. See Practical Information, Amsterdam for the ordering address and phone number for all.

Additionally, we're certain you're familiar with *Our World*. This American-published monthly magazine features lots of European destinations; it must be *the* gay travel success story of recent years. But just in case you haven't seen it, subscriptions are available from Our World Publishing, 1104 North Nova Rd., Suite 251-F, Daytona Beach, FL 32117; tel. 904-441-5367; 12 issues $44, sample copy $5. This company sells *Italia Gay* and other local European guides at discount, too.

HOW TO GET AROUND

By train, unless we tell you otherwise.

We never travel without the **Thomas Cook European Timetable: Railway and Shipping Services Throughout Europe** (available in North America primarily through Forsyth Travel Library, P.O. Box 2975, Shawnee Mission KS 66201-1375; tel. 800-FORSYTH). This classic for train travelers frees you from dependence on locally available schedules and foreign-language info negotiations with conductors and other rail officials.

If you are on a short vacation and only going to two destinations, a *Eurailpass* is probably not worth it for you. If you're covering lots of miles, however, and/or you're on a semispontaneous trip where you just walk into a station, look at the big board, and muse, "Oh, Budapest, or perhaps Vienna. Yes, that sounds like what I'm in the mood for tonight," a Eurailpass is a dream. It feels luxuriously liberating to never have to negotiate ticket purchases in an unfamiliar language—to just hop on any train, at any time, to any place that strikes your fantasy.

Anyone over 26 must buy a first-class pass. Second-class passes are about half price. But if you're under 26 and can easily afford a first-class Eurailpass, don't listen to those American guides that tell you to go second class anyway, as this is how one meets the genuine people of the country. There are plenty of genuine people of the country in first class, the seats are lots more comfy, and you don't have to listen to other American college people playing "Blowin' in the Wind" on out-of-tune folk guitars all the way to Florence.

Children under 12 can get Eurailpass first class or Flexipass for half the above fares; children under 4 travel free.

Eurailpasses are valid in Austria, Belgium, Denmark, West Germany, Finland, France, Greece, Hungary, Italy, Luxembourg, the Netherlands, Norway, Portugal, the Republic of Ireland, Spain, Sweden, and Switzerland.

The current options for a Eurailpass first class are 15 days, 21 days, 1 month, 2 months, or 3 months, for prices ranging from roughly $350 to $950. For couples not planning to break up on a vacation, a Eurail SaverPass—15 days for 2 people or more traveling together (3 people minimum from April 1 to Sept. 30), provides the same benefits as a first-class Eurailpass and will save you each approximately $100. The Eurail YouthPass, second-class travel for people under 26 years old, is available for 1 month or 2 months and costs about a third less than the first-class passes for the same amounts of time. Finally, for people who may be traveling long distances between several destinations but plan to stay put for a while once they get there (that is, who don't need or want the option to hop on a train any old time), there's the Eurail Flexipass. This allows first-class travel on a set number of individual travel days, which can be used over a longer period of time—5 days' travel within 15 days, 9 days' travel within 21 days, or 14 days' travel within 1 month. Savings over regular first-class passes range from about $80 to $150 for the same time periods, with the greatest savings on the shorter-term pass.

If you're sticking to one country or region, consider the similar but cheaper passes from France, Germany, Spain, Italy, Switzerland, Scandinavia, and Austria/eastern Europe.

$\mathscr{B}$RIGHTON

Going Down for a Dirty Weekend

$\mathscr{I}$n the mid-eighteenth century, Dr. Richard Russell of Lewes, East Sussex, discovered the therapeutic value of sea bathing. Immediately, hordes of Londoners who had never dreamed of swimming during the thousands of years when it was merely Good Fun rather than Good For You dutifully flocked fifty miles south to the nearest sea. It was thus—okay, maybe just a *tad* overcondensed thus—that the simple south-coast fishing village (and, occasionally, simple smuggling village) called Brighthelmstone evolved into the trendy spot that the London *Sun* has called "the premier gay resort of Europe": Brighton.

Brighton is actually one of a triumvirate of English seacoast resorts famous for their gay atmosphere. But staid Bournemouth, invaded by ugly public housing, has a reputation as a "giant old age home"; Blackpool's rep is worse: "Five miles of fun fair and fag-bashers," sniffs one less than entirely objective Brighton guest-house owner. "And if you think the people who go to Blackpool are cheap, you should see the buildings."

In truth, not much is left of Brighton's original seventeenth-century settlement, either, except for the narrow, twisting brick streets of "the Lanes." Today, antiques, books, and beer are hawked from the Lanes' slate-roofed, half-timbered buildings, formerly fishermen's huts. Don't bother looking for gay guest houses in these few remaining medieval streets, because there are no hotels of any sort here. One fourteenth-century pub, however, Cricketers, has reportedly been a popular hangout for the "theatrical crowd" through the ages.

The nineteenth century has survived considerably better, in the landmark Royal Pavilion's "Indian Gothic" domes as well as in thousands of dignified Regency and dainty Victorian town houses stretching back in terraces and crescents for several solid blocks from the beach. Even in this part of town, though, decay and modern times encroach. The streets do have the charmingly eclectic, eccentric look of a mini–San Francisco, but it's a San Francisco attacked by salt air, an Annie Hall thrift-store town. Paint is often a bit faded; wrought-iron work a bit rusted. Like a real Persian carpet found in a secondhand bin, Brighton is still uniquely stylish but definitely used, frayed, worn; its state is evidence of many trodding visitors and many years as a resort. It has even lost its Victorian skyline: A row of cheesy council flats, freshly unpacked from the giant celestial generic-buildings Cracker Jack box, looms ominously over all.

But there is one remnant of the town's past that has survived the centuries totally intact: a certain enduring, shall we say, *renown*. As Florence is to those seeking an art-type vacation, as Lyon is to the food-type vacation, Brighton has long been, even one hundred fifty years before Monty Python, Europe's premier destination for the nudge-nudge-wink-wink type of vacation.

"Oh yes, this town has always had quite the reputation," guest-house owner Barbara Williams chirps brightly. "The classic hotel register, you know: 'Mr. and Mrs. Smith,' 'Mr. and Mrs. Jones' . . . In London, the saying is, 'Let's go down for a *dirty weekend!*'"

This sort of revelation may not be reassuring to most gay people as a barometer for locating truly simpatico vacation spots, given the reputation of British beach towns for lower-class "Kiss-Me-Quick-and-a-Candy-Floss" vulgarity and given, too, the kind of sexist and homophobic street harassment that tends to escalate in locales packed with wild-and-crazy straight guys looking for cheap thrills. Not that the two of us haven't done all sorts of things on beaches that would make your average vulgar skinhead's hair curl. But we nevertheless are not overly partial to towns where the gay neighborhood is basically the sex'n'sleaze neighborhood, and where we're tolerated only as fellow perverts rather than as fellow people. This isn't why we, or most other gay people, or most *any* other people, blow our whole bank accounts to go to Europe. When we fantasize about Merrie England, we're thinking tea with Oscar Wilde, not live sex acts with Cornish hens.

In Brighton's case, though, there's no need to worry about either vulgarity or violence getting out of hand. "Brighton has always tolerated a certain risqué element," Barbara explains, "but always, of course, *in its proper place.*" We are, in other words, talking about very respectable sleaze here.

For example, the most famous "Mr. Jones" to go down to Brighton for a dirty weekend, back around 1784, was the future King George IV, known as "Prinny." He was actually later the prince regent of Great Britain and gave his name to Britain's Regency style of architecture. "Mrs. Jones," at the time, was really Mrs. Fitzherbert. She thought, however, that she was Mrs. Prince Regent, not entirely without reason. His Royal P.R. had, after all, gone to quite a bit of trouble to stage a bogus wedding, complete with a handsomely bribed, genuine—though jailbird—minister. Not that Mrs. Fitzherbert was George's only Mrs. Jones. Other ladies had preceded her for dirty weekends in the royal boudoir of the farmhouse that later expanded into the Royal Pavilion. Many more ladies were to succeed her, including the wife of Pavilion architect John Nash.

According to scandalized eyewitness reports, "Prinny" was one of those tacky promiscuous sorts who could not refrain from broad winks and loud sighs at girlfriends even during his own coronation. He was obviously straight. Not necessarily so Nash, who shared his London house with one John Edwardes. Despite two marriages, Nash willed his entire fortune and his knighthood to Edwardes, a young fellow who was variously explained as his cousin, his nephew, and his uncle.

It's actually quite difficult to hang out in Brighton for any time at all without running into historical mentions of Our Crowd, many of whom seem to be local heroes. Strike up six conversations in six gay pubs, and you'll hear half a dozen times about Colonel Victor Barker, who married a woman in Brighton's St. Nicholas Church in 1923. It wasn't until years later, during a strip search in the Men's Gaol after Barker's arrest for bankruptcy, that authorities discovered the local boy was actually a local girl, Valerie Arkell-Smith. She/he made news headlines in 1929 as "The Brighton Man-Woman."

Other more well-known tribe members who lived or vacationed in Brighton were Oscar Wilde, Virginia Woolf, Robin Maugham, and Radclyffe Hall. On the first of several visits during the 1920s, the normally rather proper "John" (as Ms. Hall preferred to be addressed) and her lover, Lady Una Troubridge, attended lesbian tea dances at the Royal Albion Hotel, and stayed out scandalously late (past midnight!) doing the Vampire, the Camel Walk, and other popular jazz dances of the day. Accompanying them was Barbara "Toupie" Lowther, eldest daughter of the Earl of Lonsdale, who was quite famous at the time for being one of Britain's first dykes on bikes, as well as for her alleged arrest on the Franco-Italian border for masquerading as a man. On her return across the border, the story goes, Toupie wore skirts and was again arrested, this time for masquerading as a woman.

During her visits, Radclyffe Hall stayed at the Prince's Hotel and at the Royal Crescent. And if she returned from the dead, she could no doubt get back her old room at the latter, a deluxe sixty-six-room hotel still at 100 Marine Parade. Should she want a change of venue, Hall could instead sojourn amongst the quaint fringed lamps and period Brighton paintings at Benson's, the town house hotel Barbara Williams runs with her lover, Gill Goodfellow, or take rooms at nearly a dozen other gay guest houses. The town tourist office will give you a list of them, without blinking an eye. Really.

John and Lady Una could also try one last Jog Trot at close to two dozen gay pubs and clubs; eat at half a dozen openly gay-owned restaurants; and pick up *Gay Times* plus several local freebie gay-listings papers at regular old newsstands all over town, with regular old Watney's-bellied proprietors who are obviously straight. Or are they? Estimates of the current gay population of this only moderate-sized town (150,000 total population) range from twenty-five percent to forty percent.

In Brighton, despite Clause 28, there's plenty of company in the Well of Loneliness nowadays.

"Oh my," said Frank, one half of Graham and Frank, a seventeen-year gay male couple who own Hudson's guest house. We had just arrived at Hudson's, which we'd seen described as a gay guest house in several sourcebooks. Frank was looking very distressed. "You do seem to have a little bit of a problem here."

Why are you not surprised? No doubt because you already know, especially if you're female, that gay women who blithely show up at places advertised as "gay guest houses" *often* have a little bit of a problem: that "gay" often means "men only."

In Brighton's case, though . . . Well, we won't go so far as to say that there is virtually no misogyny among gay men in this town, at least as it applies to women feeling welcome in gay male commercial establishments. But we will say that we found only one establishment where misogyny seems to hold sway, and during that brief moment at Hudson's we were just being total paranoid assholes.

Frank, you see, was addressing a far more serious problem for lesbian visitors to Brighton: parking the car. Finding a decent space is no joke in this burg, believe you us.

"Yes, you seem somehow to have gotten yourself into a *motorcycle* spot," Frank clucked. "And they are so brutal about tickets. One woman who owns a guest house here has nearly sixty now, I believe. So why don't you just nip right out and fix that, and then we'll sit down in the lounge with a map and have a chat about all the gay spots in Brighton. Coffee or tea?"

Within half an hour, Frank and Graham had not only dished us the dirt on every gay pub and club in town, but had reassured us about something we'd foreseen as another major problem in Brighton, since it's definitely one of England's major problems: the coffee. While Hudson's version isn't what you'd get in the Piazza Navona, neither was it typical British instant-compost water. Potential problems number one and number two— misogyny and bad coffee—having been eliminated, we weren't altogether surprised when potential problem number three, the famous (or infamous) Full English Breakfast, was cleared up next morning. Atypically featured were nonraw bacon, noncold toast, and noncanned fruits and veggies; equally atypically, those hideous little canned baked beans smothered in ketchup were nowhere in sight. Even totally vegetarian *or* vegan versions of the full breakfast were available, and this seemed to be the rule at most of Brighton's gay guest houses. Actually, all of you except big fans of boiled canned brussels sprouts will be relieved to know that most food in Brighton is blessedly non-British, possibly because, being a mere two-hour boat ride from Dieppe, the town has long been a French resort, too. The most prestigious local restaurant honors did seem to be the Clean Food Award and the Loo Of The Year Award, but don't let this throw you.

The bottom line is this: Gay guest houses are now, and will continue to be, the best lodgings bet in town, even if you include under "lodgings" luxury hotels. Why? Because lots of gay people live in Brighton already, and more are flooding in every day, with, as the scaffolding around town suggests, that familiar gentrification gleam in their eyes. The dream occupation seems to be gay-hotel keeper, so it's pretty safe to say that even with the usual gay-business turnover rate, a gay hotel-seeker in Brighton can count on not only competitive quality, but variety beyond imagining.

For example, what would you say to an 1800 guest house with sea views and in-house sauna—steam bath?

Not quite you? Then how about a Victorian guest house with a complete flotation-tank setup?

Or maybe you're more the type for a lesbian-owned Regency guest house with decorator-designed rooms and new heights of wonderfulness in room service: Supper at eleven P.M.? Almost anything for breakfast? "We do insist that if people want something *particularly* unusual for breakfast, they tell me the night before," comanager Katrina sighs, really putting the old foot down. "It is *so* unpleasant to try and find a grocer who carries soy milk at six A.M."

And how does this grab you theatrical types: a guest house, every room chock-full of quality antique froufrou, run as the day job of Brighton's star drag queen, David "Maisie Trollette" Raven? Local legend has it that once, when a couple of truly obnoxious flaunting hets stayed at Maisie's, he served them breakfast in full drag. In the interests of strict journalistic accuracy, we must report that when we personally checked this story out with Maisie, who was Noel-Cowarding around his patio at three P.M., still in a velour bathrobe, he said airily, "Oh, how silly. I *never* serve breakfast."

Commonly known travel wisdom has it that in Britain, even hotels that are middling expensive are often depressing: perfectly clean, perfectly respectable, but sort of Spartan and tatty. Perhaps straight guest houses in Brighton follow suit. But not the gay ones. Here, for a change, there's none of the usual gay tax and gay ghetto stuff. No "Hey faggots and fagettes, we just know you'll be thrilled to pay twice as much to stay in a place half as good, with your own kind." Odd as it seems, in Brighton, gay guest houses are where we'd send even our own perfectly straight mothers.

As an art and antiquities center, Brighton is not London, or even York. And as a gay beach resort, Brighton is . . . well, it's Britain. But between sunbathing when there's sun—which, on the south coast, is more often than elsewhere in England, honest—and sightseeing when there isn't, no couple could fail to find enough in town to fill the nondirty parts of their weekend. And if you are brave or foolhardy enough to venture out on the roads with the bloody Brit motor-maniacs, there's at least a week's worth of Norman castles, Roman ruins, Bloomsbury-group sites, and similar day trips and gay trips, no more than an hour's drive from Brighton. (Fifteen minutes, if you drive like a native.) We think Brighton is a wonderful place to start a vacation and unwind from jet lag. It's also possible to use the town as a base to see London, since it's only a little more than an hour away by train. The train, by the way, is often so gay-heavy that the locals call it the Faggot Flier.

The primo must-see sight in town is, of course, the Royal Pavilion. Though actually constructed solidly of brick, stucco and yellow Bath stone, the Pavilion looks like a mad kitchen queen's version of the Taj Mahal: a wedding cake baked from a zillion tons of spun sugar, decorated with "Brighton Rock" candy minarets, topped with whipped-cream domes. It is an absolute tart of a building, a former dumpy Cinderella farmhouse enclosed by the Prince Regent and Nash in a ball-gown shell of delirious high drag. The builder may not have been gay, but the building itself, we can assure you, is.

"Ball-gown shell," incidentally, is not merely a metaphor. In the process of reaching its present splendid state, the Pavilion's exterior went through several of those ugly-duckling evolutionary stages familiar to so many of us gay swans. Though outwardly invisible (except as reflected in certain structural shapes like the circularity of the central saloon and dome), both the original farmhouse and architect Henry Holland's overly dignified Louis XVI–style expansion of 1787 still lurk beneath Nash's exotic 1815–1822 Hindustan remodeling. Like ex-husbands, these unfortunate remnants of the past have caused problems. The water-trapping quality of the Pavilion's shell-over-an-existing-building construction was aggravated by the deterioration of Nash's ill-conceived experimental mastic roof, a total lack of rain gutters, and the natural tendency of stucco to turn into damp porridge with the slightest encouragement. Finally, in recent years, the Pavilion's walls began to mildew and to seriously rot away. Fortunately, much of the Pavilion's outside has already been cosmetically restored thanks to an organization called Friends of the Royal Pavilion. Work continues in making the exterior structurally sound.

As festive as the building's outside is, it does not begin to reflect the Pavilion's truly outrageous innards. This can perhaps be explained by the fact that while the exterior's romanticized Indian-Gothic style was quite new at the time, the interior's predominant chinoiserie, having already enjoyed various vogues in Britain for over a century, had had ample opportunity to develop to a pinnacle of glorious excess, especially in the innovative hands of a patron like George IV—who, a sign in the Pavilion's entryway proudly proclaims, "consistently refused to be bound by constraints of responsibility, taste, or convention."

It's not easy to generalize about the interior decoration without its sounding like a cartoon. But imagine an eclectic mixture of many familiar, stereotypically Chinese elements beloved of the imperialist imagination: tea wood, lace-doily fretwork screens, trilliage, huge Oriental vases, many little slant-eyed dolls with nodding heads, much simulated bamboo (painted *mahogany* yet!), dragons galore. Combine with various Indian, Arab, and Continental rococo exotica. Paint in strong Regency colors: thrilling blood reds, elegantly intense teals, more shades of pink-rose-peach than the lobby of Trump Tower. Then embellish everything within reach with enough gilt to cave in the floor of Fort Knox. Are we having Big Fun yet?

The most Chinese and most outrageous room is the music room, sort of a sheik's tent with bordello-red Oriental-tapestry walls, carved serpent columns, pagoda-roofed doors, etched-glass chandeliers that look like upside-down parasols, and a jewelbox-gold, cockleshell-domed ceiling.

Our own Personal Best room is the kitchen. Big enough to hold twenty average New York City apartments, it features the most outstanding collection of tacky plastic and rubber food we've ever seen: plastic garlic, plastic eggs, plastic vegetable soup, plastic lamb chops, a whole plastic suckling pig with a plastic apple in its mouth, even a plastic mouse scuttling across the floor looking for plastic cheese.

But we must admit that the all-around gay favorite is the Banqueting Room, if only because most of you have already seen it. What? You haven't? Turn in your tribe membership card, immediately! This was the location for the famous banquet scene in *On a Clear Day You Can See Forever*, Barbra Streisand's third movie. Remember it now? She, the reincarnated Lady Melinda, dressed by Cecil Beaton in an all-white number with sequined turban, and He, the pretty-boy fop, dressed in a tux festooned with feather boas, stare at each other across It, the Banqueting Room. Room is dressed, as always, in a copper Jack-in-the-Beanstalk-sized 3-D plantain-leaf ceiling, which sprouts from its center a crystal-and-gilt chandelier featuring a motif we can only describe as "dragons barfing up tulips."

Those of you with major birthdays or life-partnership anniversaries coming up will be thrilled to know that the Banqueting Room *is* selectively available for private-party hire.

There are few other major architectural sights in town, because Brighton had fallen out of royal favor by the 1840s. The posh crowd had left when a railway line from London brought a new onslaught of not at all posh day-trippers, and the death of George IV's successor, William IV, brought Victoria to the throne. "It is not strictly accurate to say that Queen Victoria disliked the Pavilion," an exhibit brochure hedges, but it is accurate to say that frivolity was not exactly Vicky's middle name. After waiting five years, the queen visited Brighton only twice, briefly, before putting the Pavilion up for sale in 1846. The headline in Punch read, RUBBISH FOR SALE. She were not amused.

On your way out of the Royal Pavilion, don't fail to stroll over to the west lawn for a look at the grandiose, Indian-style Dome, originally George's stable and riding school. Back when the Dome was built, around 1805, the Pavilion itself was still Henry Holland's Spartan classical-revival building. The stable's extravagant size, style, and expense led to the comment that the prince's horses were better housed than the prince.

If you're not completely breathless after the Pavilion's and Dome's flights of loony magnificence, a mini—walking tour of town should not leave out a trio of architecturally lightweight but historic fun firsts: watching the dolphins train the humans at the 1869 Aquarium, Europe's first; afternoon tea on the Victorian Palace Pier, an 1899 replacement for Chain Pier, England's earliest Atlantic City—style boardwalk; and a ride along the beach on tiny Volk's Railway, England's first electric train line.

Should the sun ever reach inspirational proportions, you can take the railway out to its terminus, England's only official nudist beach. This one hundred yards or so of sand is extremely popular with gay men, as is, for non—buff buffs, the adjacent Duke's Mound area. If you don't mind walking a bit farther and packing your own lunch (no facilities), the stretch always referred to as *the* gay beach, Telscombe Cliffs, is about four and a half miles east of Palace Pier, on the other side of Rottingdean (pronounced "Roe-dean"). Lost? Just ask for the Lower Sewer Works, conveniently located right next door to the beach, where all of Brighton and Hove's garbage spews into the English Channel.

That's about it for major in-town sights, although if you're one of those compulsives who's only happy when running around seeing and doing Exciting, Important Things, there are plenty more within commuting distance. Gay-oriented ones include Sissinghurst Castle, a formerly derelict Elizabethan manor, with its famous garden, planted by sister and brother Bloomsbury-ites Vita "Orlando" Sackville-West and Harold Nicholson; Rodmell, on the river Ouse, where Virginia Woolf lived and died; and Lamb House, in Rye, where famous closet prune Henry James lived until 1916 (the local gay rumor mill has it that Hugh Walpole propositioned him here; James would have declined, of course), and where E. F. Benson then lived until 1940. The house feels as if Benson's Miss Mapp still lives there. And there are some pretty terrific second-century Roman ruins, including remarkably intact mosaics, only thirty miles away in Fishbourne.

We ourselves spent satisfying days doing very little but strolling the streets of town, daydreaming about which town house we'd buy, if only. In this way, we discovered that a relaxed approach is a great way to discover the real Brighton.

For one thing, we came to realize that the town as a whole is architecturally vastly underrated. Casual cruising, especially in the streets of Brighton's run-together sister city, Hove (considered classier and quieter by townies), turned up whole pristine blocks, even solid unbroken squares, of classic bowfronted Regency town houses. We uncovered dozens of classic Victorian mansions, secreted in Hove's back streets and totally ignored by our guidebooks, which raved on for pages about mansions in Eastbourne that are no more impressive or interesting. Cruise around, and we're sure you'll find minor treasures of your own.

The main reason why a non-excitement-oriented approach to Brighton works is because Brighton isn't very exciting. It is simply very nice. As a gay beach resort, it hasn't got Capri's drop-dead vegetation; it's got some pleasant lawns. It hasn't got Sitges' sensational twenty-four-hour nightlife; it's got friendly pubs that close at a sensible hour. It's not a place of Important Sights like Delos, worth every ulcerous moment of the required cookie-tossing boat ride from Mykonos, but a place of small pleasures best uncovered in a relaxed, almost accidental way.

One thing about Brighton gay pubs: They are terribly unfriendly to strangers. Really, it is quite impossible to meet anyone. Ask any gay local, and he or she will tell you this. Though actually, you needn't even bother to ask, because as soon as anyone in a Brighton gay pub catches your foreign accent as you timidly order a beer, you will invariably be surrounded by hordes of unfriendly gay locals clamoring to explain to you how no one in these bloody unfriendly Brighton gay pubs will ever strike up a conversation.

The Queens Arms (no, we're not making it up) is a gambrel-roofed lesbian and gay pub with a coat of arms and a sign, hanging by the door, that reads "EST. 1757." It also sports a silver disco ball on the ceiling. Within moments of our arrival, a cute nineteen-year-old blond guy advised us on the pub's entire beer roster, returned the pittance we'd left on the bar (tipping bartenders is a no-no in England) and pointed out to us the fellow he was madly in love with, though he ended the night on someone else's lap. Within half an hour, so many folks had joined the discussion that we were forced to break the group into two parts on different sides of the room. Among them were a male nurse, who gave us the full rundown on his fucked-up love life; a woman who loves Adrienne Rich; another woman who explained at length how her mum doesn't mind she's gay, but insists she should bring home an Educated Girl . . . and the main topic of conversation continued to be the unfriendliness of the gay pubs in Brighton.

We'd braved all this notorious social viciousness because Sunday is drag night at the Queens Arms, and for some reason guys in dresses have long been considered the absolute height of humor in England. Someone told us that drag is so endemic to British culture that there was once even a famous drag *radio* show.

Since we're not among those women who have political objections to the whole genre, it made sense to catch at least one show while in England. However, we'd rarely seen a drag act, either in America or Europe, that we'd liked. And not that we don't appreciate a good Tampax joke as much as the next person, but the show at the Queens Arms was no exception. Still, most of the audience seemed to eat it up, probably because the queen, a hefty sixty-year-old guy in a sequined gown and eyelasses that looked like tarantula legs, was a local heroine who apparently knew everyone in the room. This somehow included us. Even though we'd been in town less than twenty-four hours, we got our share of bitchy one-liners, including a rendition of "New York, New York" and an "American medley": Elvis with an English accent. Then she/he broke into songs from *My Fair Lady*. Everyone, incredibly, sang along. It was all rather sweet, actually—certainly nothing one can imagine the crowd at the Mineshaft doing—and hard to resist, even for non-fans of drag. So by the end of the last Lesley Gore number it was closing hour, and we never even got to hit the Bulldog and the Oriental, the number one and number two pubs for men (though there are plenty of guys at the Queens Arms, which is known as the best women's place). Ah, well, another night.

By now, you've noticed that our own preference for British nightlife is public houses. They're just soooo English. And in gay pubs, the combination of the traditional (the crests, the shields, the half-timbered Shakespearean decor) with the bent (us) is just soooo Englishly charming, as opposed to discos, which are just soooo generically boring. But we know that dedicated followers of fashion will ignore us. So here's our tip for those seeking those who are the latest in body styles and dancing to the latest in musical styles: Club Shame. This hottest gay venue in Brighton—in the whole of England, according to *Gay Times*—is a fortnightly event at the minimalist, multilevel Zap Club. Of course, with gay "Club Nights" going in and out of fashion, not to mention in and out of business, so often, it's best to follow the London rule, and follow the promoter. If Club Shame is zapped by the time you hit town, ask for anything hosted by Paul Kemp.

If Paul Kemp has moved to Toledo by then, the hell with you. You should have listened to us and gone to the Queens Arms or Cricketers, or some other gay joint that's been around five hundred years or so in the first place.

It's the dead of night in Brighton. The gay pubs have closed. The gay guest houses have locked their front doors. It's almost midnight.

We are engaged in a last responsible-journalist attempt to see if we can scare up any skinhead gay-bashers. Although most of the other Brit-beach-town problems we'd anticipated had come to naught, this one was not mere paranoia. In Blackpool just the month before, two separate incidents had left a seventy-nine-year-old gay man barely conscious and a seventeen-year-old with a broken nose, a fractured cheekbone, and a face full of stitches.

So we have gone for a late-night walk, with our arms around each other, in Brighton's main gay-male cruising area.

This news causes, by the way, no small amount of excitement at our guest house the next morning at breakfast. Graham: "You went where? The Brighton cruising area? My word! Are you quite sure we have one? Where *is* it?"

Where it has always been: beneath and alongside the derelict Victorian West Pier, from around Hove Lawns to the Bushes. This was the location of the late, lamented "Men Only" Beach in Hove, notorious in its time. A 1907 London newspaper reported: "There are certain periods of the day when hundreds of men and boys, clad in the very scantiest of costumes, disport themselves on Brighton Beach at points where they can be easily seen from the piers and the front!" The beach was officially closed in the 1950s, when Sussex police built a retirement home opposite. But gone is not forgotten. In 1973, the Sussex Gay Liberation Front held a same-sex wedding on the site, and it continues to be a popular gay-male trysting spot. (If you are one of those occasionally expanding couples, do use caution. In an October 1989 sweep, Brighton bobbies made forty-five arrests here. A mere drop in the legal bucket, compared to Katrina's parking tickets, but still . . .)

Anyway, if a pair of hostile New Yorkers can't find a fight to pick, it's mighty slim pickins, fightwise. We found *nada* at the Pier that night. There were a few guys under the promenade, checking each other out, and there were scattered campfires farther away on the beach, which proved to belong to couples, both straight and gay, more or less looking at the water. (With the camping equipment of doom, we must add. Where else but in stalwart be-prepared England would one bring an umbrella, a Coleman stove, and army cots for a couple of hours of nighttime necking?) But no gangs cruising, unless you want to count one *huge* herd of chattering Esperantists.

That's right, Esperantists. They were holding a convention in town—two thousand people, including members of the Ligo De Samseksamaj Geesperantistoj, the Gay Esperanto League, which is over a decade old. The dream of a universal language may be forty years dead in our own self-centered superpower nation, but not in Brighton. During the day, they even had a sort of Esperanto wagon set up on the boardwalk: a guy sitting in a giant doghouse labeled in English and Esperanto (DOMO DE HUNDO) to show how accessible the language is. The combination of weirdness and sincerity in these people seemed quintessentially Brighton.

Maybe what one gay guest-house owner told us is true: Brighton is "a microcosm of an ideal world." Or maybe Brighton's just very nice. But for gay travelers, that's nice with a capital *N*.

PRACTICAL INFORMATION

BRIGHTON—NUMBER KEY

Pubs & discos

1. Liam's Club (disco; 75 Grand Parade)
2. Queen's Head (Steine St.), Aquarium Inn (6 Steine St.), and Secrets Club (disco, 25 Steine St.)
3. Shame (disco, at Zap Club underneath Arches, beachfront)
4. Villagers Club (some leather nights; 74 St. James St.)
5. Beacon Royal Hotel (bar/disco; Oriental Pl.)
6. Bulldog Tavern (31 St. James St.)
7. Cricketers (Black Lion St.)
8. Queens Arms (7 George St.)
9. The Oriental (Montpelier Rd.)
10. Black Horse (7 Church St.)

Guest Houses

11. Franklin's (41 Regency Sq.)
12. Shalimar (223 Broad St.)
13. Hudson's (22 Devonshire Pl.)
14. Benson's (16 Egremont Pl.)
15. Alpha Lodge (19 New Steine)
16. Catnaps (21 Atlingworth St.)
17. Rowlands (21 St. George Terrace)

Shop

18. Cardome (47a St. James St.)

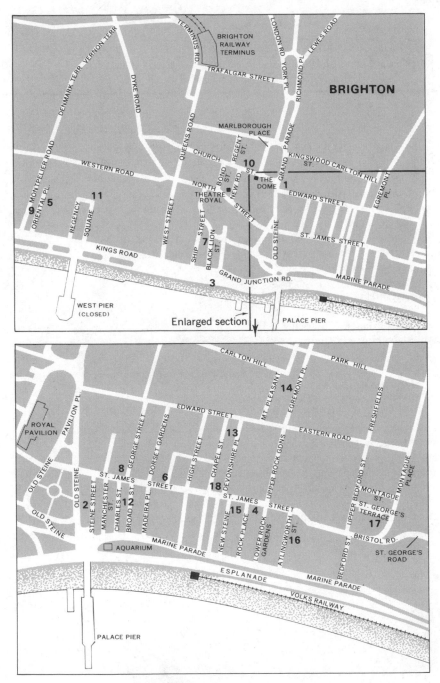

GENERAL INFO / HINTS

Brighton is located on England's southeast shore, about 50 miles from London on the A23 and M23 motorways. From London's Victoria Station, it is less than an hour by train and about two hours by express bus. From the nearest international airport, Gatwick, Brighton is about 30 miles (30 minutes) by direct rail link. The train station is a good 20-minute walk from the seafront. But unless you are planning day trips out of town, a car is both unnecessary and worrisome, as virtually everything in town is easily and pleasantly walkable, and the town authorities are strict about parking violations. If you do have a car, we found the area right above Eastern Street, from Blaker Street to Park Street, to be the least annoying (i.e., the car has to be moved only once or twice per week).

When asking for or attempting to follow directions, do beware the sort of abbreviations one normally falls into: "Hang a left at West," for example. Here there are a West Street, a West Drive, and a Western Road; a North Road and a North Street; a Queen's Road and a Queen's Way; a Steine Street, New Steine Street and Old Steine Street (of which there are two, branching off in different directions)—and if there's a system to where numbers restart, we sure couldn't figure it out. Fortunately, Brighton's a small town.

Most **gay activity** centers in two areas: around St. James Street, east of the Palace Pier, and in the blocks bordering the seafront near West Pier.

All **major banks** are located on (Brits say "in") North Street. The **main post office** is in Ship Street.

Telephone code: 0273
Currency unit: the pound (£)

WHERE TO STAY

While it is an excellent idea, in *most* European locales, to search for the most typical and atmospheric hotels in the "old town" section, there are no hotels much less gay ones, in Brighton's oldest area, the seventeenth-century red-brick "Lanes"—so don't bother. The normally reliable beachfront/sea view location option is pretty pointless here, too: There are no gay guest houses directly on the street bordering the seafront (called Marine Parade east of Palace Pier; Kings Road, west towards Hove), and you wouldn't want to stay on this traffic-packed through road even if there were. Virtually all gay lodgings in Brighton/Hove are on quieter, cuter Victorian and Regency streets within three blocks of the beach.

Prices: *Inexpensive* = under £30 per night, double; *moderate* = £30–40; *mod./exp.* = £40–50; *expensive* = over £50. All prices are for the high season (May–September, and holidays). Full English breakfast is included, unless otherwise mentioned, as are free 24-hour, and usually in-room, coffee- and tea-making facilities. Double beds, as well as single rooms and rates (usually about half price), are available at all establishments. All proprietors also provide gay maps and/or personalized advice and help. In-room plumbing varies, as indicated below; the Britspeak for "room with bath" is "en suite facilities." During the high season, reservations are recommended; but Brighton is so much a gay *weekend* destination for Londoners that it's generally possible to just blow into town on weekdays and find a room in any place listed below, any time of the year.

Hudson's (formerly Scandals), 22 Devonshire Place, Brighton BN2 1QA; tel. 68 36 42. Not visually impressive from the outside—but inside, Hudson's could not possibly be more welcoming (for women, too, though the clientele is largely male). Public areas include a smallish but comfy living room–lounge, patio garden off the breakfast room, and conservatory. There are seven rooms (six with shower, one with bathtub, two with toilet; all with color TVs), decorated in a style usually referred to as "masculine": tasteful no-froufrou grays/browns/tweeds. British Museum posters. Many thoughtful niceties, like unusually (for anywhere in Europe) thick, fuzzy bath towels; couches; individual coffee/tea-making alcoves with real milk. Breakfast was probably the best we had in Britain: choice of grapefruit or cereal; lean sausage (vegetarian available); fresh sautéed mushrooms; grilled tomatoes; eggs; whole-wheat toast and real butter (sunflower margarine for vegans); homemade three-fruit marmalade; tea or pretty decent noninstant coffee. *Moderate.*

Franklin's, 41 Regency Square, Brighton BN1 2FJ; tel. 27 01 6. Run by gay female proprietors Sandra and Katrina as mixed "because that's the way we live," Franklin's is very popular with lesbians and is our number one recommendation for women. Located on an impressively architecturally uniform seafront Regency square right off West Pier, near the Hove border (Hove's considered classier, Brighton racier), the place is proof positive that "lesbian" need not be synonymous with "low-rent." The rooms (large ones with typical Regency bowed windows, and tiled full bath, in front; smaller garden-view ones, with shower, in back—each with private toilet) are all different, but all scream decorator elegance in the best way. One features Laura Ashley–type frilly walls and curtains; another has an almost New Mexican/Native American geometric-patterned feel, in earth tones. Franklin's has a rep in town for doing "almost anything on request," whether it's room service, making you sandwiches at all hours, vegetarian breakfasts, or serving you a full evening meal. It's also fully licensed for beer, wine, and liquor. And we strongly suspect that if you can catch them when they're not working, the proprietors are great to party with. *Moderate.*

Benson's, 16 Egremont Place, Brighton BN2 1GA; tel. 69 88 52. Also highly recommended, by other guest house owners, as very comfortable for women. Female proprietors Barbara and Gill and their three resident dogs run it as mixed, and of the gay clientele, there are generally more women than men. The artwork on the walls here all evokes old Brighton, as does the delicate, impeccably kept feel of the house. The five rooms (four with double beds, one "family" room triple; three with showers; all with color TVs) are large, light, and all newly renovated with period touches like fringed wall-lamps and frilly padded headboards. *Moderate–mod. exp.*

Alpha Lodge, 19 New Steine, Brighton BN2 1PD; tel. 60 96 32. Brighton's oldest exclusively gay hotel, this is a restored house built in 1800 on a lovely Regency square half a block from the ocean. Proprietor Derrick operates the town's gay switchboard, so the place is info central. Sauna/steam room/fireplace lounge, open several nights a week for hotel guests—mostly men (as evidenced by the large statue of Michelangelo's "David") but women welcome—and friends. Though the Lodge is unlicensed, ice, mixers, etc., are available 24 hours for BYOB drinks. The 10 rooms are prefectly clean but much plainer and less "decorated" than most of those in other town gay guest houses; five have double beds and private shower, the rest are twin-bedded, both with and without showers; all with sinks and radios, some with TVs, none with toilet. Extras include complimentary drinks, and discounts during the low season and for members of some gay organizations. *Moderate–mod. exp.*

Rowland, 21 St. George Terrace, Brighton, BN1 2EE; tel. 60 36 39. Very theatrical! The clientele is mixed, but rest assured that stiff straights wouldn't last 15 minutes in any establishment run by actor/drag queen David "Maisie Trollette" Raven. The street is not as picturesque as some, but there's a nice patio and garden out back, and the most lovely, atmospheric living room–lounge in town. Of the 10 rooms, the large top-floor one is especially luxurious, but all have fantastic froufrou padded-velour headboards, old-style twin-shaded wall lamps behind the beds, sensuously thick carpeting; and all have showers and TVs. The coffee's awful. *Inexpensive.*

Shalimar, 223 Broad St., Brighton BN2 1EJ; tel. 60 53 16. Situated right off Marine Parade on a very San Francisco–looking street, this place is all lace curtains, bay windows, and cheerful yellow paint, outside; and inside, possesses the most complete private-bath facilities in town. Most of the nine rooms have large brand-new bathrooms with tubs, toilets, and even bidets. No two rooms are the same (except all have phones and color TVs), but lots of flowered prints and gold mirrors everywhere. Being excess queens, our personal fave was the large ground-floor room, no. 3, which has a bay window, antiques, plush paisley/fleur-de-lis carpeting, and plaster-swirl walls. Mixed gay and straight clientele, but proprietors Kevin and Lawrence say, "We're edging the straights out with the renovations." *Inexpensive–mod. exp.*

Catnaps, 21 Atlingworth St., Brighton BN2 1PL; tel. 68 51 93. If you get off on typical British "characters," you'll love crusty proprietor Malcolm Smith and his two friendly springer spaniels. The public lounge here is huge and hugely exotic: black marble fireplace, bird-of-paradise/peacock wallpaper and curtains, antique gold high-backed sofas, brass wall lamps, carpet deep enough to drown in. Ten rooms (three with showers and the rest with sinks; no private toilets), all nicely furnished in a well-kept old-fashioned style—none of that typical British old-and-tatty feel. The carpeted communal shower room has a condom machine. Unlike most guest houses, this one charges for coffee and tea at times other than breakfast. Most guests are gay men, but women are welcome. One- or two-pound reduction for more than one night. *Moderate.*

And finally, though it was in the process of relocating during our visit (so we were unable to check out the facilities personally), we feel we must also mention the **Floatarium,** 21 Bond St., Brighton BN1 1RD; tel. 67 95 55. After all, how often does one come across a women-run lesbian and gay-male guest house/natural therapy center where one's stay can include sessions in a flotation tank?

WHERE TO GO (DAY)

The **Royal Pavilion** is open all year, except December 25 and 26, from 10 A.M. to 5 P.M. (6 P.M. from June through September). The 1869 **Brighton Aquarium**, Britain's oldest and largest (and featuring dolphin shows) is also open year-round, except Christmas.

Aside from the **Lanes** (roughly bordered by West, North, and Old Steine Streets, and King's Road), shoppers might want to try the **North Laines** (behind Queen's Road, to the right of Brighton Station), and the Saturday morning **flea market** on Upper Gardner Street.

The brightly decorated carriages of the 1883 electric **Volk's Seafront Railway** run regularly April through September, from turn-of-the-century **Palace Pier** to the Marina. From there, it's just a hop to the gay-popular **Dukes Mound beach area** and the adjacent official **nudist beach**. Those who don't want to take the train can walk east from Palace Pier along Marine Parade, to Chichester Place, and cross the road to the sea. If you reach the Marina itself, you've gone too far.

The area referred to as the **gay beach**, Telscombe, is about four and a half miles east of Palace Pier, next to the sewer works. Walk, drive, or bus through Rottingdean, and look for a sign reading TELSCOMBE CLIFFS, with cars parked on the grass area next to it. Cross the road to the ocean side, go through the gate and follow the path down to the beach. Bring mats and refreshments (there are no facilities). If you reach Telscombe Tavern, you've gone too far.

The area beneath West Pier, from Hove Lawns to the Bushes, is also a popular beach, especially for **cruising** at night.

Gay-trippers will find Vita Sackville-West's and Harold Nicholson's **Sissinghurst Castle** and garden in Kent, northeast of Brighton, reachable either by car or via cycling path; **Lamb House**, where Henry James and later, E. F. Benson resided, at the top of West Street in Rye, East Sussex; and Virginia Woolf's home in **Rodmell**, in the Ouse Valley. (She drowned herself in the Ouse River, several miles upstream of Seaford, two towns past Rottingdean along the shore road between Brighton and Eastbourne.)

Walkers and cyclists might want to tackle at least part of the famous **South Downs Way.** This trail, passing directly north of Brighton, offers spectacular views of the sea and the Sussex downs. For a rough idea of the route, free walking and cycling **maps** of Britain are available from US branches of the **British Tourist Authority** (40 W. 57th St., New York, NY 10019; Room 450, 350 So. Figueroa, St., Los Angeles, CA 90071; 625 N. Michigan Ave., Suite 1510, Chicago, IL 60611; Cedar Maple Plaza, Suite 210, 2305 Cedar Springs Rd., Dallas, TX 75201). A more detailed pamphlet "Along the South Downs Way and on to Winchester," is about £1 at the Arundel tourist office.

WHERE TO GO (AT NIGHT)

With pubs closing at 11:30 P.M., and discos at 2 A.M. at the latest, Brighton's approximately dozen and a half clubs ought to keep anyone busy enough. Guesthouse owners can provide temporary membership for the few establishments run, for legal reasons, as private clubs.

Although most clubs draw, as usual, more gay men than lesbians, we found only a few places in town where women were unwelcome or might feel uncomfortable: the Beacon Royal and the Oriental, at any time; plus the Friday-night leather/denim-only affair run by the Sussex Lancers mens' leather group, in the cellar of the Villagers (a bar that, by the way, is on most afternoons a perfectly pleasant café). Reportedly, though, the feminist Only Alternative Left hostel in Hove (39 St. Aubyn's) is now running women-only Friday nights in their Purple Bat Café; for info, call 72 94 96. But do check with the local gay/lesbian hotlines about all the above. It was stressed to us that in Brighton, clubs' target clientele and gender policies change often, so what was true during our visit may not be true during yours.

Our own favorite is the mixed male/female **Queens Arms,** on George Street, one of those typically bent Brit gay pubs that combines Ye Olde Shakespearean decor with disco balls. Friday and Saturday are dance nights, but Sunday night's drag show is much more popular with women. If you haven't had enough by pub closing time, **Liam's Club** (75 Grand Parade) discos until 2 A.M. on Friday and Saturday and is popular with women—though be warned that this is a place that has had its ups and downs, managementwise and popularitywise. The most popular men's pub is the **Bulldog,** with upstairs/downstairs bars at 36 St. James Street. Also crowded most nights are the new and very hot **Queen's Head** and the friendly **Aquarium,** where you can get pub grub at lunchtime; both of these are on Steine Street. The Aquarium is opposite **Secrets** (25 Steine St.), a long-established membership club with a comfortable upstairs lounge for non–disco bunnies, and a 2 A.M. closing hour; but the hottest gay club night in town, possibly in all Great Britain—in terms of excellent new music, foxy clientele, and high-energy atmosphere—is **Shame** (at the Zap Club, Seafront Arches, Old Ship Beach; tel. 82 15 88 or 20 24 07 for info on which nights the club runs).

Pubs that are also open at night, but are particularly nice for afternoon ale breaks are the **Cricketers,** a wildly popular locally, fourteenth-century joint, in the Lanes (15 Black Lion St.) and the **Black Horse** (112 Church St.), mostly known only to locals though practically next door to the Royal Pavilion. Both places draw a somewhat older, mixed but picturesquely theatrical crowd.

Theatre and music buffs will want to check out the programs at the historic **Dome,** a 200-seat venue for pop and classical music as well as English variety shows, situated on the grounds of the Royal Pavilion. And famous London West End productions look even better in the red-plush Georgian interior of the **Theatre Royal,** in New Road overlooking the Pavilion's west lawn. Opera queens with a car might also want to check out the **Glyndebourne Festival Opera** in nearby Lewes, East Sussex, where most of the highly-sought-after general-public tickets are allocated by lot. Summer programs are available around January 1, which is when you should apply by mail, as annoying as it is to have to begin planning so far in advance. What you get for your trouble is international and future stars singing critically acclaimed productions of Mozart, Strauss, and Rossini, in a bucolic aristocratic-manor-house setting. And during the 75-minute intermission, you can picnic with other patrons, wearing full-evening dress, in the opera house's lakeside gardens. (Bring your own champagne, pheasant under glass, and candelabras.)

WHERE (AND WHAT) TO EAT

The restaurant even the nonvegetarian of us loved best is **Food for Friends** (17 Prince Albert St.; tel. 73 20 43. Open every day, 9 or 10 A.M. to 10 P.M.). In an informal cafeteria-style setting in the Lanes, this place—which is not gay, but has a bulletin board advertising gay as well as other "alternative" events—serves British vegetable dishes that (1) do *not* solely consist of brussels sprouts or other smelly members of the cabbage family; (2) are *not* boiled to the consistency of wet communion wafers; and (3) *are* beautifully seasoned, even with (gasp!) garlic! Dirt cheap, too: meals for two, with a full bottle of decent French wine, for around $25–$30. Really—if you think all vegetarian food has to be boring, try their buttery vegetable-cheese strudel, richly spiced Hungarian goulash pie, or feather-light cauliflower quiche before getting that opinion engraved in stone, okay?

We must mention, though, that even though this restaurant's in-house desserts are fine, you *must not miss* trying the French vanilla **Losely's Jersey double-cream ice cream,** sold at Food for Friends' retail outlet (turn left coming out of the restaurant, and it's right around the corner).

Restaurants particularly popular with gay people include **Fudge's** (127a King's Rd.; tel. 20 58 52), a moderately expensive restaurant with outdoor patio, on the sea road, run since 1984 by Dick James and Malcolm Fudge, and specializing in the freshest of local produce, fish, and meat; the **Spotlight** (33a Preston St.; tel. 25 92 8), one of the world's pinkest places, enhanced by very Fred-and-Ginger theatrical decor—gold-framed movie-star photos, ceramic masks, feather boas; and **Marmalade and Friends** (31 Western St.; tel. 77 20 89), which serves very reasonably priced nouvelle-English food like cream of mushroom and chestnut soup or poached salmon with salmon caviar and champagne sauce, and has a good wine list. Marmalade's the cat.

We personally didn't notice any other queers, though our guest-house owners assured us it's gay-friendly, but did find the freshest, lightest, crispiest fish and chips in town at **D'Arcy's** (49 Market St.; tel. 25 56 0). Located in a former fisherman's house in the oldest part of the Lanes, this elegant restaurant has a rep for the best, albeit expensive, fresh seafood in town. They do also, of course, have many more-elaborate dishes here, like a delicate, perfectly cooked halibut in shrimp sauce and a Dover sole meunière. Be warned, however, that in many of the more usual low-rent fish and chips joints in town, both the fish and the potatoes are frozen—so real chippy fans might want to get it while you can, at D'Arcy's.

Finally, although we're more afternoon beer–type ladies ourselves, our recommendation for those who want to try a traditional English afternoon tea is to take it surrounded by potted palms, Victorian period–outfitted waitresses, and (sometimes) live grand-piano music, at the **Palm Court Café,** located in an Edwardian crystallike pavilion on Palace Pier. Or if you're antique-browsing and don't want to budge from the Lanes, the **Mock Turtle** (4 Poole Valley, off East; tel. 27 38 0) is another terrific-looking old-style tea room.

WHERE TO GET THE LATEST DIRT
(INFO RESOURCES)

The big gay sources to remember are **Gay Switchboard** (tel. 69 08 25, 8 P.M.–
10 P.M. daily, except Saturday 6 P.M.–10 P.M., or write IB/Lambda, P.O. Box
449, Brighton, BN1 1UU); **Lesbian Line** (tel. 60 32 98, Tuesday and Friday,
8 P.M.–10 P.M.), and **Sussex AIDS Helpline** (tel. 57 16 6, 8 P.M.–10 P.M. daily,
or write P.O. Box 17, Brighton BN2 5NQ).

The **Brighton Tourist Information Service** is located in Room 18, Marlbor-
ough House, 54 Old Steine, Brighton BN1 1EQ; tel. 23 75 5. As well as regular
tourist info, they seemed cheerfully willing to provide help, including photo-
copies, only a year or two out of date, from the **Spartacus** guide's Brighton
section, to any visitor who expressed an interest in gay facilities in town.

Since virtually all English gay people seem to be born with a genetic urge to
open a guest house in Brighton—meaning new gay places open there every 20
minutes or so—we feel it is particularly important for visitors here to get hold
of a few local gay monthly periodicals, rather than relying completely on this or
any other *book* for the latest info. The most popular free gay rag is the London-
based *Pink Paper,* available at most gay bars along with the less well known
Action Issue (tel. 081/677 5930). The very informative *Capital Gay* newsweekly
and the comprehensive and amusing (though less timely) quarterly *Kennedy's
London Guide* also have Brighton ads and listings, and both mail internationally.
The best info source, though, is the back of *Gay Times,* which contains an
astonishingly comprehensive and up-to-date bar-and-organization list for Brighton, as well as the rest of Britain; additionally, at least a dozen Brighton guest
houses run detailed display ads in each issue. In town, buy *Gay News* at gay
shops **Cardome** (47a St. James St.) and **Scene 22** (22 Preston St.) or at numerous
regular old newsstands; or send for a single copy or subscription before you go.
(See "Practical Information, London" for mail-order addresses of all the above
publications.)

And for those interested in learning the universal language with other gay
people, write the *Gay Esperanto League* (**Ligo De Samseksamaj Geesperantistoj**).
In England, the contact is Peter Danning (G/f, 68 Church Rd., Richmond, Surrey,
Great Britain TW10 6LN). In the U.S.A., LSG's representative is Earl Galvin
(2440 Market St., Apt. 6, San Francisco, CA 94114).

WALES

The Ladies

They've taken away and burnt your caravan, they've thrown away your pots and pans and your half-mended wicker chairs. They've pulled down your sleeves and buttoned up your collar— they've forced you to sleep beneath a self-respecting roof with no chinks to let the stars through—but they haven't caught me yet! Come! Come away!
> —*Violet Trefusis, vastly underrated British writer largely known only for her youthful affair with Vita Sackville-West (largely known only for her later affair with Virginia Woolf), in a 1918 letter to Vita.*

There'll always be an England, they say. In fact Disraeli said, in 1845, that there were a couple of 'em: "Two nations, between whom there is no intercourse and no sympathy; who are as ignorant of each other's habits, thoughts, and feelings as if they were dwellers in different zones, or inhabitants of different planets; who are formed by different breeding, are fed by different food, are ordered by different manners, and are not governed by the same laws. . . ."

The great statesman was actually speaking of neither the hets and the homos nor of the boys and the girls, nor even of the English and the Welsh, but of the rich and the poor. In early nineteenth century Britain, though, all minorities were up against much the same sort of thing, in terms of not merely legal but cultural oppression.

Here's what the deal was for a pre-twentieth-century woman who was in love with another woman, and wished to make a life with her—the usual lesbian setup: Welsh country cottage, compost heap, two-cow garage, and so on.

Deal Number One: If you were of the lower classes, you had one option: to don men's clothes, get a menial men's job, and pass as a regular old straight man with a wife. Barfo. But the fact is, this sometimes worked. In England, Anne Bonney and Mary Read conducted an outstandingly successful imposture and career, at least until their arrest in 1720. The charge was, essentially, overachievement of career goals. They were pirates.

Most of our European ancestors were lower-class (really—we're probably the only two people you've ever read about who've channeled past lives as chimney sweeps rather than Egyptian royalty). So, to tell you the truth, the conditions under which poor women lived have been the catalyst for many close-to-terminal finales to our games of "Let's Pretend We Lived in the Past," variation: "If You Could Bring Only One Thing with You from Modern Times, What Would It Be?" Without mentioning names, this is how our dialogue goes:

FEMALE PERSON A: Honestly, I feel that given recent developments in plastics, it wouldn't be at all difficult to pass as a man in 1750.

FEMALE PERSON B (steam spritzing from ears): Are you actually telling me that instead of bringing antibiotics that could save most of Europe from the plague, you would bring . . . *a dildo?*

This is quite unfair, because Female Person A can assure you that she would not bring a dildo. She'd bring Tampax. But seriously, the real issue was that the poor woman's option of "passing" in order to live with one's love often did not work, and the penalties for exposure were stiff, to say the least. In early-eighteenth-century Germany, Catharina Linck was burned at the stake for trying to pass as a man and marry another woman.

But then we have . . .

Deal Number Two: Of course, if one was of the upper classes, things were simpler. One had *no* options. It was either marriage to a man, or the nunnery. Financial dependence on one's family's charitable whims left no possibility of making a life with another woman. There was changing class, of course. But in class-bound Britain, deliberately "lowering" one's status was even more inconceivable than coming out.

So one is not appalled, just terribly sad, to discover the twenty-four-year relationship between Ellen Nussey and Charlotte Brontë, for instance. Judging by their correspondence, the two had been in love from the moment they'd met at school in 1831, right up to Brontë's death in 1855. They very much wanted to live together. Yet the total amount of time they experienced alone in nearly a quarter century was one stolen week's vacation in Bridlington. This, which was supposed to have been a much longer holiday, lasted only until Nussey's distraught family tracked them down. Nevertheless, it was a week they remembered ever after with such pathetic eagerness and excitement that one wants to punch a wall for the unfairness of it, or cry.

Even in the relative freedom of 1920s Britain, class-bound Vita Sackville-West and Violet Trefusis were both compulsorily married. (To gay men, at least. They did have *some* standards.) The bottom line is that despite a plea that would have compelled anyone with even an ounce of romance in her soul to throw a few changes of underwear and a blow dryer in a carpetbag and flee the respectable real world forever, Vita never did "come away!" with Violet.

But one hundred and fifty years before, Irish aristocrats Sarah Ponsonby and Lady Eleanor Butler did just that. Where they "came away" to was Llangollen, in North Wales. And there, the idyllic, passionate union of the "Ladies of Llangollen," as they came to be known to contemporary admirers ranging from the local peasantry to the queen of England, lasted fifty years, as long as they both lived.

The life they led—what we might call Deal Number Three—depended on having money, and to a certain extent, on living in a time long before the sexologists came sniffing after female friendships, when one had to do something even more seriously outrageous than run away together before it occurred to people that you might be (gasp!) Doing It. In their day, and in the typical guidebooks of our day as well, the Ladies were described not as lezzies, but as "eccentrics." Still, they pushed the limits of the allowable much farther than most other wealthy women dared to. They got away with it.

According to a journal from the late 1700s, Sarah Ponsonby thought North Wales the "beautifullest country in the world." Less scarred by industry than the area around Cardiff and the rest of the southern part of the country, North Wales (specifically the Clwyd and Gwynedd regions, just west of Chester, England, and perhaps a three-hour drive northwest of London) is not Dylan Thomas coal-mining country. But its beauty is a hard one. This is the place where the ancient Celts finally retreated before the Saxon invaders, and it looks as though, in a last grand thumb of the old nose, the defeated people packed up all the high scenic drama and took it with them. The topography is striking, the hillsides dramatically varied: here, dense humps of wild oak, pine, and intensely green meadows; there, stubborn gray rock, purple with heather and slashed through with nearly inaccessible gorges and madly rushing wild rivers. The coast, too, is all nature contradicting itself: Rugged rock cliffs adjoin flat salt-marshes and sand dunes. The northern mountains, which Sarah called "beautifully horrid," are Brobdingnagian boulders streaked by geological wars from times far predating the human wars that left Wales dotted with more stone forts and castles, mile for mile, than any other locale in the world.

This northern third of the country also remains the most uncompromising part of Wales in matters other than scenery. It is proudly rural. Driving on major highways through tourist areas like spectacular Snowdonia National Park one is apt to crest a hill and find oneself face-to-fender with a road full of blasé munching sheep. The north is also the most nationalist part of Wales, where you're likely to hear regular people on the street conversing in Welsh. Try speaking it yourselves, kids! No one will take offense at your mistakes; this isn't France. Native speakers here have a highly developed sense of humor. People with ancestors who named towns stuff like "Llanfairpwllgwyngyllgogerychwryndrobwllllantysiliogogogoch" (pronounced the way a cat sounds when it vomits) *have* to.

In May 1780, Sarah and Eleanor settled into the then-simple, square, slate-roofed five-room stone cottage they christened Plas Newydd, the new place. (Pronounced "Plahce," as in Place de la Concorde; "New-with," to rhyme with Lewis, but with a lisp.) The view from the house and its acres of lawns and woods was, then as now, fabulous. To the north, the Eglwyseg mountains with the imposing ruins of twelfth-century Castell Dinas Bran loom over the town. The Berwyn mountains rise up to the south, and the rocky Trevors to the east. The actual town of Llangollen was, in the Ladies' time, little more than two narrow intersecting main streets lined with humble brick houses, although its situation on the main stagecoach route between London and the seaport Holyhead lent the village a cosmopolitan market-center vivaciousness. From their dressing-room window, Lady Eleanor and the Honorable Sarah had an excellent view of the coaches discharging passengers at the Hand Hotel, and in fact took great pleasure in commenting on various travelers' tacky clothes and other fashion faux pas.

Today the Hand is still in business, and though Llangollen has a few more streets and a daily instead of weekly craft market, the town retains an ungentrified feel. The eighteenth-century naturalist Thomas Pennant opined that the physical situation of Llangollen, in the vale of the river Dee, was the most romantic in North Wales. Perhaps this is why—according to only slightly exaggerated local legend—the Ladies never spent so much as a single night away from their own bedroom.

The two met back in Ireland when Lady Eleanor Butler was a hopeless spinster of twenty-nine and the Honorable Sarah Ponsonby was a recently orphaned thirteen-year-old. The Honorable Sarah had just been farmed out by her closest remaining relatives, Lady Betty and Sir William Fownes, to Miss Parkes's boarding school in Kilkenny. Since the Fowneses' Woodstock Manor was twelve miles away in the village of Inistiogue, the city-based Butlers had been asked to keep an eye on Sarah, a chore Eleanor didn't seem to mind. This initial stage of the Ladies' relationship, which seemed to consist largely of Eleanor reading to Sarah from great works of literature (a practice they later continued until Eleanor's death . . . even afterwards, if some reports are to be believed), lasted until Sarah's education ended when she was eighteen, and she was brought back to Inistiogue.

The separation lasted five years. Then things came to a head for both women. Eleanor's parents had had her educated in a convent, and now they were making definite plans to send her back to the nuns for good. Sarah's "parental" situation was worse: Gouty, fat, fiftyish Sir William was leching after her. By letter, the two made plans. Then, on the night of Monday, April 2, 1778, Eleanor sneaked out of the family castle, changed into men's clothes to deceive possible pursuers, and rode off on a borrowed horse to a rendezvous with Sarah. Their goal, initially, was Waterford, twenty-three miles away; then, the boat for England, and freedom.

They were apprehended by Sir William's servants within a mile of Waterford. Riding in a carriage and disguised in male drag, with Sarah carrying a pistol, they would have made it all the way, had it not been for the yapping of Sarah's mangy little dog, whose bark one of their trackers recognized. We cannot help pointing out that if they'd had a cat, like normal lesbians, this would not have happened. (In Llangollen, eventually, they did get one, Tatters, who slept on their bed, as God intended.)

Again they were torn apart, Sarah to Inistiogue and the disgraced Eleanor, perceived as the *real* queer, the predatory dragon lady, to the home of a married sister to await imminent shipment to a French nunnery. They were forbidden to communicate. But after three weeks of pining and sighing and doing whatever "giving attitude" was called in 1778, they were granted permission for one last brief farewell meeting. In the allotted half hour, they arranged another escape.

This time, Eleanor walked twelve miles across outlaw-infested country, and hid for days in the cupboard of Sarah's bedroom. Again, they were discovered. This time, their families threw in the towel. After all, gay people in the closet is bad enough metaphorically speaking, but when you go to put on your overcoat and there one is *literally*, seated on your jodphur boots and reading Rousseau or something, that's the last straw.

With the understanding that they'd never again set foot in sodomy-free Ireland, Eleanor and Sarah were granted a total allowance of £280 per year, just above poverty level for that time, but enough to ensure that rather than having to work to make a living, the Ladies could simply make living simply their work. We are talking major nesting here. "A life of sweet and delicious retirement" is what the Ladies had in mind.

To effect their retreat into the fantasyland version of perfect rustic simplicity that popular philosophies of the day so idealized, Sarah and Eleanor established what they called their system for daily living. This involved total withdrawal from fashionable society's vanities; charitable works among their poorer neighbors, largely of the "help them to help themselves" variety, like teaching the latest land-improvement schemes, or procuring and distributing higher-yield seeds; continually improving their physical surroundings, the house and grounds of Plas Newydd; reading, learning foreign languages, painting, reading some more; and finally, recording the whole thing.

Contemporary time travelers know so much about their life because the Ladies kept meticulous journals featuring a bewildering array of details and recipes, inspirational quotes from their readings, gardening tips, financial records, and future projects, as well as daily diaries. Literature lovers will not be impressed; these journals are accurate rather than artful. The Ladies' art did not go into the recording of their lives, but into the living of them.

Today, aside from the International Musical Eisteddfod, the Ladies and their home are Llangollen's best-known tourist attraction, and with good reason. Inside and out, from floor to ceiling, Plas Newydd is a wall-to-wall riot of elaborately carved dark Gothic oak, illuminated like a jeweled magic lantern by lead-paned stained glass windows in all colors, some dating from the 1500s.

But even during their lifetimes, the two recluses attracted considerable company. Among their more famous gentlemen callers were Sir Walter Scott, William Wordsworth, Edmund Burke, Josiah Wedgewood, Horace Walpole, and the Duke of Wellington, whose 1814 visit the Ladies commemorated with a classic teenager-in-love inscription prominently carved over the fireplace in Plas Newydd's "Oak Room": "E.B. & S.P."

To nonromantics, it might seem that something along the lines of a "D. of W." would have been a more appropriate commemoration, but obviously the Ladies' ideas about who was paying homage to whom were as clear as their ideas about interior decoration.

Most of the above male visitors contributed to the very specific home-improvement schemes of the impeccably spiritual yet not impractical Ladies, as a sign posted at Plas Newydd makes clear: "None ventured a second visit without bringing a contribution of carved oak which was the regular passport." (Wordsworth sent a sonnet instead of oak. He was *not* asked back.) None of the above stayed over. As another sign in Plas Newydd notes, "Among their many peculiarities, they never invited any gentleman to sleep at the house."

Women were another story. Although the rather snobbish Ladies were still stiffly selective, their female pajama-party roster reads like a *Who's Who* of the lesbian underground in 1800. Included were sculptress Anne Damer, accused by Lord Derby, in a notorious scandal of the day, of "liking her own sex in a criminal way" and "unnatural affection." Another overnight guest was French author and pop *savante* Madame de Genlis, whose memoirs fervidly recalled the twice-weekly socials in her childhood convent school, with nuns as dance partners. At Plas Newydd, the Comtesse was kept awake all night by an Aeolian harp hung below her window. It is displayed today in the Ladies' dressing room.

Nonvisiting admirers ranged right up to royalty level. The youngest daughter of England's George III, Princess Amelia, sent along some of her elder sister Princess Elizabeth's etchings, normally presented only to family. Their mom, Queen Charlotte, wrote to ask for a copy of the estate plans.

By 1800, the Ladies themselves were something like royalty in Llangollen. Though the local hero-worship aspect has died down considerably in recent generations, the respect in which the Ladies were held is still evident at fourteenth-century St. Collen's church, where they are buried. Beside them lies their beloved servant, Mary "Molly the Bruiser" Caryll, Lady Betty's formidable six-foot-three onetime handmaid who aided the Ladies' escape. A single headstone, describing Eleanor as Sarah's "beloved," stands over their graves. You can't miss it: It is the largest memorial in the cemetery, directly on the main path to the church entrance. When we were there, someone had left a bouquet of fuschia flowers in a marmalade jar on the grave.

Inside St. Collen's, in the middle of the right-hand wall, is a stone memorial plaque. It is permanent. It is prominent. It is a portrait of the Ladies dressed, as was their custom, in matching black riding habits, starched neckties, and short-cropped powdered hair crowned with twin tall top hats.

Ever since first reading about the Ladies more than a decade ago, we'd felt that Llangollen would make one of the world's great gay Girl Scout field trips. It didn't surprise us at all to discover that British lesbians were way ahead of us on the perv pilgrimage trail.

"Why on earth are you going to North Wales?" one woman we'd met in southern England demanded. "There's absolutely no gay life there to speak of."

Well, we began, we were going to Llangollen, and—

"*Oh,*" she interrupted with a big smile, waving her hands to indicate that no further explanation was necessary. "The *Ladies.*" We had variations of this conversation all over London and Brighton. Every lesbian seems to have made the hajj at least once.

Actually, cult followers commenced flocking to Plas Newydd almost instantly upon Sarah's death in 1831, two years after Eleanor's. The cottage's next purchasers, in fact, were a couple of spinsters who'd fawned after the Ladies in life, Amelia Lawley and Charlotte Andrew. The attempts of these two wannabes, whom Eleanor had snarkily nicknamed "the Lollies and Trollies," to emulate the Ladies consisted largely of a plethora of grotesque home renovations which are now, fortunately, gone.

An almost Lourdes-quality experience was had by one of England's first woman physicians, Mary Gordon. After encountering the Ladies by chance on one of their favorite hillside walking paths, Dr. Gordon was inspired to bribe a caretaker to let her into Plas Newydd's library later that day. According to the doctor, she and the Ladies then talked all night about birth control and other issues of the times. Did we mention that this occurred almost a hundred years after the Ladies' deaths?

It's obvious that gay role-model seekers, as well as mere cheap thrill-seeking time trippers like us, have come to Llangollen for years to play their own versions of "Let's Pretend." To deny a lesbian presence among visitors to Plas Newydd makes little more sense than denying a lesbian presence at the Michigan Womyn's Music Festival. But at the town tourist office, where we'd gone to get a general fix on the likelihood of gay visitors encountering homophobia in Llangollen guesthouses, that's exactly what the woman behind the counter did. In fact, her face went ashen when we first uttered the *L* word.

To backtrack a bit, we must tell you that there is not a lot of gay life in present-day Llangollen. What there's a lot of in Llangollen is, for example, fish. And canoe rentals. The river Dee is very big on brown trout, and is one of England's best canoeing rivers. Also, for couples whose athletic preference is carrying heavy shopping bags, there's love spoons. You cannot walk ten feet in Llangollen without passing thirty-five cute olde shoppes selling this perennially popular native craft item consisting of two oak spoons carved with your four initials. These spoons are intertwined in such a way that it's impossible to eat with them, but fans of romance and carved-oak initials will certainly want to buy a pair. A love spoon was one of Eleanor and Sarah's first purchases in Wales.

You will not, alas, find it easy to pick up Ladies souvenirs. After wading through endless commemorative tea towels, coasters, aprons, and postcards depicting the likes of Prince Charles and herds of sheep we struck out at nearly every shop in town. The lone Ladies *tchotchka* we were finally able to lay our hands on was a tiny ashtray, showing the gals strolling along together in their Fred Astaire hats.

Gay bars and hotels in Llangollen? Forget it. Instead we'd been seeking gay-friendly straight guest houses. Before we hit the tourist office, we had indeed already located several.

The woman in the tourist office, however, all but warned that gay visitors better commute two hundred or so miles each way from London if they wanted friendly quarters. "I'm *quite sure* they could not find a room. People here are very narrow-minded," she assured us, with some pride. "They're not used to seeing this sort of person."

We suggested that because of the Ladies, the town had no doubt been doing a brisk business in the queerer variety of visitor for generations.

"Oh, no," she sputtered. "I'm sure you're wrong."

We countered that several hotels had already told us that they would welcome any gay guests we sent them.

"Well don't you believe them!" she harrumphed. "They may have *said* that, but people will say anything. Why, they sometimes say they'll take *dogs,* but they don't mean it."

An antidote to this kind of small-minded meanness, and far more typical of what we personally encountered throughout Wales was Berwyn Y Coed, the homey, eccentrically decorated guest house where we ourselves stayed. To clarify "eccentric" in this instance, our room was vivid purple and green, festooned with both lace ruffles and a photo of Cypriot soldiers on a tank. The bathroom decor included a Queen Elizabeth souvenir coronation tea box and a sign above the loo reading "WE AIM TO PLEASE. YOU AIM TOO, PLEASE."

To be honest, we had been so warmly treated by charming, mother-fussy proprietor Glenfa Roberts, that we'd been reluctant to run the Drill on her, not wanting to be disillusioned. But we steeled ourselves, and Mrs. Roberts at once responded that our gay readers were perfectly welcome. Except . . . She hesitated, looking worried. ". . . There wouldn't be any people coming here who . . . had AIDS, would there?"

We said we had no way of knowing, but probably yes, there might be.

For just a second Mrs. Roberts thought. Then her jaw set, and she shook her head. "No, no, *please* forget I ever said that. Of *course* they are welcome here, *all* of them." She went on to explain: It was just that with AIDS education so spotty in Wales, people didn't know what to believe. So we had a nice chat about methods of transmission, and left with Mrs. Roberts saying how thrilled she was to be listed in our gay guide, and how we'd really made her whole day. She'd made ours, too.

If for some reason your vacation needs are not satisfied by gay people who've been dead for a hundred and fifty years, and you absolutely insist upon hanging out with a few living ones, this is do-able. Not easy, but do-able.

Action in North Wales is limited to a few more-or-less gay nights in the not-terribly-festive university towns of Bangor and Aberystwyth, (the latter really in borderline mid-Wales). But there are ample bars in South Wales, and several terrific urban as well as country guest houses in and around Cardiff. Wales being a small country, it's a cinch to do Llangollen as a day trip—or would be a cinch, if it wasn't for (1) Welsh roads, which are shoulderless and about as wide as a pack of cigarettes; and (2) Welsh drivers, who, apparently uninformed that Britain does not have a space program, are all trying to reach escape velocity in their Morris Minis.

Assuming that the prospect of dueling it out with these auto astronauts leaves you undaunted, have we ever got a gay trip find for you: a lesbian custom-made-shoe factory. Cooperatively run Marged Shoes has been located since 1981 in one of the outbuildings of a former estate in Betys Bledrws, near the little market and college town of Lampeter. Lampeter's sort of the Northampton, Massachusetts, of Wales, to judge by the number of homesteading gay women honeycombing its woods and hills. A visitable alternative-energy center in nearby Machynlleth has also attracted a sizable counterculture population to the area. "I suppose there're gay men around here, too," muses Cher Stubs, one of Marged's founders. "But I haven't seen one in years."

After measuring your weirdo feet (and don't try telling us your feet aren't weird; *everyone's* are) the Marged women will *handmake* you any of forty different styles of shoes and boots. Sandals, yuppie walking shoes, dress Beatle boots, and your basic 1920s-style fuck-me pumps are among the styles available, in any of a dozen colors and three foot shapes (normal pointy-toed, natural Earth Shoe splayed-toe, or a rounded-toe compromise). We each bought a pair of entirely handmade perfectly-fitting hot-pink-and-black boots, one pair grotesquely narrow and the other grotesquely wide, for less than we'd paid for our last pair of Nikes. These ladies do mail-order, too, and even say they don't at all mind making shoes for guys who don't mind shoes on women's lasts.

If you're a history and scenery buff who's not starved for gay nightlife, there's plenty to do within several miles of Llangollen. The romantic Dinas Bran ruin was a prominent fort in the twelfth and thirteenth centuries. Two miles northwest are a ninth-century memorial, Eliseg's Pillar, as well as the ruins of Valle Crucis Abbey, a Cistercian edifice founded in 1201 and important until the dissolution of monasteries in 1535. Six miles away in Clwyd is Chirk Castle, a splendid National Trust Property, complete with elegantly furnished staterooms, formal gardens, and a dungeon. Ten miles away is Erdigg, one of Britain's most classic *Upstairs, Downstairs* houses: The restored laundry, sawmill, bakehouse, and smithy illustrate eighteenth-century servant life; the upper classes are represented in staterooms dating from 1720, with antique furniture and tapestries.

Eleanor and Sarah, by the way, once visited all the above, except Erdigg, in one day—walking. And if this kind of walking circuit interests you, there is a Gay Outdoor Club in nearby Manchester, England, that has activities in Wales.

Naturally it's the Ladies' own home, though, that is the prime sight of interest for us. Quite a sight it is, too—a veritable Druid's wet dream, right from the canopied oak front porch elaborately carved with cherubim, flowers, and other decorative twizzles, to representations of the four Evangelists, and scenes admonishing against intemperance and obesity. To judge from their later portraits, Eleanor and Sarah paid little heed to the latter stricture.

Thankfully, the Glyndŵr District Council and Wales's Council of Museums, the organizations now responsible for the Plas Newydd restoration, appear to be free of the galloping homophobia we encountered at the tourist office. Both signs posted at Plas Newydd and the souvenir booklets sold there, carefully correct past coverup efforts. It is pointed out that the State Bedchamber, actually the Ladies' guest room, was once "also (wrongly) called Miss Ponsonby's bedroom." The "Ladies' Bedchamber" itself, gradually restored over the past decade to nearly its original state, now features a sign explaining apologetically that while the present smallish and plainish four-poster bed once belonged to them, it was evidently not *the* bed. The Ladies were more queen-size-mattress gals: "The two friends slept together in a huge four-poster bed of richly carved oak," which, over the years, had been lost.

Maybe it was just the usual minority-group tendency to be overly grateful for crumbs; such simple accuracy shouldn't have struck us as quite touching. But it did.

After viewing the house, it seemed fitting to stroll, as the Ladies did every day, through their wild garden down by the banks of the river Cufflymen. Much of the scene here is different now. Trees are cut down, rustic wooden bridges have been replaced by stone. But near the trail's end, you'll still find the ancient stone font the Ladies ripped off from Valle Crucis Abbey, and dedicated as a shrine to friendship.

Across the stream from the font is a tree which has become a sort of tourists' friendship shrine annex; more recent "friends" have, for a hundred and fifty years, inscribed their own entwined initials on its bark. Embarrassing as it is to admit, we did whip out those Swiss army knives which God issues to all lesbians at birth—well, She should—and carved our own names, and the date. This was exactly the sort of pseudospiritual sentimentality we usually avoid. But remembering the "E.B. AND S.P." over Plas Newydd's fireplace, we told ourselves that just this once, instead of being a tacky gesture, carving initials on a tree was more like adding a footnote to gay history. It *is* an oak.

ALES

PRACTICAL INFORMATION

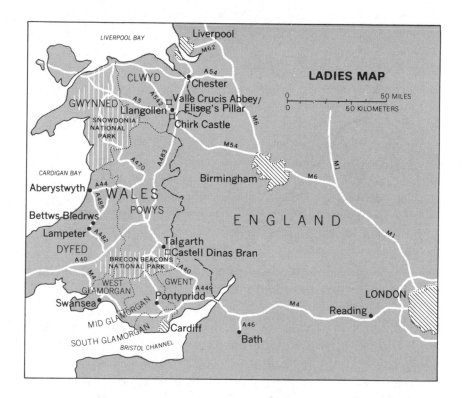

GENERAL INFO / HINTS

While many destinations in this book have modern gay social facilities as well as gay historical interest, Llangollen is not one of them. And since we'd just as soon pass on being the laughingstock of gay Britain this year, we have no intention of trying to pass the place off as gay central. Llangollen has the Ladies—and possibly their ghosts. Period. Otherwise, except for occasional events in the north coast university town of Bangor and west coast university town of Aberystwyth, there is, in fact, little modern gay life in all of North or Mid-Wales, at least of the bar/restaurant/open-to-the-public sort that would do tourists any good. Most Welsh gay life centers in the south: some in the university town of Swansea; most in Cardiff, which, by train or car, is about two hours from London. But believe us—with the beauty of North Wales, not to mention the effect of the very strong local Welsh beers you can buy in grocery stores or any old pubs, you won't miss gay bars a bit.

Llangollen is about 130–150 miles north of Cardiff, depending upon whether you take the larger M4-M5-M6-A5 routes, or the more scenic A470-A483-A5 through the Brecon Beacons. For a change, we cannot recommend the railways—they don't run to Llangollen often enough to be a practical option. But those who simply cannot face Wales's narrow, shoulderless, hedgerowed roads and manic drivers can take public transport to nearby Chester or Chirk, and from there get a bus to Llangollen for about £1.

The gay bars and organizations nearest to Llangollen are actually in England, in Chester (known for its double-decker, arcaded, row buildings) and Liverpool, roughly 25 and 50 miles away, respectively.

Currency unit: the pound (£)

WHERE TO STAY

The gay guest houses recommended are in the south part of the country. Fortunately, Wales is a small country, so all establishments are day trip distance (two and a half to three hours) from Llangollen. The three straight guest houses listed in Llangollen were, of course, put through the Drill, and are perfectly wonderful places to play at being the Ladies. Rooms in Llangollen are generally easy to come by, except during the week of the international Eisteddfod folk music festival in early July, when, unless you've reserved, you can forget any accommodations within 15 miles.

Prices: *Inexpensive* = under £25, *moderate* = £25–35; *mod./exp.* = £35–45; *expensive* = over £45. All prices are for double rooms, and include full breakfast. (As in England, the term for "room with bathroom facilities" is "en suite.")

Berwyn Y Coed, proprietor Glenfa Roberts, 66 Berwyn St., Llangollen, Clwyd LL20 8NA; tel. 0978/86 03 39. We stayed in the very bright green-and-purple back room, but try to get the larger, fireplaced front bedroom instead; warm and wonderful Mrs. Roberts is particularly proud of her restoration job on this one, and you'll see why. For the vegetarian, a nice tomato omelette was cheerfully substituted for the full-breakfast meat substances. All rooms have individual coffee/tea-making facilities. Otherwise, life at Berwyn Y Coed is informal family style, with everyone sharing a bathroom and Mrs. Roberts fussing exactly like the mother everyone should have had. *Inexpensive.*

Henllys Guest House, proprietors Nance and John Haddy, Berwyn, Llangollen, Clwyd LL20 8AL; tel. 0978/86 12 63. This 1700 house ("modernized" Regency-style in about 1805) sits on a rural three-quarter acre overlooking a valley and hillside, one mile outside Llangollen. The three bedrooms each have sinks, but share a bathroom (separate from the owners'). There's also a separate guest lounge with fireplace. Your full breakfast is served at any hour you feel like getting up, and the Haddys will make you dinner, if you want it, any time until about 9 P.M. They'll also supply advice and maps to any walkers who really want to get off the beaten track. *Inexpensive.*

Gales, 18 Bridge St., Llangollen, Clwyd LL200 8PF; tel. 0978/86 14 27 or 86 00 89; fax 0978/86 13 13. This small but full-service hotel over a restaurant is for those who want all the American style in-room accoutrements—phones, TVs, full en suite bathrooms—plus elegant extras like four-posters or brass beds, and other antique furnishings *Mod./exp.*

Lan Farm, Graigwen, Pontypridd, Mid Glamorgan CF37 3NN; tel. 0443/40 36 06. Located on a big, *big* hill between Cardiff and the Brecon Beacons National Park, this is a six-bedroom (all en suite) traditional Welsh farmhouse with cozy fireplaced sitting room, surrounded by a meadow with panoramic views. Proprietors Jamie and Eileen run it exclusively for gay men and women—mostly couples, although there is one half-price single room—and it is extremely popular, so advance reservations are essential. Evening meals, if you want them, are also bookable in advance, and quite inexpensive (about $10 per person). No alcohol sold, but they're happy to have you bring your own. *Moderate.*

Courtfield Hotel, 101 Cathedral Road, Cardiff CF1 9PH; tel. 0222/22 77 01. An elegant, impeccably-kept town-house hotel, in a Victorian street near Cardiff Castle, run as a mixed gay and straight establishment but most welcoming and helpful to gay men and women. The 17 bedrooms (nine with private bath, eight with shared bath; all with sinks, phones, color TVs, and coffee/tea-making facilities) are done in period furniture and paintings. The hotel is about a 10-minute walk from the gay bars in the center, but, for those who don't want to budge, has its own restaurant, open Monday–Saturday. *Moderate to mod./ exp.*

Finally, a very inexpensive place we did not personally check out, but which was recommended by the Cardiff Women's Centre for women who prefer **women-only lodgings,** is **Ty-Cennin** (6 East Grove, Roath, Cardiff CF2 3AE; tel. 0222/48 13 84), run by proprietors Margaret and Barbara as an alternative guest house "offering more comfort than the average" and vegetarian food.

WHERE TO GO (DAY)

Plas Newydd: Open from May till the end of September; tel. 0978/86 02 34. Located a 10-minute walk south of Llangollen's main through street, which is confusingly called Berwyn, Regent, or Queen at various points, right off Hill Street. (Warning: While reading up for your trip, don't confuse this house with James Wyatt's larger, more architecturally famous Plas Newydd near Bangor.)

St. Collen's Church: The plaque honoring the Ladies is inside (open morning and afternoon during the summer); their grave is impossible to miss from the main path to the front door.

Valle Crucis Abbey: These ruins of a Cistercian Abbey originally founded in the early years of the thirteenth century lie two miles out of town, northwest on the A542. Open most days of year. The ninth-century Eliseg's Pillar stands in a field nearby.

Castell Dinas Bran: You can't miss the ruins of this twelfth- and thirteenth-century medieval fortress (surrounded by the ditch of an Iron Age hill fort) looming above town. Begin the steep climb at Wharf Hill.

Chirk Castle: A National Trust property six miles from Llangollen along the A5. Open daily except Mondays and Saturdays, 12 P.M.–5 P.M. from Easter to September 30, and then until October 25 on Saturdays and Sundays only; tel. 0691/77 77 01.

Erdigg: In Erdigg, near Wrexham: A terrific eighteenth-century *Upstairs, Downstairs* house, with aristocratic manor and working-class bakehouse, sawmill, and smithy. There are hourly buses from Llangollen to Erdigg (continuing to Chester), Monday–Saturday. Open daily, except Fridays, 12 P.M.–5 P.M., from Easter to October 18; tel. 0978/35 53 11.

The Ladies walked all the above, except for Erdigg, in a day. And we feel certain that, had the factory existed then, they'd have ordered their footwear from **Marged Shoes**, Stable Cottage, Derby Ormond Park, Betys Bledrys, Lampeter, Dyfed, Wales SA48 8PA; tel. Llangbi 557. Proprietors Cher Stubs and Brigid Morison.

WHERE TO GO (NIGHT)

It's not gay—nothing alive in Llangollen is—but we had a swell time at the **Sarah Ponsonby** pub. To reach it, cross the bridge and take a right; it's about one city block along, on the right. The bartender here knows everything you'd ever want to know about 1960s music and beer of all nations.

The closest well-known gay venue to Llangollen is a very popular exclusively lesbian/gay bar-restaurant about a 45-minute drive away, in Chester, England: **Connections**, on Watergate Street, open every day 9:30 P.M.–2 A.M. (Sundays 8:30 P.M.–midnight); the bar's **Hungry Pilgrim** restaurant is open 11 A.M.– 5 P.M. (tel. 0244/32 06 19). Chester also has a women-run mixed gay and straight bar, the **Liverpool Arms** (79 Northgate St.; tel. 0244/31 02 32).

Tuesday is supposedly gay night at **Skinner's Bar,** located in a not-easy-to-find courtyard in Aberystwyth. As summer visitors, they sure coulda fooled us. Perhaps Skinner's gets gayer when university's in session.

There are almost a dozen gay bars in Liverpool. See "Where to Get the Latest Dirt" for hotlines, and check out the listings in *Gay Times.*

WHERE (AND WHAT) TO EAT

While there are scads of Welsh guidebooks revolving around scenery and castles, few mention food at all. There is a reason for this. Even Welsh lamb, which is among the best in the world, is difficult to find prepared in any way that isn't a culinary total waste: i.e., underspiced and overcooked.

Our advice is to eat light and save your restaurant money for Paris—which is quite easy to do, as wine-bar, vegetarian, and other alternative restaurants are becoming increasingly popular in Wales. Also, most Welsh B & Bs do include in their rates a filling "full English breakfast": juice, cereal, bacon, sausage, eggs, grilled tomato, mushrooms, toast, jam, and tea or coffee.

In Llangollen, we liked the rustic wooden-boothed wine bar/restaurant downstairs at **Gales** (see "Where to Stay" for address and phone), which serves inexpensive light meals. We had absolutely the best smoked salmon we've ever eaten, plus quiche, homemade garlic-cheese bread, a generous plate of nouvelle-y assorted salads, and a full bottle of Sancerre for about $30–$35.

We also had good luck putting together picnic lunches, in Llangollen and similarly sized towns throughout Wales. Most bakeries sell flaky, traditional Welsh meat pies (as well as vegetable, potato, and cheese variations) that make a lovely lunch to tote up the Dinas Bran hillside. We'd recommend combining these with a bottle or two of real local ale, and a few slices of cheese types that never make it to America: real farmhouse Cheddar (sharp, crumbly stuff, almost as tangy as an aged provolone, and nothing at all like the "Cheddar" you've always eaten), rich double Gloucester, younger and rarer single Gloucester, or numerous local soft sheep's-milk cheeses that town specialty and dairy shops will be happy to recommend.

WHERE TO GET THE LATEST DIRT (INFO RESOURCES)

In North Wales

The main gay info sources are: **Bangor Gay Switchboard** (tel. 0248/35 11 15, Fridays 7 P.M.–9 P.M.); **Bangor Lesbian Line** (tel. 0248/35 12 63, Tuesdays 6 P.M.–8 P.M.); **University College Lesbian and Gay Group** (Bangor; tel. 0248/ 35 37 09; nonstudents welcome at meetings and dances); and **The Women's Room** (Ty Gwydr/Greenhouse, 1 Trevelyan Terrace, Bangor, Gwynedd; tel. 0248/35 12 63).

The **Llangollen Tourist Office** is at the intersection of Parade Street and Castle Street (which leads across the bridge). Be sure to wear your 18-inch pink triangles.

In Mid-Wales

Gay info is available from: **Dyfed Gay Helpline/AIDSline** (Haverford West: tel. 0437/76 20 09; also sponsors social events), **Aberystwyth Lesbian and Gay Society** (Gayline tel. 0970/61 50 76, Tuesdays 8 P.M.–10 P.M.; or write P.O. Box 23, Aberystwyth, Dyfed; has weekly social events); **University Lesbian and Gay Society** (Aled Mandela Building, Penglais, Aberystwyth, Dyfed SY23 3DX; tel. 0970/62 42 42; meets Saturday afternoons in room 68, Barn Centre, Cambrian St.; nonstudents welcome) and **Women's Aid** (P.O. Box 38, Aberstwyth, Dyfed; tel. 0970/62 55 85).

In South Wales

The best general gay source is **Cardiff Friend** info line (tel. 0222/34 01 01; Tuesdays, Wednesdays, Thursdays, and Saturdays, 8 P.M.–10 P.M.; or write P.O. Box 179, Cardiff CF5 1YH). Women should contact the **Cardiff Women's**

Centre (2 Coburn St., Cathays, Cardiff CF2 4BS; tel 0222/38 30 24; open Tuesday–Thursday, 11 A.M.–4 P.M.), a tiny, unfunded, wonderfully helpful group, which prints an amusing and comprehensive monthly calendar of events, some mixed male and female; **Cardiff Lesbian Line** (tel. 0222/37 40 51, Thursdays 8 P.M.–10 P.M.); and the **Women's Resource Centre** (228 High St., Swansea, West Glamorgan).

In Chester, England

For health problems, call the **Chester & District AIDSline** (0244/39 03 00, Monday–Friday, 7 P.M.–10 P.M., or write CADAR, P.O. Box 315, Chester CH1 1AZ).

In Liverpool, England

This is the large gay population center nearest to Llangollen. Contact **Friend Merseyside** (14 Colquit St., L1 4DE; tel. 051/708 9552, 7 P.M.–10 P.M., or their women's line: 051/708 0234, Tuesdays, 7 P.M.–10 P.M.) for general gay info, plus hours of Café Link, an informal, friendly several-times-weekly social group at the same address; **News from Nowhere** (172 Bold St. L1; tel. 051/708 7270) is a radical bookstore selling gay books and periodicals. And for health concerns, the **Merseyside AIDS Helpline:** tel. 051/709 9000, Mondays, Wednesdays, and Fridays, 7 P.M.–10 P.M.

Gay hikers, climbers, and swimmers will certainly want to contact the **Gay Outdoor Club** (P.O. Box 41, South PDO, Manchester, England M14 5QF), which sometimes sponsors activities in Wales.

And for all Wales as well as the rest of Britain, of course, see the back of *Gay Times* (see "Practical Information, London" for subscription address).

WHAT TO READ

These Lovers Fled Away, by Morgan Graham (Banned Books). Just the sort of thing one craves on vacation for the train, the lounge chair, or the bath: the Ladies fictionalized à la Gothique. Perhaps there's a bit more poison and melodrama here, and a bit less nickels-and-dimes account-book keeping, than went on in the Ladies' real lives . . . But this is quite as it should be in any lesbian potboiler worth its salt.

The Ladies, by Doris Grumbach (Fawcett Crest). This one's also a novel, but reads like real biography in that its personal interpretations of characters' feelings and switching about of facts are done so smoothly that only a true historian would even notice that imagination rather than fact is at work.

The Ladies of Llangollen, by Elizabeth Mayer (Viking Penguin). If you want a nonfictional account of the Ladies, this one by a British author is the definitive biography.

Surpassing the Love of Men, by Lillian Faderman (Morrow). Stories of great "romantic friendships," including that of the Ladies. Also one of the best theoretical books about lesbianism, period.

$\mathcal{L}$ONDON

Second-Class Subjects at a First-Class Party

$\mathcal{I}$nstead of beginning your tour of London predictably at Big Ben or the Tower or Buckingham Palace, follow us to tiny Tite Street in the Royal Borough of Chelsea. This is a place most tourists have never heard of, but the prim brick row houses and stately gardens are dripping with typical Olde Englishe atmosphere. "Civilized"— that cliché of London descriptions—leaps immediately to mind. Tite Street is one of those mid-nineteenth-century country-lane enclaves that an increasingly Manhattanized London still manages to keep tucked behind the cranes and scaffolding in its giant Erector-set skyline. You'll immediately notice the blue plaque on the triple bay-windowed Queen Anne at number 34, noting that Oscar Wilde lived here from 1884 until 1895.

Wilde, who also lived for a time in his bachelor days down the street at number 44, moved to number 34 upon his marriage, at which point he carefully segregated his extracurricular boy-chasing to various clubs, brothels and rented rooms about town. He departed from Tite Street only after his conviction for sodomy, his forwarding address being Reading Gaol. Ironically, Wilde seems to have gone in mainly for JO parties, not "sodomy" per se, as we use the term today, but the Crown, being simply eager to fuck him over, wasn't interested in the distinctions.

Wilde was then at the height of his career. Several of his plays were smash hits in the West End at the time of his trial, and despite being impeccably hetero, were dutifully closed to protect the public from buggery by association. Wilde's fame was never based primarily on his work, in any case. As he once told André Gide, "I've put all my genius into my life; I only put my talent into my writings." His fabulous one-liners nearly carried him through his legal difficulties. During one of the trials, the Queen's Counsel tried to pin him down on why he often took semiliterate valets and grooms out to dinner. The counsel sneeringly asked, in reference to one such rough-trade rendezvous, "Was that for the purpose of having an intellectual treat?" The whole court rolled in the aisles when Wilde archly replied, "Well, for *him*—yes!"

Quoting Wilde is a little like trying to eat one potato chip, so we'll content ourselves to note that his wits of steel were apparent even at age sixteen, when, at his first ball at Dublin Castle, he nervily asked the most sought-after unmarried titled lady in the room to dance. "Do you think I'm going to dance with a child?" the belle of the ball scoffed. "Madam," replied the boy, "if I had known you were in that condition I never would have asked you."

Okay, one more chip: Even in his last days, after two years in prison at hard labor and exile to the Continent, Wilde was still giving good quote. On his deathbed, far from Tite Street in Paris's Hôtel d'Alsace, he complained about the decor: "Oh, God, that ghastly wallpaper—it's killing me. One of us has to go."

There is no blue plaque farther down the block at number 56 (or, shockingly, at any of the other houses she lived in during her many years in London, including the one where *The Well of Loneliness* was written) to tell you that Radclyffe Hall was also a resident of Tite Street, from 1909 to 1911. It's a pity that the two most influential queers of the century were never actually neighbors. It's delicious to imagine them—he the model for generations of gay dandies, aesthetes, bitchy queens, and sardonic boys in the band, she the original Killer Tailored Butch—meeting along the Thames embankment promenade and tipping identical top hats, or velvet berets. "Good evening, my dear Oscar." "And how are you tonight, John?" With regards on both sides to the missus, of course.

Hall lived in an apartment at number 56 with her grandmother during the early days of her affair with Mabel "Ladye" Batten, one of the great loves of her life; they lie buried together across town in Highgate Cemetery. Ladye, who was rumored to have been the king's mistress when she was younger, was married at the time. When Radclyffe's grandmother and Ladye's husband conveniently died the same week, Hall left Tite Street to set up house with her lover.

Just as Wilde had done a generation earlier, Hall ultimately pushed straight tolerance to the breaking point, although with less catastrophic results. While he kept up a hetero front both in his life and his work, Hall was completely out of the closet, on principle. Granted, she had the advantages of her fortune and Queen Victoria's insistence that the sodomy laws couldn't possibly pertain to women. But she also had guts about being out; which most of the rich dykes of her day, including the famous Bloomsbury crowd, did not. Wilde suffered the loss of liberty, family, livelihood, reputation, and even his health for being gay; Hall was the original Happy Homo. She parlayed her notoriety onto the lecture circuit and into various beds, and unlike the tedious Stephen in *The Well,* she almost always got the girl in real life.

Hall, too, paid a price. The first important review of *The Well,* in the *Sunday Express,* tossed around terms like "putrefaction" and "contagion," and noted: "I would rather give a healthy boy or a healthy girl a vial of prussic acid than this novel. Poison kills the body, but moral poison kills the soul." (Leonard Woolf, husband of Virginia, also savaged the novel.) The trial, in which the book was ultimately declared obscene, and then ritually burned, was so costly that Hall was compelled to sell her house.

It would be nice to report that the nastier forces that shaped the destinies of Radclyffe and Oscar are as quaintly passé as the smoking jackets they both favored. Unfortunately, brutal antigay repression still exists in Britain, arguably the worst in Europe. But the spirit of the two great lights of Tite Street also endures. There is gay brilliance, wit, and style in the London of the 1990s, even at the forefront of British culture, and there are still a few souls willing to fight back.

On May 24, 1988, Section 28 became the law of the land in Great Britain. Also known as Clause 28 (its proper name before it was passed by Parliament), it prohibits local governments from "promoting" homosexuality, or setting it up in any way as a "pretended family relationship."

The potential scope of the law is probably lost at first glance on gay United States citizens, since our own sugar tit, when we've had one at all, has tended to be the federal government. But in the United Kingdom, it's the town and district councils that control the purse strings. The British gay movement had forged particularly strong alliances with anti-Tory politicians and even with working-class labor unions; leftist local governments consequently had funded all sorts of gay community resources. Section 28 was a backlash not only against flaunting faggots and uppity dykes, but against the left-leaning (and now dismantled) Greater London Council, an early target of the Thatcher government.

Non-Europeans, especially Americans who are by now inured to the antics of the Falwell crowd, might also not realize just how regressive it is, in the postwar European political climate, to start gunning for minority groups. Europe has never been as rights-oriented as the United States, and laws that have been on the books forever sometimes change only at a glacial pace. But *new* legislation that goes out of its way specifically to discriminate against people is a guaranteed buzzer-pusher. It is an uncomfortable, taste-less-bordering-on-unthinkable reminder of World War II Nazi fascism. It simply isn't done.

When Britain did it anyway, the gay movement throughout Britain and all over Europe rose up in alarm. At the height of the debate, a lesbian zap squad even swooped onto the floor of Parliament on mountain-climbing ropes to protest the legislation's imminent passage. ("Abseiling," the official mountaineer term for what they did, is now almost a synonym in England for wonderfully outrageous queer activism.) It was initially feared that the vaguely written law could, if strictly enforced, close down every gay bar and disco in the country, and even make it difficult for gay people to get public housing or an education. Most of the more dire predictions haven't been borne out, and Section 28 seems, for the present, anyway, to function primarily as a flashing neon warning from the conservatives that gay people better not get too big for their knickers.

Not that the law has no fangs at all. Among its results: Edinburgh officials refused to sponsor a day-care center at a lesbian film and video festival; students at Colchester Institute were refused meeting space on campus; a lesbian chapter was dropped from a women's resources hand-book in Southampton; a children's book about life with a gay father was removed from the public library shelves in Wolverhampton; and teenagers in Kent were prevented from seeing Benjamin Britten's opera *Death in Venice*. Group charters have been rewritten, courses renamed, teachers hassled. Even when there's a fair amount of doubt about whether the law is applicable, some groups—like the locally funded film festival that decided not to screen *Sunday, Bloody Sunday*—opt for self-censorship over the mere possibility of a court fight.

Before Section 28, Britain was no legal paradise either. The progay reforms that have proceeded apace in other European nations have ground to a halt in the United Kingdom. Some 1,718 charges of "indecency be-tween males" were lodged in 1989. "Cottaging" (Britspeak for hanging around tearooms) and even street cruising are technically illegal and grounds for arrest on charges of "soliciting." Sodomy, i.e., sex between two consenting male adults, has been legal since the sixties, but forget threesomes or group sex: that's *two,* count 'em, *two* consenting adults. Age of consent laws for gay men are also enforced in Britain, even, absurdly, when *both* partners are under twenty-one.

If you're just a plain vanilla adult male with one steady boyfriend, Her Majesty's customs inspectors still don't want you spicing up your sex life with any Jeff Stryker videos or Phil Andros novels, and will do their utmost to nab them at the border, fining whoever tries to smuggle them in. All of these laws, incidentally, are enforced unequally against "deviants," since the definition of obscenity in Britain is based on what would offend the "average" citizen.

Britain also has had some of the most inflammatory homophobes west of the Ayatollah writing for its schlock tabloid press. One *Daily Mail* columnist not too long ago described all gay men as "potential murderers," spreading AIDS up the ass of the nation. As for oral gratification, hey, this is England, after all. A lot of the food *already* tastes like a dental dam.

Before you slam this chapter shut, however, and race off to buy your airline tickets to Amsterdam, bear with us. Yes, Section 28 is humiliating. Yes, too many gay Brits are maddeningly blasé about it, in that same apolitical way people everywhere are, always: "Oh, but it really doesn't affect my life personally." And no, the fact the we U.S. queers are illegal in a good many of our own states doesn't make Section 28 any more excusable or endurable. The cultural mindset that spawned this regressive legislation is unquestionably Olde; it is not, however, Merrie.

But despite the untenable laws, the undrinkable coffee, and our unshakable American habit of striding off the curb, diligently looking the wrong way, and then skittering like mad cockroaches to avoid being ground into Wimpyburgers by some dork in a tweed cap who feels compelled to cluck bloody this-and-that at us out the passenger window in a language which we have no choice but to understand . . . Despite these undeniable negatives, we have to admit that London is one of the great gay destinations of Europe. Among large cities, its gay facilities are second only to those of Amsterdam and Berlin, and they're vastly more accessible than those in plenty of places with much more commendable governments.

For example London is home to Heaven, the biggest, oldest gay disco in all Europe. We nearly missed it the first time we tried to go there, since it's located in an unmarked, scaffold-shrouded structure that burrows under Charing Cross Station. The building was originally constructed in the late eighteenth century as a royal gunpowder storehouse. Only after construction was well under way did the architects realize that the humidity from the nearby Thames made the site completely unsuitable for gunpowder. The fortress-thick walls make the building perfect for a nightclub, however, and Heaven has been on the site since 1979.

Inside, Heaven is a multi-environmental musical theme park. Although inspired by the now-defunct Saint in New York, it doesn't rely on the clone clichés that characterized so many American men's discos in the pre-AIDS era. When we were there, for instance, one of the three floors of the complex featured not high NRG disco or even hardcore, but a live jazz jam. Depending upon the night of the week, Heaven has drag, cabaret, go-go boys, theme parties, and an ever-changing variety of decors for every possible mood. We liked the Cave Room, with the Day-Glo dinosaur bones, and the

Hippie Pad, complete with candles, cushions, and sprawling bods. The sound system is top-notch, too. Women are definitely welcome, at least on most nights, and Heaven was also one of the few places in racially tense Britain where we encountered a fair number of gay people of color.

At Heaven we ran into John, whom we'd met at a pub in Brighton a few weeks before. John was on his way to Rhodes, in Greece, a vacation spot he claimed to prefer because most of the other gay guys are Germans. "So you like the blonds, hmmm?" we snickered. Actually, it turned out that what John likes about the Germans is that they're not British. "We're so repressed here, you know," John explained, certain that we Yanks will nod in grim sympathy.

By then we'd been in Britain long enough to expect that every wonderfully open, amusing, adorable gay person in the country would tell us how cold and repressed he or she was, just like the entire population of the United Kingdom. Since we tended to have these conversations with people who were telling us their life stories five minutes into the relationship, we'd come to wonder if this was some mass national psychosis, perhaps beamed subliminally at all watchers of the BBC. Or possibly it's just us foreigners. Maybe two Brits together, in the absence of an available German, Spaniard, American, or Australian, have the same natural magnetic properties as a pair of those little black-and-white metal Scottie dogs whose polar ends simply refuse to connect. In any case, you'll run into plenty of these poor repressed creatures on your night-crawling tour of London, possibly wearing lampshades that they've somehow decided are really bowler hats. Enjoy them.

If Heaven isn't to your taste, there are some thirty other clubs and discos to choose from. One of them, Backstreet, has to be the butchest leather/rubber club in Fetishdom. The dress code is so stringent that you're even required to wear black *socks*. Running shoes are explictly forbidden. We'd tell you about it, but we had a sneaking suspicion open-toed sandals and pantyhose didn't cut it, either.

Another true original is the Roof Gardens, a private club which has an elegant Sunday tea-dance open to the public. (No jeans allowed. In fact, you should wear something that would get you laughed out of Backstreet.) Located on the penthouse of an old office building in Kensington, the Roof Gardens has the most amazing space of any club we've ever seen, anywhere. Laid out in the thirties by a landscape architect as the roof restaurant for the department store that then occupied the lower floors, this acre and a half of garden has a huge variety of trees (including a descendant of one that grew in Thackeray's gardens), fountains, a pond, babbling brooks, several bridges, ducks, peacocks, and even live flamingoes. If you tire of the English roses or the Mediterranean palms growing a hundred feet above the street life of central London, you can go indoors to the spiffy mirrored-ceiling restaurant and disco.

And of course there are London's gay pubs, of which there are at least a few in every neighborhood. To call them "gay bars" would be like calling the Sistine Chapel ceiling "a nice coat of paint." The King William IV, a.k.a. the Willie, in the yuppified but lovely neighborhood of Hampstead, is every foreigner's fantasy of a traditional English pub: dark hardwood banquettes with high padded backs, stained-glass windows, wall-to-wall Persian rugs, ornate carved ceilings, brass lanterns hanging on the walls, theater posters, and a roaring fire. Outdoors, on sunny days, there's a beer garden. The pub is definitely gay-oriented, but it seems to attract a fair minority of straights, who can't be faulted for knowing a good thing when they see it.

For a completely different experience, try the Fallen Angel in funky Islington, a mostly-women's hangout with a stark modern California look: huge windows, lots of light, a marble bar, and white wrought-iron tables where you can dine on vegetarian food. Not that you can't find food in most English pubs. "Pub grub," it's called. And we'd certainly urge fans of overcooked day-old cabbage mixed with instant mashed potatoes ("bubble and squeak"), carbo- *and* fat filler—laden hot-dog-ish links with a side of instant mashed potatoes ("bangers and mash"), or cold, congealed sausage meat wrapped around overcooked hard-boiled eggs ("Scotch eggs") to rush right out and try it. Perhaps, as long as it's subliminally convincing the Brits that they're repressed, the BBC also suggests to them that warm ale and cold toast are appropriate commodities to put in their mouths. We'll stick to the Fallen Angel's grub ourselves. A couple of years ago a straight magazine designated it the best pub in the city. Not the best *gay* pub, just the best.

Not far away is another favorite of ours, the Cock, which has gold-painted old-fashioned lettering running above the windows the length of the building, the sort of sign that usually tells the public that the place was serving lager during the signing of the Magna Carta. This one announces that the Cock is AN EQUAL OPPORTUNITY PUB, REGARDLESS OF RACE, CREED, NATIONALITY, DISABILITY, OR SEXUAL ORIENTATION.

For more bucolic pleasures there's Hampstead Heath, the huge public wilderness area in the northern part of the city. It was, when we were in London, one of the very few areas we heard about where male cruising was relatively safe. (One of the others was the frozen food counter at the Safeway in . . . oh, never mind.) But it's you women—actually, you *ladies*—who absolutely shouldn't miss the Heath: specifically, the Ladies' Bathing Pond, on the eastern edge of the park.

The Pond is a legacy of another age, when it was unseemly for the two genders to do something as intimate as swim together. (Get married, yes; tread water in the same lake, no.) The Men's Pond is a pretty pedestrian open-air affair, with a large sign cautioning against "indulging in horseplay" and reminding bathers that their trunks better be "clean and of a recognizable type of such material and size as to not offend against public decency." The Ladies', however, feels like finding a wild orchid in with your tomato plants. It's virtually unmarked. We never would have found it if a couple of old ladies hadn't taken pity on us and given us explicit directions, clucking all the while about how they wouldn't be a bit surprised if overprotective locals, wanting to keep the pond a secret, had deliberately misdirected us. Even when you've found the right way, you need to open a creaky gate and approach down a long, leafy path deliberately overgrown with wildflowers in Vita Sackville-West's sort of "Alfriston Queen" English/jungle style. The pond is secluded from any male gazes, except for that of the odd bullfrog. Since 1976, women have been permitted to doff their tops, but only "whilst stationary" on the adjacent meadow/beach.

The Ladies' Pond has supposedly been frequented in its day by Margaret Rutherford, Fay Weldon, Margaret Drabble, and even a royal or two. Not surprisingly, it also draws a certain lesbian clientele. We first heard about the Pond in a gay newspaper column which discussed at length whether the presence of all those dykes made the ambiance "erotic" or simply "arcadian." But the Pond will now live on in our memories as the place where we finally met one of those famous English Repressives.

She noticed us copying down some information about the pond, introduced herself as one of the lifeguards, and was extremely pleasant in her hearty, beet-faced way. At least until we happened to mention that our guidebook was for lesbians and gay men—at which point she ripped a magazine article about the pond's history out of our hands, bodily hurled herself in front of the bulletin board listing such classified information as the opening times, and said she'd report us to the authorities if we dared publish a word.

"But this is a public pond," we argued, stupefied. "And anyway, this place has *already* been written up in the gay press."

"Well, they didn't have my permission, and you don't either," she harrumphed.

After a great deal of screaming, the woman finally calmed down a bit. It seems that there was once a case of two lezzies having oral sex on the meadow. Or at least there were complaints of something of the sort, but when our friend the lifeguard went to investigate, there was nothing funny going on, and no one would identify the perps. "Everyone was just being typically English, saying, 'Well, I don't like it, but it's not my place to interfere.' "

We murmur that, yes, the English do seem awfully polite. "Except me," she answers proudly.

She was, she added, gay herself. But it was still her job to preserve the pond for *nice* people.

We hope all you nice female readers enjoy the Ladies' Pond. Please bring your biggest dildoes and, perhaps, a picnic lunch hamper from Fortnum & Mason to eat off your date's crotch. (Hey, we can say this. We're not a local government.) Make sure you give our regards to Ms. Prune.

If there's a gay neighborhood in London, it's Earl's Court, where you'll find at least a dozen bars, clubs, hotels, and restaurants. One of the best is the Gazebo, the restaurant of the gay Philbeach Gardens Hotel, which serves authentic Thai food in a candlelit room with sequined quilts on the wall.

In England, we tend to stick to ethnic, especially Indian, restaurants, and to vegetarian food. But we were happy to break our own rule one night to go to Van B's. The French food wasn't bad. Not French, mind you, but not bad. The decor was fabulous: the long, narrow, brass-and-bamboo-accented dining room looks like a car on the legendary Orient Express. And where else in London can you sit next to one of the country's most famous drag queens, in full regalia, holding hands across the table with a guy who looks like a runner-up for Mr. U.K.?

You will, of course, take advantage of London's world-famous theater scene—especially since, unlike New York's world-famous theater scene, London offers better fare than just musicals calculated not to offend the straight mink-coat crowd from New Jersey. On our last trip, we had a choice of about a dozen gay-themed shows (both mainstream West End and alternative theater), ranging from a production of M. *Butterfly* to a revival of Oscar Wilde's *An Ideal Husband,* to a new play, cowritten by Richard Coles of the Communards and produced by the repertory company Gay Sweatshop, about the twenty-year friendship of an American lesbian and a British gay man.

First Out, a café-pub in the heart of the theater district, was busy further ruining London's reputation as an uptight place when we were there: The walls were covered with an exhibition of the works of local lesbian photographer Della Disgrace, who specializes in Mapplethorpian leather dykes in garter belts, with shaved heads and tattoos. Della, who grew up in California, told us that she'd tried working in other cities around the world, but ultimately realized that London is where her sensibility "belongs." If England thinks Section 28 completely discourages the sexual fringe, perhaps it had better think again.

London's other amenities include a spiffy all-women's town-house hotel, the Reeves (which offers full business services for working female travelers, as well as a resident bar and weekly public buffet/disco), several gay and women's bookstores, and what has to be one of the most impressive AIDS facilities anywhere, the London Lighthouse. Funded by national and local governments, as well as by private donations, the Lighthouse cares for several dozen resident people with AIDS and provides special services, like volunteer "nightsitters" who come to the homes of PWAs, for many nonresidents. It also offers free counseling and support groups for people with AIDS, people who are HIV positive, and their loved ones, plus a huge array of classes in meditation, nutrition, exercise, creative writing, massage, and more. All in an airy, cheerful architectural gem of a building that looks like a cross between an expensive spa and a showroom for Scandinavian furniture.

More? If you look in the classifieds of the excellent news monthly *Gay Times,* you'll find affinity-group organizations for every queer stripe you've ever imagined: unemployed gays, gay nudists, gay vegetarians, gays who are into velvet and corduroy, gay heavy-metal fans, gays who own Morris Mini automobiles, gay psoriasis sufferers, gay airport workers, gay devotees of slapstick comedy, gay people who have tattoos or pierced body parts, *two* gay biker groups (one with no dress code, and the other for serious fetishists), and even a club for gay enthusiasts of shorts . . . to name just a few.

Finally, in the heart of the city on Cowcross Street, there's the London Lesbian and Gay Centre, a huge five-story complex in an old meat warehouse that now serves as headquarters for many London organizations, including ACT UP and the Gay Switchboard. It's open seven days a week, and appears to be particularly popular on Sundays, when it's the only gay spot in town that's licensed to serve liquor all day. Among the amenities are Orchids, an extraordinarily upscale-looking wine bar for women; a more casual indoor-outdoor pub and bar area for everyone; a traditional English Sunday dinner with roast beef or leg of lamb and Yorkshire pudding (vegetarian version possible, "with all the same trimmings"); and a Sunday tea-dance, with reduced entrance rates for wearers of tuxes or drag. The entire complex is wheelchair accessible, and the main meeting rooms have facilities to aid the hearing-impaired. There is even a special arrangement with a taxi service for those who leave late at night. "We've tried to design it so it's easy to make friends here," says manager Martyn Gilbert. More than two thousand gay men and lesbians use the center every week; foreigners can take out membership by the day at a reasonable fee.

Sitting at the Centre's pub having a draught of Tennent's, we notice a startlingly beautiful young man with long brown center-parted hair and the face of a Caravaggio. There is something about him that doesn't seem quite English, and sure enough, we overhear him speaking French to his companion. His name is Daniel, his friend is Eitan, and they are both students from Paris on a quick semester-break vacation. Like all European gay people, Daniel and Eitan know about Section 28, and weren't quite sure what sort of atmosphere they would find in London.

"But *this*"—Daniel appreciatively waves his hand across the room, at the pinball machines, the stacks of board games, the sun patio—"*this* is really, really great. We have nothing like this in Paris."

————

How does one explain the paradox of gay London? Why would a nation that passed such a mean-spirited law permit such a delicious gay life-style to flourish? We ask this question of everyone we meet. Most people shrug and say that while Section 28 is appalling, it doesn't *really* affect them *personally*. We found more gut-level outrage about Section 28 in the Netherlands than we did in Britain. The hot political gossip everywhere, in Britain and abroad, is whether, in post-1992 Europe, Section 28 can be struck down by more liberal nations. Meanwhile, English gays muddle through as second-class subjects at a first-class party.

Paud Hegarty, general manager of Gay's the Word bookstore (which spent five years waging an unsuccessful legal battle to import "obscene" books from the United States), explains that it's more or less understood that the government isn't hostile to gays, per se, in the way North American fundamentalists presumably are. "It's different here. There's a *tradition* of homosexuality in the public schools, among the upper classes and the people in power. There are lots of gay people in Thatcher's cabinet, but they're not 'gay' in the sense you or I would use the word. There's that terribly English thing of falling in love with the brother and marrying the sister, the whole *Brideshead Revisited* business. It's a very plastic sexuality."

Nor, he adds, would the average Englishman dream of depriving gay people of their right to do as they choose, behind closed doors: "There's a strong belief that a man's home is his castle." A little decorum is what's wanted, not anybody's blood.

But one doesn't sense in Britain the simple double standard of the Latin countries, where gay people, especially men, can have gay sex on the side as long as they don't talk about it. If anything, England's homophobic media seem obsessed with "poofters," men in dresses, and hauling people, especially high-ranking clergy or relatives of same, out of the closet.

On a more positive note, British culture seems actively welcoming of gay men and lesbians, like Jeanette Winterson, whose novel about growing up gay in the provinces, *Oranges Are Not the Only Fruit,* was a BBC miniseries complete with a hot, wonderfully authentic love scene between two adolescent girls at a slumber party. The year after Section 28 was passed, *Out on Tuesday,* a weekly gay news show, made its debut on British commercial television. London's general-audience what's-on-this-week magazines, *Time Out* and *City Limits,* routinely list gay bars, discos, and organizations, something the city magazines of New York and San Francisco still don't do.

Where gay men and lesbians in other countries can dredge up only a handful of famous queers among their national heroes, the entire British cultural pantheon is cluttered with gays and bi's: from William Pitt the Younger, Cardinal Newman, Alan Turing, Noël Coward, Monty Python's Graham Chapman, Sir Michael Redgrave, Bloomsbury's three "V's" (Virginia Woolf, Vita Sackville-West, and Violet Trefusis), and Lawrence of

Arabia, on down to Jimmy Somerville, Boy George, Elton John, the Pet Shop Boys, and several other reigning kings of rock and roll. . . . not to mention everyone on your high school's required reading list: Bacon, Marlowe, possibly Shakespeare, Byron, Edward Lear, Saki, Forster, Housman, Auden, and more. Britain is a major, walk-in, vanity-table-with-Hollywood-lights-and-more-shoes-than-Imelda closet.

While we are talking to Paud, one of his female coworkers comes grumping into the shop. She has just had a major tiff with someone at the bank who has refused to cash a check. The check, you see, was made out to a female name, and the bank manager was convinced that Paud's coworker was actually a boy. "Oy threatened to flash moy tits at 'im," the young woman sneered triumphantly, and we all collapsed in a heap, laughing.

But the incident makes us stop and think that in fact, there's a relatively androgynous quality about much of *straight* Britain with its terribly nice, well-spoken upper-class men, its square-jawed, no-nonsense women. In a Butch Sweepstakes, both the ex–prime minister and the queen would demolish the typical male member of Parliament. Homophobia in the United Kingdom doesn't seem to have much to do with whether real men eat quiche instead of steak-and-kidney pie.

Perhaps the real sin in class-bound Britain isn't gay sex, or even stepping out of pre-assigned pink-and-blue gender roles, but something far less connected with the actions of any single individual: the pursuit of gay power. You can have a lover, a gay identity, and clubs with laser shows and live flamingoes. You can even be as eccentric as you like. What you cannot do is join forces with punks, Pakis, and striking coal miners and try to change the face of England.

LONDON

PRACTICAL INFORMATION

LONDON—NUMBER KEY

1. London Lesbian & Gay Centre (69 Cowcross St. EC1)

Pubs and Nightclubs

2. Heaven, Pyramid, Soundshaft (under the Arches, Villiers St. WC2)
3. Comptons (53 Old Compton St. W1)
4. The Golden Lion (51 Dean St. W1)
5. Bang, Propaganda (at Busby's, 157 Charing Cross Rd. WC2)
6. The Coleherne (261 Old Brompton Rd. SW5)
7. Bromptons (294 Old Brompton Rd. SW5)
8. The Drill Hall (16 Chenies St. WC1)
9. The Bell (259 Pentonville Rd. N1)
10. Paradise Club (Parkfield St., near Pentonville Rd. and Upper St., N1)
11. The Fallen Angel (65 Graham St., off City Rd., N1)
12. Market Tavern (Market Towers, Nine Elms Lane SW8)
21. Reeves (48 Shepherds Bush Green W12; women's hotel/restaurant/disco)

Restaurants

13. Gazebo Restaurant (at Philbeach Hotel, 30–31 Philbeach Gardens SW5—off map)
14. Van B's (306b Fulham Rd. SW10)
15. The Gardens (top of old Derry & Tom's bldg., Derry St. off Kensington High St.)
21. Reeves (48 Shepherds Bush Green W12; women's hotel/restaurant/disco)

Bookstores

16. Silver Moon Women's Bookshop (68 Charing Cross Rd. WC2)
17. Gay's the Word Bookshop (66 Marchmont St. WC1)
18. Sisterwrite Women's Bookshop (190 Upper St. N1)

Hotels

13. Philbeach Hotel (same address as Gazebo Restaurant: 30–31 Philbeach Gardens SW5—off map)
19. Halifax (65 Philbeach Gardens SW5—off map)

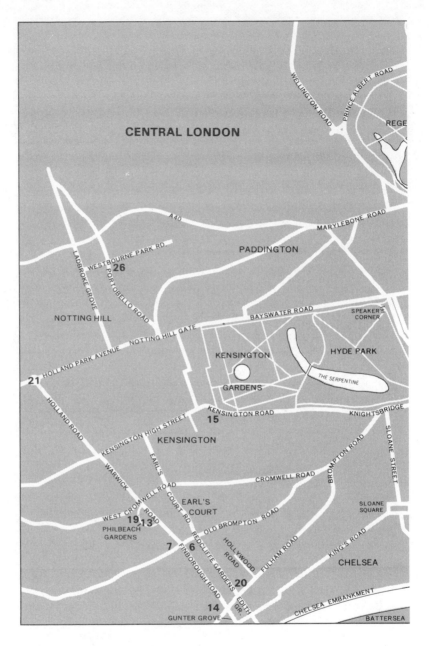

CENTRAL LONDON

20. Redcliffe (268 Fulham Rd. SW10)
21. Reeves (48 Shepherds Bush Green W12; women's hotel/restaurant/disco—off map)
22. Elizabeth (37 Eccleston Sq. SW1)
23. St. Athans (20 Tavistock Pl. WC1)

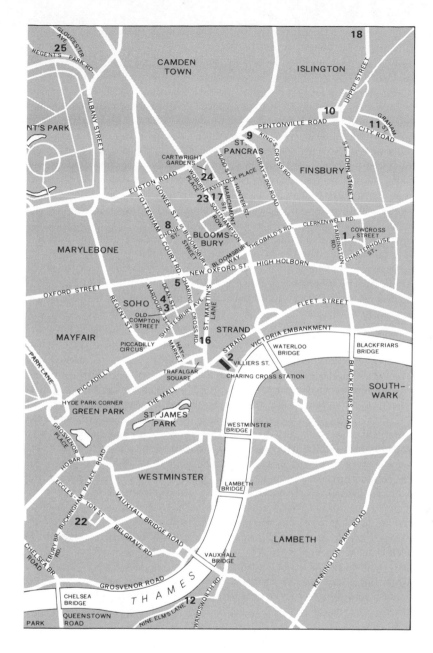

24. Jenkins (45 Cartwright Gardens, WC1H 9EH)
25. Primrose Hill Guesthouse (14 Edis St. NW1)

Etc.

26. Marc Saint Tattoos (201 Portobello Rd. W11)

There are more gay establishments and groups of all kinds in London than anywhere on earth. So although Earl's Court is the gayest area in town, to say this is largely meaningless. We doubt that there's a neighborhood in London that doesn't have several absolutely to-die-for classically English gay pubs.

To get around to these places, London taxis are adorably quaint and cost a fortune. Take the tube. It stops at midnight but then you can get a night bus; these run to most parts of London. A "Buses for Night Owls" schedule is available free from London Transport Information at Heathrow airport as well as Piccadilly Circus, Victoria, and several other central city locations you're bound to be passing through.

The city's main tourist-information center, at Victoria Station, also has lots of other useful free maps and brochures, a bookshop where you can get many of the general entertainment guides (with gay listings) in our "Information Resources" section, and a hotel booking service if you need it.

Best Map: *London A–Z* (pronounced "zed")—booklet form, very detailed, and a much better idea in this town than large one-page maps.

Telephone code: 071 (central London), 081 (outskirts)

Currency unit: the pound (£)

WHERE TO STAY

London lodgings can be a bit of a problem for those of us who go for maximum atmosphere. Basically, what we Americans think of as traditionally English rooms—aristocratic Queen Victoria–type decor—are readily had at a price easily affordable to those willing to mortgage their homes, cars, and children. We're not, so you won't find luxury hotels listed here. "Budget" rooms at prices that make us normally $30–$45-a-night types gag, are also readily available and perfectly clean, but often rather tatty, with worn carpets and depressing non–color schemes—hardly the affordable yet super-atmospheric standard we always look for in European lodgings, and generally manage to find. And unlike those in Brighton, gay hotels in London are no exception to this clean-but-tatty rule. However, we have found you a few rare prizes—and naturally, all nongay hotels have been Drilled.

If you really get stuck for a room, you might try **Check-In**, a free hotel booking service for gay men and women; tel. 01/278 6846.

All prices for double rooms with full English breakfast, unless otherwise mentioned.

Prices: *Inexpensive* = under £35; *inex./mod.* = £35–40; *moderate* = £40–50; *mod./exp.* = £50–60; *expensive* = £65–75.

Jenkins, 45 Cartwright Gardens, London WC1H 9EH, U.K.; tel. 387 2067. This is not a gay guest house, but we think you'll love it. You'll immediately notice personal touches like the flower arrangements when you walk in—but they're just the tip of the iceberg. This whole 1805 brick Georgian town-house hotel is a jewel. Some of the 15 rooms have private bathrooms and/or their own balconies; most have fireplaces; all have TVs, phones, fridges, coffee/tea-making facilities, patterned/molded walls, and super-cheerful coordinated floral decor. The full breakfasts include small but nice touches like whole-grain bread. The tennis courts in the front crescent are available to guests. *Moderate.*

Primrose Hill Guesthouse, c/o Gail O'Farrell, prop., 14 Edis St., Primrose Hill, London NW1, U.K.; (Chalk Farm station, Northern train line) tel. 722 6869. This place just off Gloucester Avenue is quite a find: in a nongay but welcoming guest house, a lovely two-room suite—bedroom and sitting room/kitchen, with skylights, Klee prints, pine furniture, and fresh flowers always—for less than the price of an average regular London hotel room. There's a garden, too. If this suite is taken, don't despair: the proprietor has just gotten together a selection of similar properties in central yet peaceful Primrose Hill (five minutes' walk from famous Regent's Park Zoo, 10 minutes' walk from Camden Town's antique shops, and not far from Hampstead Heath), varying in size and price. *Inex./mod.–moderate.*

The Philbeach Hotel, 30–31 Philbeach Gardens, London SW5, U.K.; tel. 373 1244. On a quiet Earl's Court residential circle, this 40-room town-house hotel is probably London's most popular gay hotel. And we do mean gay: We happened upon the desk staff demanding, of a male/female couple who claimed to be just colleagues from the same opera company, renditions of various arias from their favorite productions as proof that they weren't just sneaky hets. Obviously, the staff is terrific, as is the antiques-and-red-carpet ground-floor decor. The decidedly nondecorated rooms are not as wonderful, especially the less expensive ones without private baths, and the upstairs hall carpeting has seen better days. We also could not understand why, with a fair number of lesbian couples resident, such a percentage of the male clientele couldn't remember to bloody shut the doors of the shared bath/shower rooms. There's a great Thai restaurant on premises (see "Where to Eat" section), and a small bar/disco in the cellar. *Inex./mod.* and *mod./exp.*

Hotel Halifax, 65 Philbeach Gardens, London SW5 9EE, U.K.; tel. 373 4153, is another town house on the same circle as the Philbeach, and seems to be the first choice for gay people when the Philbeach is full. The 15 "modernized Victorian" rooms are of varying quality, some grandmother-nice with gilt mirrors, some tatty. About a third of the rooms have a private bath. Breakfast is Continental, with egg and cereal added. *Inex./mod.* and *moderate.*

Elizabeth Hotel, 37 Eccleston Sq., Victoria, London SW1V 1PB; tel. 828 6812. This nongay hotel close to Belgravia is the nicest town house on a mid-nineteenth century square of neoclassical buildings, one a former residence of Winston Churchill. Rooms are both with and without private bath. Guests can arrange to use the square's central garden/park and tennis courts. *Moderate, mod./exp.,* and *expensive.*

The Redcliffe Hotel, 268 Fulham Rd. (corner of Redcliffe Gardens), London, U.K.; tel. 823 3494; fax 01 351 2467. Props.: Jack, Ian, and Co. This 16-room hotel is London's newest large gay hotel—so new that unfortunately, it wasn't open while we were in town. But we had a nice phone conversation with the friendly owners, and it sounds like a good bet to us. The modern-decorated rooms have lots of amenities: private baths, direct-dial phones, color TVs, hairdryers, and even irons. And there's a very popular gay bar on premises. *Mod./ exp.*

St. Athan's Hotel, 20 Tavistock Place, Russell Sq., London WC1H 9RE; tel. 837 9140. A friendly basic nongay B&B in Bloomsbury, near the British Museum. The 36 rooms are small but pleasant (all with sinks but shared baths), and there's a TV lounge. The Georgian-fronted house is protected by the Historic Buildings Act. *Inex./mod.*

Reeves Hotel, 48 Shepherd's Bush Green, London W12 8PHJ, U.K.; tel. 740 1158. From the patio/garden to the sauna to the restaurant/lounge bar to the high ceilings to the stylish peach/pink/aqua decor, this nine-room town house is *the* class-act hotel for women. All rooms have private bath, telephone, and TV. For business travelers, they'll arrange fax, telex, copying, and typing services; they can also arrange for a masseuse to come to your room. Breakfast is expanded Continental. *Expensive,* but some spectacularly reduced "weekend break" rates for two nights, bringing prices into the *moderate* range.

WHERE TO GO (DAY)

Our idea of a perfect day in London would be a late-morning visit to the wonderful food halls of **Harrod's** for some of their festive little canapés and other picnic supplies, and then a jaunt out to 800-acre Hampstead Heath, for an afternoon's swimming, boating, and sunning at the gay-popular **Ladies' Pond.** You guys will, of course, have to settle for the **Men's Pond**—not so idyllically private, but larger and not bad at all, we hear, for some casual cruising. In the summer (third Saturday in May to third Sunday in September), pond hours are 7 A.M.–9 P.M. for the Ladies' (Kenwood) Pond and 6 A.M.–9 P.M. for the Men's (Highgate). And remember: no "indulging in horseplay."

A Sunday-afternoon London institution is the **Speakers Corner** at Hyde Park, by Marble Arch, where people gather to hear and heckle as speakers orate from soapboxes. You won't want to miss the regular gay contingent, **Hyde Park Gays and Sapphics;** catch them from 3 P.M. on.

If you've been thinking that a tiny flower, or perhaps a wee pair of handcuffs, would be just the thing on the back of your shoulder, **tattooist** Marc Saint (201 Portobello Road, London W11; tel. 727 8211) advertises in all the gay media, and does great-looking work, from what we could see in his window. Unfortunately, he was "gone for 10 minutes" for over half an hour when we stopped by, so we didn't actually get the tattoos we'd been planning on.

We've always been perfectly happy ferreting out old Radclyffe-and-Oscar hangouts by ourselves, with our *Pink Plaque Guide* of historic gay addresses. But if you'd prefer company, Gary Chambers at City Walks and Tours (9 Kensington High St., London W8 5HP; tel. 937 4281) guides three different-themed **"Pink Walks":** *A Walk on the Wilde Side, Dancing with Mr. Sloane,* and *London's Pink Bohemia.*

To see what a truly first-class AIDS/ARC/HIV+ support facility looks like, drop by **London Lighthouse**, 111–117 Lancaster Rd., London W11 1QT; tel. 792 1200.

For day **cruising**, gay men report good results at the frozen food counter of the Streatham Safeway supermarket, Tooting, South London.

WHERE TO GO (NIGHT)

The long-time institution in London is "club nights," wherein different promoters produce theme events at different venues, for one night only. This means: (1) a venue that's totally "in" on Monday night can be totally "out" on Tuesday, (2) one should therefore generally follow promoter's name and "club" name, rather than the venue's name; (3) one really must consult the periodicals listed below, like *Gay Times*, as these clubs' venues and nights get switched around constantly. A well-known promoter is Colin Peters. Examples of well-known gay club nights are "Pyramid" (the club) at Heaven (the venue), an alternative-music gay male/female dance event that's fashionable, outrageous, and considered possibly *the* hottest in town; the multinational bhangra/alternative music "Asia" at the Paradise; and Europe's largest nightclub for women, "Venus Rising," at the Fridge. (By the way, "women-only" clubs are increasingly allowing lesbians to bring gay male guests.)

Heaven (under the Arches, Craven St., Charing Cross, London WC2; Charing Cross or Embankment tube) is London's most famous gay disco, and for once the place is worth the hype, with a variety of musical styles and promoters on different nights as well as in the huge venue's several separate performing, dancing, and drinking areas. Saturday is currently the men-only "Troll" club, Friday "Garage" is gay men with women guests, Thursday is straight/bi, Wednesday is "Pyramid." But do check to make sure these nights are still accurate before going. Patrons can also munch at the snack bar, and catch up on their T-shirt, magazine, greeting-card, and condom shopping at the on-premises Heaven Shop, open when the disco is.

The **London Lesbian and Gay Centre** (69 Cowcross St., London EC1; Farringdon tube; open Monday and Tuesday 5:30 P.M.–11 P.M., other days from noon, and till 2 A.M. for weekend discos) is out of the way, but so friendly and casually classy that we're sure we'd hang out here constantly, night *and* day, if we lived in London. Five floors of bars (all with great beers—one with outdoor "beer garden" and one, "Orchids," women-only), discos, meeting rooms (for groups ranging from political to wrestling or folk-dancing folks), bulletin boards, theater cabaret space, a restaurant/café—you name it. Visitors can buy a day membership for about 60 cents. On certain disco nights with an additional charge, women in tuxes or men in drag get in for £1 less.

After a day at the Hampstead Ponds, you couldn't do better than to wind up at one of Hampstead's most traditionally English gay pubs, the **King William IV** (75 Hampstead High St., London NW3). It has an outdoor beer garden, which draws a certain number of harmless straight locals, if the smoke gets to you in the gayer inside.

On Sundays, we would not miss the gay disco/dinner, 8:30 P.M.–2 A.M., at the **Gardens** (99 Kensington High St.; actually on Derry St., on top of the old Derry and Toms department store building; London W8 5ED; tel. 937 8923 or 937 7994). There are three gardens on this roof, each totally different botani-cally: polite Tudor, wild English woodland, and tropical Spanish—with live flamingoes. Dress.

The trendy, light, and casual **Fallen Angel** pub (65 Graham St., N1; Angel tube; open daily 10 A.M.–midnight, except Sundays till 11:30 P.M.) is popular with both genders, but Tuesday night is for women only and is packed. After 10 P.M., bring your own toilet paper.

Lesbian artist Della Disgrace recommends the women-only pool games Mon-days at **Angel's Pool Club** (1B Parkfield St., London N1).

Also for women, the restaurant/bar of the **Reeves Hotel** (see "Where to Stay" section above) is known as a space for non–bar bunnies who prefer quieter relaxation and conversation to hard discoing. But for dancers, there's also a weekly Friday-night social, with vegetarian buffet in the hotel's bar/dining room and a later disco, 48 Club.

We didn't feel particularly drawn to enter **Brompton's** (294 Old Brompton Rd., London SW4)—but we feel it only fair to you guys to mention that this was because leather-y sorts of men and thumpy-humpy sorts of music were virtually spilling out the doors here. The Earl's Court location is convenient to most of the gay hotels; in fact, Brompton's itself has a few hotel rooms upstairs. An even more well-known leather/denim pub in the same neighborhood is the **Coleherne** (261 Old Brompton Rd., London SW5), tremendously popular with tourists as well as locals, especially for Sunday lunch.

You will, of course, have your own theater preferences. (And you do know about the **half-price same-day ticket booth** in Leicester Square, yes?) But watch out for productions of the **Gay Sweatshop Theatre Company** (P.O. Box 820, London NW1 8LVV). **The Drill Hall Arts Centre** (16 Chenies St., London WC1; Goodge St. tube; Mondays women-only) is a good venue to watch for live gay alternative-theater productions. So is the **Duke of Wellington** (119 Balls Pond Rd., London NW1) Sunday through Wednesday nights. (The rest of the week, there's generally live music here—jazz on weekends, women-only nights on Thursdays, with live rock bands.)

Movie buffs will want to know that there's an annual **Lesbian and Gay Film Festival** at the National Theatre, sometime in late October–early November. Movie theaters that often show films of interest to gay people include **The Scala** in King's Cross, the **Rio Cinema, Hampstead Everyman,** and the **Brixton Roxy.**

WHERE (AND WHAT) TO EAT

We found London's best gay restaurant right in our own hotel: the Thai **Gazebo,** at the Philbeach (see "Where to Stay" section above for address). Don't get thrown off by the menu, which, probably due to some sort of translation prob-lem, reads like the sort of selection you'd find at a 1955 pseudo-Chinese joint on Route 46, New Jersey: "sweet and sour" shrimp soup, etc. The food is actually the most splendid Thai cooking we've ever had, anywhere. And the hours make after-theater dining possible: Last orders aren't taken until 11–11:30 P.M., midnight on Saturdays.

In the interest of self-preservation, you will be eating ethnic quite a bit in London; and if you don't want to eat at the Gazebo every night, international meals we love are the sophisticated, unusual regional Indian dishes at nongay, cooperatively run **Last Days of the Raj** (22 Drury Lane, London WC2; tel. 836 5707; thankfully, open late: last orders 11:30 P.M.); and Hungarian **The Gay Hussar** (2 Greek St., London W1; tel. 437 0973), which isn't gay either, but where the spicy *szegedi* fish soup, chicken *paprikás* with *galuska* (noodles), cheese pancakes, and chocolate-raspberry *eszterhazy torte* are all better, say some foodie experts, than one can find in Hungary.

Fish and chips is traditional Brit food that can be either cheap and very tasty, if made with fresh fish and light, crispy batter, or cheap and very nasty, if made, as is more common, with frozen fish and near-rancid oil. Two places where fish fans will be completely happy are the **Sea Shell** (49–51 Lisson Grove, NW1; open Tuesday–Saturday noon–2 P.M. and 5:15 P.M.–10:30 P.M.), which many consider London's best chippie (and we found pleasantly reminiscent, in ambiance, of old-fashioned shore places of our childhood); and the **Upper Street Fish Shop** (324 Upper St., London N1; open 11:30 A.M.–2 P.M. and 5:30 P.M.–10 P.M. Monday–Saturday; bring your own alcohol), where the crispy chippie fare is supplemented, for the combination artsy/neighborhood clientele of this homey local handy to the Camden Passage antique shops, by new additions like poached salmon and Perrier.

Those who want to try the Brit institution of **afternoon tea** may be interested in taking it, from 3 P.M. to 6 P.M., in the polished dark-wood clubby **Edwardian Room of the Cadogan** (75 Sloane St., London SW1X 9SG), the hotel where Oscar Wilde was arrested.

The very gay **Van B's** (306b Fulham Rd, SW10; Earl's Court tube; tel. 351 0863—reservations advised) was for us the rare elegant English restaurant experience that did not disappoint. Hopefully the light nouvelle-cuisine main dishes, perfectly undercooked veggie garnishes, and festive gay ambiance will remain the same under new management.

Cooperatively run **First Out Coffeeshop** (52 St. Giles High St., London WC2; tel. 240 8042; open 11 A.M.–midnight, Monday–Saturday) is an art gallery as well as a young, smart gay café; we saw an exhibit of Della Disgrace's lesbian-erotic photos there. First Out serves salads, sandwiches, quiche, pastries, and full vegetarian as well as regular evening meals, all inexpensive. You can also pick up all the free gay papers here, and reduced-price tickets to popular discos like Heaven and the Garage.

For those fond of merrie olde congealed sausage meat and so on, "pub grub" is available at a number of gay pubs: **King William IV** [see "Where to Go (Night)" for address]; **King's Arms** (23 Poland St., London W1); **Compton's** (53 Old Compton St., London W1) where, towards 11 P.M. closing, you can often pick up comps to Heaven, The Bell, Bang, and other popular gay disco clubs and pubs; and **Golden Lion** (51 Dean St., London W1), among others. Actually, we hear the food is much better at these places than at the average straight pub, though we admit we had not the courage to attempt it. But for a total redefinition of the term "pub grub," try the vegetarian eats at the **Fallen Angel** [see "Where to Go (Night)" for address; main meals 11 A.M.–3 P.M. and 5:30 P.M. on, snacks otherwise].

A traditional English Sunday roast midday dinner is served at some gay establishments, popular ones including the amusing **George IV** (7a Ida St., London E14; tel. 515 7339), a drag pub where lunch includes a cabaret show; the mostly gay male, American-style, deliberately downscale **Market Tavern** (Market Towers, 9 Elms Lane, London SW8; tel. 622 5655); and the docklands guppie **Ship & Whale** (2 Gulliver St., London SE16; tel. 237 3305). Our recommendation is the lunch at the **London Lesbian and Gay Centre Café** [see "Where to Go (Night)" for address], which has all the Yorkshire pudding–type trimmings, and a trimmings-only version for vegetarians. In the summer, there's a Sunday afternoon beer-garden barbecue. Regular café food hours (normally, they serve at least four different great salads, pies, snacks, and full hot-meal specials) run until about 10 P.M. daily.

There's also a Sunday buffet supper included in the admission price to the **Gardens** [see "Where to Go (Night)" for address]; there's a full menu and wine list nightly as well as a Friday veggie buffet at the **Reeves** (see "Where to Stay") for women; and a vegetarian restaurant, the **Greenhouse**, downstairs at the Drill Hall [see "Where to go (Night)"] which is mixed gay men and lesbians, except Mondays, for women only.

WHERE TO GET THE LATEST DIRT (INFORMATION RESOURCES)

The Lesbian & Gay Switchboard: 837 7324, 24 hours a day.

An outstanding gay bookstore, where you can buy all the listings periodicals below plus lots of hard-to-find (in America) European-published gay books, and get a halfway decent cup of coffee as well, is **Gay's the Word** (66 Marchmont St., London WC1; tel. 278 7654—near the Russell Square tube). They do mail order, too.

Good women's bookstores/info centers are **Sisterwrite** (190 Upper St., London N1 1RO; open Monday–Saturday, 10 A.M.–6 P.M.), a two-story place with crafts (T-shirts, socks, stationery, pottery, prints) as well as books—and with a welcome sign requesting men not to use the lesbian fiction section, unlike **Silvermoon** (66 Charing Cross Rd., WC2; open Monday–Saturday 10:30 A.M.–6:30 P.M.), a perfectly nice, friendly feminist bookstore where we nevertheless could barely contain ourselves from totally smushing a sleazoid straight fellow who was cruising the lesbo trash section, obviously looking for cheap thrills.

As already mentioned in "Practical Information, Brighton," three London-based gay periodicals have good club, hotel, and organization listings/ads for all Britain (but London especially): the astoundingly complete monthly *Gay Times* (283 Camden High St., London NW1 7BX U.K.; tel. 267 0021; fax 071/284 0329); and the weekly *Capital Gay* (Gay Community Distribution Services, P.O. Box 44, Welwyn Garden City, AL7 2DE U.K.). As GCDS is a volunteer group that gives any profits to gay and lesbian organizations, the paper is available free in bars and other gay venues, and for minimal cost by subscription. Another free bar weekly is **The Pink Paper** (42 Colbrook Row, London N1 8AS; tel. 226 8905). The feminist monthly **Spare Rib** (27 Clerkenwell Close, London EC1R 0AT, U.K.; tel. 253 9792) also has events and resources listings, as well as news and reviews.

International mail-order is available for all the above, if you enjoy reading up and planning in advance.

In addition, two regular old slick local London weekly entertainment-guide magazines have good gay listings sections: **Time Out** (Tower House, Southampton St., London WC2E 7HD; tel. 836 4411) and **City Limits** (8–15 Aylesbury St., London EC1R 0LR; tel. 259 1299). You'll want to buy both of these anyway, for the theater schedules. They're available at any newsstand.

Being a quarterly gay guide, **Kennedy's London Guide** (Phase Four Productions, same address as *City Limits*, tel. 622 2130; available by mail) is naturally less timely, but extremely comprehensive—and, with general travel tips and gay-related interviews and other features, most amusing. Included in the guide is a "Gay Business Association Directory" which lists everything from gay travel agents to gay opticians, photographers, locksmiths, and tattoo parlors. The guide also features a page of discount coupons to various gay stores, restaurants, pubs, and discos.

For travelers with AIDS-related conditions, useful numbers to know are the **National AIDS helpline**, 0800 56 71 23, 24 hours; **Terrence Higgins Trust**, 242 1010, daily 3 P.M.–10 P.M.; and London **Ealing AIDS Response Service**, 993 0011 or 993 8872.

London Lesbian Line, 251 6911, dispenses advice 2 P.M.–10 P.M. Mondays and Fridays, 7 P.M.–10 P.M. Tuesdays, Wednesdays, and Thursdays.

Although it's not hard to meet people in London gay bars, it occurs to us that some people might enjoy "meeting" and corresponding with gay friends before going. Other kinds of vacation planning and anticipatory learning are fun, so why not? **G.L.I. "Couples Link"** (BCM-GLI, 27 Old Gloucester St., London, WC1N 3XX, U.K.) is a service especially for couples who want to meet others already in a one-to-one relationship; it's not available to single people. The same company's **"Gaypen"** is for everyone. In both cases, they send you a form to fill out, asking about your own interests as well as your preferences in friends. "Couples Link" then sends you a list of members (with descriptions from the above form) to select from yourself, while "Gaypen" matches you with three members they pick and informs others with the right requirements about you.

WHAT TO READ

The Pink Plaque Guide to London, by Michael Elliman and Frederick Roll (GMP). The indispensable companion for the queer-about-town in London, telling who lived where, when, and with whom.

The Swimming-Pool Library, by Alan Hollinghurst (Random House). A novel about lust, race, and class in pre-AIDS London.

Oranges Are Not the Only Fruit, by Jeanette Winterson (Atlantic Monthly Press). Growing up English, fundamentalist, and queer.

Oscar Wilde's London: A Scrapbook of Vice and Virtues, 1880–1900, by Wolf von Eckardt, Sander L. Gilman, and J. Edward Chamberlin (Anchor). A portrait of the gaslit Victorian age, in all its splendor, and also all its squalor, from kiddie porn to Jack the Ripper. Great vintage photos.

The Oscar Wilde File, compiled by Jonathan Goodman (Allison & Busby). A collage of playbills, letters, news clips, trial testimony, photos, and drawings relating to Wilde's rise and fall.

Lord Alfred Douglas, by H. Montgomery Hyde (Dodd, Mead). You read it to find out what in the world Wilde ever saw in this twit. You never find out.

The Importance of Being Oscar: The Life and Wit of Oscar Wilde, by Leslie Frewin (W. H. Allen). An all-Wilde version of *Bartlett's Familiar Quotations.*

De Profundis and Other Writings, by Oscar Wilde (Penguin). Exactly what it says. "De Profundis" is Wilde's lengthy, betrayed letter-from-prison poem to Bosie.

The Well of Loneliness, by Radclyffe Hall (Avon). The critics of the day were right about one thing—don't give it to a kid. Not any kid you'd like to see turn out queer, anyway. What a bummer.

Our Three Selves: The Life of Radclyffe Hall, by Michael Baker (Morrow). A sympathetic bio by a true admirer.

Una Troubridge: The Friend of Radclyffe Hall, by Richard Ormrod (Carroll & Graf). Even if you're not fond of Hall's writing, this book's portrayal of her relationship with Troubridge must make you admire how "out" these two were in a time when it was neither usual nor considered morally admirable for upper-class gay people to be uncloseted.

Orlando, by Virginia Woolf (Harvest). Her queerest novel.

Our Sisters' London: Feminist Walking Tours, by Katherine Sturtevant (Chicago Review Press). Fascinating tours past the historic dwelling places of queens, prostitutes, suffragists, artists, even a bearded female saint.

The Buddha of Suburbia, by Hanif Kureishi (Viking). From the scriptwriter of *My Beautiful Laundrette,* an irreverent, avant-garde bildungsroman about a bisexual East Indian/English boy growing up in middle-class suburban London.

$\mathscr{A}$MSTERDAM

Fighting for the Last Quarter-Inch

$\mathscr{T}$he Taveerne de Pul is a typical example of what the Dutch call *bruine kroegen,* or "brown cafés": bars with traditional cozy settings of dark wood paneling, richly varnished walls and floors, and the nicotine stains of generations on the tables. According to custom, every inch of these cafés drips with Netherlands knickknacks, from brass ship's-lanterns to Rembrandty reproductions of cigar-box seventeenth-century burghers. The Taveerne de Pul is no different, except that it's in Kerkstraat, one of a half dozen Amsterdam neighborhoods with especially high concentrations of gay bars, saunas, hotels, restaurants, shops, and discos. Since the Taveerne de Pul is, in fact, a *gay* brown café, the decor has a bit of extra pizzazz: Hanging from the ceiling, amid the blue-and-white-ceramic Delftware, the idyllic scenes of tulips and windmills, and the traditional wooden shoes is an enormous wooden dildo.

Like San Francisco, Amsterdam is a weird mix of the quaint and the queer. Its monarchy, its art treasures, and its high-rise—free center of gabled brick town houses and picture-postcard canals make it one of the most graciously Old World of European capitals. Its red-light district, its marijuana bars, its huge hippie-squatter counterculture, and its unbeatable gay scene also make it one of the most free-wheeling. Both sides are the real Amsterdam, and what we personally find most charming about the city is precisely the trash-and-tradition, dildoes-and-Delft juxtaposition.

Some people—even some gay people—disagree. If you have a low threshold for honkytonk and you're really looking for Hans Brinker and the silver skates, you'd be better off going to an unambiguously picturesque town like Bruges in Flemish Belgium. On the other hand, if what turns you on is dirty, sordid sex-in-the-shadows, go to England or Italy, not Amsterdam. Sexuality in Holland is about as unsavory a topic as the weather.

In making gay life in the Netherlands special, the local gay people have some help from the atmosphere created by Dutch straights, 87 percent of whom say they support full equality for gay men and lesbians. And not because they think we're this year's liberal fad, or because they want to come to our discos and party, either. In the Netherlands, a country surprisingly full of churchgoers, stay-at-home housewives, and other latter-day burghers, values like individual freedom and tolerance are themselves traditions going back centuries.

Historically the Dutch never put curtains in their windows, the idea being that if you were a good Calvinist with nothing to hide, the curtains were superfluous. The same sensibility survives in the modern mindset, even where the activities in question might have made a Calvinist of old dive for the draperies. Whatever the issue—abortion, homosexuality, prostitution, pornography, recreational drugs, euthanasia—the Dutch generally prefer to have things out in the open, where everybody can keep an eye on them.

For gay people, this openness translates into the giddy sensation that you can actually go about your business, just like a real person, without getting bashed or even accused of flaunting it. The two of us aren't consciously aware of roaming our own turf under a cloud of dread, but there's something about being in a city where the average person you encounter is probably on your side (or at least doesn't give a shit) that palpably lightens our psychic load.

The first time we came to Amsterdam as a couple, we stayed in a gay-owned hotel purely by chance, and found a lesbian "brown bar" within minutes of our arrival, just by walking around the block. Instead of the classic closety pre-Stonewall knock-three-times-Joe-sent-me exteriors you still find in many European as well as American cities, Amsterdam gay spots often have touches like outdoor terraces for spillover crowds, huge plate-glass windows, sing-alongs that the entire block can listen in on, and rainbow flags flying from the gables. Or they have signs like the one in the entryway of the lesbian-owned mixed disco Homolulu, cautioning pick-pockets, gun-toters, drunks, druggies, and "antigay people" that they're emphatically unwelcome. Another disco, with an enormous neon sign on the roof, is actually *called* Gay Life.

Of all the countries in the world, Holland has the lowest percentage of its population in prisons and the highest per-capita number of bookstores; one bookstore for every day of the year in Amsterdam, according to a local saying. The Dutch strongly believe that knowledge informs, rather than corrupts, that if contraception is made available to straight teenagers, say, they might actually behave more sensibly than if they had simply been told to just say no. It works, too. White American teenage girls are seven times as likely to get pregnant as their Dutch counterparts.

The Dutch have attacked AIDS not by closing the baths, but through education, the ready availability of condoms, and the development of especially strong multilayered rubbers—double-bagging the groceries, so to speak. When Jesse Helms and friends were trying to keep Robert Mapplethorpe's work out of American museums, the Dutch response to the controversy was to publish the photos in the mainstream press. The whole country got to gaze, muse, discuss, and individually decide whether the now-famous erect black dick emerging from the polyester pants was, indeed, art.

At the Taveerne de Pul, an Irish tourist at the next table to ours is getting depressed because he has to leave tomorrow. He has a suitcase full of porn, to tide him over until his next trip—which, he assures us, will be as soon as possible, unless he's busted by Irish customs. Meanwhile, he is draped over his chair on the sidewalk café outside the tavern, watching the passing parade of men—less in cruising gear than with a sort of reverent expectancy that something wondrously nonrepressive might happen any second. "It's such a crazy city," he smiles dreamily.

We're here on this particular night with Peter Glencross, the British-born editor of the English-language *Top Guide to Amsterdam,* one of the best and most meticulously researched local European gay guides we know. Since Amsterdam has such a huge number of gay night spots, Peter has offered to squire us around to some that he thinks are the cream of the crop. First, he wants to introduce us to the owner of the de Pul, an older, fat, hearty, typical blond Dutchman who, Peter adds, is straight, and runs the place with his wife. We're puzzled, our New York reference point for straight owners of gay bars being guys with diamond pinkie rings and access to cement shoes.

Peter laughs, calls the owner over, and asks him how he feels about having so many gay people as patrons. The man grins broadly. "Well, it depends." He twinkles at us. "If they're under fourteen, I don't want them, and if they're over eighty, there's a problem going up to the top step." Then he cheerily wishes all of us and the already home-away-from-homesick Irish guy a lovely evening.

Our next stop is across the street in geography but a few centuries away in decor: Route 66, a small modern bar with a jukebox. On this particular evening it seems to be frequented entirely by very young, very blond Dutch guys who could pass for California disco bunnies, or possibly California disco chickens. One baby-surfer type puts his hands lasciviously underneath the T-shirt of an "older" guy in his early twenties, who looks at him mock-askance and says, "Go back to grade school."

He makes this joke in English, so that all of us can be in on it. Since Amsterdam seems to be on the itinerary of every gay tourist, the gay scene here is the most international of any urban center in Europe. English is absolutely the lingua franca, which is just one more reason Amsterdam is such a relaxing stopover for anglophones. The Dutch themselves are historically a nation of linguists, a legacy of their role as a nation of traders, and most of them seem to speak not only excellent English but also fluent German and at least a Romance language or two. Be prepared for lots of bilingual puns, most of them with punchlines involving fingers stuck in dykes. For the record, "dyke" in Dutch, that is, the lesbian-type as opposed to the seawall-type, is *"pot."* The operative word for men, aside from "homo" and "gay," is *"flikker."*

The host at the next bar on our itinerary is in fact a fellow American, Tony De Rosa, owner of De Spijk, a.k.a. the Spyker Bar. The clientele is overwhelmingly male and butch. "The Spyker is the only bar in the world to host jack-off parties," proclaims a sign, this one put up by the Amsterdam Jacks, the local JO Olympic team. It adds: "Don't you want to be part of history?"

Peter pops into the backroom for a second to make some quick notes for inclusion in the next edition of his guide. He's a balding man with soulfully deep blue eyes, a gentle smile, and both the crisp demeanor and the organizational skills of the British Rail manager he used to be before he got into the gay-guidebook business. But his customary English manners desert him completely as he comes yelping out of the cavelike space where the Jacks have their safe-sex parties several times a month, with the official approval of the Dutch Ministry of Health. "There's some graffiti on the wall that says, 'Peter Glencross knelt here,' " he reports indignantly, "but I've never been in there before in my life!"

While Peter recovers his aplomb, Tony, who looks like your basic teddy bear, tells us that before he was a born-again jack-off party host from Amsterdam he was an old hippie from San Francisco turned middle-aged screenplay editor from Los Angeles. In 1985, he took what was to be a two-month trip to Europe. He didn't like Britain, his first stop. His next destination was Amsterdam, and as he was exiting Central Station, he knew in a flash that he wanted to live here. He never got any farther. Today he says he only misses two things about the United States: American aspirin, and yellow legal-sized pads.

The easiest way for a gay American to stay in Amsterdam is to hook up with a Dutch lover. Although the Dutch were beaten to the punch by the Danes on gay marriage, they support gay relationships in every area from family discounts on bus passes to official status at embassies around the world for the lovers of gay diplomats. If Tony had had a Dutch boyfriend, he could have applied for permanent residency after five years. He didn't have a steady, and anyway, he notes with distaste, "Your passport is stamped HOUSEWIFE."

The other way for a gay (or straight) American to stay in Amsterdam is to prove that he or she is engaged in a job that no Dutch or European Community citizen is qualified to hold. So Tony opened a gay *American* brown café, from whose ceiling hang such items as an upside-down inflatable Statue of Liberty, a strand of New Orleans Mardi Gras pearls, six boxes of Aunt Jemima pancake mix, and a rubbing of Rock Hudson's signature from the sidewalk outside Graumann's Chinese Theater.

The bar serves American cocktails, plays American music ("from Billie Holiday to Leon Redbone to the Grateful Dead, and absolutely no disco"), and shows Hollywood cartoons and old movies (*King Kong,* Bugs Bunny, Road Runner, Laurel and Hardy) every night before the porn loops start. "I'd love to show *Oklahoma!* and *A Chorus Line,*" Tony enthuses. Then there's the sign over the bar that flashes "OINK ALERT!" whenever a particularly hot man walks in.

Tony has even introduced the concept of American holidays to his patrons. No one thought his Halloween-party idea would work, but when he offered cash prizes for the most unusual costumes, people quickly got into the spirit. Ethnic joke alert. For those of you who didn't catch that: The term "Dutch treat" doesn't come out of nowhere. In Belgium, we heard one about how you squeeze a dozen Dutch people into a Volkswagen: *You throw a guilder into the backseat.* For tourists, the most visible ramification of the Dutch desire to hold onto cash is the dearth of places that accept credit cards.

"Here," Tony beams, thrusting glossies of the Halloween party in full swing. We are especially struck by the shot of the prizewinner in a gauze fairy-princess number from the waist up, and not much of anything from the waist down. He is standing by a pool table, and is indeed playing pool. Sort of. Robert Mapplethorpe would have admired the fellow's pool cue, we're certain.

Even more heavy-duty than the Spyker is the Old Harbour, a mostly-men's leather/rubber bar with an all-men's hotel upstairs. The place used to be a hooker-addict hotel, although street hooking and hard drugs are among the things the Dutch government seriously does crack down on. Out of sentiment, the women still return to the Old Harbour to shoot up in the ladies' room. The new owner, an Englishman whose couture is so studded and spiked that he clanks when he moves, explains that he has recently tried to discourage these old-timers by installing red lights in the john, so they won't be able to see their veins.

We get into a conversation with Willy, a sweet-faced, muscled young Dutch guy who is sitting at the bar with his cocker spaniel, Sonia. He and his boyfriend also have two male cats at home, he adds, and all of their pets are gay. "When Sonia is in heat, she lifts her rump only for the girl dogs," Willy insists, sliding off the bar stool and pointing his butt in a little show-and-tell demo.

We notice the red hanky in his back pocket. "I *love* getting fist-fucked," Willy explains, in the same wonderfully animated, wholesome, unself-conscious tone of voice that someone else (someone not Dutch, anyway) might talk about their favorite flavor of ice cream. After a discussion about what sorts of latex gloves one's safe-sex fisting partner should wear, Willy decides he's going to teach us to drink the Dutch way. As near as we can remember, this sometimes involved leaning over a brimming glass of beer and slurping, and other times involved hoisting and toasting (*"Proost"* being Dutch for "Here's looking at you, kid") and chugging.

We also come away with a flyer called "the World's Most Comprehensive Hanky Code," a list of at least fifty colors and their meanings. We nod along absently, reading the usual fuck-suck-tits stuff, the codes for armpit freaks, for guys who like to eat meals off their tricks, and for those who want to give head to policemen (magenta worn on the right, lime-green on the left, and medium-blue on the right, if you absolutely *must* know), and even the gray-flannel hanky on the right for those who are into guys in suits. By the time we get to handywipe-on-left ("gives hot motor oil massages"), cocktail-napkin-on-right (for those who dig bartenders), and mosquito-netting-on-left (for tops who like to do it outdoors), we realize we've been had.

Peter, whose guidebooks also cover other European cities, tells us that the Amsterdam leather/rubber scene is far more playful than those in cities like London and Berlin. In Berlin, he was once refused entry to a club he simply wanted to report on for his readers. His sin was the wearing of regulation street clothes. "They suggested I go back to my hotel and change," he recalls. "I was so annoyed that I told them the only other outfit I'd brought with me was my best pink frock." Compared to other parts of Europe, we notice that drag seems relatively unpopular in Amsterdam, too. But then, so does any kind of dressing up. The rather elegant black-and-mirrored Homolulu is about the only club in town where anyone, male or female, can wear a suit jacket without feeling like the very conspicuous winner of the Asshole of the Week Award.

When we were there, the hot fashion statement for men was skintight black nylon bicycle shorts that made a person's legs look like matched sets of licorice sausages. In contrast to the American yuppie-couch-potatoes-in-mountaineer-gear syndrome, though, everybody in Holland really does seem to ride a bike everywhere. We'd been taken aback more than once by riders whose bikes lacked bells, and who sidled up behind us, politely chirping "Brrrnnng, brrrnnng." Bicycle theft is also one of the few rampant crimes in the Netherlands. A standard joke is that if you need a new one, you should go to a crowded section of Amsterdam and scream, "Hey you! That's my bike!" Then take your choice of the machines abandoned on the spot by fleeing "owners."

When the Dutch aren't biking, or reading, they're eating. Breakfasts are enormous (and snotoid soft-boiled eggs in jaunty little cups unavoidable, though it's easy to ignore them and just concentrate on the customary mountain of cold cuts, cheeses, and fresh-baked breads). If you can tear yourself away from the gay cafés and restaurants, we highly recommend Dutch junk food, especially the *pannekoeken* (light pancakes roughly the size of an ice-skating rink) which are served with everything from apples to bacon to whipped cream, and the many varieties of *broodjes* (literally, "little bread")—sandwiches, usually served on soft buttered rolls and sold in special fast-food shops called *broodjewinkels*. Carnivores will want to try the *filet américain* version (succulently spiced steak tartare). Herring fans can buy the real thing from stands all over the city during the warm-weather months, although the "new" or "green" herring is best in May. When the herring isn't in season, hearty Dutch pea soup *(erwtensoep)* that a spoon can stand up in probably is.

Probably the most interesting foodie experience of all in Amsterdam is the *rijstaffel,* or Indonesian rice table: a large bowl of rice served with up to two dozen condiment dishes of various meats, fish, fruits, nuts, and vegetables, both hot and cold, sweet and sour, pickled and fresh, in sauces ranging from curry to hot pepper to peanut. The idea is to pile your plate with rice, and then mix and match with whatever condiments you please. You'll read about the restaurants Bali and Sama Sebo in every guidebook and probably decide that they're the Trader Vic's of *rijstaffel,* but in fact they really *are* better than the more authentic-looking holes in the wall. These include the glamorous-looking gay-oriented one on Utrechtsestraat *somebody's* bound to try to steer you to, where nearly all condiments were so "authentically" incendiary we couldn't taste a thing, or use our breath for anything except lighting people's cigarettes, for days.

Then, of course, there's Dutch beer. This brings us back to our diligent research on Amsterdam's night life. As the night wore on, our notes got more and more illegible, but we do remember being mightily impressed by the mostly-lesbian bar Vivelavie. Very crowded, very cruisy, very deco-look sophisticated, Vivelavie was full of beautiful young women with perfectly sculpted, immaculately moussed punk haircuts, each one more gravity-defying than the last. In general, like everywhere else in the known universe, women's venues are far fewer in number than men's, but the ones that do exist are fine.

Amsterdam is also practically the only place we've ever heard of that had a lesbian bar with a backroom. Unfortunately, it had come and gone by the time of our visit. According to one woman we interviewed, the place had briefly been a smash hit, but as the patrons inevitably met, paired off, and reverted to infamous lesbian nesting mode, business in the backroom slacked off. By and by the owners began to feel they couldn't really spare the space. Still, they did keep it technically open for a while, our source reports. By then, however, it doubled as a storage area; you had to make your hot contacts next to the mops, buckets, and brooms.

As for the wide open hetero porno–hooker–live sex show scene, those of you who are of the feminist persuasion might be surprised at its relatively low sleaze quotient. At home, we're definitely not good open-minded liberals on the subject; in fact, Women Against Pornography was founded in our living room. We later parted company with WAP on the censorship issue, but just because we think the sex industry has a right to exist doesn't mean we think it's harmless, charming entertainment. Aside from often degrading the women involved, most straight porn seems to feed exactly the piggy, hostile straight-male attitudes that affect *us* every time we walk down the street and some asshole invites us to sit on his face.

But in prosex, egalitarian Amsterdam, our buzzers simply don't get pushed very hard. The red-light district—in the usual breathtakingly beautiful canal-crossed neighborhood, with regular museums and restaurants and so on mixed in with the sex shops and brothels—is as clean and orderly as the rest of the city. Although it's noisy and sometimes even rowdy, we've never once been hassled there. The vibes are more like the crowd at Disneyland than the one in Times Square.

Dressed as cartoon Frederick's of Hollywood hookers in their high heels and baby-doll negligees, the prostitutes stand or sit in picture windows actually lit with scarlet bulbs. From there they beckon potential clients with all the subtlety of carnival barkers. The women don't have to worry about violent johns and the like, since the whole system is run by the state with the same efficiency as the railroads. The hookers are even unionized. (On our tours of inspection, we even saw a few who were middle aged and decidedly chunky, although we never figured out if this was a matter of client taste or some sort of government-stamped equal-opportunity job protection.) In the commerce-driven culture of Holland, sex appears to be a commodity like any other, and prostitution is a *job*, a state of affairs that not everyone might admire, but which seems to have more to do with the evils of capitalism than with those of sexism. One of us was in a bank in Amsterdam one morning when a hooker, still in her fishnet stockings, got on the line to make a deposit, a crisp wad of guilders in her fist. No one batted an eye.

At some point during our tour of the town, we asked Peter Glencross about the many "houses with boys" we'd seen ads for. Were these male brothels licensed in the same way as the hetero bordellos? Did they encourage safe sex? He suggested we go to the source for the answers, and before we knew it, we were bounding up the stairs to the Blue Boy Club, the oldest male whorehouse in the city, established in 1973. After an initial double-take, a sinuous little Mediterranean philosophically assumed we were potential clients and slithered up behind one of us to describe his qualifications in a feverish, moaning stage whisper.

The Blue Boy is actually part of a sleek modern complex that also includes several bars and theaters. A flyer tells us that the club sells poppers, souvenirs, and videos starring the staff ("EIGHT HORNY YOUNGSTERS strip down and oil up their smooth young bodies for your home entertainment"), and that you're welcome to stop by for a beer, with no obligation to hire a hustler. On the other hand, if you want takeout to your hotel, that's available, too. Live sex shows are featured several nights a week, and there's a free nightly strip show.

Tonight's stripper has just finished his routine as we arrive. He's a hunky blond with an enormous basket, by then reencased in green short shorts of approximately the same dimensions as an airmail stamp. Peter asks how old we guess the fellow is. Twenty-five? Twenty-eight? In fact, he's forty-five, and works by day as a lawyer with a big bank. However, this day job leaves him only partially fulfilled. We ask, jaws dropping, if the bank has any idea that he moonlights as a rent boy. "Oh, they could care less," says Peter. This is *Amsterdam*, silly.

Tommy, a clean-cut high-school-swim-team type with curly black hair, offers to show the visiting journalists his room. "This . . . is where it all happens," he exclaims dramatically, flipping on the mood lighting. In fact, the place is nicer than most hotels: about the size of a small airfield, designer-modern, and spotlessly tidy, with a pink tub for two next to the bed, a separate bathroom, and porn flickering discreetly on the VCR/TV.

We ask how the house finds the boys, but Tommy insists that it's the other way around. The boys find the house. The important thing is to have many types, from British bulldog skinheads to Oriental flowers. "Today, we had a Russian boy come by," he adds proudly. Most of the clients are American or British gay male tourists, though there's a small but steady stream of local married men, and occasionally a straight woman. Peter points out a fiftyish, chubby, bald, very middle-class man who is adjusting his tie in the main reception room. The man is Swiss, and he's been a client of the banker-with-the-basket for as long as anyone can remember. Once a year, the two sit down with their calendars and plan out their twice-a-month weekend trysts together.

All credit cards and foreign currency are thoughtfuly accepted, and condoms are free. Getting men to go along with safer sex was a problem a few years ago, according to Tommy, but now it's assumed.

Finally, he shows us the brand-new upstairs "SM Loft," with its slings and wall-manacles. We inspect a large open tub, which, presumably, will be used for scat and golden-showers scenes, although Tommy can't bring himself to say so. "It's for . . . whatever," he punts. "This isn't *my* scene," he adds. "I'm a romantic, myself."

On the last Saturday in June, Dutch gay men and lesbians honor the anniversary of America's gay pride–birthing Stonewall riots with a march, which takes place in a different city each year. But the long-time traditional gay holiday—like the Mardi Gras in New Orleans or Halloween in much of the rest of the United States—is the queen's birthday, April 30. Actually, her real birthday is in January, but, like a racehorse, the queen has an official birthday, too. According to custom, all the minor laws are suspended on Her Majesty's Day. In times long since past, the dispensation meant that gay men could prance through town in evening gowns while their lesbian sisters strutted about in tuxedoes, and queers of both genders could dance with their lovers in the streets. In the modern era, it tends to mean all-night parties at most of the bars.

The truly racy thing about the queen's birthday, though, is that all commercial laws are suspended as well. During the other 364 days of the year, the country has a tightly regulated economy: Establishments are licensed to be open only during particular hours, and never 'round the clock (which is why some gay bathhouses are "day saunas" and some are "night saunas"). Merchants must be licensed, and their licenses limit what they can sell. For an entrepreneuring grocer to start carrying videotapes on the back rack of the shop would be unthinkable, under ordinary circumstances. But on April 30 all bets are off. Anyone can sell anything, and everyone does. People get up before dawn to find prime locales to hawk their old jewelry or their home-made pastries.

People in Amsterdam, including gay people, get very excited about this. In a country where people peddle their asses in red-light picture windows under the strict supervision of the authorities, the *real* thrill apparently is Shopping Without a License.

Regardless of what time of year you come to Amsterdam, don't leave town without a visit to the Homomonument, which "commemorates all women and men who were ever oppressed and persecuted because of their homosexuality," particularly the thousands of men who were forced to wear the Pink Triangle in Nazi concentration camps. Designed by Karin Daan, it's one of the most graceful pieces of public sculpture anywhere.

There are other European memorials to the gay victims of World War II—in Bologna, and in West Berlin, and in several of the camps themselves. The Amsterdam monument, however, dedicated in 1987, is easily the most prominent. It was deliberately situated near the Anne Frank House, a center and symbol for antifascist and antiracist movements from all over the world (many of whose members, unfortunately, probably don't know that Anne's father censored her homoerotic musings from the famous diaries).

Since it's less a "monument" in the bowling-trophy sense of the word than a sort of staired terrace jutting into the Keizergracht canal, you could miss the Homomonument altogether, or mistake it for an oddly shaped, rose-colored dock. But if you know what you're looking at, you see a giant pink granite triangle, 107 feet on each side. The large triangle in turn contains three smaller triangles. One points to the Anne Frank House; a second points toward the headquarters of the country's major gay-rights organization, the Cultuur-en Outspannings Centrum (Center for Culture and Leisure), or COC (pronounced "See-Oh-See," incidentally, *not* "cock"); the third triangle extends down the stairs and into the canal, forming a wharflike space where people loll on their backs in the sun, read, and eat lunch. But nobody forgets where they are. The day we were there, someone had left a bouquet of roses and white daisies, along with a little piece of paper that simply said "Gay Indonesia."

Across the way, on the stone canal wall, there's a huge piece of graffiti that's obviously been there for some time without the authorities scrubbing it off. It refers to the antigay law passed in Great Britain in 1988: "STOP CLAUSE 28."

Why Amsterdam? The standard response is that the Dutch are "tolerant," a people who've given safe haven to Jews, Huguenots, Puritans, Quakers, and anybody else who ever needed it.

"We're a merchant culture with lots of ports, which means we've always been open to outside influences," explains Juriënne Ossewold, cocurator of "Two of a Kind," an exhibit on the history of gay people in Holland that was shown in 1989–1990 at the Amsterdam Historical Museum. Her colleague, Paul Verstraten, adds: "Most Dutch people regularly read books and articles in English, German, and French. Our ideas are constantly fertilized by other cultures."

All of this is true, although we ourselves have never really sussed out the formula for what makes a gay mecca in Europe. Tolerance certainly helps, but London manages to have a booming gay scene smack in the middle of narrow-minded, explicitly antigay Thatcherism. Copenhagen activists say the main reason they managed to pass their domestic-partnership law is that organized religion is practically dead in Denmark. How then does one explain the fact that the single largest progay force in East Berlin before the fall of the Wall was the Evangelical Lutheran Church, or that the largest gay and lesbian organization in Paris is a Christian center? The gayest places in Italy are the strongholds of the Communist Party, the very folks who in other lands consider us a symptom of capitalist decadence. In Mykonos, half the population seems to be royalist. You figure it.

The other problem with the "tolerance" theory is that it doesn't explain why Dutch tolerance didn't extend to the gay community until the sixties. Amsterdam was a gay backwater for most of this century, even when Paris and Berlin were awash in queer culture. According to the official booklet published in conjunction with "Two of a Kind," Dutch gays in the teens, twenties, and thirties were vulnerable to blackmail, with bars frequently raided and the names of patrons placed on a police list. In those few pre-sixties Amsterdam clubs that did flourish, bartenders developed a danger signal in the form of a small model owl. If a stranger entered the bar, the owl's eyes would light up; or, alternatively, the bird would be prominently placed where the regular clients would notice it and moderate their behavior accordingly. For years, the Dutch slang word for straights was "owls."

The Nazi occupation brought far more brutal antigay policies. Paradoxically, the war also served as a cover for gay couples, since Amsterdam's eight P.M. curfew made it normal for friends to stay overnight at each other's homes without incurring suspicion. In 1946, a social group was formed that much later became the COC. It was tolerated by the authorities, but hardly encouraged. Only in the sixties, when the entire society bloomed into a giant Haight-Ashbury with windmills, did gay men and lesbians begin to gain real acceptance.

In *The Embarrassment of Riches,* the Harvard historian Simon Schama makes an interesting argument: that the Dutch spirit of tolerance was forged by the constant, pressing need to keep the sea at bay. While the rest of Europe fiddled around with feudal hierarchies and religious wars, the Dutch learned to cooperate with each other to build, maintain, and repair the seawalls, dams, dikes, and pumping windmills that served as the lines of defense against the ever-threatening water. At the same time, the Dutch carved out a national identity around images of survival of the floods. Sermons were full of comparisons to Noah and to the Chosen People for whom the seas had miraculously parted. For centuries, the Dutch prospered in the secure belief that they had made a covenant with God, who in turn protected them from the deluges.

Then, in 1726 and 1728, the country suffered a catastrophic series of floods, and in the winter of 1731, part of the dike along the north coast of Holland collapsed altogether. The cause of the erosion was a colony of pile worms, creatures with voracious, termitelike appetites, who up until that time had been unknown to scientists.

In 1730, two men were caught having sex in the tower of Utrecht Cathedral. One of the arrested men was persuaded to provide a list of his contacts, and he turned out to be a slut of major proportions. Sex between men was hardly unknown in the Netherlands—indeed, the great Dutch humanist Erasmus had been accused of seducing his young male pupil at the end of the fifteenth century. Nonetheless, the authorities were completely stunned to discover what seemed to be a national network of dedicated practitioners who cruised each other day and night in the marketplaces, churches, and town halls of Amsterdam, the Hague, Leyden, Rotterdam, and other major cities. Gay life had infiltrated the very heart of the nation.

The government proceeded to embark on a Bible-thumping witch-hunt totally at odds with Holland's centuries-old history of tolerance and moderation. Over the next two years, hundreds of men and boys were arrested or forced to flee. Dozens were hanged, burned, thrown into the sea, or publicly garrotted—the latter supposedly the most humiliating execution of all, since it was usually reserved for women.

Schama suggests that the two phenomena were related: The "sodomites" were scapegoated by a nation that happened to be terrified about its physical vulnerability. Like the pile worms, gay men could be seen as previously hidden agents of destruction who all along had been invading the churches and other foundations of society. Even the act of anal sex itself became a ready metaphor for insatiable, burrowing incursions into the pure body politic. The rotten wooden dikes were eventually replaced with stone, but sporadic waves of antigay persecution continued throughout the century.

The last flood disaster suffered by the Netherlands was in 1953, when eighteen hundred people drowned in Zeeland, near the Belgian border. Since then the brilliant Dutch engineering of the Delta Project, which closed off the Maas and Scheldt Rivers from the North Sea, has finally made the country completely secure. The Polders, vast tracts of land east of Amsterdam that had been reclaimed by the earlier closing-off of the Zuyder Zee, have also been settled and farmed.

If we can turn Schama's theory on its head, is it possible that it was only in the sixties that the Netherlands at long last felt high and dry enough to welcome the sodomites?

Today the first article of the Dutch Constitution reads that discrimination of any kind is against the law. The town of Utrecht is known not for its anitgay pogroms, but for its university, which has a famous department of

Gay Studies. The COC, now officially named the Dutch Society for the Integration of Homosexuality COC, has seven thousand members, gay centers in forty cities, and, since 1973, legal status as part of Her Majesty's government. Gay writers and performers have come out and been hailed as cultural heroes. It all seems too perfect. We ask everybody we meet where the flaws are.

"I'm sure discrimination against gay people *happens* here," says Luc Lucas, a translator for Radio Nederlands. He is trying hard to be helpful, although he can't personally think of a single area in his life where he suffers from homophobia. He finally adds that when he was a boy in the 1950s, growing up in the heavily Catholic southern part of the country, it was definitely not cool to be queer.

But now?

"Well, now you'll find policemen wearing little earrings, and a year ago one of the small towns actually elected a gay mayor. That *was* a break-through, not something that happens every day, although lots of cities now *do* have an active policy of hiring homosexuals and lesbians as teachers, and advertise in gay magazines. Of course we have openly gay people in the army here. They have their own organization, set up with the approval of the ministry. I think there's a sense in Holland that there *should* be gay people in all the major institutions, just as a reflection of society."

But, um . . . the negatives?

Luc acknowledges that gay people still can't marry in the Netherlands. Of course, that's partly because the COC hasn't especially pushed for it: Many radicals think gay marriage is hopelessly bourgeois. "A gay couple did apply for a marriage license at the Amsterdam Town Hall," he adds. "The man at the desk was terribly sorry that he couldn't comply, and he agreed with them that it was *ridiculous,* since there are so many different kinds of relationships nowadays." Finally the clerk offered to do all the preliminary paperwork to help the couple mount a court challenge to the present civil code. "I thought that was very Dutch," Luc smiles.

Someone else tells us about a man who was rejected for a position at the Royal Palace. It turns out the problem wasn't that the man was gay, but that he was in the closet. This was perceived as an unwholesome trait, which might leave him open to blackmail.

A gay restaurant-owner glumly confesses that it took him an uncon-scionably long time to come out to his parents because he knew it would be "a blow." But it turns out that when he finally told them, he was all of twenty-one, and now they adore his boyfriend. The president of the Am-sterdam COC complains that the churches aren't doing enough to help gays. Well, no, they're not waving placards and swearing that we're all going to fry in hell, but they should be taking *affirmative* steps, and they're not. We also hear about some teenagers who wrote antigay slogans on the side of the COC building a few years ago. The vandals were caught, and forced by the authorities to wash the slogans off.

Several people tell us about an incident in the town of Zwolle, where a group of Muslim immigrants from Holland's former South Pacific colonies got clearance from the local government to hold religious services in a public building. Then the Muslims found out that a gay group was meeting in the next room, and they balked. When they were told that the gays had just as much right to be there as they did, the Muslims apologized and said that it wasn't that they didn't want to worship next to a *gay* group. The problem was that it was a *social* group. They wouldn't want to worship next to *any* social group, no matter who it was.

Nobody believes them, of course, and the story is told to us as an example that anti-gay prejudices still surface in Dutch society.

But it seems to us that what the story is really about is the fact that Dutch society finds homophobia unacceptable. In the Netherlands, gay people are simply another minority subculture, like Jews in New York or Hispanics in California. Not everybody loves us, but even the worst hardcases learn fast that they don't get a free pass to call us the abomination of the earth, either.

It shouldn't be a big deal, but it is. And Amsterdam is as close to the other side of the rainbow as it gets.

AMSTERDAM

PRACTICAL INFORMATION

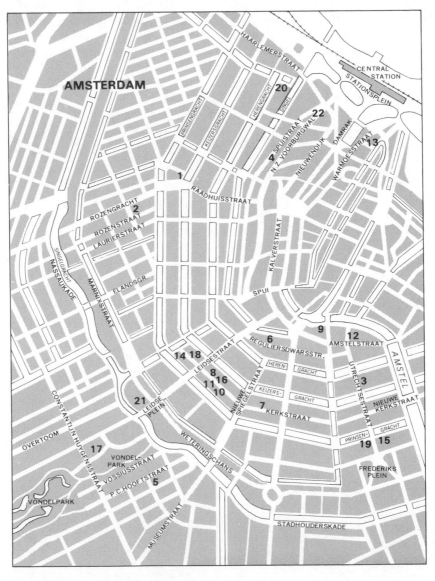

AMSTERDAM—NUMBER KEY

1. Homomonument (at edge of Keizersgracht near Raadhuisstraat)
2. COC (Roxenstraat 14) Gay Center

Restaurants and Coffee Shops

3. Chopin (Utrechtsestraat 21)
4. 't Sluisje (1 Torensteeg, off Spuistraat)
5. Sama Sebo (P.C. Hooftstraat 42)
6. Downtown (Reguliersdwarsstraat 31)
7. Françoise (mostly women; Kerkstraat 176)

Bars

8. De Pul (Kerkstraat 45)
9. Amstel Taveerne (Amstelstraat 54)
10. Route 66 (Kerkstraat 66)
11. Cosmo Bar (Kerkstraat 42; same address as West End Hotel)
12. Vivelavie (mainly women; Amstelstraat 7)
13. Old Harbour (leather; Warmoesstraat 23)
14. Spijker (Kerkstraat 4)
22. Why Not Bar/Blue Boy Club ("house with boys" N.Z. Voorburgwal 28)

Hotels

11. West End Hotel (Kerkstraat 42; same address as Cosmo Bar)
15. Prinsenhof (Prinsengracht 810)
16. Aero (Kerkstraat 49)
17. Engelande (Roemer Visscherstraat 30a, near Constantin Huygensstraat)
18. Unique (Kerkstraat 37)
19. ITC (Prinsengracht 1051)
20. New York (Herengracht 13)
21. Quentin (Leidsekade 89, off Marnixstraat near the Leidseplein)

GENERAL HINTS / INFO

To orient yourself, picture one of those diagrams of the solar system they always used to show us in science class when we were kids. Chop it in half horizontally, right through the middle of Our Friend Mr. Sun, and throw away the whole top half. What you have left, which should look like a multilined half circle with the straight part on top, is central Amsterdam: The remaining half of Mr. Sun (in the middle of the straight top part) is the Central Rail Station, and the planet orbits semicircling around it are the main ring canals, named, from the inside out, the inner Singel, Herengracht, Keizersgracht, Prinsengracht, and the outer Singel. Pay absolutely no attention to the leftover planet orbits; to tell you the truth, we always preferred the dinosaur-science classes.

Although gay life is really everywhere in Amsterdam (even most ordinary bookstores have a gay shelf or two), there are a few **particular areas of gay** concentration, arranged around scenes for different tastes—which are naturally not, in this tolerant town, strictly separate.

Male brothels ("Houses with Boys and Escorts"), as well as sex shops, SM shops, and male porn theaters, center around Nieuwezijds (usually abbreviated N.Z.) Voorburgwal/Spuistraat.

The heaviest leather area is along Warmoesstraat. This neighborhood also has a large concentration of Amsterdam's famous marijuana bars, formerly marked by reefer-leaf signs, but now more discreetly identified by large potted plants in the front windows. Buyers still choose openly from a large sample book of available varieties.

Both the latter areas are located in Amsterdam's inner core, between the Central Station and the inner Singel. The other main gay areas are in the more picturesque part of town, between the inner and outer Singels.

One major gay-bar area is Amstel/Rembrandtsplein, which centers on river-side Amstel, on parallel Amstelstraat, and on Halvemaansteeg and Paardenstraat (side streets connecting the other two). A couple of bars here are leather, but there are also many, many decidedly less heavy-duty places—several well-known sing-along pubs, for instance, as well as a glamorous women's bar. In all, more than two dozen gay establishments are located here.

Another long-time major gay area where variety is the key is Kerkstraat. Here there are at least a dozen and a half establishments ranging from gay hotels (several) to gay versions of traditional Dutch "brown cafés" to gay yuppie bars, saunas, and discos. We came to think of this area as the "normal" gay neighborhood, for us regular vanilla-type pervs.

A newer gay locale with over a dozen hotels, bars, coffee shops, and discos (like the super-smart Exit), which draw a trendier, younger guppie in-crowd is Reguliersdwarstraat. This area includes parallel Singel and perpendicular Beulingstraat.

Telephone Code: 020.
Currency Unit: the guilder, or florin (Hfl)

WHERE TO STAY

Amsterdam has two or three times as many gay-owned and gay-oriented hotels as we are listing. These are just our favorites. All prices are for a double room, with full Dutch breakfast. Off-season (roughly November through March), some hotels discount.

Prices: *Inexpensive* = below Hfl 85; *moderate* = Hfl 85–110; *mod./exp.* = Hfl 110–160; *expensive* = over Hfl 160.

ITC (International Travel Club) Hotel, Prinsengracht 1051, 1017 JE Amsterdam; tel. 23 02 30. Traditional eighteenth-century canal house outside, tastefully simple Scandinavian-style modern inside, the ITC is exclusively gay—although a straight couple with androgynous names once did slip past. They liked the place. So do gay guests. Of the 15 rooms, all doubles have bathrooms, and some have canal views. The real prizewinner is a huge suite which accommodates one to four people, at varying prices, although we'd probably go for the mirror room (walls *and* ceiling) ourselves. There's a plant-filled ground-floor lounge and a guest bar open from morning until after midnight. Owners John and Grant give a gay map/guide to all, and a helpful lesbian-Amsterdam portfolio to gay female guests. *Moderate–mod./exp.*

Hotel Engelande, Roemer Visscherstraat 30a, NL 1054 ES Amsterdam; tel. 18 08 62. Part of a row of seven turn-of-the-century hotels, each designed to represent the architecture of a different country, the Engelande, on a quiet street almost right next door to Vondelpark, is only a 5- to 10-minute walk from Kerkstraat. Run by its gay owner as a mixed hotel, it was, in fact, a tad too discreet for us: gay maps are available, but you have to ask for them. Straight tourist info is on a front-hall rack. That said, though, it's a lovely place, especially the traditional antique dark wood–furnished breakfast room, with glass doors to the private, enclosed back garden (which comes with lurking monster cat). The 28 cheerful rooms are available both with and without bathroom; without is about a third less expensive—but still very nice. Light, roomy bathless rooms 1 and 2, for instance, both have terraces with table overlooking the garden, artsy Scandinavian designer/hippie tie-dye bedspreads, pen-and-ink naked-people drawings on the white sandpaint walls, and shellike sconce bed lights. Many niceties: Laundry service is available, as is the *International Herald Tribune* with breakfast. *Moderate–mod./exp.*

The Quentin Hotel, Leidsekade 89, 1017 PN Amsterdam; tel. 26 21 87. Named after Quentin Crisp, this renovated 100-year-old canal-front hotel has a largely actor/artist/musician and gay clientele; the gay male owners wrote us that they're particularly welcoming to lesbians. Of the 16 rooms, five with double bed, only one has a private bathroom, but most have canal views. We wish we could tell you actual specifics about the rooms, but the snippy petty bureaucrat at the front desk, citing the always ever-so-interesting "if we let you we'd have to let everybody" justification, wouldn't show us any. There's a 24-hour house bar and a canal-front terrace; and you can stumble down to breakfast as late as 1 P.M. *Inexpensive–moderate; with bath, mod./exp.*

Hotel Prinsenhof, Prinsengracht 810, 1017 JL Amsterdam; tel. 23 17 72 or 27 65 67. You won't find this hotel in other gay guidebooks. In fact, the two guys who run the place initially didn't want to be in ours, either, until we explained it fully. So you might not want to stay here if you have your heart set on heavy cruising, showing up at breakfast with a hustler dressed only in a loincloth, or some of the other more outrageous behavior we heard about in some of Amsterdam's other gay-owned hotels. Not personally being all that big on loincloths, however, we loved our beautiful old gable-windowed, beamed-ceiling room on the top floor, when we happened on this old canal-house hotel by accident on our first visit. They crank your luggage up the narrow stairs on a pulley. *Moderate.*

Hotel New York, Herengracht 13, 1015 BA Amsterdam; tel. 24 30 66; fax 20 32 30. Exclusively gay, this 20-room hotel, consisting of three renovated and modernized seventeenth-century houses, is a bit more expensive and probably the most American in amenities. So, if you are one of those guppies in a stressful business, to whom room service and a telephone–umbilical cord is an important part of vacation relaxation, this very comfy canal-front place is definitely where you should stay. The hotel has a garage, TV lounge, guest bar, laundry service, and hot or cold snacks on request; all rooms have showers (some full bathrooms) and direct-dial phones. *Mod./exp.–expensive.*

As you've no doubt gathered, we personally prefer picturesque, typically Dutch-looking hotels in a quiet location, preferably on a canal and/or with a garden, like all of the above. We'll mention in passing, however, for those whose priority is to be smack in the middle of busy gay central, that a good bet is the **Unique Hotel** (Kerkstraat 37, 1017 GB Amsterdam; tel 24 47 85; *moderate*), which claims to be Amsterdam's first exclusively gay hotel (established 40 years ago); on Sundays, they serve a champagne breakfast. The **West End** (Kerkstraat 42, 1017 GM Amsterdam; tel 24 80 74; *moderate*), across the street and upstairs from the gay Cosmo Bar, is also exclusively gay, serves breakfast in bed, and is slightly cheaper. The mixed **Aero** (Kerkstraat 49, second floor, 1017 GB Amsterdam; tel. 22 77 28; *inexpensive–moderate*), next to the gay Taveerne de Pul, has one of the world's great breakfast rooms—a queeny red-and-gold, chandeliered and mirrored Victorian extravaganza—but the rooms are just modern.

The Old Harbour Hotel and often-listed John's Place do not welcome women.

Visitors who are planning stays of at least three days can save some money and get larger accommodations by renting a **furnished apartment.** There are several gay agencies that handle this, a good one being Gay Interhome Services (Keizersgracht 33, 1015 CD Amsterdam; tel. 25 00 71). Prices depend on location and luxury, but average around $40/day, $250/week—lower for a month.

WHERE TO GO (DAY)

The pink granite three-triangle **Homomonument** is located on the Westermarkt, jutting into the Keizersgracht, with one triangle pointing to the COC building, one to the Anne Frank House (both very nearby, and worth a visit), and one to the national memorial to victims of fascism on Dam Square.

As for day trips, we've always filled our days just walking around Amsterdam. In our several trips here, we've hardly found time to wander outside the central ring canals, much less out of town—even to the Netherlands' other major gay centers like Utrecht, Rotterdam, and The Hague.

We can tell you from experience, however, that between the flat land and the sane drivers, Holland is a joy for **biking,** even for out-of-shape couch potatoes. With a few tourist-office brochures you can pick your own destinations. But gay men especially might enjoy pedaling to the secluded dunes of the **Nieuwe Meer** parkland, only six miles from central Amsterdam, where there's a major gay sunbathing and cruising area near the Oeverland entrance parking area, by the lake. No facilities.

Zandvoort, roughly 19 miles from Amsterdam, on the North Sea (30 to 45 minutes by train), has what is purportedly the biggest gay nude beach area in Europe. When you hit the beach, hang a left on the boardwalk. The gay part of the nude beach is about a five-kilometer walk. For refreshments, look for bars/restaurants Zeezicht, Eldorado, and Amerika.

WHERE TO GO (NIGHT)

Most bars in Amsterdam are open until 1 A.M. (2 A.M. on weekends), while discos are open until 4 A.M. (5 A.M. on weekends).

Bars/discos mentioned in the text: the **Taveerne de Pul** (Kerkstraat 45) is a very friendly traditional "brown café" with pool room, outdoor tables, and small snacks. The charming-looking **Saarein** (Elandstraat 119), is a lesbian brown café with pool table, whose bartenders are known for being particularly helpful to travelers in need of gay info. Small **Route 66** (Kerkstraat 66) draws a big crowd because of its prodigiously stocked bar and 1950s and '60s American nostalgia jukebox . . . not to mention its location next to the night sauna. **De Spyker** (Kerkstraat 4) is a comfy/cruisy "American-style" gay bar mainly for men—though the owner insists women are welcome, contrary to rumors we heard about occasional troublesome doorpeople—featuring good nondisco music, early-night vintage cartoons and later-night porn videos, plus bimonthly jack-off parties in the world's smallest backroom. The **Old Harbour** hotel bar (Warmoesstraat 23) is a seriously leather-clothes joint with an outgoing, mostly male clientele (lesbians are welcome in the bar, though not in the hotel). Every European lesbian who's ever been to Amsterdam swoons at the mere mention of the mainly, though not exclusively, female bar, **Vivelavie** (Amstelstraat 7). The clientele *is* fabulous-looking. **Homolulu** (Kerkstraat 23) is a sophisticated women-owned disco which includes a candlelit Continental restaurant (open until 3 or 4 A.M.!); it has occasional Sunday all-women's evenings, but is normally popular with both gay men and lesbians. The fashionable newish guppie fave **Exit** (Reguliersdwarsstraat 42), a bilevel disco with separate barroom, is located in a venerable building that combines old and new: high half-timber beamed medieval-castle ceilings, state-of-the-art sound system and light show. **Gay Life** (Amstelstraat 28–30) is a very popular modern disco with free admission, reasonably priced drinks, some sporadic women-only nights, a separate, plush lounge/bar, and a video room with dim lights and dirty movies, plus a low-priced café/restaurant, Café Mokum, downstairs.

If you go for boisterous summer-camp atmosphere, gay camp style, the most famous of the traditional gay sing-along bars is the **Amstel Taverne** (Amstelstraat 54, corner of Halvemaansteeg), one of Amsterdam's oldest gay bars (est. 1960). **'T Pandje** (Korte Reguliersdwarsstraat 6, just off Rembrandtsplein end of Reguliersdwarsstraat) is a smaller version of this foot-stomping genre of bar, drawing a big local crowd including quite a few transsexuals. Big fun. Right around the corner, the very popular **Chez Manfred** has a typical Dutch house-party atmosphere and an outrageous singing owner.

On Friday nights from 10 P.M. to 2 A.M. and Saturday nights from 8 P.M. to 2 A.M., **COC** runs a disco at Rozenstraat 8. Saturdays are women-only, and very popular. Women come from all over Holland. The COC building has a couple of bars, one of which opens pleasantly onto an enclosed garden during good weather.

There are almost half a dozen male brothels in town. The one we visited is the **Blue Boy Club** (Spuistraat 3-H; tel. 27 43 74; open noon–2 A.M. daily). First-time bordello visitors might be more comfortable using the entrance at N.Z. Voorburgwal 28, which is the Blue Boy's **Why Not Bar**. Beers are reasonable, the friendly, fluently English–speaking bartender can tell you all about the way things work, and there's no obligation to buy a guy—or even patronize the cinema, live striptease shows, or sauna—if you don't want to.

Incidentally, if this sort of thing has ever interested you fellows, we *would* recommend Amsterdam as the safest, cleanest place to try it. But do, do, do use a house like this one, rather than responding to, for example, the rent boys who hang around Central Station and in several of the hustler bars on Paardenstraat —the sleazoid Festival in particular, and the Cupido. In both the straight and gay prostitution scenes here, streetwalkers are largely drug addicts looking to support their habits.

Finally, while it's not in the text, we nevertheless want to call your attention to the monthly **women's "borrels"** organized by Lesbisch Archief (Lesbian Archive) Amsterdam. These get-togethers are a combination presentation and party, organized around a cultural theme. Past themes have included Gay Pride Day San Francisco, Jazz and Blues, cross-dressing rebel writer Gluck, and a lingerie/erotic accessories sort of Schtupperware party. Events are on the first Friday of each month, beginning at 5 P.M., and are scheduled five or six months in advance. A calendar is printed in the archive's *Nieuwsbrief*. For info: Lesbisch Archief Amsterdam, Postbus 10870, 1001 EW Amsterdam; tel. 24 37 47.

WHERE (AND WHAT) TO EAT

The Netherlands are not known for flutesnoot haute cuisine. There are indeed some restaurants in Amsterdam that serve very expensive food. But, from experience, we feel that with few exceptions, they're not worth it, when one can eat very well in this town for very little money—and almost entirely in gay-owned restaurants, or, at the least, places that actively seek gay business.

Service is already included in Dutch menu prices. However, "service" and "tips" are seen as two different things in Holland, and it is important not to use the wrong word. In both restaurants and bars, it is customary to leave extra small change; in fact it's considered rude not to. However, we did more than once hear foreigners ask if "tip" rather than "service" was included, be told no, and leave, in their confusion, a whole extra 12–15% rather than just "rounding up" the bill.

If you do as the Dutch do, and eat only a light *broodje*-type lunch after your enormous breakfast, try Amsterdam's most popular gay coffee bar, **Coffeeshop Downtown**, located in one of the town's trendiest gay streets, at Reguliersdwarsstraat 31. The food is mainly of the classic salad–sandwich–eggs benedict brunch type, and you can eat it outside, at one of the tables surrounding a nude male sculpture, or in the tiny, bilevel, casual, California-look interior, where you can try to ignore the music—usually described as "pleasant jazz," actually petrified AOR. (Remember "Feelings"?) Newer in town is hi-tech **The Eighties** (Brouwersgracht 139), a gay coffeehouse located on a canal in Amsterdam's oldest residential section, the Jordaan. There are outdoor tables, and art exhibits inside as well as magazines, if you like to linger and read with your cappuccino.

For very elegant crepelike variations on *pannekoeken* in a tiny, dramatically romantic setting, go to **Chopin**, at Utrechtsestraat 21. Up the spiral staircase, there are a few tables and a grand piano. They do serve full dinners, but we never managed to tear ourselves away from the beautiful floral ground-floor room . . . and the crepes.

Those who want to try typical Dutch food absolutely could not do better than 't Sluisje (Torensteeg 1, off Spuistraat), a bistro/grill where enormous amounts are served at unbelievably painless prices, in a most festive gay-camp/old-fashioned-pub atmosphere. The total population of Rhode Island could not have finished the daily special: warm cheese bread with herb butter, several types of perfectly grilled meats and sausages with several dipping sauces, *frites and* potato croquettes, a mixed vegetable salad, *and* a fruit salad. Plus, Sluisje is open until 1 A.M., in a very hot gay-bar neighborhood.

It is almost always an expensive disaster when foodies who have eaten their way around most of France try to duplicate the experience in other countries. If you suddenly get a gotta-have-it French food attack in Amsterdam, however, reserve at **Bistro 109** (Spuistraat 109). The fish preparations at this intimate and upscale gay-popular spot are especially good.

For *rijstaffel,* our fave is nongay **Samo Sebo** (P. C. Hooftstraat 27). This eatery is very popular, so reserve, especially if you want to sit in the more atmospheric dining room instead of the bar—and they do a very nice vegetarian rice table without advance notice and without the usual fussing that this variation could only be done for the whole table. Our second fave is old standby **Bali** (Leidsestraat 89, nongay but quite handy to Kerkstraat). Many people like the incendiary *rijstaffel* at gay-popular **Tempo Doeloe,** but unfortunately we did not.

Indonesian may be the best known, but it's not the only ethnic food in Amsterdam. If you've only had Thai food in America, for instance, it's entirely possible you've never tasted it as it should be. You can correct this at **de Kooning van Siam** (Oude Zijds—usually abbreviated "O.Z."—Voorburgwal 42), a knockout, relatively new place. Sophisticated decor and authentic Thai cooking make this restaurant one of Amsterdam's hottest recent culinary success stories. Ask charmingly, and owner Jan, whose Thai boyfriend is the chef, will show you how to do a trick with the napkins which you will duplicate at all your own parties for the next 40 years.

WHERE TO GET THE LATEST DIRT

Our favorite Amsterdam gay bookstore, and recommended first info stop in town for both men and women, is **Boekhandel Vrolijk** (Paleisstraat 135, 1012 ZL Amsterdam, near the Royal Palace; tel. 020/23 51 42; closed Sundays). This shop offers a decent-sized selection of English-language gay books (including a larger lesbian selection than any other bookstore in town), many from British publishers difficult to find in the USA. Vrolijk carries **De Gay Krant** (international mail-order available from P.O. Box 161, 5680 AD BEST; tel. 04998/96 233; fax 04998-72638; modem 04998-71647), the largest gay newspaper in the Netherlands—in all the Low Countries, actually. This biweekly publication is entirely in Dutch, but the gay listings section, for virtually all towns in Holland, Belgium, and Luxembourg that have any gay facilities whatsoever, is the most complete to be found anywhere. And since it's just an address/phone/hours list, it's quite comprehensible to non–Dutch speakers, just so you know enough to recognize the days of the week.

A similar complete listing of gay bars throughout the Netherlands is published in the monthly **GA** *(Gay Agenda)* magazine (P.O. Box 10757, 1001 ET Amsterdam; tel. 27 88 08; international mail-order available). *GA* is also Dutch-language. With the *Gay Amsterdam News* no longer publishing, there are currently no major, locally published, English-language gay info periodicals. However, England's **Gay Times** does, in its rear listings section, have a sizable Amsterdam section that includes very brief capsule descriptions as well as addresses. See "Practical Information, London" for mail-order address.

Another good bookstore carrying *De Gay Krant* and English-language books is **Intermale** (Spuistraat 251; tel. 020/25 00 09; closed Sundays)—more male-oriented than Vrolijk, but quite respectable despite its sex-shop-ish name. For men, info on the commercial gay scene is also available at **Man-to-Man Book/ Video Shop** (Spuistraat 21, or for mail order Box 10419, 1012 SR Amsterdam; tel. 25 87 97), which publishes its own guide. This complex near the Central Station, which is really more sex- than literature-oriented, also shows gay male films in a twin theater, and sells male porn magazines and videos.

Lesbians will find one of Europe's largest selections of women's books (many in English) at **Xantippe** (Prinsengracht 290, on a canal close to the Homomonument and the Anne Frank house; tel. 23 58 54). This is also a terrific source of all sorts of local information—a bulletin board and stacks of leaflets for the terminally shy, as well as spoken help from friendly staff members who welcome questions.

A **free "Holiday Help" packet for lesbians** is available from P.O. Box 22643, NL 1100 DC Amsterdam. Enclose two International Reply Coupons for postage.

Also for women, the summer edition of the Dutch-language magazine *Ma'dam* (c/o COC, Rozenstraat 14; tel. 020/268300—co-coordinator Petra Van Dijk) carries holiday addresses throughout Europe, and contacts to travel agencies that run lesbian tours.

For an annual book carrying specific bar/baths/brothel/bookshop/sex shop/ hotel/restaurant information that is far more detailed and accurate than all the far better known English-language European guidebooks, send for (or buy at Vrolijk or Intermale) Peter Glencross's **Top Guide to Amsterdam.** The direct address is Excellent Publications, P.O. Box 22643, NL-1100 DC Amsterdam, The Netherlands (tel. 011/3120/90 56 91). From the U.S.A., however, it's easier and cheaper to order through *Our World*'s book service: Traveler International, 1104 N. Nova Rd, Suite 251, Daytona Beach, FL 32117 (tel. 904/441-5367). The guide includes info for lesbians as well as gay men; but separatist women who are interested only in women's stuff can order, direct from the publisher, a special Amsterdam lesbian info portfolio.

The **Gay and Lesbian Switchboard** is a live 24-hour info source; tel. 23 65 65. For 24-hour pretaped information on important gay dates, call the **Amsterdam Gay Info Line,** 75 30 26.

COC is at Rozenstraat 14; their coffee shop and information phone number is 23 40 79; the office number is 26 30 87. The organization's national office is next door at Rozenstraat 8 (tel. 23 45 96 or 23 11 92).

For medical info: **Body Positive Hotline** (tel. 24 50 05, Wednesday and Saturday, 8 P.M.–11 P.M.), **AIDS Hotline** (tel. 321 2120, Monday through Friday 2 P.M.–10 P.M.), and the Women's Health Center **Vrouwengezondheidscentrum,** Obliplein 4 (tel. 93 43 58).

The regular old **VVV Amsterdam Tourist Information Center** (info offices open Monday through Saturday at Stationsplein 10, right outside the Central Rail Station, and at Leidsestraat 106; tel. 26 64 44, Sundays 22 10 16) publishes *Amsterdam A–Z,* a free multilanguage newsprint publication actually intended for young travelers, but containing in its listings lots of gay addresses: help/info lines, bars, dancing spots, galleries, etc., as well as women's and other interesting alternative-culture establishments (like squatters' bars). Info on theater, films and other cultural events can also be obtained from the VVV. Ask for the free monthly *Uitkrant* (it comes in either English/German or Dutch/French), and *This Week in Amsterdam,* about Hfl 1.50.

Most gay-oriented hotels can provide you with a gay map of Amsterdam, too. The ITC's is especially good.

WHAT TO READ

The Embarrassment of Riches: An Interpretation of Dutch Culture in the Golden Age, by Simon Schama (University of California). Only in small part about gay people per se, but the best book in print in English about what makes the Netherlands the way it is.

The Homomonument, by Pieter Koenders (Intermale). A history in both Dutch and English of the famous landmark, available through the Intermale bookstore in Amsterdam.

Gay Life in Dutch Society, ed. A. X. van Noerssen (Harrington Park Press). An English translation of essays by Dutch gay men and lesbians about their culture, from the origins of the gay movement to the present.

COPENHAGEN

Where Fairy Tales Come True

oward the end of one of our first trips together to Copenhagen, we were strolling hand in hand one night in Tivoli Gardens. As usual, jolliness abounded. In the old-fashioned gazebo across the way, a full-dress orchestra swung into a Strauss waltz, followed by a Benny Goodman number. Healthy, smiling old ladies with white braids wrapped around their heads tapped their feet in time to the music, while adorable blond children drank mugs of hot chocolate and waited for the end-of-the-evening fireworks display. Bowers of colored lights twinkled over the artificial lake, where a family of tame ducklings slept like contended housecats in a clump on the shore. We turned down a lane along the lake and ran right into a flasher.

Normally this sort of encounter flips us into Killer Dyke Karate Mode. But we'd been in Denmark too long.

On a previous trip, we'd lost a wallet, which among other things held our Tivoli season passes with the address of our Copenhagen hotel written on them. We were on a ferry boat. Before we even got back to our room, someone had phoned to report that the wallet had been found and turned in to the boat company—with all the money. On the way to pick up the wallet, Pam stopped to window-shop on the Strøget—Copenhagen's long, snaking, goodie-filled pedestrian street. A guy who was looking in the same window started up a genuinely friendly, amusing conversation in four different languages. When it finally dawned on Pam that he was trying to pick her up, she told him she was going out that night with her girlfriend. He politely doffed his cap, wished her a very good afternoon, and went cheerfully on his way. Other encounters with straight men had been equally painless.

A few days earlier, Lindsy had suffered a corneal abrasion and gone to a public hospital for treatment. There was no waiting, no blood on the floor, no surly emergency-room receptionist practicing triage; the doctor was wonderful, and the treatment was absolutely free. And a few nights before *that*, Lindsy's seven-year-old daughter had disappeared in Tivoli. We freaked out with visions of her face on Danish milk cartons, and couldn't understand why the park guards were being so blasé instead of calling Interpol; meanwhile, the kid had been rescued by the first Dane who spotted her and treated to an ice-cream cone on the way to the Lost Children's Station. . . . Then there's the time the cabdriver gave back a proffered tip, explaining that in Denmark this sort of thing really isn't necessary, and . . .

We could natter on for several more paragraphs about how well Denmark works. We've now been there, separately or together, six times, and we keep waiting for some dreadful under-the-scab inequity to surface. So far, we've been disappointed.

Which is why, when we encountered the leering, lurking Tivoli flasher, we viewed him not as Macho Standard-Bearer of a Sick Society's Core Misogynist Aggression, but simply as an isolated schmuck. Instead of kneeing him in the groin, we gave him an earnest lecture about his inappropriate behavior.

On the first Sunday in October 1989, the world's paparazzi descended in swarms on Copenhagen's copper-spired Town Hall to memorialize the first "gay weddings" in Europe. At the time, a poll of the Danish population showed that 57 percent supported the new domestic-partnership law and only 17 percent disapproved. In a survey of Americans around the same time, only 23 percent favored *any* legal recognition of gay couples, and 69 percent were opposed.

Most Danes we met seemed a bit surprised at all the fuss. Gay partnership rights was an idea whose time had come, and the Danish Parliament had simply responded. What else would a sane, decent society do? Denmark is a little like an older sibling, proud but also slightly bored with the endless chore of serving as role model. The parliamentary notes accompanying the law even *say* that it's intended as an "example" that other countries will inevitably follow.

When we asked the woman in the Copenhagen tourist office if gay visitors needed to anticipate any problems, she could barely contain her mirth. "This is *Denmark*," she explained to us emissaries from the land of the barbarians. Case closed. We were reminded of the media expression "postfeminist"; Denmark may be the first truly "postgay" country.

Other places have more dramatic architecture or more famous art, but no northern country is more relaxed than Denmark, and few cities anywhere have the happy-go-lucky charm of Copenhagen. What other capital has an amusement park and a permanent circus right in the center of town? And Scandinavia is one of the few places we know where everyone really does speak some English, since it's the agreed-upon language for communicating among Danes, Norwegians, and Swedes. (Many of them speak it so well that they have a distinct British or American accent, depending upon which course of study they elected at school.) Things are so effortless that after about five minutes in Copenhagen, we slip into a trance and become good for nothing but shopping for housewares. About your worst hassle will be deciding whether you prefer Carlsberg or Tuborg.

Gay life in Copenhagen is equally laid-back. Unlike Amsterdam, Berlin, or other cities with progay political underpinnings, Copenhagen has a relatively modest assortment of exclusively gay bars and clubs, and only a couple of gay hotels (these nonexclusively so). One reason seems to be that most gay men and lesbians—including those who aren't out at work—are extremely assimilated into straight social life. After giving us a printed list of the town's gay hotspots and cruising areas, the desk clerk at our gay-oriented hotel added, "But of course you are now in the most liberal country in the world. In Copenhagen, gay people can also meet in straight bars."

By the same token, we heard minor grumbling among some of Our Crowd about the huge numbers of straights hogging space at Pan, the gay café and disco run by the country's largest gay civil-rights organization. "For some reason, it has recently become very trendy to come here," one patron shrugs. What can you do? The place is as close to a glitzy fashion find as you'll ever get in a country where the entire population appears to live in jeans, anoraks, and sensible shoes, but Pan is also friendly: multi-level, for maximum freedom of choice (dancing, talking, and bar games all comfortably coexisting in separate areas), and with a casual modern/minimal fern-bar sort of decor that projects the message "Everybody welcome here."

Most of Copenhagen's gay bars have this relaxed noncategorical, or multicategorical, look and feel. Hardly any bars are even just exclusively bars—they tend to be café/disco/cabaret/bars, with maybe a lecture event every week or two, and some light snacks. There *is* an all-woman's space, but it's still multicultural, multipurpose, and multisexually-oriented—and, fittingly, partially government-subsidized. The Pan complex has a weekly all-lesbian disco, too, but if the bartender on duty that night happens to be a guy, nobody (except us foreigners) even seems to notice, much less to care.

Denmark's number one home-grown pop singer, Anne Linnet, has recorded hit love songs addressed to the woman in her life (although we're told that she studiously avoids using the L word in describing herself). The more virulent forms of homophobia also appear to be rare. "In Germany, I met lesbian women whose children have no grandparents or aunts and uncles," a lesbian philosophy student told us with a shudder. "Here, your family might not *brag* about you being gay, but they're still your family." A position paper put out by the main gay organization states that to the extent that harassment does exist, it isn't reported by gays at a greater rate than by any other Danish minority. Nor is there a lower rate of successful prosecutions.

To foreigners, one of the most bizarre manifestations of assimilation is that nowhere else in Western civilization is it harder to figure out who's queer. Yes, yes, we know: *Lots* of us are, to use the crass shorthand of the personals ads, "straight appearing." But everyplace else we've ever been in Europe, the United States, or Canada, there are also certain tribal looks that you see over and over again: clone, lezbo-punk, pretty boy, tofu dyke, leatherman, lipstick lesbian, screaming queen, etc.—plus a whole huge array of more subtle styles and details. In Copenhagen, the visual clues are so few and far between that you'll think your gay-dar is busted.

One thing you can be sure of is that you won't run out of things to do, even if you never get near a gay bar. Go to the world-famous ballet, or get a tattoo in Nyhavn, the old, now gentrified sailors' quarter. Check out the brewery tours, the open-air museums in Lyngby and Odense (actual thatched-roof cottages from ancient times), the impossibly adorable fishing villages of Dragør and Køge (actual ancient cottages currently lived in by real Danes), the king's deer park at Charlottenlund, and the shopping—especially Illum's Bolighus, the Tiffany of Tupperware. Normally we're the kind of people who tote home souvenir mustard pots in the shape of toilets with bawdy Italian verse inscribed on the bowl, but Copenhagen will bring out the tasteful in anyone. This is the place to buy teakwood pepper mills, silver salad bowls, nutcrackers, mobiles, candlesticks, corkscrews and a zillion other things you didn't realize until this moment that you can't possibly live without.

Luckily, you don't have to spend a lot of money on food in Copenhagen.

In fact, if the weather's nice, you barely need to go indoors to eat. The famous Danish *smørrebrød* (buttered bread) open-faced sandwiches are available to go all over downtown, looking like sandwich landscape paintings and tasting like nothing of the same name you've ever had in the United States: rare roast beef with béarnaise sauce and *stegte løj* (crisp-fried onions); *leverpostej* (liver pâté) with sautéed mushrooms, lettuce, crumbled bacon, and a square of jellied consommé; Danish blue cheese *(blåost)* with sweet onion and hard-boiled egg slices; steak tartare with cucumber salad and horseradish sauce; a mound of fingernail-sized pink shrimp with mayonnaise and white asparagus. You can also follow your nose to unbelievably light and buttery Danish pastries, known here as *wienerbrød* (Vienna bread), and not to be confused with those sodden cellophane-wrapped globs of dough sold as "Danishes" in American coffee shops; and to some of the world's other great carbo junk food, from pancakes to soft ice cones.

Nonkosher carnivores should by all means try a *ribbensandwich* (crunchy loin of pork on a soft bun, with fresh marinated sweet cucumbers —the best ones are in Tivoli, near the Tietgensgade entrance) and the many sausages *(pølse)* and franks sold on the street from wagons. The fat, grayish-brown *medister pølse* looks dubious, but it's one of the tastiest. There's an entire sausage etiquette in Denmark. Some are served on a roll, some with bread on the side, and they're available with various combinations of fried or raw onions, pickled cucumber slices, sweet and hot mustard, *rémoulade* sauce, and other condiments. There's even a vegetarian version called a *"Kradser":* a hot dog with everything, hold the hot dog. (The homegrown ketchup and mustard, by the way, are the best in the world, and we regularly schlep home a few bottles. The secret ingredient seems to be apples!) According to a brochure we picked up at the Youth Office, several of the leading sausage types have nicknames "connected with the male's reproductive organ," but we leave that up to you owners of actual male reproductive organs to research.

In our opinion, "gourmet" restaurants are generally not worth the money in Denmark. But you will want to try at least one sit-down meal— a smörgåsbord (cold and hot buffet), which, again, bears no resemblance to American impostors, except for being all-you-can-eat. And even here there's a big difference. In Denmark, one does not make a Big Rock Candy Mountain of mixed'n'mushed all-you-can-eat, on the same plate. One hits the herring first, then other cold fish dishes, then cold meats and salads, then hot dishes, then desserts, using a new plate—the waiter clears away the old one—for each trip to the table. Fortunately, this kind of meal doesn't have to be a break-the-bank experience, either: There's an inexpensive, elegant, old-fashioned one-hundred-plus-dish smörgåsbord restaurant in the main train station, right next to Tivoli.

North Americans who are used to the scale of Walt Disney World are usually amazed at how tiny Tivoli Gardens is—one city block, albeit one so brilliantly laid out by its designers in 1843 that it feels much bigger. If you're expecting an "amusement park" in the roller-coaster sense, you'll also be in for a surprise. Tivoli does have a thrill ride or two (and more, alas, than it used to), but it also has old-world gingerbread pergolas, big-name jazz concerts, mimes, acrobats, fountains, flowers, boy soldiers on white ponies, balloons, a giant Chinese pagoda, a Moorish castle completely festooned with Christmas-tree-bulb-styled colored lights, slot machines, a bank, a small branch of Illum's Bolighus, some of the fanciest restaurants in Copenhagen, absolutely orgasmic fireworks three times a week, and more fairy-tale charm than you've seen since the last time you rented *The Wizard of Oz*. Don't miss it.

If we had to pick one thing that we *didn't* like about Copenhagen, it would be that everybody everywhere smokes. Actually, no one on the entire continent of Europe seems to have heard yet that Cigarettes Are Hazardous to Your Health, but this lapse seems especially incongruous in a country that exudes wholesomeness. One night at the Kvindehuset (Women's House), we talked for hours with a lesbian with whom we seemed to be in synch on every other subject under the midnight sun. Finally, timidly, not wanting to trash her as a pathetic addicted pawn of the tobacco industry, we asked her why she still smoked. Equally timidly, she replied that she was surprised that we *didn't*—since we seemed so progressive.

Huh?

"Oh, you know," she explained. "Americans are so puritanical, so *anti* everything. Antidrinking, antidrugs, antismoking, antigay, antiabortion . . ."

The comparison between Denmark and the Netherlands is inevitable, and every time we're in either country, we end up having the same argument about which of the two we'll try to defect to someday when we can't stand living in President Quayle's America. The main difference is that Holland is a tolerant nation, whereas Denmark is liberal.

A joke we heard repeatedly in the Netherlands was that if you get one Dutchman in a room, you've got a political opinion; with two Dutchmen in a room, you've got a political argument. Dutch society seems composed of wildly disparate religious and ethnic elements, many of them downright reactionary—the Netherlands are, remember, the country with one of the lowest rates of women in the labor force in the industrialized world. But the Dutch have agreed on one thing: their absolute right to disagree, loudly, at all times, and to respect each other's craziest opinions.

In homogeneous Denmark, people appear genuinely to agree, or at least to put a high value on consensus and keeping the peace. Over and over again we heard that when it comes to *pushing* for gay rights, "Danes aren't like that." Easygoing wins every time; the other side of the equation is that one can usually expect to get easygoing treatment from straights. "It's due to nature," one gay man sighed. "Just look at this country. *Tiny* hills. Everything soft and sweet shapes. The only rough side is what's *around* it: the sea. Nothing bad happens here."

Overt vicious homophobia in Denmark now has about the same legal status as yelling "Fire!" in a crowded theater does in the United States. There was recently a move afoot to prosecute two people under the terms of the national civil-rights law, which forbids "threatening, humiliating, or degrading" someone in public on the basis of their race, religion, ethnic background or, since 1987, their sexual orientation. One of the targets of the prosecution was a Christian woman in western Denmark who had written a series of homophobic letters to a newspaper trashing the domestic-partnership law as "ungodly" and homosexuality itself as "the ugliest kind of adultery," and opining that since AIDS robs people of their lives, gay men can be considered "thieves." Also targeted was the editor who published her letters.

Curiously, from an American perspective, the law in question doesn't explicitly protect gay men and lesbians from, say, being quietly and unpublicly fired, although people assured us that hardly anyone ever *is* fired for being gay per se. "You'd only be fired," explained one Danish lesbian, "if your gayness made it difficult for your colleagues to work with you."

One of us (by sheer coincidence the member of the couple who happens to be of Dutch ancestry) feels far more comfortable among the homophobes of Holland, where the basic deal is that people *can* be different and difficult. The other of us finds the bedrock feminism and the light-heartedness of the Danes utterly seductive. Denmark may be the only country in the world where we feel most people are pretty much on our wavelength, and so we don't have to do a lot of tedious bitching.

In real life, we'll defect to whichever country asks us first. Let's start the bidding.

The most important gay political organization in Denmark is the Landsforeningen For Bøsser Og Lesbiske/Forbundet Af 1948. That translates as National Organization for Gay Men and Lesbians/Union of 1948. It was founded, obviously, in 1948, when there was enormous sympathy in Denmark for any group that had been persecuted by the Nazis. In 1988, the organization received from the Danish government the equivalent of $360,000 for AIDS work and $250,000 for other programs; this in a country with about 2 percent of the population of the United States. (Just try to imagine Congress giving the National Gay and Lesbian Task Force $30 million or so.)

In Copenhagen alone, the gay union's activities include the Pan café/disco, a radio station, switchboard, magazine, library, bookstore, athletic association, extensive AIDS and HIV+ help, and numerous other services, all run out of a complex of several buildings and a table-filled courtyard in the heart of the old town. But the organization is probably best known for its lobbying efforts on behalf of gay men and lesbians—bearing in mind that "lobbying" in a country as small and as liberal as Denmark usually means engaging in reasoned dialogue with some concerned official with a listed phone number whose kid brother you may have gone to high school with.

In addition to persuading Parliament to pass gay civil-rights legislation, the group has worked closely with the authorities to develop sensible, effective AIDS policies. Virtually every country in northern Europe had aggressive government-sponsored safer-sex information campaigns at a time when the U.S. Congress was still arguing about spending taxpayers' money on such nasty, immoral stuff. But only Denmark's safer-sex info rose to the level of art. Our personal favorite: a poster showing a macho muscleman whose entire face has just been slathered with a whipped-cream cake. The hunk is grinning deliriously as great gushy gobs of whipped cream drip from his eyebrows, his hair, his chin. The tag line reads: "On him, not in him."

"In Denmark," explains Dorthe Jacobsen, a legal counselor on the staff of the Gay Union, "the best way to reach people has always been with humor."

Although Holland has long offered many protections for gay and lesbian couples, Denmark was the first country to put gay and lesbian relationships on a near-equal legal footing with heterosexual marriage. Thousands of couples have already registered their partnerships, four hundred in the law's first month alone.

To our distress, the registration law stipulates that at least one of the partners has to be a Dane. Years ago, after we realized that the extra taxes and health-insurance costs of being "single" were taking thousands of dollars a year out of our joint bank account, and after one of us couldn't visit the other in the hospital because she wasn't a "family" member, we made a decision that the next legal wedding ceremony we attend will be our own. No political stand we've ever taken has caused so much bad feeling. Several straight friends and relatives have reacted with deep hurt that we don't want to be there on the day they stand up in front of the whole world and make a "special commitment." We respond that as long as our relationship gets classed as a lesser commitment, asking us to witness theirs is like inviting Jewish or black friends to pick up a doggie bag at the back door of a restricted club while the bride and groom enjoy the wedding feast inside. If Denmark ever amends its law to cover foreigners, we'll be there in a flash with the brown rice, the twin tuxedoes, and the cake with two brides on the top.

The Danish legislation gives gay couples the same insurance, pension, inheritance, and other legal and economic rights that other married couples have, with two exceptions: They can't marry in church, and they can't adopt children. We didn't meet a soul who gave two kroner about the first limitation, but the second one has seriously pissed off Danish lesbians, who, in the months after the law went into effect, seemed to be staying away from Town Hall in droves.

"This is a nice, straight, middle-class law that addresses the concerns of middle-aged gay men with enough money and property to make a difference," acknowledges Dorthe Jacobsen, who is both a long-time feminist and the Gay Union staffer who has worked most intimately on the partnership legislation. Although lesbians are more likely than gay men to see parental rights as crucial, she notes, they're also more likely to have a healthy distrust of marriage, an institution that was used for centuries to make women into men's property. In the days when feminism and gay liberation were heady new topics, the prevailing politically correct radical line was that the state should treat everyone as an equally worthy individual: *No one* should get married, or at least no one should be allowed to benefit from marriage.

This isn't a totally crazy idea in Denmark. Although the 1989 law does give gay couples certain financial benefits, Dorthe estimates that most of its value, given the compromise on adoption, is symbolic. Vast numbers of straight Danes don't bother to get married, even when they have children, since many services, like health care, are provided regardless of nuclear-family status.

The problem with pushing the no-marriage-rights platform is that the straight unmarrieds aren't organized. In the seventies, when both radical lesbian-feminists and anarchist gay men splintered off from the Gay Union into their own movements, they had no heterosexual consituency. The radical platform collapsed. Meanwhile, the Gay Union was left in the hands of precisely those who were (a) male, and (b) more interested in shielding their lovers' pensions than in a life of sex, drugs, and rock and roll, compliments of the welfare state. Although the current law reflects age-old stereotypes about gay people and kids, it's also a legitimate reflection of the priorities of the people who worked hard for it for years. Axel Axgil, the seventy-somethingish founder of the Gay Union, and his lover were among the first group of men to tie the knot.

The rationale for the no-adoption clause, officially, is that some countries, especially Catholic countries, might cut off the flow of adoptable children to Denmark if they couldn't be sure the kids wouldn't land in homo homes, and that this would unduly penalize the kids and the straight parents. But, Dorthe points out, there's no loophole to allow a Danish lesbian to adopt her partner's biological child if the child's father isn't part of the equation. "There are lots of children of lesbians already around; why not let them have two legal parents?" she asks, and then answers herself:

"They're afraid our way of life will rub off on the children when the children have free choice and see how their parents can live and survive with self-respect. They're scared shitless!" (Dorthe lived for a year in San Francisco, and her English is very, very good.)

When, we wonder, will things change? We expect the reply to be phrased in terms of decades, possibly generations. Dorthe looks suitably grim. "We have to build up our credibility again, and let people see how the law is being used," she says. "I don't think we can start for four or five years."

We decided to seek out the radicals in this most liberal of all countries. We met Gitte Pedersen at a dance at the Women's House. She is thirty-one, small and round-faced, with granny glasses and stick-straight shoulder-length blond hair. Her baby daughter Signe has short hair and no glasses, but otherwise she looks a lot like her mother. Gitte has recently organized a group of lesbians who want to change the laws about artificial insemination "so that others don't have to go through what I did."

At present, sperm banks are operated under the same restrictions as adoptions, and are only open to screened, heterosexual women who have been married for several years. There's a brisk business in black-market sperm, and unfortunately, one of the consequences of AIDS is that the lesbian demand for HIV-negative semen outstrips the supply.

Gitte spent two years trying to connect with the available sperm at the right time of the month, as well as talking men into donations to her turkey baster. ("Suddenly they had all these *feelings*," she snorts.) Then she happened to go out for a drink with a coworker, a straight man whom she was in fact planning to hit on. He startled her by volunteering that if she ever wanted to have a child, he'd be honored to be the donor. He's seen Signe twice, but there are no legal problems should he decide to play a larger role than the one he and Gitte agreed on. Under Danish law, no woman, gay or straight, is required to share custody with a man she hasn't lived with.

Danish women also get free abortions, and the kind of maternity and child-care benefits that make it relatively easy for mothers to be single. There are even childcare facilities in some supermarkets and movie theaters. Women still don't make as much as men, but in the Reagan years, when American feminists were wearing little buttons protesting that we made 59 cents for every dollar a man made, the equivalent figure in Denmark was already 86 cents. There are plenty of women in Parliament, and women's studies are part of the high-school curriculum. About the worst discovery we've personally made about the status of Danish women is that there aren't any little girls in the nerdy toy soldier–suited Tivoli Guard Drum Corps. "What we say about organized feminism," one lesbian told us, "is that it was so successful here that it died."

Copenhagen: Where Fairy Tales Come True / 119

Thousands of gay male activists belong to the Gay Union, about twenty others belong to the Bøssehuset. *"Bøsse"* (pronounced "bursa") means "gay men," although it also means "guns"; *"huset"* is "a house." The Bøssehuset is part of the "Free City of Christiania," a mostly-straight hippie commune on Christianshavn Island just a few minutes' walk from Copenhagen's famous shopping street, the Strøget. "There is no antigay harassment here," say the Bøsse. "It's a *society* of outcasts."

Formerly an army base, the area was taken over by squatters in 1971. The government decided that since the city wasn't using the land anyway, and since the young squatters needed housing, there was no good reason not to let them stay. While the place has been intermittently controversial for decades, some eight hundred men, women, and children now live in the town-within-a-town year-round. Several hundred more camp there in the summer. It's as if Woodstock had never left Max Yasgur's farm.

Christiania is a major blast from the past. For starters, it's the drug capital of the city. Grass, hash, and what the authorities usually call "paraphernalia" are sold openly from booths near the entrance, although there's been a crackdown on harder stuff. Cabs pull up all night outside the main gate of the complex and wait while their fares race in, cop some loose joints, and then head off to party elsewhere.

What irritates the public about the commune isn't so much the drugs per se but the fact that the residents of Christiania don't pay taxes on their property. This is serious business in a country where even the queen coughs up. Nobody minded much when the perception was that the residents were poor dropouts, but lately there have been mutterings about rich drug dealers building million-krone waterfront houses on what's really public land. Now there is talk of turning Christiania into a public entertainment area of some kind.

Inside Christiania, weeds grow up through the cobblestones and huge dogs roam at will. The communal bathhouse has no windows, and you can peer in and gape at naked showerers in the gender of your choice. There's a lot of the official 1968 Haight-Ashbury Day-Glo silver-and-black color scheme, many candles melted creatively in empty wine bottles, and building-sized murals of blissed-out people with rainbows and sunbeams emanating from their heads. There's even a banner across one street that reads, in English, DON'T WORRY, BE HIPPIE. Most of the red-brick warehouse that serves as the Bøssehuset is devoted to a stage containing a beat-up piano and several vintage Peavey amps, and an approximately fifty-seat auditorium. The radical gay men are very into theater as their preferred form of political action. Their current project is dancing lessons for gay couples in tango, jitterbug, and cha cha.

"We're all so bored with marching," one of them tells us. "We've been doing it for forty years. There has to be a different way now." The last time he and his confrères were in a demonstration, when the minister of war was once again threatening to kick the Christianians off the military base, "we turned it into a sort of picnic. We brought sandwiches and champagne. When people came by we toasted them and told them they were free to read our literature. If they wished."

The Bøssehuset was originally founded in 1971, according to one old-timer, by men who "were very deeply inspired by the Christopher Street liberation movement." In its prime it had five hundred members, but now only a dozen or so show up at the group's regular weekly meeting. The ones we met, all of whom looked like every straight Deadhead you've ever seen, tended to have a low opinion of the politics of the Gay Union. "They want to be the Ministry of Gays," scoffed one. Yet even the rads were proud of Denmark for passing the domestic-partnership legislation. "After 1992, when the borders are open and all Europe is one big happy place," one man enthused, "let us say I go to Spain with my husband: Spain has to recognize that marriage. This leads to legal questions concerning Spanish gays.

"We can make a lot of trouble, and it's going to be fun!"

The really far-out radical queers in Denmark aren't the baster brigades or the pothead hippie squatters. The true fringe group is the Metropolitan Community Church.

We were able to meet the entire national membership—the pastor, Mia Andersen, her French-born lover Laurence Vergez, and four other people, including the heterosexual mother of one of the parishioners—at Sunday services one night in the basement of the local Unitarian Church.

It isn't just *gay* Christians who are a minority. Despite the presence of an official Lutheran state church, poll after poll shows that in terms of actual belief, Denmark is one of the most secularized countries in the world. "I find it easier to come out at work as a lesbian than as a Christian," ruefully notes one of the congregation, an electrical technician.

"In Denmark," adds the pastor, "talking about faith is considered a bit obscene." Her own parents are typical, upstanding Danish atheists.

"The church has no real power," according to Laurence. "If it did, we probably wouldn't have the domestic-partnership law." The church is Danish only, with no official ties to other bodies and no missionary purpose. Bishops are forbidden by law to take political stands. Even those Danes who do practice tend to check in only for what Laurence calls "hatch, match, and dispatch"—i.e., baptism, wedding, and funeral. "The church isn't a *force* here like in other countries," she adds. "It's just sort of there, as a service. Like the trains."

Mia and Laurence think they might get married soon, if only to save

Laurence the trouble of dropping by the immigration folks to renew her papers at regular intervals. Are they planning, we wonder, to have a big celebration? The fiancées look at each other blankly. Clearly they do not view their wedding as the Most Important Day in a Woman's Life.

"Oh, maybe not," Mia finally says. It seems that it's a tradition in Denmark for friends to play tricks on each other before their weddings. When a straight friend got married, they took her on an "enforced swimming lesson," and she has vowed revenge. Mia and Laurence start to giggle at the memory. Better perhaps, they think aloud, to elope some lunch hour and avoid a dive in the Baltic.

We can't leave Denmark without mentioning the country's favorite son, Hans Christian Andersen. There's a statue of him in front of Town Hall, with well-worn copper knees that generations of Danish children haven't been able to resist hoisting themselves up on. He lived most of his adult life in Nyhavn. We've heard repeated rumors that Andersen was That Way, but we haven't been able to pin down the specifics. We decide to ask Dorthe Jacobsen. She says that she can't name names either.

"But in my heart, I think he is," she adds. "I often reread "The Ugly Duckling": the story of growing up, and feeling so different, and then all of a sudden, finding yourself among your own kind—and realizing that you're beautiful.

"What could be more gay?"

COPENHAGEN

PRACTICAL INFORMATION

COPENHAGEN—NUMBER KEY

Lesbian and Gay Center

1. Pan (Knabrostræde 3)

Bars

2. Cosy Bar (Studiestræde 24)
3. Madame Arthur (Lavendelstræde 17)
4. Pink Club (Farvergade 10)
5. Jeppes Club 48 (mainly lesbians, Fridays; Allégade 25)
6. Café Babooshka (Turesensgade 6)

Women's House

7. Kvindehuset (women only; Gothersgade 37)

Men's Cruising

8. Ørstedsparken (near corner of Vester Voldgade and Nørre Voldgade: evenings and nights; caution. Popular toilets are also at City Hall Square; Israels Plads, at the intersection of Vendersgade and Linnésgade; and the subway at Nørre Voldgade and Frederiksborggade.)

Restaurants

9. DSB Bistro (Central Station)
10. Greens (Grønnegade 12–14, at Pistolstræde)
11. La Rose de Tunis (Vesterbrogade 120)

Hotels

12. Hotel Windsor (Frederiksborggade 30)
13. Hotel Jørgensen (Rømersgade 11)

Etc.

14. Bøssehuset (no exact address; ask in Christiania)

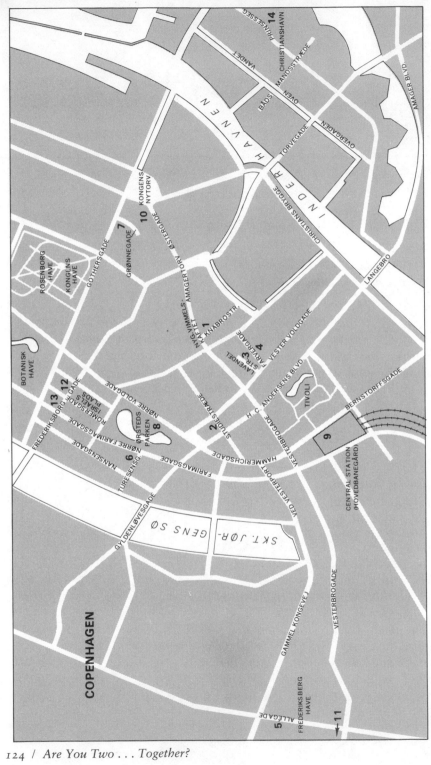

GENERAL HINTS / INFO

There aren't an overwhelming number of gay establishments in Copenhagen. But what there is, is nice. In fact, the Pan Café/Disco might be the most elegant gay space in Europe.

Everything in central Copenhagen—meaning most of the gay stuff—is walkable. If you'd rather not schlep, S-trains, which are suburban commuter trains, are fast, safe, and free with Eurailpass; they stop at several inner-city stations. Buses go everywhere (see "Information Resources" section for obtaining bus map), and drivers who see would-be passengers running actually stop and wait for them, instead of slamming the door on said passengers' fingers the way they do in New York.

Orientation: Denmark is a peninsula-and-islands country jutting into the North and Baltic seas at the northern tip of continental Europe, with Germany to the south and Sweden to the east. Copenhagen is located on the east coast of the easternmost island, Zealand (Sjælland) right across the narrow Øresund from Malmö, Sweden. For rail-riders, the ferries linking Germany with Denmark are free to Eurailpass holders; in fact, the train drives right onto the rail-equipped boats. Copenhagen's Central Station is right in the heart of downtown, virtually next door to Rådhuspladsen (the square in front of City Hall, from which the world-famous shopping street Strøget begins) and Tivoli, the universe's most magical amusement park. For fliers, Copenhagen's airport is Kastrup, about a 20- to 30-minute drive from the city center. Public airport buses, costing under $2, run from Rådhuspladsen, and faster, double-price SAS buses run from the Central Station, roughly every 15 minutes.

Although Copenhagen is a relaxing place for gay people year-round, we strongly recommend you schedule your visit sometime between the beginning of May and mid-September, when Tivoli is open. It's kind of touching and inspiring to go early in the day, when the park unofficially belongs to Copenhagen's senior citizens. They look great; what a place to grow old in! However, Tivoli is most enchanted at night, especially if you steer clear of the overrated roller coaster and other annoyingly noisy second-string "thrill" rides. Instead, stroll around the lake looking at the border lights in colors you've never seen before, the illuminated Chinese tower, and pseudo–Taj Mahal, and all the rest of the fantastical architecture.

If you get stuck short of cash after the banks close (normally 4 P.M., occasionally 6 P.M.), **late-hours currency exchange** is possible until 10 P.M. at the Central Station, and until 11 P.M. at Tivoli's exchange office next door to the station.

Telephone code: 01 (city), 02 (suburbs)
Currency unit: the Danish krone (Dkr)

WHERE TO STAY

There are only a couple of gay-oriented (though mixed) hotels in Copenhagen. Fortunately, they're not listed on the hotels board at the central station used by every arriving tourist, so it is sometimes possible to arrive without reservations even in August, as we did, and get a room. We'd definitely advise reserving, though, if your schedule allows.

If you find these hotels completely booked, the tourist office assured us that gay people would encounter no homophobia at any hotel in town. For the most part, this is probably true. We certainly had no trouble at the Dan Hotel (near Kastrup airport), the in-town Saga, or any other straight hotels we've stayed in, and we are hardly discreet. Nevertheless, the very nice Hotel d'Angleterre specifically requested *not* to be listed. And for what it's worth, we also had a lower rate of return to our Copenhagen hotel mail inquiries than for any other destination in this book, including Clause 28–saddled London.

We'd additionally advise room-hunters not to stay in the area right around the Central Station. A number of Copenhagen's most reasonably priced hotels are located here, and even the most middle-class straight guidebooks say that despite the fact that it's sex central in terms of porn stores, the neighborhood is quite safe. Probably it is. We didn't get hassled when we stayed here once. But it's scuzzy. We like atmospheric, picturesque vacation lodgings that are fun to come home to—and this place wasn't, with female hookers and male hustlers all over the streets and hotel steps, even though they didn't bother us.

As far as decor goes, the Scandinavian hotel-room norm is clean-enough-to-eat-off, but quite simple, functional, and often small. Don't expect fabulous froufrou in this town.

There are no real hotel bargains in Copenhagen. The good news is that at least you don't have to pay the "gay tax" here: The gay-oriented hotels below are among the most reasonable in town. All prices are for double rooms, and include breakfast.

Prices: *Inexpensive* = under 325 Dkr; *inex./moderate* = 325–475 Dkr; *moderate* = 475–650 Dkr; *mod./exp.* = 650–850 Dkr; *expensive* = over 850 Dkr.

Hotel Windsor, Frederiksborggade 30, 1360 København K; tel. 33/11 08 30. Probably the gayest hotel in town (the second floor is all men), this 25-room hotel fronting on Israels Plads square has both small budget rooms, which are spare but perfectly cheerful, and larger ones with amenities like refrigerators and color TVs. The front-desk personnel are delightful; the atmosphere in the breakfast room is dishy and encouraging of cross-table conversations with strangers; and the location is not daunting for walking home from Tivoli or the gay bars. If you're feeling lazy, the Nørreport S-train station is a block away. Don't let the fact that the hotel starts on the second floor mislead you into thinking it's not nice inside; this over-store lobby stuff is common in smaller European hotels. Breakfast is Continental. *Inex./mod.–moderate.*

Hotel Jørgensen, Rømersgade 11, 1362 København K; tel. 33/13 81 86. A block from the Windsor and also on Israels Plads (convenient to the ever-popular Rømersgade toilets), this hotel used to be known as the studentish sort of place where you could get a cheap but not-so-great room. Although there's still dorm space, many of the hotel's rooms have been newly renovated and are now quite nice; 10 have private bathrooms. There's even one apartment. The gay-popular Adagio Café and Piano Bar is in the hotel. Full Danish breakfast. *Moderate; apt. mod./exp.*

For new gay guest houses, check the local gay guides and newspapers listed in the "Information Resources" section.

During the high-season summer months, **Værelseanvisning,** the hotel-booking service in the Central Station, can find you a room in a private home, if you insist. Their job, after all, is to fill hotel rooms. Private rooms cost considerably less money. The disadvantage is that many are somewhat out of the center of town, but you may luck out: We checked out the location of one top-floor room with a panoramic view, near Christiania, for instance. **Use It** (see "Information Resources" section for address and description) can also help you locate a private room, often costing even less than Værelseanvisning's listings.

WHERE TO GO (DAY)

Particularly popular with gay men for sunbathing/cruising in the summer is **Amagerfælled,** reachable via bus no. 31 from Kongens Nytorv. Get off at Vejlands Allé, follow the road west, and then go into the woods on the right.

Also popular for gay beaching is **Tisvildeleje nude beach.** Take the "E" train to Hillerød, where you change for the local railroad. At the sea, walk for about a half hour along the forested side of the road from the parking lot, until you reach the fifth stone, which is marked "TROLDESKOVEN." From here, head towards the beach and when you get there, take a right. There's cruising in the woods behind the beach.

Because the streetlights are not what they could be, especially around the lake where the most successful drug sellers have built their mighty upscale hippie houses, the "free state" of **Christiana** (Fristaden Christiania, 1432 København K) is best seen by day. The 20–30 minute walk from the city center is pleasant, or take bus no. 8 from Rådhuspladsen to Bodenhoffs Plads. The entrance to this partially walled settlement is at the corner of Bådsmandsstræde and Prinsessegade, and you can't miss the hash sellers lining the main path only a few hundred feet from the gate. **Bøssehuset,** the alternative gay organization, is here; to find out if the guys have any shows, gay tango lessons, or other events going on, call 31/95 98 72. They meet every Monday at 8 P.M.

WHERE TO GO (NIGHT)

Tivoli. Fireworks are on Wednesday, Saturday and Sunday nights, at varying times between 11 P.M. and the park's midnight closing hour. Exact shoot-off locale also varies daily, but the best fireworks are those launched over the lake, on Sundays.

Of late, the deluxe-class **Pan Café/Disco,** located in a terrific courtyard complex at Knabrostræde 3, has become so hot that even straight people are finding it irresistible. There goes the neighborhood. The hi-tech disco room is blessedly separate from the rest of the bar, which is itself a multilevel affair connected by spiral staircases, so conversations—or just relating over pool or pinball games— can happen without yelling. The café is open every day from noon (1 P.M. Sundays), until 3 A.M. Sunday–Tuesday, 4 A.M. Wednesdays and Thursdays, and at least 5 A.M. Fridays and Saturdays. The disco runs from 10 P.M. nightly. After this hour café entrance is also through the disco, and there's an overall admission charge to the complex—though not if you're already inside, so everyone comes early. Thursdays are lesbian-only, big fun, and enormously popular.

The "Women's House," **Kvindehuset** (Gothersgade 37, 1123 København K; tel. 33/14 28 04) runs sporadic discos for women only; call for their schedule. Drawing mainly lesbians but mixed are **Jeppes Club 48** (Allégade 25, 2000 Fredericsberg; tel. 31/87 32 48), on Fridays only, 9 P.M.–3 A.M.; and the newer fern bar **Café Babooskha** (Turensgade 6; open 11 A.M.–midnight daily), just a quick catty-corner cut from both of our listed gay-friendly hotels, across H. C. Ørsteds Parken. The Nørre Voldgade/Vester Voldgade side of the park is itself a popular gay male evening-to-late-night cruising ground. Caution is advised, however, as incidents of hassling and outright violence by teenagers are not unheard-of here.

The **Adagio Café,** in the Hotel Jørgensen, is a nice, light, tropical-feeling space, mixed male/female and gay/straight, but more gay during the winter months.

Otherwise, the rest of Copenhagen's mere dozen or so gay bars have a mostly male clientele, though women are tolerated. The favorite for festivity, and fairly close to Tivoli, is **Pink Club** (Farvegade 10). **Cosy Bar** (Studiestræde 24) is also very popular. The only two specialty role-playing bars are the very leathery **Stable Bar** (Tejlgårdsstræde 3) and the drag club **Madame Arthur** (Lavendelstræde 17).

WHERE (AND WHAT) TO EAT

We won't repeat ourselves here about Copenhagen's world-class fast food, except to reemphasize that meat-eaters who do not try a *ribbensteg* sandwich (spit-roasted pork with marinated cucumbers) at Tivoli will never forgive themselves. And late-night bar denizens, as well as early-morning train catchers, should know that **Centrum Smørrebrød** (Vesterbrogade 6c), a pretty wonderful *smørrebrød* shop right across from the train station, has a machine thingy where you can get open-faced sandwiches 24 hours a day.

For *smørgåsbord*, the **DSB Bistro** (at the Central Station; tel. 33/14 12 32; open 11 A.M.–9:30 P.M.), in a traditional old high-ceilinged room with a fountain in the middle, serves a great, typical all-you-can-eat assortment. This includes cold dishes like gravlax, smoked fish, five kinds of herring, and roast beef (all with sauces and different veggie garnishes); six hot main dishes; plus desserts, cheeses, and breads—for about $15.

An informally elegant, upscale, and tasty vegetarian restaurant is Crank's Grønne Buffet, usually just called **Green's** (Grønnegade 12–14, at Pistolstræde). In a newly renovated building, the place was packed with gay people and alternative culture-type yuppie locals the night we went, no doubt due to the All-You-Can-Eat special they run once weekly. This includes a salad bar (fantastic potato salad) and cheese rolls, plus half a dozen hot entrees like polenta, quiche, and a veggie stir-fry.

Our favorite gay-owned restaurant in Copenhagen is **La Rose de Tunis** (Vesterbrogade 120, 1620 København V; tel. 31/24 06 51)—very popular, so best reserve. Børge and Moktar's couscous is wonderful, and the rich, delicate tuna *brik* (layered puff pastry) is so far above any we've ever had (ordinary run-of-the-mill *briks* can indeed be bricklike) that it's hard to even think of this one by the same name.

Gay foodwise, the already-mentioned **Café Babooshka** and **Adagio** both serve food; the **Kvindehuset** has women-only dinner nights; and **Pan Café** has snacks.

WHERE TO GET THE LATEST DIRT (INFORMATION RESOURCES)

For gay info before you go, the Nordic gay magazine *Reporter* publishes an up-to-date guide to Denmark—as well as Norway, Sweden, Finland, and Iceland—in every issue. In the June/July and August issues, the guide is in English. An exciting possibility you might want to consider is that the magazine also offers small ad spaces free to foreigners, for couples who might want to correspond with and eventually meet and socialize with their Scandinavian counterparts. For rates on single copies by mail order (about 25 Swedish kroner): *Reporter,* Box 170, S-101 22 Stockholm, Sweden.

In town, **Pan Information,** run by the Landsforeningen for Bøsser og Lesbiske, is located in this national gay organization's complex at Knabrostræde 3, 1210 Köbenhavn K; it's open 8 P.M.–12 A.M., Friday–Monday. Also in the complex are the Landforeningen's **offices** (second door to the left after entering the main portal), **library** (first door to the right; open Mondays and Fridays, 5–7 P.M., Wednesdays 5P.M.–8 P.M., and Saturdays 1–3 P.M.), and **bookstore** (first door to the left; tel. 33/11 19 61; open Monday–Thursday 5P.M.–7 P.M., Fridays 5P.M.–8 P.M.), as well as gay **Radio Rosa** (which broadcasts every day on 101.7 Mhz, 3 P.M.–5 P.M. and 9:30 P.M.–11:30 P.M., and the already recommended **Pan Club/Disco. Pan's free monthly newspaper,** which you can pick up here, is in Danish but has an events calendar and some gay establishment ads that are useful to English-speakers.

For lesbians, the **Kvindehuset** (Gothersgade 37, 1123 København K; tel. 33/14 28 04) has sporadically scheduled disco nights, restaurant nights, and other special events. It also publishes a newspaper, *Hvidløgspressen* ("Garlic Press"), in Danish but with a calendar of women's events that English-speakers can to some extent decipher.

The **Gay Switchboard,** which is Pan Info's phoneline, is: 33/13 01 12, weekends (or alternatively, during the week, 33/13 19 48).

If you stay at the Windsor, they will supply you with their own small gay map of Copenhagen, which includes a bar–sauna–porn cinema list.

Oddly, the most complete gay info booklet in town is from a youth organization: **Use It,** the travel division of Huset, located at Rådhusstræde 13; tel. 33/15 65 18. Use It publishes a free 23-page *Copenhagen Gay Guide,* containing the latest info on lesbian and gay organizations, bars, discos, cafés, saunas, cinemas, cruising spots, and escort services, plus a fairly detailed keyed map. While you're picking up the gay guide, you might as well also grab copies of their *Playtime* (which has more gay info), *Copenhagen by Foot,* and *Copenhagen by Bus,* check out the rest of this very impressive building, which includes several nightclubs for diverse musical tastes; and maybe use the toilets (to the right of the entrance door). You can also get the free *Copenhagen This Week* standard sightseeing guide here, if you don't want to bother with the tourist office.

Danmark's Turiströd (the tourist office) is conveniently located right at the Rådhuspladsen Tivoli entrance, at H. C. Andersen Blvd., tel. 33/11 13 25. While not terribly knowledgeable about gay Copenhagen, the staff there is helpful and totally nonhomophobic. Ask them anything.

MISCELLANEOUS:
WHERE TO STAY ON YOUR WAY

If you're coming to Copenhagen from anywhere in southern Europe, it's a long trip—basically an uncomfortable all-nighter on the train, unless you break up the journey somewhere in northern Germany. The obvious stop is Hamburg, which, though it's an industrial port city, does have a lot of gay life. As an alternative, we suggest Lübeck, a canal-encircled, tower-guarded Hanseatic city with an extensive old-town section—and a gay-oriented hotel as well as several gay bars.

Gay Hotels in Lübeck
Hotel-Restaurant Astoria (Fackenburger Allee 68, D-2400 Lübeck; tel 045/4 67 63 or 47 81 00; fax 0451/476488) is a 100-bed hotel in an impressive detached brick house, with lots of wide-board paneling throughout the interior, located near the old town. Rooms are both with and without bath. *Inex./mod.–moderate.*

Gay Bars in Lübeck
Chapeauclaque (Hartengrube 25–27; tel. 77371), **Man** (Fischergrube 23; tel. 75456), **PapaGay** (Marlesgrube 61; tel. 72144).

Gay Organizations/Info Resources in Lübeck
Homosexuelle Initiative Lübeck (**HIL**) (Postfach 1823, 2400 Lübeck) meets Wednesdays 8 P.M.–10 P.M. at Königstresse 23, third floor, and has a gay map of Lübeck. The group's "Rosa Telephon" hotline is 0451/7 45 19.

The **Lübecker AIDS-Hilfe** hotline is: 19411.

BERLIN

The Last Days
of the Raj

We're standing with Peter Hedenstroem, comanager of one of West Berlin's leading gay bookstores, in a working-class neighborhood that bargain-sniffing yuppie businesspeople have recently been trying to gentrify. "But do you know what *that* is?" Peter points with some satisfaction toward a disreputable-looking dive right in the midst of the upscale fern-bar touches. *That* is a new bar run by hippie-punk squatters. And while it definitely mars the middle-class plastic, it also piques one's curiosity, and maybe even gives the plastic a little character.

"Berlin is *rotten!*" Peter exclaims cheerfully, smiling through his blondish beard. "It always has been. It always will be. That is what I love about it!"

"*Berlin bleibt noch Berlin,*" as the local saying goes: Berlin is still Berlin. The city's official symbol is the bear, but its true spiritual mascot would be a slightly scuzzy alley cat that keeps landing on its feet. You can overrun Berlin with Nazis, bomb the shit out of it, chop it in quarters, blockade it, build a wall through the middle, fill it with modern architecture, and try to make it an example to the world. But some cozy kernel of earthiness, some perverse divergence from the Plan—something less heroic than deliciously *rotten*—will sprout up to spoil your scheme. Berliners like Peter count on it, stocking their survivalist cellars with large supplies of irony.

For gay people, the most dramatic evidence of the city's staying power is the Nollendorfplatz, the grand intersection that was the site of most of the gay bars in the twenties and thirties. The bars were closed by the Nazis, the square largely demolished by Allied bombs. Today new bars and discos have risen from the ashes, and the neighborhood is, once again, one of the great gay corners of Europe. A small pink triangle on a wall behind the U-bahn station commemorates the gay prisoners who were beaten, starved, and worked to death in concentration camps. Around the corner, on a frumpy brown stucco apartment house at Nollendorfstraße 17, you can find another, happier plaque: This is the building that was memorialized as Sally Bowles's boarding house in Christopher Isherwood's *Berlin Stories* and later in *Cabaret*.

Both our fathers fought in World War II; one of us is half Jewish, and the other is the mother of two half-Jewish children. But when we visited the Nollendorfplatz, we felt like honorary Berliners. Our kind survived, too.

Since before World War II, Berlin has been to the rest of Germany something like what New York is to the rest of the United States: hypersophisticated, tough, convinced of being the center of the universe, and at the same time of being a world apart. Like New York, Berlin was also mightily resented. It had become the capital overnight in 1871, not because of its illustrious past (it had none) or because its location was central (it wasn't), but purely on the basis of brute politics; the Prussians dominated the new united German states, and Berlin had been the residence of their kings. Hitler was only one of many non-Prussians of a later era who regarded the city as arrogant, degenerate, and way too Jewish. That is, much the same way many rural and suburban Americans regard us New Yorkers.

For centuries, Berlin had been a melting pot. In addition to the Jews, it had welcomed waves of Huguenots, Bohemians, Salzburgers, Poles, Russians, and others. During the era of the Wall, West Berlin remained a magnet, although many "normal" West Germans regarded it as a Siberia —one reason why citizens got an eight per cent tax-free bonus just for living there. In the postwar era the newcomers were the troops of the occupying nations, plus Yugoslavs, southern Italians, Greeks, and a huge Turkish immigrant population . . . as well as punks, draft dodgers, hippies, radicals, and other sociopolitical misfits from everywhere in Germany. Including, of course, gay men and lesbians.

According to a local government pamphlet, by the time the Wall fell there were up to fifteen thousand Berliners employed in approximately fifteen hundred "alternative culture" projects, from theater collectives to ecology groups. There were more women than men in the Senate, and a special ministry for gays had just been inaugurated as part of a joint "Red-Green" coalition victory of the left and environmentalists. Berlin even had a special "Rock Commissioner" to help coordinate the activities of the enormous numbers of New Wave bands performing in the city.

Like most Americans, we had very little understanding of any of this before we traveled to Berlin. We grew up with the Wall as a staple of civics-class lessons, the only high point being JFK's pompous double entendre faux pas announcing that he, too, was a jelly donut. (That should have been our first clue that the town was okay. Who but complete mad loons wouldn't mind sharing a title with a piece of pastry?) We thought of modern Berlin as (a) the showroom of the Cold War, and (b) a place whose history had been smashed to bits. It sounded sterile, quasi-American, and full of the ugly skyscrapers and urban stress we go to Europe to get *away* from. All in all, Berlin sounded about as fascinating as the sixth-grade class trip to the United Nations, but without the fun of singing "One Hundred Bottles of Beer on the Wall" in the bus on the way home.

Yet there has always been, and we suspect always will be, some curious fascination that draws many people to Berlin in spite of themselves—nothing as easy to explain as the warmth of Italy or the romance of France or the wit of Britain, but just as compelling. For a lot of us, the roots of the attraction probably started simply with reading and loving the works of Isherwood, who first came to Berlin from England in 1928. An uncle whose shipping business was based in Germany had earnestly warned him that the city was a shameless sexual sewer, a Sodom openly catering to "the vilest perversions." Isherwood instantly perked up. Although he was ostensibly traveling abroad to write, the fact, as he notes in *Christopher and His Kind,* was that "Berlin meant Boys."

It also meant Girls. In the Weimar era there were a staggering *sixty* (count 'em, Six Oh!) bars, social clubs, and other meeting places for lesbians, including notorious weekly butch-femme costume balls. There were two competing lesbian magazines—*Frauenliebe* ("Women Love") and *Die Freundin* ("The Girlfriend")—which ran hot personals ads, and arty photo spreads of naked ladies.

Most of the scene was social, but there was far more to prewar queer Berlin than Liza Minnelli and Joel Grey types slinking around cabarets in the Tuxedoes of Doom. The city was also the cradle of the modern gay-rights movement, generations before Stonewall and Harvey Milk. There was even serious talk at the time of organizing a gay political party and winning a gay seat in the Reichstag, the German parliament.

The single greatest figure in the struggle was a walrus-moustached physician named Magnus Hirschfeld. In 1897, he and his supporters had submitted a petition to the Reichstag demanding the repeal of Paragraph 175, the criminal law prohibiting male sodomy. (Sporadic attempts to put women under the jurisdiction of the law were defeated, usually out of squeamishness and sexism, rather than justice. At one point a Reichstag commission explained in an official statement that such a law would be unfair, since lesbianism was really nothing but a form of masturbation— something men weren't forbidden to do.) The appeal was signed by thousands of prominent citizens, including Albert Einstein, artists Käthe Kollwitz and George Grosz, writers Heinrich Mann, Rainer Maria Rilke, and Herman Hesse, philosopher Martin Buber, and psychiatrist Richard von Krafft-Ebing.

Hirschfeld believed that gay men and lesbians were genetically a "Third Sex," deserving of understanding, not censure. As the pioneering founder of Berlin's prestigious Institute for Sexual Science, he also worked for general sexual reform, researching and counseling the problems of prostitutes, fetishists, and even plain vanilla straight married couples. He was an early advocate of nationalized health care and the rights of the disabled, and in 1919, he presciently urged that smoking be banned in all public places. But the doctor, who was discreetly gay himself, worked most tirelessly and controversially for the cause of the Third Sex. His lectures were sometimes interrupted by stink bombs, and he himself was spat on and even stoned. In 1920, Hirschfeld (who was Jewish as well as gay) had his head bashed in by a gang of Munich Nazis who left him for dead, fortunately without sticking around to make sure. His attackers were never arrested.

In one of those flukes that sometimes make it seem as if there are only a dozen gay people in the universe and they've all shown up at the same brunch, Isherwood happened to rent a room from Hirschfeld's sister when he first settled in Berlin. The room was in a building directly adjoining the Institute for Sexual Science, and the writer vividly remembered his tour of the Institute's museum:

> Here were whips and chains and torture instruments designed for the practitioners of pleasure-pain . . . lacy female undies which had been worn by ferociously masculine Prussian officers beneath their uniforms . . . the lower halves of trouser legs with elastic bands to hold them in position between knee and ankle. In these and nothing else but an overcoat and a pair of shoes, you could walk the streets and seem fully clothed, giving a camera-quick exposure whenever a suitable viewer appeared.

There were also Hirschfeld's colorful clients: when André Gide came to visit, he was visibly dismayed at the young male patient who greeted him by opening his shirt and flashing a pair of female breasts.

But what Isherwood was especially struck by was the museum's photo gallery of gay couples: Wilde and Bosie, Whitman and Peter Doyle, Ludwig of Bavaria and Kainz, Edward Carpenter and George Merrill. It was, Isherwood later wrote, the first time he was forced to think of himself not as a man who happened to have sex with other men, but as a member of a gay tribe.

During the year Isherwood lived next door to the Institute, the Reichstag came close to reforming Paragraph 175. A survey of all major political parties had yielded mostly positive responses on the issue. Unfortunately, the crash of the American stock market in late 1929 triggered a panic in Europe that in turn led to paralysis in the fragile Weimar government. All legislative reform was tabled indefinitely.

One of the few parties that had been dead set against reform was the Nazis. Their blood-chilling official statement read, in part: "Anyone who even thinks of homosexual love is our enemy. We reject anything which emasculates our people and makes it a plaything for our enemies, for we know that life is a fight, and it is madness to think that men will ever embrace fraternally. . . . Might makes right, and the stronger will always win over the weak." Tight-assed Nazi policy also held that Jews, gay men, and all women were ruled by undisciplined, immature passions, because *they liked sex*, whereas a "real man," an "Aryan" heterosexual, had more important things on his mind.

Hirschfeld was out of the country lecturing on May 6, 1933, when the Nazis invaded the Institute and trashed it. All the books, papers, photographs, and exhibits in the library were flung into a bonfire, including a symbolic bronze bust of the sex reformer that had been presented to him on his sixtieth birthday, Hirschfeld himself died of a stroke in exile in Nice two years later. His long-time lover and assistant, Karl Giese, committed suicide not long afterward.

Surviving them both was Paragraph 175, which remained on the books in both East and West Germany until the late sixties. After the Nazis took power, the scope of the law was vastly extended to criminalize as little as a kiss, a touch, or a love letter between men. Even *fantasies* were prosecuted: one man was convicted for watching a straight couple make love in a park, and admitting that he had only watched the man.

We arrived in Berlin less than three months before the Wall came down. Hungary had just begun to let vacationing East Germans use its borders to defect to the West, but the crisis-hardened Berliners we met didn't have a whiff that they'd be partying on top of the barbed wire by the New Year. It was business as usual—which meant partying everywhere *but* the Wall.

Our gay-oriented hotel was our first clue that perhaps Divine Decadence wasn't totally dead. Maybe it was the posh hetero bordello on the floor below ours. At least that was what we assumed it was, since no one ever came out of the "club" except good-looking, fashionable young women and old-fart businessmen . . . and a lot of music and smoke. Or maybe it was the elegant dwarf who lurked outside the building, apparently directing traffic into the whorehouse.

Even more surprising to us was the architecture of the place. Although our hotel was right in the middle of the Ku'damm, West Berlin's main drag, the building was from the turn of the century. With its high ceilings, carved-wood banisters, an open-grille elevator that looked like a canary cage, and elaborate decorations of fruit, flowers, dragons, and birds on the moldings and ceilings—it was exactly the sort of hotel you'd be thrilled to find in Vienna or Florence. We had repeatedly read that "nothing" was left of old Berlin. Where was the Manhattan milk-carton we'd expected to stay in?

Well, they're there, too. But you'd be surprised how many of the old buildings are still around, especially after looking at endless American guidebook photos that never show anything but skyscrapers, the Wall, and the Kaiser Wilhelm Memorial Church with its sawed-off steeple. Allied bombs actually annihilated less than half of the city's structures, and they often wrecked capriciously, leaving gaping holes next to rows of still-standing houses. Today Berlin is a historical hodgepodge. One soon finds oneself paying attention to details, a roof ornament here, a door there, with a focus that drop-dead beautiful cities never demand.

This is not to say that Berlin wasn't without some pretty dazzling vitality. At night, the whole city shimmered: Runaway neon signs clashed with each other on the roofs of the Ku'damm, and searchlights crisscrossed the heavens. (Looking for planes? For spies?) The East Berlin Television Tower, a classic piece of Whose-Dick-Is-Bigger architecture with a revolving restaurant on the top, winked its red lights over the Wall. Towering above everything in the West was a giant urban Cyclops eye, the luminous blue and white Mercedes logo, as much a part of the Berlin sky as the moon.

"Lots of people do the comparison between New York and Berlin," according to Peter Hedenstroem, who with three other men collectively runs the gay bookstore, Prinz Eisenherz. "Like New York, Berlin has energy, and it gets its energy from contrasts. But in New York the contrasts are of money: rich and poor, black and white. In Berlin, the contrast is of east and west, old and new."

Like most Berliners, Peter is from somewhere else; in his case, a small town in the heath lands south of Hamburg. He told us that when he was growing up in the fifties and sixties, his parents never, ever mentioned World War II. He learned about the Nazis the way other kids learn about sex: in the gutter. When we asked him if we, as foreigners and women, would be welcome in certain Berlin men's leather bars, Peter shrugged and flashed us a wicked grin: "If they give you trouble, just remind them who won the war."

In Berlin, it's hard to rewrite recent history, since its messy legacy is always in your face. The city also has even more self-consciousness of its past than Athens or Rome has. Everywhere, you see postcards and books with loving photos of *alt Berlin,* old, before-the-bombs Berlin. A permanent signboard display on the Savignyplatz, near Prinz Eisenherz and many of the bars, painstakingly maps out which houses on the square are survivors. Soon you begin to walk into major streets and plazas with a kind of time-warped double vision, half-consciously comparing what is with what was before.

Another reminder is in the Grunewald, one of the extensive lake-and-forest greenbelts that form the city's western borders. You walk down a long path from the main road into deep woods. Suddenly, right in front of you, is the huge hill the Berliners call Teufelsberg, or Devil's Mountain. At first glance, it looks like any other mound of land, dotted with little ski trails and crowned by a radio signal tower. But if you look at the ground, you see, among the buttercups and Queen Anne's lace, countless little shards of brick.

The Teufelsberg is a landfill, built entirely of the rubble that was *alt Berlin.*

We could natter on, comparing Berlin with New York, or Munich, or Amsterdam, or Rome—or even with *Planet of the Apes,* and the famous scene where the astronaut realizes that he's standing on the ruins of a nuked-out New York harbor, with the Statue of Liberty's arm poking through the muck. But what we constantly compared Berlin to wasn't some other place we'd been but was another category of past experience altogether: that of being mildly high on psychedelic drugs. From Day One in Berlin, we had a slight physical sense of disorientation. Perhaps the past is so palpably a part of the present that the present seems, in consequence, to be hurtling into the future, throwing you off.

Berlin is also simply *weird.*

On our second night in town, before we had our bearings, we bought tickets for a late-night gay cabaret on the far edge of the Tiergarten, another of the city's parks. In the middle of the park we crossed a massive traffic circle, with an immense phallic victory column in the center. Our map told us that this was the Siegesäule, commemorating the defeat of France in the Franco-Prussian War. Around the perimeter of the circle were dozens of overblown marble monuments. Several were column-fronted pseudo-temples containing public restrooms and the entrances to underground pedestrian walkways for getting across the expanse of the intersection. This was serious fascist architecture, even though it predated the Nazis by decades: Everything was on so ponderous and larger-than-life a scale that it made us feel puny.

We knew we'd seen this place before. It took a minute to register: this was the famous *Klo* from *Taxi Zum Klo.* (And if the number of bikes parked outside is any indication, it's still a prime cruising spot.)

The "theater" materialized suddenly, in a clearing in the woods. To our delight, it turned out to be not a concert hall, but a red-white-and-blue circus tent festooned with garlands of Christmas lights. Inside, the mixed gay-straight crowd was absurdly hip: a girl whose head was shaved bald on the sides with a Victorian upsweep on top; a boy who was one hundred percent skinhead punk from the waist up, but was also wearing baggy bermudas, knee socks, and mountain-climbing shoes. An elderly woman with obviously home-bleached blond hair and a gold lamé suit was licking mustard off her fingers. The guy she was with looked like he worked for IBM and had been born in a tie. The audience was sprawled around the stage on wooden benches, folding chairs, and white wrought-iron ice-cream-parlor ringside tables and chairs. The inevitable Eurosmoke from a hundred Marlboros hazed up to the big top and made patterns in the klieg lights. Someone was filming the event.

The show was called *Concentrated Camp*. (Get it?) It was in English: The players turned out to be from New York, the remnants of the seventies glitter group Hot Peaches. The opening number (to the tune of the Andrews Sisters' Yiddish hit, "Bei Mir Bist Du Schön") featured a latter-day Joel Grey in raccoon makeup, bicycle shorts, and a stylized little tux-and-bow-tie top. He was flanked by two ladies in spangles. One of them was the gorgeous drag queen International Chrysis, whose death from cancer we would be startled, and saddened, to read about in a gay newspaper a few months later.

The straights, here and everywhere else in West Berlin, didn't seem terribly intrusive. We found ourselves wondering if the city in fact lacks the usual Sensibility Gap, since being straight in postwar pre-Unification West Berlin was a little like being gay anywhere else: surrounded by hostile enemies, misunderstood and written off, but determined to survive. *All* Berliners of that era feel special and different and proud, despite living lives that most Germans wouldn't want. As in the gay world, it's the outsiders who are the insiders.

The audience on this night was bilingual enough to laugh at most of the right lines, including tons of gay slang. Still, there's definitely something about being a couple of *americanische* girls watching a bunch of Germans watch a bunch of Americans belt out a song about an imaginary conversation at a Paris café among the British writer Oscar Wilde and the French poets (and lovers), Verlaine and Rimbaud, followed by endless puns on the subject of concentration camps . . . something that made us feel we were inviting nosebleeds.

By the time the show was over, it was almost four A.M. As we tried to find our way back out of the Tiergarten on foot, we took a series of wrong turns. Soon we were hopelessly lost, and the map was no help, since there were no real landmarks—only long, dimly lit, deserted boulevards through the woods.

Suddenly scores of wild rabbits scampered across the path in front of us. They spotted us and froze. Little brown ears twitched in the moonlight. The nearby shrubbery quivered. Little glittery eyes were everywhere, reflecting from all the bushes lining the sidewalk, waiting for our next move.

There are times in life where reasoned thought flees, leaving nothing in one's mind except the theme from *The Twilight Zone: "bee*-bee-bee-bee, *bee*-bee-bee-bee." . . . Feeling a tad disoriented—actually even rudely intrusive—we stumbled from the rabbit tableau onto the wide adjoining roadway, which we'd been avoiding since it was blocked off by what looked like police barricades. But once we were actually in the street, the barricades seemed to be not so much a blockade as a pointing arrowhead, a surreal art statement, a beacon of sorts: Down the road's center, as far as the eye could see, was a line of structures that looked like thirty-foot-high red-lit goalposts. A quarter of an hour's walk later, the goalposts abruptly stopped. At the end of the trail, instead of civilization, or even a sign directing us out of the Tiergarten back to the realm of human life, was a huge, shell-white, semi-inflated geodesic dome lying on its side across the road. A concession stand under repair? An igloo from Mars?

We turned around and hiked back the way we had come . . . and found ourselves virtually on top of the Berlin Wall.

This was our first glimpse of it, and if it were still there, instead of in shards on coffee tables all over the world, we would by all means urge you to see it, for full dream-sequence effect, in the dead of night. Just you, the guys with the machine guns, and five million rabbits. Signs in four languages warned us—ACHTUNG!—not to go another step. Behind us the blazing goalposts hulked like giants with their arms crossed, glaring across the Wall, which looked much too short for its mythology: maybe ten feet tall. The harsh lights of the East glowered back.

We eventually managed to get back to our hotel, or course. The next day, we decided to try to find the site of Hirschfeld's Institute for Sexual Science. We knew it had been destroyed, but we had the address, and we looked up the street on our map of modern Berlin.

As near as we can tell, it was almost precisely on the spot where we'd gone to the cabaret the night before. That seemed like an astonishing coincidence. But by then, the whole city seemed like an acid flashback.

In Swiss-German they used to call us *Warmi*—"warm people." Another delicious old euphemism for our kind is *"anderes Ufer,"* the other bank of the river. Today it's the name of one of West Berlin's most popular men's bars. One's *Freund* is a very good friend indeed, and the universal "gay" is understood. For women, *"Lesbierin"* (or slang *"Lesbe"*) is the noun, and *"lesbisch"* the adjective. The most common expression you'll hear among gay people themselves is *"schwul"*—which roughly translates as "queer," and has, like the insult words in English, been resurrected as a badge of pride. The gay center, which for years has been *the* place for men to go on Saturday nights, is called the *Schwulenzentrum,* affectionately nicknamed *Schwuz.*

In both quantity and quality, Berlin gay nightlife is among the best in Europe. In addition to the Nollendorfplatz area east of the Kaiser Wilhelm Memorial Church, and the streets both north and south off the Ku'damm near Savignyplatz (west of the church), there are gay places galore in Kreuzberg, the funky neighborhood south of the old Checkpoint Charlie. The party goes on at least until four A.M. every night.

As you might expect, the bars are as various as the rest of Berlin. Hudson is almost a parody of an American men's bar: a neon sign that says "STROH'S SPOKEN HERE" (just what you want to drink in Germany!); halogen lighting; a minimalist white-tile and chrome environment that looks like an incredibly elegant bathroom; men who could be from West Hollywood as easily as West Berlin. Be sure to check out the coasters, guys: If you look long enough at the artsy, stylized insignia spelling out the name of the bar, you realize it's actually a circumcised penis. We bet you'll figure it out quicker than we did.

For a completely different experience, go to Elli's Bier-Bar, one of the few prewar taverns that's still around. In fact, we heard it stayed open even *during* the war, as a resource for those hapless homos who had somehow made it into the Nazi high command. It's in a Turkish working-class neighborhood, and the building looks like a typical tenement. You walk up the steps and ring the bell. A raspy-voiced older woman peeps out. If she thinks you're straight, you get no farther. But if you pass, a wonderfully glitz-free environment awaits you: old sofas draped with shawls, a coal stove, tacky tinsel party steamers across the ceiling, ancient peeling Tom of Finland posters on the wall, and a jukebox that plays sixties girl groups.

If you don't like either of these places, there are more than sixty other men's bars and discos, plus several saunas and at least a dozen gay-oriented restaurants.

Thanks to the foreign influences, Berlin is one German city where you could probably go years without resorting to the ususal ham-on-bacon-with-a-side-of-porkchop German fare (although you might want to try the famous local street-stand sausages anyway.) Our favorite place to eat was the mixed lesbian and gay male Hofgarten, a typically cozy, wood-paneled little place, strong on veggie food and curries, with great salads and great prices, too.

If you want to spend more Deutsche Marks and you don't mind mingling with straights (although they did seat us in a section of the room that appeared to be intentionally reserved for gays), we recommend the Paris Bistro, where everyone looks like, and maybe is, an artist, a model, or a rich patron of the arts. The food is French, and so is the ambiance: waiters zoom about yelling things like, *"Ja, ja monsieur,"* and you can read French newspapers while you wait for your table. We went there on our first evening in Berlin; the place was solidly, exuberantly packed with tanned trendies, and the table we'd reserved was very far from ready. Where we come from, that would have been a sign for the faggot behind the bar to shrug, give poseur attitude, and suggest a long walk around the block. The faggot behind the Paris Bistro's bar instead apologized and treated us to complimentary champagne. It was a lovely welcome to the city.

Lesbian Berlin includes about a dozen bars and discos, including one of the most appealing women's spaces we've ever been to. Actually, our first encounter with the management of Dinelo wasn't promising. It was about ten minutes before their scheduled opening time in the evening, and it had just started to rain. We banged on the door, making frantic, drowned-rat noises. A burly, butchish woman in her fifties finally came and grudgingly let us in, screaming at us in German. Without the aid of a dictionary, we could tell that she thought we were major pains in the ass. We nodded meekly.

The inside was luxuriously spacious (why are most lesbian bars the size of a file cabinet?), with high ceilings, white walls, light wood, lots of green things growing, and plenty of candlelight. There's a bar area, and another section where you can flopse around with your friends on sofas and ottomans. Or you can sit at tables of various heights, diameters, and artistic styles to suit your mood, on short rustic stools made out of beer-barrel bases or tall mod ones of tubular steel, and order snacks or play cards. The place seats from seventy-five to a hundred women all together. There's no dancing, but that's a plus: The total effect of Dinelo is more like a lounge on a cruise ship than a bar.

A frosty-blonde lipstick lesbian in her twenties came over to take our orders. She spoke English, and when she realized we were foreigners, she was aghast that the dyke at the door had yelled at us. She introduced herself as Lisa. The older door dyke, who waved sheepishly at us from behind the bar, was Kris, and—by now we should be used to these Berlin contrasts—the two of them have been lovers and business partners for eight years.

The name "Dinelo," Lisa explained, "means 'crazy' in the gypsy language [Romany]. It's because Kris is part gypsy, and also because it's crazy that she ended up here." From 1963 to 1973, Kris owned a lesbian bar at the same location—a typically depressing pre-Stonewall place, with too much boozing and a lot of gloomy, closety paranoia. She dreamed of running a place like Dinelo, "but in 1963 it wasn't possible." For a decade she got out of the bar business, and even ran a pet shop for a while. In 1983, she found out that her old space was available, and recycled it as Dinelo.

While we had been scratching at the door in the downpour, we'd noticed a sign forbidding entry to men. Is this legal? "I don't know," Lisa shrugged disdainfully. "I just tell them not to come in." Straight women, on the other hand, are encouraged. "We've got a reputation as a 'mummy place,' where a daughter can bring her mother, and have her mother learn that it's okay to be a lesbian."

One of the bar's other claims to fame is its theme parties, especially the ones inspired by places that Lisa and Kris have vacationed. We were personally sorry not to have been in Berlin for their Morocco event, complete with tents, couscous and a real live belly dancer. If you move fast, you might catch the Walt Disney World party.

Berlin has some of the most efficient information services for gay tourists that we encountered in all our travels. The government-sponsored Frauen-infothek bureau isn't specifically lesbian, but it's a marvel of a resource on anything connected with women in Berlin. They gave us a printed list of lesbian bars, a brochure from a women's hotel, and information on a lesbian history archive. They'll also help you network with women's groups, arrange tours, recommend places to see . . . and pretty much anything else you can dream up. They speak English, and their services are free.

The Prinz Eisenherz bookstore, near Savignyplatz, isn't an information service, but the men who work there are so eager to please that it might as well be. They sell numerous guidebooks and local magazines in German, as well as a large selection of gay fiction and nonfiction in English. When we were there, they were planning to bring out an English-language calendar of gay events for their customers. The name, incidentally, comes from the German version of Prince Valiant. "We knew it would be more politically correct to name it after Magnus Hirschfeld or somebody like that," one of the collective members told us. "But the night before we were to go to the lawyer's office to draw up the papers, we were in a bar, and . . ."

Make sure you also get the bookstore boys to point out the spot under the bridge, down the block, where a scene from *Cabaret* was shot—the one where Liza Minnelli teaches Michael York to vent his frustrations by screaming as the train rumbles by overhead.

Mann-O-Meter operates an information switchboard for gay men. It's more oriented to local men than to tourists, and is especially involved with providing AIDS and safer-sex information, but they put out an excellent map of the gay bars in central Berlin. The guy behind the desk even tipped us off that Boy George was going to give a surprise show that night at a lesbian disco. On the side, they sell terrific gay political posters. We dragged one home as a present for our best gay male friends: a grainy, Thirties shot of two trench-coated men kissing passionately in a crowded train station while the Orient Express steams in the background.

———

For modern-day rail travelers, Berlin is now, obviously, a much less formidable destination in terms of political borders. Geographically, though—being considerably closer to Poland than to any other major German city—it'll always be quite a schlep. From Paris, Amsterdam, or Copenhagen, Berlin is roughly twelve hours by train; even from Munich, it's almost ten hours. It's do-able in one marathon stretch. But it's more pleasantly done with an overnight break, especially since so many German towns on the way from anywhere else to Berlin are the stuff of which fairy tales are made.

On our way to Berlin, we stopped overnight in the tiny town of Goslar, which has a beautiful setting in the Harz mountains, right on the former East-West border, and a medieval core of brightly-painted half-timbered houses. The first bed-and-breakfast we tried was full, but the grandmotherly woman who ran the place insisted on calling around town on our behalf and finding us an equally nice room somewhere else. Her English was hesitant, and our German is worse, but we did manage to communicate our thanks, and our distress that we couldn't be her guests. She told us cheerfully that we should send all our American friends.

We mentioned that, as a matter of fact, we were writing a travel book. And we would love to send lots of our friends . . . as long as it was okay that they were gay.

The word drew a blank.

Our friends were *Schwule*. Still a blank.

We began hauling out dictionaries and phrase books, while the woman, now dying to find out just what sorts of friends we had, hollered for her daughter, who had lived for a time in England, to come help translate. Just as the daughter came through the living-room door, Pam shouted out, *"Lesbisch?"*

While the daughter tried to figure out what was going on, the mother threw up her hands in delight. *This* was a word she understood. And she was either so happy to get it or so genuinely nonhomophobic that we completely passed over the usual coming-out awkwardness. She and her daughter absolutely welcome you, as it turns out—and if you'd like a stopover, we think you'd love her place, and the whole fairy-tale town of Goslar, too.

Of course, we went to the East.

We had already walked along the western side of the Wall, and along the grim border of the Spree River, taking note of the row of crosses commemorating the desperate leapers and swimmers who had been shot down. The newest crosses were only a few months old.

We also knew from a previous trip to Prague that legal crossings into Eastern Europe could be tedious and even mildly scary. So we weren't entirely unprepared for the endless lines at East Berlin's antiseptically drab Friedrichstraße Station, the surly bureaucrats who made us change Western currency into eastern Monopoly-money, the goose-stepping armed soldiers, the bag searches, and even the Kafkaesque scrutiny by the border guards.

They call it *Gesichtskontrolle:* face control. You hand over your passport to some unsmiling uniformed types in a high windowed booth. They look at your passport picture. Then they look at you. They look at the photo again. At you again, a longer look this time. They study each feature individually, flickering back and forth from your eyebrow, your nose, your chin, to the one on the passport. If you're wearing glasses today, but you took them off for the passport shot, you're asked to take them off for the guards. God help you, presumably, if you've switched to contacts. The guards confer. We wonder if gay people, with our habitual layers of masks, are better at toughing out the scrutiny than the rest. Or are we that much more paranoid? After an agonizingly long wait, during which it seems certain that they have somehow discovered that you're really not who you say you are, you're waved through.

Incidentally, gang, don't get your hopes up merely because there's no more border. One still must go through an only slightly less rigorous version of *Gesichtskontrolle* at Buschallee and a few other of the more studiously "in" East Berlin gay bars.

The other side of the Wall was another country, but more dramatically, it seemed to us to be another decade. The streets were full of confident, flashy people, obviously reflecting East Germany's status as the most prosperous of the Eastern-bloc countries—except that they were strutting around in denim suits, wide lapels, and bell-bottoms, the height of Western fashion circa 1975. We felt as if we'd stepped behind the Polyester Curtain.

In the windows of fancy stores, everyday items like bananas and canned pineapple were lovingly arranged in artful pyramids, like the merchandise at Tiffany's. An East German version of Crazy Eddie, complete with flashing neon come-on lights, was selling 45 rpm hi-fi phonographs, reel-to-reel tape recorders, and other remnants of our postwar New Jersey rec room childhoods. Even the automobiles looked insubstantial, like amusement-park bumper cars, but there were a lot of them. It was rampant consumerism without capitalism—a paradox which only began to make sense to us a few months later, when the myth of all those happy communists went up in smoke. These folks were junior mall-bunnies-in-training, lacking only their Amex Gold.

We knew that homosexuality was legal in East Germany, but we weren't up for flaunting our Western decadence at the border guards—at least not in the form of a gay guidebook with bodybuilder-clutching-his-crotch cover and cockring ads. Instead we had discreetly copied down some addresses. Our first stop was the Alt Berliner, a typical little Berlin neighborhood bar. The front room was full of men of all ages standing and drinking; the backroom had tables where nuclear families were eating lunch. If we hadn't known we were in a gay bar, we would have assumed, at first glance, that the men in front were straight, working-class guys tossing back a few beers.

The second we set foot in the door we felt distinctly like aliens. No one did anything rude, but not a soul in the place would make eye contact with us, including the bartender. Was it because we were women? Westerners? Americans? Queers who might blow their cover with the nuke-fams in the back room? We got a partial answer a few moments later when we noticed two other people (Western and queer, but British and male) huddled together in the corner looking as uncomfortable as we did. They introduced themselves as Steve and Andy, from London. Andy was tall and dark; Steve was wiry and blond and almost Germanic looking himself. They were both thirty, a long-time couple, together nearly a decade.

We decided to join forces and check out another bar, the Café (Peking) Ecke Schönhauser, described in our guidebook as *"eines der elegantesten Cafés in Ost-Berlin."* Elegant it was, with flattering pink lighting, black leather sofas, and, to our distress, no beer on the menu, an apparent stab at classiness. We felt this might have come off more successfully, all in all, had the champagne kirs we ordered to get rid of our funny money tasted a bit less like grape soda. The Alt Berliner had German folk-dance music on the tape system. Here it was Tina Turner. Desperately fashionable people in gold jewelry and the de rigueur killer denim openly checked us all out, amid much hissing and buzzing excitement about "Vesterners." The two of us were a little sorry that we happened to be in Dyke Drab; we had visions of the entire clientele racing home to their sewing machines, trying to duplicate our Chi pants and ratty Gore-Tex jackets.

Unlike the other bar, this place seemed to contain a few people who were unequivocally gay. In fact, two women were necking furiously at the next table, right in the front window in full view of all passersby. In one of the rare moments when they weren't making out, one of them took out a clunky desk calculator, no doubt a prized purchase from Crazy Otto's Low-Tech Warehouse down the street, and elaborately added up their bill.

They were part of a larger group, mostly male, and when we tried to catch the women's eyes, we instead caught one of the men's. He spoke some English, and we asked him if he would ask the women if they knew of any lesbian bars in the East. The guy went over to confer with one of them, who looked across at the two of us with great interest. We smiled. The women got up to leave, and the guy came back to report to us. He paused, obviously searching his English vocabulary for *le mot juste.*

"I am not what you call a smooth operator," he finally said, "but yes, I think I can get you a wife for tonight."

Huh? We hurriedly explained that we didn't want a *"Frau,"* that we each *had* a reasonable facsimile already, that something had gotten hopelessly lost in the translation.

He took that in, switched gears, and asked us if we'd like to change some money illegally. No, we didn't. Then he told us a little about himself. He was straight, and so was the male friend he had come in with, but one of the passionate calculatrixes was apparently the friend's sister. The two guys were out drinking to the possibility that the friend's very pregnant wife would have a boy. (Makes perfect sense. *Hey, where would be an appropriate place to drink toasts to a sexist pig sentiment? Oh, I know! A gay bar!*)

Mr. Non-Smooth managed one of the big hotels off the Alexanderplatz, and aspired to be a yuppie (pronounced "you-pee"), although, he admitted, that wasn't easy in East Germany. He enumerated all the boring things one has to put up with as a communist: required Russian in school, vacations in the armpits of Bulgaria, hassles acquiring nice clothes. We nodded along sympathetically. Was there anything he was curious to know about us and our lives, we asked? Well, actually, yes: He wanted to know why Lindsy— a mother and former wife, after all!—has turned "abnormal."

Fascinated though we were to find that some things know no cultural bounds, we signaled to Andy and Steve that it was time to split. Our next stop was dinner in the only place around that was open. It was, we supposed, a you-pee restaurant. The "salad bar" summed up the pompous pathos of the East better than anything we'd seen all day. You had your choice of five kinds of greens: two bowls of coarsely ground cabbage, two bowls of cold canned string beans, and a bowl of rotting apples.

"I think every Western-nation citizen who doesn't vote should be required to come here," Andy muttered.

We tromped around after dinner to some other bars, but everything was closed. We still had tons of eastmarks and a few hours before we had to return to the border, so for lack of a better idea, we went back to the Peking Schönhauser. Mr. Non-Smooth had left, at least. We sat at a table next to a tall blond boy with an earring. The four of us braced ourselves for either hostility or a hustle.

Instead, the fellow shyly asked us if he could buy us all coffee. His English was far more limited than Mr. Non-Smooth's, but Steve had studied German in school, and we all whipped out our dictionaries. The boy told us his name was Maik, that he was twenty-two, and that he worked as a tram driver. Since he had no relatives in the West who might sponsor him for a visit, he said, he probably wouldn't get out of East Germany until his sixty-fifth birthday, when he would receive a special senior-citizen's travel dispensation. The guys at Prinz Eisenherz had already told us about the old gay men who somehow found their way into the bookstore, and looked longingly at all the books they couldn't begin to afford. One man, in the West for the first time, had even broken down and cried when he saw that such books even existed.

Maik and Steve chattered on in German until it was perilously close to the time that we four Westerners would turn into pumpkins. The Brits had to go back the way they came, through Checkpoint Charlie, and we had to make our way back to the Friedrichstraße Station.

Maik insisted on escorting us girls. Without Steve to interpret, our conversation was fairly limited, but we'd already established that we all liked rock and roll. For the duration of the tram ride, we shouted the names of gay bands at each other—"Bronski Beat?" "*Ja ja!* Pet Shop Boys?"— and then hooted with joy when we liked each other's choices.

At the station, we hugged Maik good-bye, and bade him *bis bald,* the slang expression meaning "See you soon." And then we all giggled ruefully, in acknowledgment that we lived in two different worlds, and that we'd probably never meet again.

POSTSCRIPT

The Wall cracked open, of course. A few weeks later, our phone rang. It was Steve, calling from London. "You'll never guess who's here," he cackled.

He and Andy had been corresponding with Maik, and had already gone back to Berlin for a long weekend and met up with him again. When the East German government gave citizens permission to travel, they had bought him a ticket; he was going to come back again in the winter for the big blast they were planning to celebrate their tenth anniversary. Maik was too shy to come to the phone and speak English, but we got a letter from him a few weeks later: "My first time in UK was very very very beautiful. It's was indescribable for me. All all so NEW . . . The WALL is to fall. We are FREE."

Six weeks later, Steve phones again, sounding glum. The anniversary party is off. He and Andy have broken up. We're stunned.

Then Steve says, "Remember how when I called you before, you asked me to give Maik a kiss for you? Well . . . I did. I still am."

The situation for gay people in what used to be the East has been changing at a bewildering pace—and despite "liberation," the change hasn't been entirely for the better. The fall of the Wall made it easier for our side to express itself, but it's given neo-Nazis the same option. On the plus side, there are at least fifty gay political groups in East Germany (before 1989, the only above ground organizations were a few connected with the Lutheran Church). There are also active gay groups in Poland, Czechoslovakia, Hungary, and elsewhere in the Eastern bloc.

If things have improved politically, however, they sound far more dismal socially, even in the West. One West German lesbian we'd met wrote us that women were increasingly worried about straight men from the East, whose concept of freedom in West Berlin included plenty of porn and free sex. When they didn't score, they sometimes took out their frustration by hassling lesbians on the street.

A lesbian leader of the new East German gay group Courage gave us an even bleaker report: "We were on the edge of getting people used to men kissing each other good-bye or walking hand-in-hand in the street. That has largely stopped . . . Within the last months and weeks there have been attacks on gay clubs and bars by skinheads who support the [extreme right wing]. Significant too is that the GDR-wide demonstration to mark the Christopher Street anniversary, due to have been held in Leipzig, was cancelled out of fear of the possible consequence."

As the months went by, we heard more and more reports of bashings— of leftists, Jews, and people of color, as well as gay men and lesbians. Even without the violence, the isolated City of Weirdos is no more. We worry that the effect on gay people of Berlin's post-Reunification capital status will be akin to what would happen if Congress, General Motors and the National Council of Churches suddenly relocated to Castro Street.

In the summer of 1990, Hot Peaches, the very troupe we'd gone to see in the Tiergarten, made what was supposed to be a triumphal return to Berlin. Director Jimmy Camicia published his disillusioned diary in the New York gay newspaper *The Native*. "For months, I sat in my Sixth Avenue apartment watching TV where Berliners toasted and drank champagne on top of the Wall," he wrote. "I expected a celebration . . . Nothing could be further from the truth." Instead he found hostility between Eastern and Western gays, fear of homophobia everywhere, and so much emotional overdosing on Reunification that whenever he mentioned the fall of the Wall in his act, he could physically feel the audience's energy dip. The party, as he and we knew it, seemed to be over.

By the time you get to Berlin, the situation probably will have changed again, and again. We can only keep the faith that the city will once again survive itself, that *Berlin bleibt noch Berlin*.

PRACTICAL INFORMATION

BERLIN—NUMBER KEY

Organizations
1. AIDS-Hilfe (Niebuhrstr. 71)
2. Fraueninfothek (Leibnizstr. 57)
3. Mann-o-Meter (Motzstr. 5)

Bars and Discos
4. Andreas Kneipe (Ansbacherstr. 29)
5. Tom's Bar (Motzstr. 19)
6. Pool (disco; Motzstr. 25)
7. Hofgarten (Regensburgerstr. 5)
8. Lipstick (Richard-Wagner-Platz)

Restaurants and Hotels
9. Paris Bistro (Kantstr. 152)
10. Savigny Café (Grolmannstr. 53)
11. Hotel Artemisia (Brandenburgischestr. 18)
12. Arco Hotel (Kürfürstendamm 30)
13. Bistro 25 (Kantstr. 25)

Bookstores
14. Lilith Frauenbuchladen (Knesebeckstr. 86–87)
15. Prinz Eisenherz (Bülowstr. 17)

Shopping, Etc.
16. KaDeWe (Tauentzienstr. 21)
17. Europa Center
18. Mantours Travel Agency (Motzstr. 70)

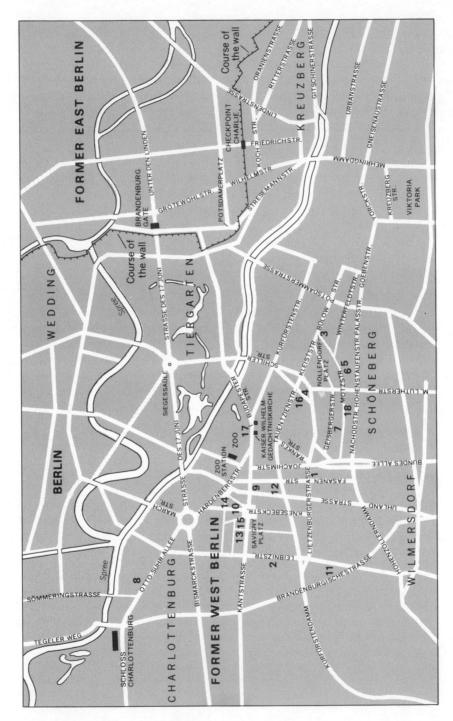

GENERAL HINTS / INFO

For orientation, it's interesting to remember that although the Kurfürstendamm was always Berlin's fashionable shopping/café street, before the war many of the most old-money luxurious as well as the most no-money sinful neighborhoods were in what was until recently East Berlin. And in what was West Berlin, many gays have reestablished themselves after the war in the areas gay places have always been: the formerly working-class, now more alternative-culture Kreuzberg (which is actually far enough east to be due south of former East Berlin); middle-class Schöneberg just west of that, like Kreuzberg an old Isherwood neighborhood; and to some extent Charlottenburg, even farther west and north of the Ku'damm.

While Berlin has plenty of appealing gay establishments—of both the rustic or decadent old types, and the fashionable or alternative new types—that welcome everyone, it is also a town where a great many gay places take their stiff little roles and rules very seriously: men only, leather/denim only, cruising only (for conversations, try the place next door), and so on. And Berliners admit that striking up casual conversations with strangers in gay bars is not always easy here—even for newcomers who are outgoing and speak German. This is particularly unfortunate since we cannot think of another city where local guidance and insights are more valuable to understanding the place's psychological and physical complexities, especially in these times of political change. So we'd like to especially push, in this town, for you to obtain a few of the inexpensive local guides recommended in the "Information Resources" section, and ask the store owners to personally mark these booklets with their own suggestions of places friendly to foreign travelers.

Very few establishments of any sort in Berlin take credit cards.

Telephone code: 030

Currency unit: the Deutsche Mark (DM)

WHERE TO STAY

Because of Berlin's location, and also because the city attracts an awful lot of major international business conventions, advance hotel reservations are strongly recommended.

All prices are for double rooms and include breakfast.

Prices: *Inexpensive* = under DM100; *inex./mod.* = DM100–125; *moderate* = DM125–150; *mod./exp.* = DM150–200; *expensive* = over DM200.

Arco Hotel Pension, Kurfürstendamm 30, 1000 Berlin 15; tel. 881 99 02 (or 882 63 88). The 20 rooms in this 1890s building are gargantuan high-ceilinged affairs, many with balconies overlooking either the Ku'damm or a much quieter tree'd courtyard, and lots of lovely old moldings and other elaborate decorative touches. Some have private baths, but most have showers and sinks. Breakfast is expanded Continental. The hotel has some straight guests, too, but feels largely gay. Ask for the free gay-Berlin maps they keep behind the desk. *Inex./mod.– moderate.*

Hotel Pension Brenner, Fuggerstraße 33, 1000 Berlin 30; tel. 24 83 43. A 15-room mixed but mostly gay hotel in a turn-of-the-century building, recently renovated by the owners personally. It's not as nice inside as the Arco, but is friendly, pleasant, and in a particularly convenient location for a number of the most popular Schöneberg men's bars. Rooms are large and some have in-room showers; none have full private bathrooms. *Inex./mod.*

Artemisia Frauenhotel, Brandenburgische Straße 18, D1000 Berlin 31; tel. 87 89 05 or 87 63 73. A very stylish, modern hotel for women only. There are eight white/pink/turquoise rooms, all dedicated to different famous women. One is a suite, and one a four-bed dorm that's much less expensive; all but the dorm and one other room have private baths, plus other niceties like hair dryers, desks, and phones. The breakfast is a sumptuous buffet with yogurt, cereal, meat, and cheese as well as breads. It's served until 11 A.M. or noon, bar-hoppers will be happy to know. The hotel also has a pleasant, sophisticatedly decorated bar, open from 5 P.M., and a roof garden/sundeck. *Moderate* (bed in dorm room *very inexpensive;* suite *mod./exp.*).

Schloßhotel Gehrhus, Brahmsstraße 4–10, 1000 Berlin 33; tel. 826 20 81. Nongay, but responding well to our usual are-gays-welcome Drill, is this absolutely exquisite 1912–14 castle-hotel in the Grünewald, the quiet, green-forested section of Berlin where aristocrats always did and still do have their estates. The 40 rooms do vary in fabulousness (some of the inexpensive, bathless ones being small); but one step inside the carved-and-coffered, crystal-chandeliered Great Hall, which looks like an ornately enameled two-story jewelbox, and you will simply die. There's an on-premises restaurant and bar. *Inex./mod., moderate,* and *mod./exp.* (suites *expensive*).

WHERE TO GO (DAY)

For literary pilgrims, probably the most famous of the old Isherwood addresses mentioned in his books and our text, is 17 Nollendorfstraße—landlady Fraulein Thurau's house, where Sally Bowles/Liza Minnelli and the author lived in the movie *Cabaret.* Other former Isherwood residences include Admiralstraße 38 in Kottbusser Tor; and a couple of apartment buildings that, postwar, no longer exist, though their neighborhoods are worth a visit: the house adjoining Magnus Hirschfeld's Institute for Sexual Science (in Den Zelten in the Tiergarten, now, rather eerily, all parkland), and Otto Nowaks's family's slum tenement at Simeonstraße 4 in Hallesches Tor (in *Goodbye to Berlin* called Wassertorstraße, which was actually a continuation of Simeonstraße—though we couldn't find either street anymore). The Cozy Corner bar was at Zossenerstraße 7, in Hallesches Tor. Kleist Casino is still at 35 Kleiststraße. Teufelsberg (Devil's Mountain), the spookily peaceful mountain of war rubble Isherwood speaks of in *Christopher and His Kind,* is in the Grünewald.

For work breaks, Isherwood's idea of a really Big Fun time was to skip out to the Berlin Zoologischer Garten (the zoo). Ours, too. In truth, we only came here because we'd read the train schedule wrong and had a few hours to kill— the zoo is right next door to the station—but the circus-Oriental buildings, the unusual species, the greenery, and the great deal of space given to the animals' environments all combine to make this one of the most magical zoos we've ever visited.

Don't miss the world-famous department store **KaDeWe** (pronounced "kah-day-vay), especially the food floor, which makes Harrod's look anemic. Afterward, depending on whether you go early or late, you can either take your food haul from the food halls and picnic at the zoo, or else nip around the corner to Andreas Kneipe [see "Where to Go (Night)"] for a beer.

WHERE TO GO (NIGHT)

While residents of, say, New York City or Detroit will no doubt still find late-night Berlin relatively safe, do remember that there's currently a good deal of post-Wall transitional tension in town—roaming gangs of sexist, homophobic neofascist skinheads from the East, for instance. So don't turn the radar off, okay?

In (former) West Berlin

As pointed out in the text, the nicest, most elegant yet comfortable women's bar/ restaurant we've ever been in, anywhere, is **Dinelo** (Vorbergstraße 10, 1000 Berlin 62; tel. 782 21 85; open from 6 P.M. except Mondays).

Mixed lesbian/gay male, but particularly exciting for men who prefer a young alternative-culture feel to an old cruisy one, is the **Schwuz,** short for Schwulen-zentrum (Hassenheide 54, 1000 Berlin 61; tel. 694 10 77). This friendly, high-energy club on the fourth floor of the gay center (which is also a good information source), is in Kreuzberg.

A 50-year-old knock-three-times-and-ask-for-Josephine-type Berlin nightspot that atmospherically calls up all the weird, decadent little dives Isherwood wrote about, is **Elli's Bier-Bar,** at Skalitzer Straße 102, in Kreuzberg near the Görlitzer U-Bhf. stop.

If you want an afternoon or early-evening gay beer in Kreuzberg, **Café Graefe** (Graefestraße 18, near U-Bhf. Kottbusser Tor) is a small, pleasant café with a few outdoor tables, open from about 1 P.M.

A typical old-fashioned raucous Berlin pub, open from midday on and a good bet for afternoon coffee and conversation, is **Andreas Kneipe** (Ansbacher Straße 29, in the Schöneberg district, handily located near Wittenbergplatz and KaDeWe department store). The gay café **Anderes Ufer** (Hauptstraße 157) is also in Schöneberg, also open from midday, and also very popular with men.

Things start happening fast at about 9:30–10 P.M. at **Hudson** (Elssholzstraße 10, in Schöneberg, near U-Bhf. Kleistpark), a sleek urban-American-looking bar that draws an attractive younger crowd.

For dancing, **Lipstick** (Richard Wagner Platz 5, in Charlottenburg), a large complex with a couple of bars and a game room as well as a dance floor, is mainly known as a lesbian disco, and weekends plus some weekdays are indeed women's nights. But it's quite fashionable for men, too, especially younger ones. Boy George was even holding court there one night when we were in town. Actually, we'd recommend it over most of Berlin's boy bars for male couples whose priority is high-energy dancing rather than cruising.

Since you've no doubt heard of world-famous megadisco **Metropol** (5 Nollendorfplatz—not to be confused with the men's hustler-boy disco **Metropolis,** at Kleiststraße 35), we should mention that it has not for some time been as gay as it used to be; now it's mostly just a mixed young-crowd hangout. But the sound system is still impressive, the huge prewar former theater building is terrific-looking, and Nollendorf is old Isherwood territory, as well as modern gay turf, so you'll be in the neighborhood anyway.

In case you're interested in a real traditional prewar Berlin experience—drag bars intended for straight tourists—you can't beat the "ladies" at **Chez Nous** (Marburger Straße 14, only 100 yards or so from the Europa Center).

Musts-to-avoid for women include Levi/leather Tom's Place and the even heavier leather Knast, both men-only backroom clubs. Would-be gay male patrons of these places are advised to leave the Chi pants, beach sandals, and any light-colored cotton apparel in their hotel rooms; Dad's World War II hand-me-downs might be just the thing. Actually, if you're as vanilla as we are, hanging out next door to Tom's at **Pool,** a hot dancing bar that draws a young and pretty crowd, would be an even safer idea.

For outdoor cruising, film buffs will certainly want to check out the popular *Taxi Zum Klo* **public toilets** near the Siegesäule (Victory Column), and the surrounding *Tiergarten.*

In (former) East Berlin

The most attractive gay cafés are the coffee-and-wine bar **Ecke Schönhauser,** also referred to by locals as Café Peking (Kastienallee 2; U-Bhf. Dimitroffstraße; tel. 448 33 31; open daily 11 A.M.–11 P.M. or midnight), and **Café Senefelder** (Schönhauser Allee 173; U-Bhf. Senefelder Platz; tel. 282 77 85; open from 7 P.M., except Mondays).

Also near the Dimitroffstraße U-Bhf. stop is **Schoppenstube** (Schönhauser Allee 44; tel. 448 16 89; closed Sundays and Mondays), especially popular with young, attitudinous gay men. A place more popular with lesbians than with gay men is the **Bänsch Café,** on Bänschstraße in the area of the Frankfurter Tor U-Bhf. station.

A particularly rustic-looking traditional gay local is **Altberliner Bierstuben** (Saarbrücker Straße 17; U-Bhf. Senefelder Platz; tel 282 89 33; open from 11 A.M.).

Mixed gay and straight but somewhat gay-popular is the **Opern Café** (Unter den Linden 5; open at 5:30 P.M.).

The most popular disco by far, for both lesbians and gay men (though usually there are more men) is **Buschallee** (Buschallee 87), which is actually used as a school canteen during the day. There's serious *Gesichtskontrolle* (face control) here—they prefer good-looking people, as well as those from Western countries; so let the doorfolk overhear you speaking English, and/or arrive early in the evening, when it's easier to get in. (To get there, take the no. 70 tram from Friedrichstraße station, and get out at the second stop in the Buschallee. The building is near the school and set back from the road, behind the Kaufhalle supermarket.)

WHERE (AND WHAT) TO EAT

Gay-oriented restaurants mentioned in the text include: **Dinelo** [see "Where to Go (Night)" for address], for women only; and **Hofgarten** (Regensburger Straße 5, corner of Ansbacher Straße; tel. 24 18 83) for reasonably priced, inventive, and extremely tasty internationally-oriented vegetarian and lighter meat dishes (plus great salads). This dark, cozy neighborhood bistro draws *many* gay men and women.

Also popular with gay people and with the arts crowd in general, is the very fashionable but friendly **Paris Bistro** (Kantstraße 152), which serves foie gras, salade niçoise, and other nice, nouvelle-ish French preparations—strong on fish.

A gay-oriented restaurant near Savignyplatz in Charlottenburg that is quite inexpensive and recommended for meat-eaters who want to try typical German specialties is the small, casual **Bistro 125** (Kantstraße 25). The regular menu does not offer any vegetarian or fish dishes. And for those who want a second breakfast, or just a cup of dynamite cappuccino, the cute Vienna-esque **Savigny Café,** just north of Savignyplatz on Grolmannstraße, attracts a relaxed, magazine-browsing gay clientele.

Conveniently near the Schwuz in Kreuzberg is restaurant **Hasenburg** (Fichte-straße 1), a gay-friendly, elegant place (waiters in tails) with "nouvelle *Kuchen"* food: gravlax in lemon cream sauce, veal with wild mushrooms, steamed broccoli, and rye in tomato sabayon.

WHERE TO GET THE LATEST DIRT (INFORMATION RESOURCES)

Mann-o-Meter (Motzstraße 5, 1000 Berlin 30) is a gay (and lesbian, in theory, but in practice mostly for men) info center that has its own café, where both men and women are welcome. Info hotline: 216 80 08, Sunday–Friday 3 P.M.–11 P.M. They say they'll answer inquiries by mail, too.

Lesbian info line: 215 20 00, Monday–Thursday 5 P.M.–8 P.M.

AIDS info line: Berliner AIDS-hilfe, Meinekestraße 12, Berlin 15; open 10 A.M.–6 P.M.; tel. 883 30 17 (24 hours) or 882 55 53.

Frauen Infothek (Leibnizstraße 57, fourth floor, 1000 Berlin 12; tel. 324 50 78; open 9 A.M.–9 P.M., except Sundays until 3 P.M. and closed Mon.) Near the Ku'damm, this service can help out in all sorts of ways. They can advise you on addresses/descriptions of women's bars and restaurants, as well as good places to shop. They'll design and/or arrange women's bike and walking tours of the city (and actually, guys, there's even one woman who's an Isherwood address buff). Prefer a super-safe hotel? The organization keeps a list of places in all price ranges, meeting certain standards of lighting, etc. They can help groups to set up a feminist conference, or individuals to set up a visit to Berlin's lesbian archive, Spinnboden.

A newer women's info center is **Lesberlin,** Kohlfurther Straße 40, D-1000 Berlin 36, Germany. They publish a directory of women's groups and a newspaper.

For the address and phone number of the **Schwuz** (Schwulenzentrum), see "Where to Go (Night)."

A few local city guides and periodicals are most useful. A very inexpensive pocket book is **Berlin-Report Für Freunde** (published by Club 70, Eberstraße 58, 1000 Berlin 62; tel. 784 17 86). Club 70 is a cruisy men's hustler bar/pension, but the guide is for all sorts of places, mostly male-oriented saunas, sex shops, boutiques, and clubs, but many establishments welcoming lesbians too; there's even a little general tourist info. For women: **Blattgold** (Potsdamer Straße 139, 1000 Berlin 30; tel. 215 66 28), has an events calendar and list of women's resources. The relatively new male-oriented monthly **Magnus** (Monumenten-straße 33–34, 1000 Berlin 62; tel. 784 30 31) also has some events listings and ads. All the above are in German; but if you know that *"geöffnet von 11 bis 23 Uhr ausser Sonntag und Montag"* means "open from 11 A.M. to 11 P.M. except Sunday and Monday," and can manage the other days of the week *(Dienstag, Mittwoch, Donnerstag, Freitag, Sonnabend)*, you've pretty well got it.

An absolutely wonderful gay bookstore, for Berlin or anywhere else, is **Prinz Eisenherz Buchladen** (Bleibtreaustraße 52, 1000 Berlin 12; tel. 313 99 36). The place is spacious and has an outstanding selection of English-language gay books; not many are lesbian, but many are in ordinarily hard-to-find areas (like gay-related theater, and both fiction and nonfiction about early twentieth-century Berlin), and there's a complete selection of international periodicals and guides, too. The English-speaking people who work here are also extraordinarily friendly, offering information and recommendations for nightspots; and if you want any publications before hitting town, they take credit cards and do mail-order.

For women, **Lilith Buchladen** (Knesebeckstraße 86–87; tel. 312 31 02) is where to pick up your *Blattgold* and perhaps the German lesbian review *Lesben-stich*, which also contains an updated resource list. A friendly place, though English books and English-speakers are almost as minimal as our German.

Gay-rights and self-help organizations include: **Schwulenberatugsstelle** (Kulmer Straße 20a, Berlin 30, in Schöneberg, tel. 215 90 00); and the Berlin **government's gay office,** the Stelle fur Gleichgeschlechtliche Lebensweisen, Senatsverwaltung fur Frauen, Jugend und Familie (Am Karlsbad 8–10, D-1000 Berlin 30; tel. 26 04).

In what used to be East Berlin, an excellent gay resource is **Courage** (PSF 121, 1051 Berlin for mail; or, for drop-ins, Knaackstraße 7 [Prenzlauer Allee], from 5:30 P.M. to 7:30 P.M. Monday through Friday; tel. 588 08 33 or 449 11 84). This organization offers opportunities for gays and lesbians to meet and talk, as well as advice, gay-rights work, lectures, meetings, and more. Other long-standing gay groups are the **Sonntagsclub** (PSF 229, 1030 Berlin) and **Lesben in der Kirche (LIK)** (c/o Dagmar Harmsen, Str. d. Pariser Kommune 34, Berlin 1035; tel. 589 64 07). Additionally, there is now reportedly a gay center in this part of town, housed in a squat on Mainzer Straße.

For general Berlin info **Informationszentrum Berlin** (20 Hardenbergerstraße, second floor) has several impressive free booklets (one almost 100 pages long), far better than the average shallow tourist fare, that go into some depth about Berlin's history, cultural life, organizations, facilities for minority groups (including ours), and political situation—in English. Maps and more tourist-oriented brochures are available at the **Tourist Information Office** in the Europa Center, on Budapesterstraße; they'll also book a room for you, if you need one, for a few marks' fee.

WHAT TO READ

Before the Deluge: A Portrait of Berlin in the 20s, by Otto Friedrich (Fromm). Not a gay take, but a good history of the era.

Lost Berlin, by Susanne Everett (Galley). A picture book showing the city as it was.

Lesbian Feminism in Turn-of-the-Century Germany, ed. Lillian Faderman and Brigitte Eriksson (Naiad). Although Germany was indeed the primary place the first sexologists emerged, at the turn of the century, you'll nevertheless be astonished at the lesbian doings there, back in a time when American women didn't even exist below the waist. Some stories, some essays—all a good read.

Magnus Hirschfeld: A Portrait of a Pioneer in Sexology, by Charlotte Wolf, M.D. (Quartet). Turgid and not terribly illuminating of the private man, but the most complete work in English of his life.

The Pink Triangle: The Nazi War Against Homosexuals, by Richard Plant (New Republic). The most up-to-date account on the subject.

Mephisto, by Klaus Mann (Penguin). Actor deserts politics, morals, and loved ones for fame in Nazi Germany. Based on Mann's real-life brother-in-law/lover (though the real-life homosexuality is disguised in the novel).

The Hustler, by John Henry Mackay (Alyson). A novel colorfully evoking the flavor of the lower-class gay hustler subculture in 1920s Berlin.

The Pious Dance, by Klaus Mann (GMP). An important 1920s semiautobiographical novel, portraying Berlin between the wars: the art scene, the disillusioned youth, the gay underworld.

Berlin Stories, by Christopher Isherwood (New Directions). The classic; includes the "Sally Bowles" segment on which *Cabaret* was based, without the show's gratuitous heterosexuality. Most interesting if read back to back with the book below.

Christopher and His Kind, by Christopher Isherwood (Farrar, Straus & Giroux). In retrospect, the older, wiser, and more secure Isherwood rejected his earlier closetiness in the *Berlin Stories* and other works. In this book, he laughs at his young self quite endearingly, corrects the pronouns, and tells the real stories.

WHERE TO STAY ON THE WAY

Our wonderful lady in fairy-tale **Goslar** is Margot Schünemann, who runs the very *inexpensive* **Haus Schünemann** (Claustorwall 18, 3380 Goslar; tel. 05321/ 233 69). The charming old house is in a garden, and some rooms have private bath. Vacation apartments are also available, if you want to hang out and really eyeball the town's muraled houses for a while.

If you eat at Goslar's Ratskeller (Markt 3), where the food is fine, don't believe it if your waiter tells you, as ours told us, that service is not included on your bill. It is.

ℬAVARIA

A King and
His Dream Castles

*Once upon a time, in a forested mountain kingdom way in
the south of Germany, there lived a handsome young
prince. He grew up in a gingerbread castle, which he liked so much that he
built three other castles that were even more magical-looking. He had
beautiful curly ringlets, and a golden coach, and even a boat shaped like a
swan, just like in a fairytale. But better! Because this prince was real . . .*

We've always wanted to begin a piece with "Once upon a time," because our favorite childhood stories, from the *Book of Knowledge*, started
out that way. This was an old-fashioned encyclopedia that must have been
popular in its time, since every grandmother on both our blocks owned a
set. Each volume was full of useful real-life information we'd naturally
ignore in order to pore over the fairy tales, which were full of beautiful
princesses we'd also ignore, as they never did a blessed thing except get

themselves locked in towers from which they'd have to be rescued by handsome young princes.

These were different creatures altogether. These we'd daydream about. Not about marrying them, though; gross! About becoming them.

It was the illustrations in the *Book of Knowledge* that made this fantasy possible. In a sense, they were our first gay pinups. Because instead of broad-shouldered fledgling "real" men, they invariably depicted delicate multiringleted cuties wearing tunic-and-pump ensembles that looked like modified ballet costumes. Obviously, to an already odd but shrewd seven-year-old mind seeking the best options, these princes were *girls!* Or better: some sort of evolved eternal boy-girl hybrids, who got to do all the best girl stuff like flounce around in sissy clothes, and not have whiskers, and get good haircuts (this was the 1950s, when little boys' barbers had all apparently trained at the Perdue School of Chicken Plucking); but who also got to do all the best boy stuff like tear around the kingdom on horseback—or in golden coaches, or in boats pulled by swans—having adventures that were gloriously exciting yet safely idealized. They involved dream dragon-fights rather than boring, bloody real-life territorial warfare, and chivalry rather than sex . . . Well, at least until considerably after the final "And They Lived Happily Ever After."

Sure, none of the above was reality. But for very young potentially gay people, reality sucked. Fantasies and dreams were all we had.

Thus it was with the prince in our story above, who never stooped to substance when style was available, and who was at least as charming as any guy Cinderella ever brought home. His hairdo, for instance. "If I didn't have my hair curled every day," he once explained, "I couldn't enjoy my food." Even his best friend, Empress Elizabeth of Austria, could not sway him from his resolve though she laughed uproariously one day when the prince showed up for an army function with his helmet in one hand and a large open umbrella in the other. "I've no intention," he scolded her angrily, "of spoiling my coiffure."

One of the most famous operatic composers of all time—who wouldn't have had the chance to complete many of his most important works had it not been for the support of the prince—wrote to a friend, "You cannot begin to imagine the magic of his eyes." This admirer was, by the way, quite hetero otherwise: Richard Wagner, composer of *Tristan und Isolde,* every straight frat boy's favorite music to seduce girls by.

Another emotional captive, a young Hessian officer who only glimpsed the prince once, briefly, during an insultingly overdue review of his troops (the prince thought modern warfare hideous), later told his grandchild, "He was so divinely beautiful that my heart stopped beating. I was so deeply moved that a terrible thought seized me: This godlike youth is too beautiful for this world."

Unfortunately, this appraisal turned out to be quite true. And it's why we can't end with "And So He Lived Happily Ever After."

Because as we already mentioned, this story is not a fairy tale but mere real life. It is the story of Ludwig II, ruler of the former kingdom (now province) of Bavaria, known to most people only as "Mad King Ludwig" —an appallingly unfair description. Better to describe him, as the French press did, even while France was still licking its wounds from a humiliating defeat by Germany in the Franco-Prussian War, as a Fairytale Prince. "He is not a wicked king," *Figaro* pointed out during Ludwig's visit to Versailles in 1874. "He has never even accompanied his soldiers, apart from on the piano."

To be more specific, he was Ludwig the generous, who was hated by his fellow royals but adored by his peasants; Ludwig the dreamer, who would spend his money on beautiful castles and beautiful music, instead of ugly wars; Ludwig the real-life fairy martyr, who had to die because his gay sensibilities wouldn't permit him to live as a bargain-hunting boor or a war-mongering bully, much less as a breeder of future royal boorish bullies; Ludwig, the physical dead-ringer for Vivien Leigh; Ludwig, the king who would be queen.

Ludwig was not Germany's only gay monarch, or even the most famous. There was, for example, Frederick the Great, King of Prussia from 1740 to 1786. By the time Frederick was eighteen, his annoyed father, King Frederick William I, had already attempted to teach his son a lesson by having his lover of several years, twenty-six-year-old Lieutenant Hans von Katte, publicly executed. As the young officer was marched to the block, Frederick, from his balcony, blew his *Freundin* a kiss and called, "A thousand pardons, please, my dear Katte." The lieutenant called back, "My prince, there is nothing to forgive"; and was promptly beheaded.

Ludwig's diaries indicate no sexual activity until he was at least twenty-two, and even then, his liaisons—with his equerry, Richard Hornig, and actor Joseph Kainz, among others, mostly social underlings—appear to have been alternately ecstatic and religiously guilt-ridden. The journals are filled with anguished attempts to "purify" himself by going cold turkey on sex altogether. Although, fortunately, the decor of Ludwig's castles doesn't reflect any of this religious fanaticism, he was apparently quite spiritual from his childhood. His mother Queen Marie's diary noted that at age six, little Ludwig particularly enjoyed dressing up as a nun.

Frederick's sexual attitudes were a good deal more tolerant, as well as pragmatic. Once, upon noticing an excellent cavalry soldier in chains, he discovered that the man's offense was bestiality with his horse. "Then don't put him in irons, fools," Frederick exclaimed. "Put him in the infantry."

Frederick's military genius also placed him squarely in the real world, as did his willingness to accept an arranged political marriage with Princess Elizabeth Christine of Brunswick. Ludwig, however, was not able to go through with a marriage to his cousin Sophie, sister of his buddy the Empress of Austria. And though he did twice commit Bavaria to war, he only did so reluctantly. From an early age he'd been fascinated by the medieval concept of chivalry. Murals relating the sagas of the Holy Grail, Tannhäuser, and Lohengrin fill the walls of Hohenschwangau castle, where Ludwig grew up; some legends even claimed that the Swan Knight had lived there. But real warfare Ludwig found repugnant.

The twenty-one-year-old monarch's reaction to his first military conflict, the disastrous Seven Weeks' War against Prussia in 1866, was to first flee to Switzerland, with the idea of possibly abdicating, and then to retire with his current favorite, Prince Paul von Thurn und Taxis, to strict ostrichlike seclusion at his summer residence Schloß Berg. There, the pair set off nightly fireworks. On the very day war was declared, a minister who had been denied access to confer with Ludwig forced his way in and found the king and Prince Von T. & T. in a darkened room lit by an artificial moon; they were dressed as Barbarossa and Lohengrin. (Ludwig's personal correspondence includes numerous notes to the Court Theater, requesting the temporary loan of period costumes.)

At the conclusion of Ludwig's second, and more successful, military venture, the Franco-Prussian War, he couldn't even bring himself to go to Versailles for the crowning of Wilhelm of Prussia as Emperor of Germany. Claiming he had a toothache, Ludwig sent his younger brother, who doubtless made quite an impression as an emissary: Otto was far enough into insanity by then that he was subject to fits of weeping, making terrible faces, and barking like a dog. For what it's worth, Prussian chancellor Bismarck nevertheless commented, on the basis of correspondence with Ludwig, that he "had always had the impression of him being a businesslike and clear-cut ruler." Formal affairs of state, Bismarck felt, simply bored the king.

What Ludwig found fascinating was, first, the romance of the theater, particularly heroic opera—and most particularly the operas and person of Richard Wagner. By the age of thirteen, the prince had memorized the libretti of *Tannhäuser* and *Lohengrin*. At sixteen, the first time he actually saw a live production of Wagner's works, he became so convulsed with emotion at one point that observers feared he was developing epilepsy. When he became king at age eighteen, in 1864, one of his first acts was to seek out Wagner to offer financial support. This couldn't have come at a better time for the sybaritically inclined composer, who was in hiding from his creditors with an unfinished *Ring des Nibelungen* and a *Tristan* whose extravagant staging had made it impossible for any opera house to produce.

What followed was an intense six-year love affair. It was possibly, even probably, unconsummated, unless you want to count as "issue" *Das Rheingold, Die Walküre,* and *Siegfried* from the Ring cycle, and *Die Meistersinger,* all of which were birthed during this time, thanks to Ludwig's patronage. But it was certainly by all accounts a mutual infatuation, though cynical analysts would have to conclude that from a practical standpoint—with Ludwig paying Wagner's enormous debts, buying him several houses, building him theaters, and giving him a generous allowance as well as a horse carriage, a Lohengrin picture–pocketwatch, swan cufflinks, and other gifts—Wagner did a whole lot more receiving than giving.

Still, what is one to think of letters like the one from Wagner to a friend in 1864, describing the first meeting between composer and king as "one great love scene"? Or how about this extract: "Shall I be able to renounce women completely? With a deep sigh I confess I could almost wish it! Now he is everything to me, world, wife, and child!" Or: "It is a beautiful relationship. . . . Often we sit in complete silence, lost in each other's eyes." And in return, from Ludwig, on the occasion of Wagner's first visit to the king's childhood home, Hohenschwangau: "What bliss enfolds me! A wonderful dream has become a reality. . . . I am in your angelic arms!"

By 1871, the honeymoon was over. Wagner's jingoistically pro-Prussian wartime sentiments and his other political meddling had long made him remarkably unpopular in Munich, and the new success rendered possible by Ludwig's support now made it also possible for Wagner to desert both Ludwig's capital city and Ludwig. Like an unfaithful lover who's reluctant to desert his ex until his new affair is a certainty, Wagner spent much of the Franco-Prussian War covertly negotiating for a base in Bayreuth, only informing Ludwig he was leaving when his control of the new theater was a fait accompli.

The disloyalty hurt Ludwig deeply, though he continued to support Wagner financially, making possible the completion and production of *Götterdämmerung* and *Parsifal.* Fortunately, the king had already developed a new romantic interest: building his castles.

If you've been to Disneyland or Walt Disney World, you've already seen Ludwig's first and most famous castle—or at least, something a lot like it. Neuschwanstein, started in 1868, is the model for Fantasyland's castle-entrance, although even Uncle Walt couldn't duplicate its Alpine setting, with towers cleaving the clouds on a mountaintop high above the Alpsee.

We should perhaps mention here that *See* means "lake" in German. It's a word one encounters often in Bayern (the German name of Bavaria). While much of this huge southern German province, which covers between a third and a quarter of what used to be West Germany, is rolling meadow and forest land, the extreme southern Bavarian Alps and foothills around Munich where Ludwig built all of his castles, are dotted with dozens of deep blue lakes left behind by retreating glaciers during the last ice age. Surrounding the lakes are green valleys also carved by glacial action; and these in turn are surrounded by jagged snow-capped mountain peaks rising to heights of almost three thousand meters. In some of southern Bavaria's villages, the steep mountain bases literally run right into the town streets. This is dramatic country, to say the least.

In the same town as Neuschwanstein, though in a less precipitously pinnacled setting, is lakeside Hohenschwangau, Ludwig's gingerbread-castle boyhood home. There are two other castles as well on the compleat Ludwig tour: Linderhof, the only one of his creations totally completed during Ludwig's lifetime, is 15 miles from Neuschwanstein, and Herren-chiemsee is on a lake within an hour's drive.

In his last years, the king developed a passion for all-night sleigh and coach rides, often in Bourbon-era or medieval costumes, during which he easily more than covered the distance between his castles. Although we don't advise it, present-day visitors could certainly also hit all three in one day, if pressed for time, or if they were just giving Germany a trial run, and weren't quite sure how it was going to turn out.

This is admittedly how we, as a gay couple, felt before our first stay in Germany—especially the half of the couple that's of part-Jewish ancestry. We realize it would hardly be fair of us, as citizens of the country that brought the world Vietnam and numerous Central American atrocities, among others, to get politically self-righteous. But we also know that the idea of vacationing in Germany makes some historically-aware gay travelers uneasy, even when they know perfectly well that, realistically, right-wing extremists in Britain and in our own country are probably more of a threat to sexual and other minority groups today. Looking around at those fairy-tale landscapes and thinking, "If we lived in one of these cute gingerbread houses fifty years ago, we'd have been turned into smoked salmon," just affects some of us like that, emotionally.

We got over our Germanophobia years ago, but if you have any such tendencies, you ought to know that Bavaria was Hitler's power base and favorite region. The site of his "Eagle's Nest" is in Berchtesgaden, right in the heart of Ludwig country. Bavaria is and always has been the most conservative, traditional province in the country—and the traditions aren't all folksy cute stuff like lederhosen, brush-feathered loden hats, and Okto-berfest. Until appallingly recently—we're talking twenty or thirty years after World War II—the famous once-per-decade Oberammergau Passion Play retained a centuries-old anti-Semitic "Jews killed Our Lord" tone. Oberammergau is less than eight miles from Schloß Linderhof, and cute as a stag-horn button. One could easily be tempted to base oneself at one of the town's painted-front guest houses. We didn't. Most recently, the province of Bavaria distinguished itself by becoming one of the few places in the West to require HIV antibody tests of foreigners who want to move there.

Still, history is seldom simplistically black and white. Bavaria was also the home of sexual-emancipation pioneer Karl Ulrichs, arguably the first gay person to publicly come out, in the sense of defining gayness as a whole sexual and emotional orientation, rather than as an occasional sex act. After an 1854 sex scandal forced him to quit his job as a civil-service attorney, Ulrichs argued several times with Munich juries, in favor of de-criminalizing sex between men; he based his arguments on the ground that gays were an actual class of people subjected to legal persecution for merely being themselves. He was also responsible for several other gay "firsts": drafting, in 1865, a set of bylaws for an "Urning Union," the first plan for a homosexual-rights group; and, in 1870, publishing one issue of the first gay male magazine.

For gay visitors today, it's undeniable that Bavaria isn't Berlin, or even Hamburg. But the gay scene in relaxingly cosmopolitan, liberal Munich is exciting, varied, and ample. There are almost forty gay bars catering to all tastes in decor, music, atmosphere, clothing, and gender preference. There is a women's bookstore, center, and hotline. There are over half a dozen gay restaurants, and even a couple of morning-after cafés where one can go to drink suprisingly decent cappuccino, while comparing eye bags and other damages with fellow disco denizens.

Hardcore gay-history buffs will also find indispensable a visit to Munich's 1859 Hofbräuhaus, which, while not a gay bar, is the local where Ludwig's earthy mom, Queen Marie of Prussia, used to hang out drinking, banging her stein to the live Bavarian music (still oompah-ing away nightly) and majestically dispensing tokens for free liters of beer to the general populace. *Bier* is, by the way, what all gay imbibers with their heads screwed on straight will drink in Bavaria. But terminal-case *Weißwein* (white wine) sippers will want to know that the only way to get a bottle of anything that does not taste like it ought to be poured over waffles is to forget all the usual phrasebooook terms for "dry," and order your wine *pfurztrocken*. That means "dry as a fart." It also means that your *Kellner* or *Kellnerin* (waiter or waitress—addressed as *Herr Ober* or *Fräulein*) will totally crack up on the spot, and give you great service.

There are a few gay-oriented hotels in Munich. But we strongly recommend that all but the most hopeless nightlife addicts stay instead at a gay-friendly establishment in one of the small towns near Ludwig's castles, and commute up to Munich for an occasional live fag or fagette fix. We find particularly charming the less-gentrified Garmisch half of Garmisch-Parten-kirchen, coupled Alpine-valley resort towns surrounded by towering mountains, where many guest houses still look as though Rumpelstiltskin vacated the premises only yesterday. This visually spectacular area at the base of the Zugspitze, Germany's highest peak, was the inspiration for one of Ludwig's earliest Oriental-style building ventures, an 1870 Turkish-Bavarian renovation of one of his father King Max's hunting huts. You can still climb to the site, right below the six-thousand-foot Schachen, on one of the Wetterstein mountains just south of Garmisch-Partenkirchen.

From a practical standpoint, having a base near the castles makes it lots easier to arrive near opening hour, beating the hordes of tourists commuting from the cities.

From an emotional standpoint, staying in the sticks is what will best enable you to understand why all those fairy tales were written in rural Germany, and why Ludwig so loved all those solitary moonlit sleigh rides around his prototype Magic Kingdom.

Neuschwanstein has been featured on roughly two out of every three Bavarian travel posters printed in the last, oh, hundred years or so. So it's hardly surprising that German tourist personnel consider the almost unbelievable picturesqueness of this structure a rather mixed blessing, at this point—even more of a Bavarian pictorial cliché than those rustic red-cheeked fellows in lederhosen, jovially hoisting ceramic beer steins. In fact, the last time we wandered into the German National Tourist Office in New York for a few pamphlets, a wild-eyed female official, who was evidently in charge of new publicity-poster designs, actually had one poor photographer who'd innocently asked about possible subject matter backed clear against the office wall. "Anything!" she hissed. "Anyplace! Any picture at all would be fine . . . except *that castle* again!"

Most posters feature the long view of this nouveau-medieval German knights' castle perched atop a craggy foothill of the Tegelberg, which sure doesn't feel like any foothill when you're struggling up its heights on your own two feet, as you must, to visit the castle. Still, the breathless climb enables you to get a view that is breathtaking even on a miserably overcast day: tall, circular, witchy towers rising high above you, illuminated only by an occasional narrow beam of sunlight that has managed to spear through the surrounding fog and dark forest foliage.

The castle was intended by Ludwig as a shrine to Lohengrin, Tannhäuser, Parsifal, and the age of German chivalry in general. Also as a place Ludwig could get away from his mother, who was too often in attendance at Hohenschwangau. It's well worth making time, incidentally, to visit the latter. Hohenschwangau, the twelfth-century headquarters of the Schwangau Knights, was renovated by Ludwig's father, King Max, in Biedermeier (very romantic Gothic) style. While not as spectacular as Ludwig's own creations, Hohenschwangau is not exactly a toilet. Ornate gilded-wood carvings, florid full-wall murals, and even some Oriental touches make it quite clear that Ludwig's flamboyance didn't come from nowhere.

Not infrequently, we've read critiques indicating disappointment with Neuschwanstein's interior. Except that the late-Romanesque-revival exterior and magical setting are hard to beat, it's difficult to understand where that disappointment comes from. To us, what's invariably disappointing is the inside of every *authentic* medieval castle we've ever been in. Stark, stiff, no style, no pizzazz, no time-trippy atmosphere—the real things just don't look anywhere near as good as our dreams of them.

What's really needed for the perfect high-melodrama effect is a Hollywood-type rendition of a castle. And that's exactly what Ludwig got at Neuschwanstein and at his other two castles as well, by employing the Munich Court Theater's stage and costume designers, Christian Jank and Franz Seitz, to work with his regular court architect, Georg Dollmann. Each of the three castles does have a very different real historical style as a jumping-off point; but all three finished products are Ludwig's own personal vision of the genuine style—outrageous, dramatic stage-set versions.

Neuschwanstein is a Byzantine–Romanesque–late Gothic combo, with overdone Teutonic overtones over all: much ornately carved dark oak paneling, colorful vaulted ceilings enameled with stars and various Oriental designs, intricate mosaic floors, and fake (painted) "tapestries" of Wagnerian opera themes, like the Parsifal and Holy Grail murals in the Singers' Hall. During the sadly brief time Ludwig lived to enjoy his creation, no singers ever got to play in the Singers' Hall. But modern opera queens can hear Wagnerian concerts here, every September.

In contrast to Neuschwanstein's Alpine exhibitionism, Linderhof, a former hunting hut intended, like the Grand Trianon, as a poetic retreat and private pleasure sanctuary, is securely tucked into an idyllic green clearing amid the deeply wooded hills of the Graswang valley. The style is a sort of impure German baroque-gone-bozo on the outside, combined with an interior of riotous Bavarian, Franconian, *and* French rococo. It's not easy even to make out walls beneath the layers of gold froufrou twizzles, mirrors, tapestries, crystal chandeliers and candelabra, lapis and malachite mosaic-like designs, exotic Oriental vases, and trompe l'oeil murals. If we had to choose only one of the three castles to visit, it would be this one.

Everybody's favorite Linderhof gimmick is the dining room's *Tischlein deck-dich* ("little table that sets itself"). This elevator table could be lowered through the floor to the kitchen below, enabling servants to clear and reset courses without intruding on the privacy of shy Ludwig. Not that he always dined alone. Often, according to kitchen boys, Ludwig ordered food for three or four, maintaining that he had guests—usually Louis XIV, Louis XV, Madame de Maintenon, and Madame de Pompadour, with whose ghosts he would occasionally even carry on dinnertime conversations.

What makes Linderhof especially wonderful, though, is its outbuildings. There's a Moorish kiosk (from Paris) with peacock throne, to which the king and his retinue would retire to smoke hookahs. And, best of all: an all-artificial underground grotto complete with a secret "open sesame" boulder door, cement-coated cast-iron stalactites, a waterfall, a lake with artificial waves and a swan boat, a backdrop from the first act of *Tannhäu-*

ser, a heating system, and the first electric-light installation in Bavaria—red for Tannhäuser's Grotto of Venus, blue for the Blue Grotto in Capri. To make absolutely sure of the correct shade of blue, the king actually sent a personal representative to Capri. Twice.

Herrenchiemsee, modeled after Versailles as a more expansive public-feeling state palace, is set on a flat island surrounded by sculptured formal gardens. Don't allow this dignified setting to lure you into thinking that Herrenchiemsee is boring, however. Tasteless, Ludwig could do. Boring, never. The decor is in the style of Ludwig's idol Louis XIV, run rampant—half again as big, twelve zillion times as colorful. As one of the palace's first royal visitors graciously put it, "The palace of Versailles seemed by comparison almost like a desolate ruin in its pallid splendor."

An extra at Herrenchiemsee is a museum of Ludwig's life, all in German, but easily accessible to non–*Deutsch* speakers. The king's sexual orientation is not gone into in the museum's printed material. Surprisingly, though, the English-speaking tour guides at all three castles seemed quite familiar with Ludwig's boyfriends, and willing to talk. One female guide at Linderhof voluntarily and quite matter-of-factly brought up the subject herself, in answer to a question about possible reasons for Ludwig's undeserved bad rep with his fellow royals—much to the surprise of the pot-bellied straight redneck Texan who'd asked.

Simultaneously amusing and sad are the museum's drawings of three new palaces Ludwig was planning when he died: a mock-Gothic robber-baron's eyrie, a Byzantine number, and a Chinese summer palace, in which the whole court would be required to wear Chinese dress. These plans were the last straw for his humorless cabinet and greedy extended family, who could see the entire House of Wittelsbach fortune, which had been built up over eight hundred years, blown in one generation. The king had spent no state money, only his own royal income of about five million marks annually, on his building projects. But he *had* borrowed a tad: roughly twenty-one million marks.

To put this sum in perspective, it was less than the amount of reparations Bavaria had been compelled to pay Prussia for losing the totally pointless Seven Weeks' War, which Ludwig hadn't even wanted to fight. These same cabinet members and nobles had considered those reparations a miraculous bargain. But fairy-tale castles for fairy princes were a reckless extravagance. The aristocrats were looking for an excuse to rid themselves of this big spender. And given Ludwig's eccentricities, they didn't have to look too far.

They first came for the king on June 10, 1866, at Neuschwanstein. They didn't get him.

Alerted by a groom, who'd been alarmed when one of the conspirators had forbidden him to hitch up the horses for the king's nightly ride, assorted peasants and the volunteer fire brigades from all the surrounding villages flocked to protect their sovereign when a state commission showed up at the castle, at four A.M., to take him. The volunteers' defense efforts were aided by one of Ludwig's lovelorn local groupies, a certain Baroness Spera von Truchsess, who arrived in quite a state of indignation, verbally abused individual members of the commission ("You, Graf Törring: your children must be ashamed of you! And Minister Crailsheim: with you I shall never again play piano duets!"); and then, wielding her parasol as a weapon, forced her way into the castle after inviting all to join her in a resounding "Long live the king!"

The commission retreated in confusion; its members were immediately arrested by Ludwig, who then relented and let them go after a few hours. But two days later they returned—and, with the help of a trusted servant, who, unbeknownst to the king, was one of the conspirators, captured him.

The damning medical report read, in part: "His Majesty is, in advanced degree, insane and is suffering from that form of derangement known as paranoia . . . Because of his illness, his Majesty is not able to make decisions of his own free will."

Now admittedly, there had been a good bit of inbreeding in the Wittelsbach family. Ludwig's truly unbalanced brother, Otto, was a victim. Otherwise, though? Well, okay, there *was* that sister of the king's father, Max, whose whole life had been confused by her firm conviction that at some point early on, she'd swallowed a grand piano made of glass. But to cite as evidence of congenital insanity, as this 1886 medical report did, a relative who had died sometime in the 1500s? Paranoia is supposedly an unjustified persecution complex. What do you call it when they're really persecuting you?

The report condemning Ludwig was signed by a panel of doctors from Munich, none of whom had ever personally examined or observed him. Their judgment was based entirely upon reports of out-of-favor lackeys, who had been instructed to spy and to steal any personal papers they could get their hands on. Bismarck characterized the evidence as "rakings from the king's wastepaper-basket." But there was quite a bit of it, since many servants did have grudges—the prince being no less imperious, and a good deal more deviously imaginative, than other monarchs. For example, one sore loser whom Ludwig found stupid had been compelled to wear a wax seal on his forehead, to indicate that his mind was sealed. Another, whom Ludwig considered an ass, had to don jester's clothes and sit on a donkey.

The most enthusiastic grudge holder was Ludwig's personal valet Mayr, who'd had to wear a black mask for the better part of a year, when the prince became annoyed and simply did not want to see Mayr's face. Believe you us: This vindictive poor sport would have to pay a *fortune* on Christopher Street for a mask like that today.

The main conspirator was Graf Max Holnstein, a former aide widely regarded even then as an unscrupulous adventurer. But probably the most heartbreaking betrayer, from the king's point of view, was his trusted equerry, Karl Hesselwerdt, whom Ludwig had purposely left in Munich to keep him informed of possible plots. Instead, the turkey sang. Who never did talk was Ludwig's last cabinet secretary Schneider, though he very much wanted to. He had collected three hundred messages the prince had sent to the cabinet over the last three years, none of which showed any sign of derangement. Schneider was never called for questioning. Paranoia?

Among assorted so-called evidences of insanity:

(1) Bad table manners. "His Majesty," testified Mayr, "splashes the gravy and vegetables all over his clothes."

(2) His hours. The king preferred to sleep during the day, rise at midnight, and party. He reveled in nocturnal rides, during which he often dropped in on peasant families, who were delighted to see him. He also favored moonlit picnics, to which he often invited grooms and lackeys, who were delighted to come. But the commission felt it was not normal to be a night person.

(3) His choice of dinner companions. Ludwig once invited his favorite horse to dine with him, on a menu of soup, fish, a roast, and wine—which, reportedly, the horse ate all of, with good appetite. (Personally, we think she sounds like superior company to the rest of Ludwig's court, even if she did finish by stepping on the dinner service.)

(4) Still at it after the prince's death, the Chamber of Councillors stated, on June 21, 1886, that it should be considered special proof of Ludwig's mental illness that he'd commissioned an inventor to build an aircraft to fly over the Bavarian mountains. The first airplanes began testing ten years later. Of course, Ludwig had sort of had in mind a chariot drawn by peacocks . . . But still.

As for Ludwig's inability to make decisions of his own free will, the problem was obviously exactly the opposite. This is how the king himself saw it. "It seems to me that in the household of life, there is room for only a single type of person. He who wants to be someone must be rough, coarse, or phlegmatic. Whoever is different is called eccentric by friend or foe."

When Ludwig asked how long the proposed insanity treatment might last, head commissioner Bernhard von Gudden replied that a year was the minimum time. "No, it won't take that long. They can do as they did to the Sultan," Ludwig replied, refering to a well-known political assassination of the day.

He was taken to Schloß Berg, which had already been equipped with spy holes in the doors, and holes for iron bars drilled in the windows. But Ludwig's keepers didn't have to bother with fitting the bars. On June 13, the king and Dr. Von Gudden failed to return from an evening walk, and were later discovered floating, dead, about twenty yards offshore on the

Starnberg lake. The king, according to a letter from Graf Philipp zu Eulenberg, secretary of the Prussian legation in Munich (who had just coincidentally happened to be in Starnberg that fateful day), had "an insane smile" on his face.

There was some talk of a bungled escape attempt: carriage tracks were found around the lake; and there were reports of flickering torches around the lake the previous night, as well as attempted signals from the undergrowth during the king's walk that morning. Some of the most reliable researchers feel Ludwig's death might have been a combination of all the above. No one has ever discovered what really happened.

The authorities called it suicide. The common people called it murder. In a display of weeping and fainting that was not equaled until Judy Garland's memorial service, they packed their Dream King's funeral chapel by the thousands.

King Ludwig's final smile? Take it from two who've seen the death mask in the Hohenschwangau museum. No way is this smile insane. Insufferably smug, perhaps. Ironic, definitely. It looks like the expression of someone who in his last seconds might have been remembering with great satisfaction and certainty a letter he wrote to Wagner back in 1864: "When we two are no more, our work will serve the world as a shining example. It will delight distant generations, hearts will glow with enthusiasm for the artistic genius which is God-given and eternal."

It's not "And They Lived Happily Ever After." But it's probably the best epitaph a fairy-tale prince in the real world could ever have: " 'Mad' King Ludwig II of Bavaria: They All Laughed—But Who Has the Last Laugh Now?"

PRACTICAL INFORMATION

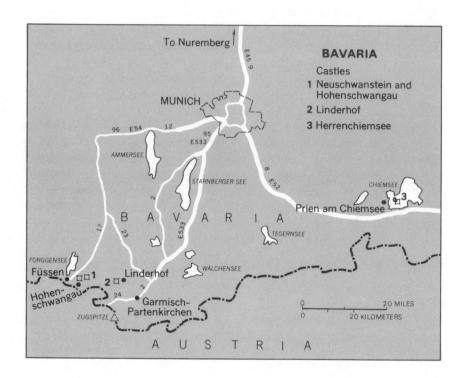

To Nuremberg

MUNICH

BAVARIA

Castles

1 Neuschwanstein and Hohenschwangau

2 Linderhof

3 Herrenchiemsee

AMMERSEE

STARNBERGER SEE

CHIEMSEE

Prien am Chiemsee

B A V A R I A

TEGERNSEE

FORGGENSEE

Füssen

Linderhof

WALCHENSEE

Hohen-schwangau

Garmisch-Partenkirchen

ZUGSPITZE

20 MILES

20 KILOMETERS

A U S T R I A

GENERAL HINTS / INFO

If gay life—meaning actual living gay people—were our vacation priority, we wouldn't go to Bavaria. Not that there aren't plenty of exciting bars in Bavaria's two major cities, München (Munich), the metropolitan area nearest to Ludwig's castles, and Nürnberg (Nuremburg) about 100 miles to the north. And certainly not that Munich and Nuremberg are awful cities. But we think the real enchantment of Bavaria is rural, in all those cute little Alpine towns that look like skierdwarfs built them. There really aren't any gay establishments in the sticks, at least none we or any of our German sources could identify. If you want to try out your own gay-dar while there, however, the verbal shrugs-of-the-shoulder

"Na denn," Na und" (So what?"), and "Why not?" are good bets for gay bar names, as is "Mylord," variously spelled.

For us, Bavaria is a historical destination focusing entirely on King Ludwig's dream castles; to get the feel, it's best to immerse oneself in the countryside near them.

Orientation: The nearest international airport is Munich-Riem. Linderhof castle is about 60 miles southwest, near Oberammergau, and reachable by car or bus from Munich via the A-95 autobahn. Neuschwanstein and Hohenschwangau castles are about 70 miles southwest of Munich, via the smaller roads B-12 to Landsberg and B-17 to the village of Hohenschwangau and larger town of Füssen three or four miles away; alternatively, the train trip from Munich to Füssen, via Kaufbeuren or Buchloe, takes about two hours. Herrenchiemsee castle is on an island in the Chiemsee, Bavaria's largest lake, about 60 miles southeast of Munich via the A-8 autobahn to Prien (on the lake); or take a one-hour train ride from Munich to Prien.

Currency unit: the Deutsche Mark (DM)

WHERE TO STAY

Not Munich. Ludwig himself spent as little time as possible in his Munich Residenz. You can always day-trip in, if you need a gay fix. There's only one exclusively gay hotel, Pension Eulenspiegel, anyway; and aside from the fact that the manager didn't want to be listed, it's located off a sort-of parking lot, and the interior has all the charm of a college dorm.

For hitting all of Ludwig's castles by public transportation, one Schloß per day, we found an ideal base to be Garmisch-Partenkirchen, a small-enough-to-be-cute town sunk in Alps at the foot of the Zugspitze, Germany's highest mountain. This sprawling village, split down the middle by the Partnach River, is actually two resorts that grew together. Being kitsch fans, we personally prefer the predominantly half-timbered Snow White–ish Garmisch side of town. Sophisticates, however, will no doubt opt for the fancier ski chalet–type hotels and restaurants in somewhat more gentrified Partenkirchen, to the east.

Most people who are interested in only seeing the Disneyesque Neuschwanstein, as opposed to doing the complete circuit of Ludwig's castles, stay in Füssen. However, the lodgings there tend to get quite packed in summer. We suggest instead staying right in Hohenschwangau, the small town in which the castle's located. This will enable you to get up to the Schloß at opening hour and beat the commuting hordes. It also gives you plenty of time to see Ludwig's fairly fantastic boyhood home, 1,000-year-old Schloß Hohenschwangau, in the afternoon—a disastrous time to visit Neuschwanstein, but fine for Hohenschwangau, which never gets the same cattle-pen sort of crowds.

Seasonal hotel rates remain constant except in summer mountaineering/winter skiing center Garmisch-Partenkirchen, where spring and fall prices are about 25 percent less. All prices include breakfast, and, are for a double room *(Doppelzimmer)* either *mit* or *ohne Bad* (with or without bath). And do remember that throughout Germany, a *Doppelbett* will never be a real double bed; your hotelier is not just being homophobic.

Listed hotels are not gay-oriented, but have, as usual, been Drilled as to whether us queers are welcome.

Prices: *Inexpensive* = under 60 DM; *moderate* = 60–90 DM; *mod./exp.* = 90–120 DM; *expensive* = 120–200 DM.

Haus Kellner. Alleestraße 19; tel. 13 44. This charming rose-covered seven-room guesthouse, with its equally charming proprietor Sonja Davis, couldn't be more fairy-tale–Bavarian perfect. Located on a narrow, quiet, wooded dirt road-let by the side of a rushing river, it seems idyllic yet is really only a block from the center of Garmisch. Our large sunny room had its own balcony overlooking an extensive lawn and garden, a lace-clothed table perfect for picnic dinners (and evidently watched over by elves; the day after we'd drunk wine from the room's water glasses, two wineglasses magically appeared) . . . and decor by Heidi. *Inexpensive.*

Schloßhotel Lisl und Jägerhaus. Hohenschwangau; tel. 08362/81006 or 81008; telex 541332 Lislh d. Schloß Hohenschwangau is an easy 10-minute walk, and one of the more strenuous of several mountain paths up to Neusch-wanstein is practically within spitting distance of this rustic hotel. Some of the large rooms are tastefully modern, while others have the more quaint decor we personally prefer: floral-garlanded wallpaper, scalloped easy chairs. Rooms come both with and without bathroom, and rates range widely. The hotel has a cute and reasonably priced porch restaurant where you can get lake fish and typical Bavarian dishes. *Moderate to expensive.*

Pension Weiher. Hofwiesenweg 11, 8959 Hohenschwangau; tel. 08362/81161. This seven-room pension at the foot of the castles is cheerful on the inside, a bit motelish on the outside (though much improved by flowered terraces and window boxes). Rooms come both with and without bathroom, and most have balconies from which one can see Neuschwanstein. If you show up without a reservation and the Weiher is full, the nice Oswald family who run the place says they'll help you find a room elsewhere. *Inexpensive–moderate.*

For those who want to visit **Schloß Linderhof** only, there are no hotels in Linderhof itself. There are, however, a number of accommodations in Graswang and Ettal, two towns seldom mentioned in American guides, but only three and six miles away respectively, and on the Europabus route. Walkers will be pleased to know that there are also numerous hiking trails connecting the towns in this rolling green hill country. For a list of guest houses in both towns, as well as private rooms to let (recognizable by a *"Zimmer frei"* sign), write the cordial Ettal tourist-info office (Gemeinde Ettal, Ammergauer Straße 8, 8107 Ettal; tel. 08822/534) and ask for their current *Gästezimmernachweis (Hotels, Privatver-mieter und Ferienwohnung).* They will also provide a little Linderhof/Ettal/Gras-wang map, to orient you.

For accommodations near **Schloß Herrenchiemsee,** write the tourist office in the lake's main town, Prien: Verkehrsverband Chiemsee, Rathausstraße 11, D-82 10 Prien.

If you must stay in Munich, there's a very popular older *mod./exp.* hotel/restaurant/bar with about 20 rooms and a large gay following (mostly men, but women welcome), called the **Deutsche Eiche** (Reichenbachstraße 13; tel. 089/26 84 77); it's well known among gays, so reservations are advised.

WHERE TO GO (DAY)

Schloß Linderhof is open 9 A.M.–5 P.M. in summer, 9 A.M.–4 P.M. in winter. **Neuschwanstein**'s hours are 8:30 A.M.–5:30 P.M. in summer, 10 A.M.–4:30 P.M. in winter; **Hohenschwangau**'s are 8:30 A.M.–5:30 P.M. in summer, 10 A.M.– 4 P.M. in winter. **Herrenchiemsee** is open 9 A.M.–5 P.M. in summer, 10 A.M.– 4 P.M. in winter. Admission to each is about $3–4.

For those relying on public **transportation**, Linderhof and Neuschwanstein/ Hohenschwangau are both served by Europabus, which is free with a Eurailpass and otherwise costs about $5 round-trip for Linderhof and $11 for Neuschwanstein. From the front of the Garmisch-Partenkirchen train station, four buses leave daily for nearby Linderhof (at 8:50 A.M., 10:15 A.M., 12:10 P.M., and 1:10 P.M.) and three to Neuschwanstein (at 8 A.M., 12:10 P.M., and 4:30 P.M.). But you will check these times, yes? And to avoid the worst castle crowds take the early bus, no matter how painful it is to arise at that unspeakable hour.

As we already mentioned, the town of Prien am Chiemsee (from which you catch the steamer to the Herreninsel, the island where Herrenchiemsee castle is located) is on a rail line. From the main rail station there, you can either take a little wooden-seated private steam train (not covered by Eurailpass), or follow the tracks on an easy walk down the main road to the lake.

If you're staying in Garmisch-Partenkirchen and have extra time after castling, there are fabulous **hikes** from here. One particularly spectacular and only mildly athletic one is through the Partnachklamm Gorge. Here, one walks along a high ledge trail—which often passes *behind* waterfalls—looking down at the river and up at 3,000 feet of mountains. Lots of **cable-car** and **funicular** rides leave from Garmisch-Partenkirchen, too. The **Verkehrsamt** (**tourist-information office**), just a little to the left of the *Bahnhof* (train station) on the way into Garmisch, can provide pamphlets and details.

For those staying in Hohenschwangau, the town has a lake **swimming** beach on the Alpsee, with snack bar, dressing rooms and showers, and nice lawns, as well as boat rentals. And the open-air beer garden, near the bottom of the main road up to Neuschwanstein, is as quaint as all get-out.

WHERE TO GO (NIGHT)

To bed, that's where. You have an early Schloß bus to catch.

If you absolutely must have night life, you can play baccarat, roulette, blackjack, or try the one-armed bandits, at Garmisch-Partenkirchen's popular **Spielbank** (casino), at 74 Bahnhofstraße, open from mid-afternoon to 2 A.M. Or play "find the *schwulen*" at **Jürgens Pilsbar** (Bankgasse 2).

If you insist on real gay nightlife, Munich, with several dozen gay establishments, is the nearest place you'll find serious action. Nuremberg is also a possibility. But unless you stay in these cities you'll need a car; the last train from Munich to Garmisch-Partenkirchen is at about 11 P.M.

For dancing, the best Munich nightspots for gay men are **New York** (Sonnestraße 25), and **Together** (Hans-Sachsstraße 17), the latter of which women also patronize. Most popular for gay women are **Karotte** (Reichenbachstraße 37; open from mid-afternoon), almost exclusively lesbian but welcoming gay men and **Mylord** (Ickstattstraße 2a), a very comfortable mainly-women pub that's been around forever, and also welcomes men. There are also a number of gay establishments along Müllerstraße, though it's hard to imagine a street more unpicturesque. For gay pubs with food, see "Where (and What) to Eat."

The (straight) **Hofbräuhaus,** where Ludwig's royal mom used to drink, is at Platzl 9. There's also a brass band here, and food of the sausage/sauerkraut/soup genre.

WHERE (AND WHAT) TO EAT

Gourmet food–wise, Germany is not France—or even Austria, where at least the grill craze has largely supplanted boiling as the favorite cooking method in recent years. Nevertheless, Bavarian food is not the overcooked, underspiced, starch-laden cannon fodder it used to be. The region has gone quite nuts for salads, for example; one desperate night, we even found radicchio in a McDonald's side salad. And you can get *einen grünen Salat* (a green salad) or *einen gemischten Salat-Teller* (a plate of roughly half a dozen different vegetable salads, like dilled cucumbers in light cream sauce, marinated green beans, celery rémoulade, German-style potato salad, and sweet-and-sour cabbage) at any restaurant.

In Garmisch, we liked the **Alpenhof** (74 Bahnhofstraße; tel. 59055), next to the casino. Here one can find better-than-average versions of usual Bavarian specialties like *Hochzeitsuppe* ("wedding soup," a rich yet delicate broth with pancake strips, and complicated combinations of meats and vegetables) and *Leberknödelsuppe* (little *Bayerische Leberknödel*–minced liver, bacon, onion, and bread dumplings—in bouillon), *Geschnetzeltes in Rahm* (sauteed veal tidbits in cream sauce), an elaborate *Schlachtplatte* of various sausages (like Munich's delicate *Weißwürste* and *Nürnberger Brätwürst),* or the famous Munich *Sauerbraten.* But the Alpenhof also features some more nouvelle-y dishes: fresh *Forellen* (trout) half a dozen different ways; a *Schnitzel* (cutlet), made of salmon rather than the usual pork or veal, in a light mousseline. The place also has the all-you-can-eat buffet salad bar of doom. Best of all, they have Fürst von Metternich, a dry (*trocken* in German) sparkling wine *(Sekt)* that we find somehow more sensual than most other champagnes. Try it, and do let us know what it does for *your* love life.

In Munich, some gay bars serve meals, too; a few for both genders are: **Na Und?** (Unterer Anger 16; mainly women), **Warsteinerschänke** (Klenzerstraße 45; about 80 percent women), **Karotte,** and the **Deutsche Eiche.** And for morning-after casualties—or gay visitors to Munich looking for lighter-than-the-usual-Bavarian brunch munchies and drinks in a gay daytime pub-café environment: the **Zarah Café Bar** (6 A.M.–1 P.M.) and **Sebastianstubn** (10 A.M.–midnight), on small hidden courtyard Sebastianplatz.

For snacking, Bavaria is to German cheeses what Normandy is to French ones; the sign to look for, meaning cheese specialty store, is *Käsegeschäft.*

If you're still not a major Bavarian-food fan, remember that the German *Frühstück* (breakfast) included in your hotel rate is nearly always substantial enough that it's hard to think of eating again until dinner. This repast supplements the customary Continental coffee and breads with cold cuts, cheeses, and often an egg and juice (though never, for some reason, fresh juice).

And also remember: Beer is food.

Service, by the way, is included in German menu prices; but nonrubes round up the bill to the next 50 pfennigs in inexpensive and moderate restaurants, and add 5 percent in snazzy joints.

WHERE TO GET THE LATEST DIRT
(INFORMATION RESOURCES)

For gay women, a Munich info hotline: **Lesbentelefon,** Güllstrasse 3, 8000 München 2; tel. 089/725 4272, 6 P.M.–10 P.M. They also publish a helpful two-page "München für Lesben" handout. (And at this same address, on Fridays from 6 P.M. to 11 P.M., is an exclusive *Lesbencafe* with vegetarian food—and *bier,* naturally, for lesbians; on Thursdays, a café for all women.)

Also for women: Lots of lesbian books in English, a coffee-and-reading lounge, and any local info you could possibly want (including the little handout above) are all yours at **Lillemor's Frauenbuchladen,** Arcisstraße 57, 8000 München 40; tel. 089/272 1205.

For men in Munich, local gay information is available from the gay phone line, **Rosa Freiheit** (725 6878), and at **Max & Milian Bookshop,** Gabelsbergerstraße 65, 8000 München 2; tel. 089/52 74 52.

In Nuremberg, gay and lesbian bar and hotel info is available from the gay liberation organization, **Fliederlich,** at Luitpoldstraße 15; tel. 0911/22 23 05. They have a cafe on Saturday and Sunday afternoon. They also publish a monthly newspaper, *Nürnberger Schwulenpost,* that has current information on gay activities and bars all over Bavaria.

And for women only, the very helpful English-speaking management of **Frauenbuchladen Nürnberg** (Innerer Kleinreutherweg 28, 8500 Nürnberg 10; tel. 0911/35 24 03) can provide you with books, newspapers, and verbal info on special events, discos and bars—including what "gay" establishments women should avoid.

WHAT TO READ

The Dream King, by Wilfred Blunt (Hamish Hamilton). Since most know Ludwig II only as "Mad King Ludwig" if at all, it is not surprising that this is virtually the only truly scholarly and writerly English-language biography of him existing. Published by a British house, it's available by mail order from Prinz Eisenherz bookstore in Berlin (see "Practical Information, Berlin" for address) if you can't find it in the U.S.A.

Castles, Mystery and Music, by Anton Sailer (Bruckmann München). More a coffee-table book than a serious literary effort, this volume reads like a translation from the German, which it is. Nevertheless, real Ludwig fans will enjoy it, especially for the photo reproductions of Ludwig's boyfriend Kainz, Ludwig in full knight regalia in his swan boat, and other period gems.

$\mathcal{B}$ELGIUM/ BELGIQUE/ BELGIË

Where "Bi" Means Lingual

$\mathcal{J}$acques Brel once wrote a song describing his native Belgium as the land where Frida the Blonde becomes Margot. He was referring not to an overly merged long-time lesbian couple, but to the meeting ground of the Germanic North and the Latin South.

Imagine a landscape of early Renaissance art–drenched Mediterranean hill towns, minus the hills, plus a few windmills, painted by Edward Hopper in foggy industrial grays, and you begin to get the idea. Belgium is an austere, underdressed country with a few spectacularly tarted-up accessories, including some of the most interesting food and municipal architecture in Europe. Tourists who whiz through nonstop on their way to Paris or

Amsterdam are missing a place like no other; where devout Catholics practice the Protestant ethic with a vengeance, trains run on time through timeless scenery, and beer and garlic appear at the same meal. And with gay bars, restaurants, hotels, and organizations in nearly three dozen Belgian towns, gay social life is also not only alive but thriving, very openly, in this conservative little country—possibly because in the midst of the Belgian cultural collision, we're low on everybody's hit list.

Like a potato sliced jaggedly down the middle, Belgium is divided into slightly larger French-speaking Wallonia in the south, and slightly smaller Flanders in the north, where the lingua non franca is Flemish, a dialect of Dutch. There's also a tiny German-speaking pocket in the east. Some economic tensions exist between the two main regions, since at present, Flanders's service economy is far more prosperous. Wallonia is pretty much the Midwest of Europe, with a lot of once thriving, now dying coal, steel, and other smokestack industries, plus some up-to-the-minute nuclear-power plants. Except for the Ardennes forest region, most Belgian tourist destinations, including the art cities of Ghent, Bruges, and Antwerp, are within Flemish borders.

Flanders also contains Brussels, the capital of both Belgium and Europe, a linguistic enclave that's officially bilingual, but only in terms of menus and street names. To the Flemings' distress, everyone actually *speaks* only French—of a variety far more understandable, incidentally (at least to the American ear) than you'll hear in Paris. (A tip, however, to visitors who need to count beyond sixty-nine: Seventy in Belgian is *septante*, not *soixante-dix*.)

The Walloon accent will be the only break you get in Flanders. Although the lines about what language gets spoken where were drawn decades ago, there's still an incredible amount of bad blood festering between these Van Hatfields and De McCoys. You think Switzerland is linguistically confusing? You think Canada is a battleground of the tongue? Just wait until you hit Brussels. That's Bruxelles to you, hon, or possibly Brussel.

A tiny but typical example: On the main train lines that go through Flanders, the conductors *only* announce the Flemish names of the destinations—except for the three station stops in Brussels, when they magically become bilingual. As soon as the train passes beyond the city limits and back into Flemish Flanders, they once again forget every French word they ever knew. This can be disconcerting for the tourist: If you want to go, say, to Liège, you'd better know that you're bound for Luik. Then we have such nonintuitive pairs as Bruges/Brugge (pronounced BROOG-ha, just to confuse you), Gent/Gand, Ypres/Iper, Courtrai/Kortrijk, Tournai/Doornik, Malines/Mechelen, and Anvers/Antwerpen. And who would ever guess that Mons and Bergen are one and the same city?

The linguistic constipation of the Flemish train conductors, writ large, becomes especially puzzling when you consider that the two most potent political forces in Europe today—the reintegration of the East with the rest of the Continent, and the post-1992 united Europe—are really about moving *beyond* frontiers. Belgium's family quarrels seem like a throwback to the days of assassinated archdukes. On the other hand, as gay people who know all too well the tricky tap dance of trying to maintain our difference while pushing to be part of the mainstream, we sometimes found ourselves identifying with even the most exasperating Flemish insularity. Without some heel-digging, their culture probably *would* be swallowed by the francophones.

A little background here: Originally part of the Holy Roman Empire, and then acquired by Burgundy, Flanders, along with the rest of the Low Country lands, became a Spanish possession in the mid-sixteenth century. The northern and mostly Protestant provinces rebelled and managed to secure their independence as the present-day Netherlands. The southern provinces, including Flanders, Wallonia, present-day Luxembourg, and a sliver of what's now northern France, remained under Spain's yoke as the Catholic Netherlands for more than 150 years. The area has since been conquered, either militarily or in giant international Monopoly games like the Congress of Vienna, by Austria, France, Holland, and Germany. In 1830 Belgium became an independent country, but only as a political move on the board—its separate parts had and have about as much cultural cohesion as Alaska and Hawaii.

Basically, the Flemings' position is that because their language isn't a worldwide biggie, the Walloons don't bother to learn it—or at best, as one Fleming told us in all seriousness, "they only bother to learn it as perhaps their fourth language, never their second." The Flemings return the favor by not speaking French ever, even if they were required, as most of them were until recently, to learn it in school.

We spent the better part of an afternoon with a lovely lesbian couple from the university town of Leuven (a.k.a. Louvain) twenty minutes outside of Brussels. One of them had to sweat for hours translating the interview questions to her girlfriend, who spoke very little English. Both the girlfriend and Lindsy are near-fluent French speakers, which in theory could have taken at least half the pressure off the translator—but the Flemings made it clear that they preferred to do it the hard way. We also heard from a Ghent activist that we had committed a major faux pas . . . er, *mistake* by writing letters to Flemish gay organizations in both English and French. English alone would apparently have been the preferred form, *even if the reader of the letter understood French but not English*. He or she would rather bring the letter to an English speaker for translation than put up with what was evidently our obnoxious reminder that French, not Flemish, is the language taught in American high schools.

In fact, English is widely spoken in Flanders, since it's one of the parts of the Continent closest to Britain. But we've also encountered several nonanglophones, including young people and workers in the tourist industry. After much trial and error, and badgering of all our new Flemish friends, we figured out the least inflammatory course for the non–Flemish speaker:

(1) Abandon the multilingual approach. Start by asking any stranger, "Do you speak English?" If the person says yes, proceed in English, no matter how bad their version of it turns out to be.

(2) If they say no, you might try German, although the Germans are not exactly beloved in Belgium, either.

(3) If you or they don't speak German, but you do speak French, shrug as if you were about to suggest diving into something truly distasteful but also beneficial—perhaps a bowl of beet-flavored macrobiotic boiled wheat germ. Say, offhandedly, *en français*, "I can also speak a very tiny bit of French, if this is at all possible." Having established your credentials as someone being pulled by wild horses, you can probably then proceed in as rapid-fire French as you can muster.

If Flanders only had it in for the Walloons, the situation would be relatively simple, but matters are far more convoluted than that. The easiest way to understand Flanders is to imagine a very burnt-out lesbian activist, smoldering at all the straight feminists who expect her to show up at abortion demos even though they never march on Gay Pride Day; equally pissed at her gay male friends who think AIDS is her issue, but breast cancer isn't theirs. The Flemish, you see, also get it from the Dutch.

On paper, Dutch and Flemish look the same, but from all we can gather, they sound about as similar as Bob Marley and Princess Margaret. The dialects also vary widely from town to town, so that some Flemings can't even easily communicate with each other, much less with anyone from the Netherlands. Even worse, especially in the westernmost part of Flanders, people do something exotic with "g" and "h" sounds that's the basis of an entire subcategory of Dutch national humor. Example: The Flemish pronunciation of "holy" sounds like Dutch slang for "horny," making every reference to, say, the Holy Ghost, an instant laff-riot.

The normally sporting Dutch also love to tell jokes about Belgian drivers—who, okay, granted, until recently didn't need to have licenses—and about a characteristic Belgian mannerism: a sort of "pfuhfp" sound made by puffing up the cheeks and exhaling through nearly closed lips. It's a little like a sigh, but with some gale winds behind it, and it's usually produced when one is pondering the answer to a question, eyes rolled heavenward.

The last time we were in Amsterdam, we actually heard a joke combining both of these motifs:

Q: Why do Belgian cars have the windshield wipers on the inside of the windows?

A: Because Belgians drive like this [frenetic six-year-old-child steering motions]: *"PFUUUUUHPH!"*

One thing you will hear about Belgians is that they are aloof, hard to get to know. That they will never invite you to their homes, at least not until they've known you a few years or decades. Don't believe it. We had more invitations than we could handle from complete strangers, even including some guy in a small-town tourist bureau who was apparently thrilled to meet foreigners who were interested in medieval Belgian history.

When we wrote to a women's café-disco in Leuven asking for suggestions about the area, they put up a notice in the john inviting the locals to come meet us when we were in town. The notice did not mention that we were writing a travel book; it simply touted us as a pair of American lesbians. An entire barful of curious women showed up, and we spent the whole night gabbing. We learned, among other things, that "hairdresser" means the same thing in Flemish as it does in American; that much of the industrial dance-music flooding American gay clubs—which, like vogueing, will doubtless trickle down into the hipper straight clubs within a decade or two—was spawned in Belgian gay clubs, by native "New Beat" groups like Belgian Front 242, Confetti's and à;Grumph; and that the numero-uno crush object among Belgian dykes is Tina Turner.

The only remotely unfriendly moment was the mass of vomit sounds when we informed the group that the most popular imported beer in America is Heineken. Belgians may be shy, but only until you draw them out. What, we asked the Leuven group, is the best way for American visitors to break the ice? "Buy beer," they replied. *Belgian* beer.

If there's a key to the Belgian psyche, it might be that from Napoleon to the Nazis, their nation has been the wartime punching bag for all sides. People don't assume that fighting is a good thing; they know it leaves victims in its wake. Not surprisingly, this isn't the kind of country where you get your way by sitting in on the steps of Town Hall. Abortion wasn't legalized until 1990, after feminists had been semi-openly running abortion clinics for years and everyone had had plenty of time to get used to the idea. Even the language issue seems to be dealt with mainly by keeping the sides as far away from each other as possible.

The Belgian gay movement is still at the stage where it's a big deal to get people to come out for a gay pride march. This seemed odd to us, at first, since these folks do, after all, live next door to the gay Mecca. But as one person after another cautioned us, "Belgium isn't the Netherlands."

"We're less political than the Netherlands," a Flemish lesbian therapist told us in Leuven, "because we have a history of always being an oppressed people. It's a different mentality. We're more suspicious, less out-speaking. The Dutch look for ways to confront. We look for ways to escape underground."

Brussels is exactly the kind of city we'd normally steer you away from. Although its core, the jewelbox Gothic/Baroque Grand' Place, is indeed one of the grandest places in Europe, and although the city contains some of the finest examples of Art Nouveau interiors on the Continent (especially the work of Victor Horta), there are way too many hideous modern multinational HQs hulking on the fringes of the old town, and too many still-unspoiled smaller towns an hour or two away with equally gorgeous town halls and market squares.

But we have to bend the rules just a little, because inch for inch, central Brussels probably has more gay facilities than any downtown we've ever been in. *Anywhere.* We're not talking gay neighborhood here. We're talking smack-in-the-center-of-Touristville, as if the Castro and the Mission had been grafted onto Fisherman's Wharf and Union Square. Within walking distance of the Grand' Place are a terrific gay hotel, a trilingual lesbian-feminist bookstore, the headquarters of several gay publications and a radio station, several saunas, and a staggering array of gay and mixed bars and restaurants. You could probably walk into downtown bars at random and still find the gay ones.

A local gay paper complains that politically the Brussels movement suffers from *"la torpeur,"* and we believe them. But it's also possible that gay men and lesbians can't possibly march while they're digesting great meals—which they're doing constantly.

How to begin describing Belgian cuisine? The first time we went there, a friend of ours who used to live in Brussels whispered rapturously behind the back of his cholesterolophobe boyfriend: "Ohhhh, you're going to *love* it: French food . . . with German portions."

A very short list of Belgian classics would have to include *waterzooi* (a hearty stew of chicken or fish and finely sliced vegetables in a custardy broth of cream and white wine); *carbonnades à la flamande* (a sort of boeuf bourguignon simmered with onions in beer); salads of tiny baby watercress and lacy chicory; witloof or *chicons* (endive) braised and buried in béchamel sauce; famous Belgian waffles, Ardennes ham, and just about every kind of seafood, but especially mussels *(moules)*. Don't pass up the chance to order them *à l'escargot*, broiled in garlic butter. French fries *(frites)* bear no resemblance to anything you ever ordered under the Golden Arches. They're a junk-food maven's dream and a cardiologist's nightmare: probably deep-fried in animal fat, which the vegetarian one of us prefers not to dwell on, and usually available from stands, in paper cones, with a choice of at least a half dozen flavors of mayonnaise. Try the *sauce andalouse*, with a hint of hot pimiento.

The two very, very best Belgian oral gratifications are chocolate and beer. Belgian chocolate is better than French chocolate or Swiss chocolate, which is saying a great deal. The streets of Brussels have *chocolatières* every block or so, like dry cleaners or drugstores. "Chocolate is one of the most effective restoratives," according to the legendary chef Brillat-Savarin. "All those who have to work when they might be sleeping, men of wit who feel temporarily deprived of their intellectual powers, those who find the weather oppressive, time dragging, the atmosphere depressing; those who are tormented by some preoccupation that deprives them of the liberty of thought; let all such men imbibe a half-liter of chocolate . . . and they will be amazed." We couldn't have said it better ourselves, but we'd add that our favorite chocolates (dark, milk or white) are those filled with just-made *crème fraîche* flavored with vanilla, hazelnut, coffee, orange, raspberry, or still more chocolate.

As for the beer, it too is the most remarkable in the world: better than Dutch or Danish or even Czech or German. Most of it never gets to North America, unfortunately, because it's unpasteurized—which is also one of the reasons it's so tasty. People pay the kind of attention to beer in Belgium that's usually only given to fine wines. Each brand (and they say that there's one for every day of the year) is served in its own specially shaped snifter, with little indentations in the bottom to trap sediment when necessary. Some of it, like Belgium itself, may be an acquired taste, but we've yet to meet a Belgian bartender (or any Belgian, period) who isn't thrilled to play mentor in your educational process. Skip the ubiquitous, good-but-not-great Stella and Jupiler, and try the exotica: smoked beer, cherry and peach beers, wheat beer, and the dark, malty abbey-brewed Trappist beers. If you enjoy getting knocked on your ass, order, very respectfully, a thrice-fermented *tripel,* some of which top 11 percent alcohol (American beers average 4.2 to 5.3 percent). If you don't indulge at all, order *alcoholvribier.*

The best beer we had in all of Belgium, and the known universe, was at the De Garre, a tiny restaurant-bar in an alley in Bruges. In addition to 124 kinds of bottled beer, there are a couple of homebrews on tap, including the fabulous Tripel van de Garre, a deceptively smooth, incredibly complex, faintly gingery number that's 8.5 percent alcohol.

We think you should go to Bruges in any case. At least a half dozen European cities with canals try to pass themselves off as "the Venice of the North," but only Bruges has the same time-trippingly evocative magic. Most perfectly preserved towns in Europe (like Rothenberg, Germany, and Les Baux and Carcassonne in France) are a fraction of its size. In Bruges you can walk for miles past medieval belfries, ancient houses with stair-step roof gables, windmills, stone bridges, horse-drawn carriages, and gliding swans. The town drips with Flemish art, and there's even a Michelangelo "Madonna and Child" in the Eglise Notre Dame. The pouty young Jesus stands in the folds of his mother's dress in the classic S-curve Greek boy—seductress pose—right hip out, knee bent, left shoulder forward. Mary's expression is equally classic: Clearly, she's realizing this kid is major jailbait.

Bruges has several nice gay bars, and a gay-oriented hotel, the Hans Memling, which is in the process of being turned into a mini-Versailles by its proprietors. When you spy into the ground-floor rooms at night, with the crystal chandeliers lit, the portraits of King Baudouin and Queen Fabiola on the walls (names which, we feel, are surpassed among royals only by "Babar" and "Celeste"), the sweeping hardwood staircase, and the guests sipping aperitifs, it looks exactly like what you hoped, as a kid, that being an elegant grown-up would look like.

We stopped by for a visit with owners Gilbert Moerman, a former hospital worker, and his lover, Marc Devaux, a former glazier who is now in charge of the decorating scheme, along with their collie, Rajah, and their black Persian cat, Lady. After checking out the antique canopied beds and candelabras, we asked Marc and Gilbert a lot of nosy questions about their relationship, and they—typical aloof Belgians—were only too happy to spill the beans. It turned out to be one of the most original "how we became a couple" stories we'd heard in a long time.

It seems that in 1976, Marc got married . . . to a woman. "I was really in love with her brother," he assures us, whipping out a scrapbook. There we see Marc—same crinkly brown eyes and sandy moustache—in period-piece bellbottoms, standing next to a pretty girl in a bridal dress. She is glowing. He looks utterly downcast. They spent their honeymoon at the seashore, where, fourteen days into marital bliss, Marc was spied lolling about on a towel by Gilbert. The rest is history.

If you can tear yourself away from Bruges, take a paddle steamboat ride to the village of Damme through some of the most idyllic scenery in Belgium: grazing cows, old guys fishing from the canal banks, and green lollipop trees that look as if they were painted by Seurat. Damme is also the site of a museum honoring Tyl Ulenspiegel, the storybook hero who suffered a thousand tortures at the hands of the Spanish but managed to emerge smiling.

Since we'd already blown our chance to visit the Leather Museum in Northampton, England (where the truly hard-core can sniff Queen Victoria's saddle), we wanted to make sure not to leave out any of you readers who may be also be fans of Tyl. Aside from being the national hero of Belgium, Tyl is the inspiration for the New York City SM group the Eulenspiegel Society. According to a flyer we picked up at the last Gay Pride Parade, masochists have a special fondness for Tyl's tendency to prefer laborious uphill climbs over easy downhill strolls during which "he could not help thinking of the effort and toil involved by climbing the next hill."

We can report that in Damme, Tyl groupies can also see pix of people boiled alive in pitch, bare-chested torturers, chains, scaffolds, boot licking, whole Flemish cities burning while Spaniards cackle ecstatically at the sound of the victims' screams, and other light-hearted entertainment.

In the twelfth century, as a result of the Crusades, Europe had what historians insist on referring to as "surplus women." Even if there had been a few more potential husbands floating around, one needed a dowry to marry. Convents also required dowries, which left a lot of poor women in the lurch; the main non-upper-class female career opportunity at the time was prostitution.

Around 1170, the first beguinage *(begijnhof* in Flemish) was founded, in Liège. It was a radical departure: a community of women who lived, worked, and prayed together, but outside the church hierarchy. Beguines weren't required to take lifelong vows, and could leave at any time. They apparently had relative privacy, living in their own cottages, or in pairs in the villagelike beguinages. Unlike nuns, who were largely cloistered, Beguines cooperatively supported themselves by caring for the sick, running schools, and spinning, weaving, mending, lace-making, and laundering in the towns. Some Beguines banded together as urban beggars, like the Franciscan friars.

The communities quickly attracted thousands of women from all classes who couldn't or didn't want to live lives dependent on husband or church. Within a century, there were some two hundred beguinages in Europe, about half of them in Belgium. The beguinages are certainly where *we* would have gravitated, and for that reason alone, we consider the Beguines part of lesbian history, even if someone could prove to us that none of them ever had sex together. Without the ability to make a living, one can't even begin to dream of living a lesbian life.

Not surprisingly, when the church fathers realized that an entire movement of independent women had mushroomed, completely out of their control, they panicked.

The twelfth and thirteenth centuries were a time of huge spiritual unrest in Western Europe generally. Movements that were later snuffed out as heresies were rife, and many of them had (or were accused of having) elements of sexual unorthodoxy. The Cathars or Albigensians in southwestern France, for example, believed that the life of the world—especially heterosexual intercourse—was the work of the devil. They refused to eat meat or other "products" of straight sex, and since gender was just a mirage cooked up by the Evil One, they let women become sect leaders. Male leaders swore off heterosexual intercourse, but there were rampant accusations that they practiced gay orgies (which, not producing more Satanic products, theologically didn't count).

Papal witch-hunters tended to lump all the heretics of the day together, and some historians claim that the word "Beguine" has etymological connections with "Albigensian." Others say the word simply refers to the women's beige habits. We personally wonder if there's any connection between "Beguine" and *gouine,* the French word for "dyke." Actually, we've also fantasized a connection with Cole Porter's "Begin the Beguine," but we realize that's stretching it a bit.

In any case, the Beguines were way too uppity for the church. They were said to have translated the Bible into the vernacular and preached it, a definite no-no for women, and to have claimed that the Holy Spirit would come back next time in female form. They were accused of being loose women, and, naturally, of being lesbians. To be fair, lesbianism was not seen as strictly a beguinage problem. As early as the fifth century, St. Augustine chastised his sister, a nun, saying that the love she bore her fellow handmaidens of Christ "ought not to be carnal, but spiritual"; and the 1212 and 1214 councils of Paris and Rouen, respectively, forbade nuns from sleeping together and introduced rules requiring lights to burn all night in convent dormitories. Not subject to these regulations, though, Beguines had even more potential to be erotically threatening. Many of the religious Beguines were mystics whose favorite scripture was the Song of Solomon, and their sexual energy unquestionably freaked out the authorities. The medieval churchman Jacques de Vitry improbably claimed that some Beguines stayed in bed reciting the lustier verses for years on end.

In 1273, the bishop of Olmutz officially complained to the pope about the Beguines' refusal to marry. His assholiness and other church henchmen tried over the years to limit what tools the Beguines could use, who could join, and whether new orders could be established. Things came to a head in 1310 when a Belgian Beguine leader, Margaret Porete, was burnt at the stake as a heretic. The following year, the Council of Vienne decreed that "since these women promise no obedience to anyone," they should be excommunicated. Pope John XXII did just that. A loophole was created in the Low Countries, allowing the beguinages to stay open, but only if they came under church authority. Some beguinages were transformed into regular Catholic convents. Others technically remained Beguine orders, but bearing little resemblance to their former feminist selves.

The door may have slammed on the Beguines seven-hundred years ago, but some twenty of the beguinages are still standing. Apart from their history, they offer the tourist some of the most beautiful and peaceful townscapes anywhere.

In Bruges, the ancient beguinage is currently occupied by Benedictine nuns. Set behind high walls, across a swan-filled lagoon, and back several centuries in time, the Vineyard, as the beguinage was originally christened in 1245, is an oasis of rural calm in the midst of this bustling medieval merchants' town. Small, quaint whitewashed brick houses with red "flowerpot" tile roofs, each with its own tiny walled cloister garden, surround a great public lawn filled with beech trees and daffodils, and intersected by peaceful walking paths. Rebuilt after a fire in the sixteenth century, the beguinage church is largely Renaissance in style, but retains vestiges of the 1300s. You can actually visit one of the early seventeenth-century houses, reconstructed to illustrate how a typical pair of Beguines lived, where you and your main squeeze can play Let's Pretend. ("Babe, do you think we could bring the laptop computer back in time with us, and put it here by the spinning wheel and the foot warmer used during the Offices of the Church?")

If you get gung-ho enough to hit the beguinage trail, you'll find that each one is architecturally different. Behind the walls of Leuven's much larger and more urban Great Begijnhof, for example, the houses are immaculate red brick, and set not around a grassy courtyard but in block after block of narrow cobblestoned roads. At night, every corner is lit by old iron gaslights, adapted to electricity. The individual cottages—over a hundred of them with typical arched doorways, most dating from the 17th century—have been turned into housing for visiting University of Leuven professors. This worldly, cosmopolitan adaptation is probably fitting: it was after a visit to this particular beguinage, after all, that a scandalized archbishop complained of "a serious lapse of zeal . . . too much going out" and "too many meals eaten in the city," by Leuven's Beguines. Lier has a similar miniature-city-within-a-city layout, although the cottages (which now house a mixture of old people and young families) have a funkier, less decorator-restored look, with flashy geraniums on the sills, lots of the famous local lace in the windows, and kids playing in the streets.

The town of Diest has turned its eighty-house beguinage, which has more of a small-town feel, into a sort of walled artists' sanctuary and community cultural center, with old-fashioned crafts shops (like that of a costumed lace-maker) as well as more modern painting, etching, and other fine-arts workshop-galleries. Among the other visitable buildings is a typical modest thirteenth- or fourteenth-century beguinage church, and the *engelenconvent,* a three-room furnished Beguine's house-cum-workshop with medieval herb garden. There is also a wonderful traditional Flemish restaurant dating from 1618, whose castlelike interior is decorated with stained-glass windows, old guild banners, and an open central fireplace. What we enjoyed the most, though, was the inscription, from the Song of Solomon, on the beguinage's monumental arched baroque outer gate. COMT IN MYNEN HOF MYN SUSTER BRUYT ("Come into my garden, my sister bride").

There are important beguinages in Ghent, Antwerp, Arschot, and other Belgian towns, as well as one in downtown Amsterdam. But the one that remains most memorable to us is the one in Kortrijk a few miles from the French border. A regular Beguine community operated here until the population dwindled in 1971; now, it is mainly a refuge for widows and single women. With a profusion of both flowering greenery and cobblestoned alleys, this largely seventeenth-century cloister feels like a mix of town and country. There's a snazzy 1698 Grand Mistress's house with double stepped gables, a brick-roofed 1682 recreation hall, and many other houses from even earlier in the century. The interior of the small baroque chapel is touchingly, naïvely simple: stiff-backed chairs, a blue-sky starred ceiling, a heroic statue of St. Godelive (who looks like a dead ringer for Wonder Woman), and walls that very badly need paint—the place is dying, like the profession.

We remember this beguinage so vividly, however, not because it looked more picturesque than any of the others we'd visited, but because it was there that we met Sister Marcella, or Mademoiselle Marcella, as she prefers to be called, one of fewer than two dozen actual Beguines left in Belgium.

Now in her late sixties and nearly blind, Marcella is one of only two women in her order left in Kortrijk. Her "sister" sits outside the chapel door, collecting admission fees from tourists, while Marcella sells souvenir postcards as well as crocheted stuffed animals and pillows from her cottage. It's a simple room with an army cot, a tiny wood stove with just enough room for a teakettle, a small cabinet, and a crucifix on the wall. The only modern touch, aside from the postcard rack, is a discreetly hidden hi-fi.

The daughter of a chicken farmer, Marcella had considered becoming a regular nun when she was a girl, but had been told her eyes wouldn't stand up to the strain of reading religious texts. In any case, she was attracted to the notion that Beguines could do real work in the world. Although no one has joined the Beguines for a generation, she added, it does not make her sad to be the last of a dying breed, because their ideas about the contributions of working women are now part of the culture. They have done their work, well.

She also knows that before too long, she and her sister will be buried in the remaining two plots of the beguinage cemetery. But this doesn't seem to bother her, either. In fact, there's much jesting about her former Beguine comrades being planted in their graves like so many potatoes, and apparently a good deal of jesting between her and her sister about which one will be the next potato, and which one the old maid.

"It has been a hard life, but I have been very happy," she told us. "As a Beguine, one does not make much money. But someday, when I'm a *pomme de terre*, we'll all be equal. Until then, life is hard, so it is important to enjoy oneself."

Having picked Sister Marcella's brain, we asked her if she had any questions for *us*. Indeed, she nodded, she was glad we'd asked. "I am Flemish-born, and I drink beer with my meals," she said. "My sister is French, and she prefers wine. Tell me: What *is* it that Americans drink?"

————

We're sitting in the Falstaff, a gaudy noisy Belle Epoque restaurant in downtown Brussels with a mixed but definitely gay-oriented clientele. Marian Lens, who looks like a young Rita Mae and who runs the feminist bookstore—art gallery—lesbian information center Artemys, is introducing us to some of her favorite Belgian beers. Also at the table are her friends Claudia and Bizoux (the nickname means "little kisses"), two fashionably coiffed young women who teach lesbian martial-arts classes. All three of them are militant lesbian separatists of a sort rarely seen in Belgium. "I don't want to change just a few things in this society," Marian had cheerfully told us a bit earlier. "I want it be to broken . . . *destroyed*."

But even these three revolutionaries are unprepared for the Sani-Fem Freshette we pull out as soon as the subject turns to peeing, which in Brussels it's sooner or later bound to do.

Maybe it's all that beer. Whatever, Brussels is the only world-class capital whose most famous tourist attraction is (attention, water-sports fans) the breathtakingly tacky Manneken-Pis statue-fountain of a small boy taking a leak. According to legend, it's the legacy of a rich merchant whose small son disappeared, and who frantically promised a search party that he'd donate to the city a statue of the kid in whatever pose he was found.

The M-P has become a sort of international Ken Doll, regularly dressed up in an array of outfits including British Beefeater Guard, Indian Chief, Toreador, French Courtier, Kilted Scottie, and much, much more. If this turns you on, you can see his entire wardrobe at the Museum of the City of Brussels in the Grand' Place. Souvenir hunters meanwhile can well imagine the treasure trove of M-P kitsch, from Belgian-chocolate versions of His Splashiness, to clever corkscrews that let you open your wine bottles with his curlicue dick, to the extremely tasteful urinating Grand Marnier dispenser, which Pam actually bought for her gay brother.

Feminists, we're sure, will be relieved (so to speak) to learn of the separate but equal Jeanneke-Pis status of a squatting little girl, installed in an alley off rue des Bouchers, the main drag of tourist-oriented restaurants. We personally feel her waterworks aren't as impressive as some of the squirting-boob statues we've seen in Italy and Germany, but it's probably just a matter of taste. Throw a few coins into the fountain; they'll be donated to AIDS and cancer research.

In any case, there we were, a buncha lesbian chicks sitting around talking about peeing envy, and what a pain it is, if you're a woman, to find a public toilet, and how half the time when you *do* find one, you'd sooner sit down on an anthill. But we're delighted to tell all you traveling gals that a solution is literally at hand.

The Freshette, which we first discovered in a camping catalogue, is a deceptively narrow cup that fits snugly over your crotch. There's a small spout in the other end, and most of the time, that's all you need. Just stand there like one of the guys, unzip your fly, cup, and go. We've now christened both the Amsterdam Herengracht and Venice's Giudecca Canal, as well as numerous horrible French "ladies'" rooms consisting of a trough in the floor and two footrests. If you're a size queen, or if you need to pee somewhere other than a toilet, there's a plastic extender that fits in the spout and that in turn can slide onto a specially-designed disposable plastic bag. (Pam once used the latter method, sitting down, on a crowded bus in Bavaria—undetected.) The Freshette, extender, bags, and a washable tote pouch weigh about six ounces all together, and we don't leave home without it.

The Belgians shrieked when they first laid eyes on it. But they were intrigued with our show-and-tell demo, as were most of the neighboring tables; and after a few more beers, we were all plotting mass airlifts for every Freshette-deprived female in Brussels, starting with Jeanneke-Pis. After still more beers, when Bizoux got up to go to the john, we insisted that she take one of our devices with her. She promptly sat down and ordered a few *more* beers, to get her nerve up. We understood completely. No matter how liberated you think you are, now matter how butch or how cool, and no matter how badly you have to go, the first time you try this thing you will lose all faith, and your bladder will behave like the Sahara.

So we weren't surprised when this tough-and-together Belgian radical-lesbian-feminist separatist was away from the table for quite a long time. And we weren't surprised at the silly grin on her face when she finally did come back.

Now," she exclaimed, handing back the Freshette with a grand flourish, "we are *truly* equal."

$\mathscr{B}$ELGIUM

PRACTICAL INFORMATION

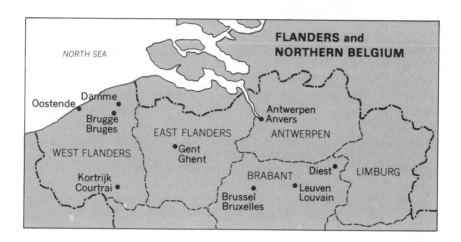

FLANDERS and NORTHERN BELGIUM

NORTH SEA

Oostende
Damme
Brugge
Bruges
WEST FLANDERS
EAST FLANDERS
Gent
Ghent
Kortrijk
Courtrai
Antwerpen
Anvers
ANTWERPEN
BRABANT
Diest
LIMBURG
Leuven
Louvain
Brussel
Bruxelles

BRUGES — NUMBER KEY

Hotels

1. Hans Memling (Kuiperstraat 18)
2. Uilenspiegel (Langestraat 2–4)
3. Het Geestelijk Hof (Heilige Geestraat 2)

Bars

4. Plexat (Hoogste van Brugge 1)
5. Bolero (Garenmarkt 32)

Best Beer Bar in Universe

6. De Garre (1 De Garre)

7. tourist office (intersection of Hoögstraat and Breidelstraat)
8. Church of Our Lady (with Pièta) (intersection of Kerkhof-zvig and Katelijnestraat)
9. Beguinage (across bridge from Wijngaardplein)

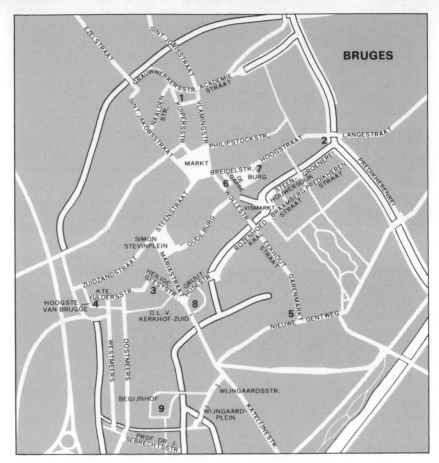

GENERAL HINTS / INFO

Although neither a large country nor one that's a prime vacation destination for gay Americans, Belgium has enough gay establishments to make your head pop off. For this reason—and because we visited a number of different Belgian locales, since our own priority was following the *béguinage/begijnhof* trail—the practical information for this chapter is arranged a bit differently: by town.

The "Venice of the North," Bruges (Brugge) is our favorite Belgian town. It's a relaxing canal-crossed place virtually free of French/Flemish language hassles (most people speak English, anyway), where almost no nasty modernity except an excess of cars disturbs the medieval look and feel. Most Americans who have visited Belgium feel the same, much to the annoyance of Belgians from other perfectly nice cities, who feel we should give their hometowns a chance, too. Nevertheless, we strongly recommend that you base yourselves in Bruges. Assuming that you will follow our advice, Bruges will be our main listing below (with all the usual categories), followed by listings of nearby Brussels—an easy one-hour train trip for those who want more varied gay life than Bruges' three gay bars and one gay hotel provide.

As it happens, however, many beguinage towns also have gay facilities. So we're also providing much sketchier rundowns on some of these. Most will be simply gay information sources—organizations and publications—rather than addresses of bars that probably will have turned into hetero truckstops or wedding halls by the time you get there. We will, of course, tell you about any totally irresistible establishments that are especially friendly to foreign visitors.

Hope we haven't terminally confused you, sweeties. Have a glass of Belgian beer and fan yourselves.

Apropos of other general Belgian stuff: Those for whom sex without dirty magazines/videos is like a day without sunshine should think about bringing their own—very carefully. While homosexual activity (over the age of consent) is legal in Belgium, pornography is not.

As for language tips: Since Brussels is the only francophone town we're listing, it's the only place to drag out your high school French at the outset. Otherwise (since we assume no one knows Flemish), begin in English, which most Flemings know. If you wish to be more polite by attempting to begin with a salutation in Flemish, *"Goddag"* (pronounced "goe-DAH" or "goe-DAI," depending on locale) or just *"dag"* will suffice for both hello and good-bye, though you'll additionally hear *"Godmorgen"* ("goe-MOAern") in shops during the morning.

In Flanders, the term for gay male is *homo* (for "homophile"); lesbian is *lesbisch* and *lesbienne*. *Begijnhof* is pronounced "beh-HANE-hoff," but this naturally is also subject to regional variations.

Now about Bruges' mosquitoes. This, of course, is the downside of having picturesque canals running through the city. The portable mosquito-zappers sold in the USA—those electronic soundwave things that imitate mosquito-eating bugs, and so on—may have proven ineffective in tests, but don't fear. In Europe, you can buy tiny plug-in devices that smushify them critters just great. We got ours in a Boots drugstore in England, their own brand; Bayer in England makes one, too, and other brands are sold in Belgian drugstores (or hotels—Het Geestelijk Hof carries them, for instance). The devices come with little rectangular tablets that release some faint-smelling, mosquito-killing substance into the air all night. Probably it's a noxious gas that eventually causes people to sprout green hair and grow horns, but we don't care. It works.

Currency unit: the Belgian franc (BF)

In Brugge [Bruges]
telephone code 050

WHERE TO STAY

Only because it isn't the sort of thing that would ever occur to an adult person not accustomed to staying in youth hostels, do we suggest that you check hotel closing hours in this town. It is *not* necessary to do this in any hotel we list below (or for any other city); all our hotels that don't have 24-hour reception give guests keys. But we did wind up once in a perfectly charming-looking hotel in Bruges, the Rembrandt-Rubens, that had a midnight curfew—inflexible, no key or negotiations possible. This is clearly ludicrous in late night-life towns like Bruges and Brussels.

A typical Belgian breakfast (ham, cheeses, and many types of breads and croissants with butter and jam, plus coffee, tea, or hot chocolate) is included in hotel rates, unless otherwise mentioned.

Prices: *Inexpensive* = under 1,100 BF; *inex./mod.* = 1,100–1,600 BF; *moderate* = 1,600–2,200 BF; *mod./exp.* = 2,200–2,900 BF; *expensive* = over 2,900 BF.

Hans Memling (formerly Cosmopolite), Kuipersstraat 18, 8000 Brugge; tel. 33 20 96. This is Bruges' only gay hotel—but what a hotel! Outside, an unimpressive plain white stucco building with red trim; inside, a homemade palace. The building is from 1835; it's been a hotel since 1920, and was all lovingly hand-renovated, Louis XV-style, by the charming gay male owners in 1986. There's an elevator, and 17 rooms, all with phones, big bathrooms, and antique furniture—canopied French beds, marble tables, crystal chandeliers, ornate candelabras, lace tablecloths, parquet floors, Oriental rugs, etc. We won't, although it's tempting, go into individual room decor; but if we show up here and one of you readers has taken room number 1, there's gonna be big trouble. In summer, reserve two weeks ahead; in winter, it's possible to just show up. *Mod.–mod./ exp.*

Het Geestelijk Hof, Heilige Geetstraat 2, 8000 Brugge; tel. 34 25 94. This is an old, typical stepped-roof brick Flemish town house in jewellike condition, with small but precious decorating touches throughout—like swan-patterned lace curtains. The seven largely antique-furnished rooms are *huge*, and come both with and without bath, for only a few dollars' difference. All are decorated differently, some in charmingly eccentric style. One has a fireplace with a couch *in* it. Another has Persian rugs on top of wall-to-wall carpeting. The room we last stayed in had three beds, but proprietor Greta DeWulf explained she would charge us only for a regular double room, "Because of course, you only use one bed! Ha, ha, ha!" Greta is totally charming, a real fox, and speaks so many languages that, as she circulates around the breakfast room talking to guests of all nations, you'll think you're still asleep and dreaming. *Inex./mod.*

Ulenspiegel, Langestraat 2–4, 8000 Brugge; tel. 33 85 06. Directly on the junction of three canals, this cute hotel with ground-floor bar/restaurant is picturesquely decorated with curioes and good old furniture. There are six rooms, all with phones and bathrooms. *Moderate.*

Die Svaene, Steenhouwersdijk (Groene Rei), 8000 Brugge; tel. 34 27 98; fax 33 66 74; telex 82.446 Swaene B. Higher-budget travelers (those who don't blanch at spending $125–$150 for a double room) can time-trip in the lap of gay-friendly luxury at this canal-front medieval patrician house, which was exquisitely and very romantically restored as a hotel-restaurant in 1981. *Expensive.*

WHERE TO GO (DAY)

The seventeenth-century beguinage, **The Vineyard,** is located just left of Wijngaardplein, about five minutes' walk from the train station (up Oostmeers to Begijnvest or Prof. Dr. J. Sebrechtsstraat, and the first left off either).

Michelangelo's (other) junior-jailbait **"Pieta"** is located in the south transept (hang a right from entrance, and straight on) of Eglise Notre Dame. The church is on a major north–south road, Katelijnestraat (from the beguinage, east on Wijngaardstraat, then left).

For an excursion to the **Tyl Ulenspiegel Museum,** across from the town hall in Damme, head north out of the main "Markt" square on Vlamingstraat until Academiestraat, where you take a right and then follow the canal that starts at Jan Van Eyckplein forever, over the big bridge to Noorweegse Kaai, where you'll eventually see the Damme boat. Don't worry about the factories you'll pass at the start of the half-hour boat ride; the countryside gets bucolically rural again soon. About Tyl's name, by the way: You have indeed seen it spelled differently elsewhere (Tyl Eulenspiegel, Tijl Uilenspiegel, etc.). Belgium and Germany have the best citizenship claims, but almost every country in Europe has some version of this hardluck SM hero. Don't miss, in the museum's international room, the posters of Tyl in a gondola, playing Welsh bagpipes, fighting a bull, and discussing something or other (favorite handcuff brands, perhaps) with a busby-hatted Buckingham Palace guard.

In the English Channel passenger port and beach resort **Oostende (Ostend),** where ferries from Britain dock, there are lots of gay bars and a sandy beach that might interest day-trippers; it's only 20 minutes from Bruges by train. Frankly, we didn't like it. There are few charming old buildings even along the seafront promenade, due as much to misguided modernization as to war damage, and despite the well-known and supposedly glamorous ugly modern casino, the town's general feel is dime-store sailor-scuzzy. If you want to give it a try yourselves, though, the main queer concentration is on easy-to-remember San Franciscusstraat (particularly around its intersection with pedestrian-only Kadzandstraat), which begins right across the bridge from the ferry terminal, on the right of Vissers Kaai. A friendly bar conducive to meeting people is **Byblos** (Kadzanstraat 2), a smallish houseplant-festooned sort-of ferndump with a nice sound system and some mighty weird tapes. (See if they still have the "Ome Jo Medley" by Hans Versnel, and don't laugh so hard you choke on your beer.) Upstairs are three hotel rooms, all with bath, where, as at the bar, lesbians are welcome though most patrons are gay men. Avoid the very pink hotel/restaurant **San Francisco,** St. Franciscusstraat 63—formerly gay, but now run by a hostile, homophobic straight couple.

WHERE TO GO (NIGHT)

Plexat (Hoogste van Brugge 1; street sometimes referred to as " 't Hoogste") is perfectly nice at night but known as the afternoon/evening bar, gay-wise. The place is small but cute-elegant; the visuals include dark blue walls, a marble bar top, comfy cushioned bar stools, two beautiful old-fashioned-looking flipper pinball machines, and fresh flower bouquets all over. Open until whenever, from 1 P.M. on weekdays and 5 P.M. on weekends, closed Tuesday. **Bolero** (Garenmarkt 32)—open 9 P.M. to whenever everyone leaves, every day except Sunday —seems to be the most in, or at least most exclusively gay, night bar. Don't miss the gorgeous painted tiles on the wall, in the hall on your way to the toilet.

Klein Verschil, a friendly and nonattitudinous bar run by Bruges' gay and lesbian political organization GOCA, has recently moved to the Homo and Lesbiennecentrum (St. Clarastraat 43, 8000 Brugge; tel. 33 47 42). While hours here always depend somewhat on size of the crowd and bartender's energy level, as all workers are volunteers, the bar is generally open to all on Wednesdays from 8 P.M. to midnight, Fridays and Saturdays from 8 P.M. to 1 A.M., and Sundays from 4 P.M. to midnight. Mondays, from 8 P.M. on, are lesbian nights. To actively try to draw more women to the bar, GOCA is also just starting to do special women's events; the first was a movie night, with *Desert Hearts!* Women can also check the **Vrouenhuis** (Westmeers 22; tel. 33 70 96). This "Women's House" occasionally hosts a *vrouwenkaffe,* **Tunia's,** run by lesbian *vrouwenpraatgroep* "Timas." During our visit, the café was being held the first and third Saturdays of the month from 8 P.M., but best call.

Our highest bar recommendation goes to the nongay but most cordial **De Garre** at 1 De Garre, a tiny alley to the right, between two lace shops, off Breidelstraat, which leads to the tourist office from the main square. They've been making their own beer about five years, and have two homebrews on draft, including the world's without-a-question best beer, Tripel van de Garre. Also available are 124 bottled beers. All beers are served with complimentary nibbles of cheese.

WHERE (AND WHAT) TO EAT

Typical Belgian specialties to try in restaurants include: *waterzooi; gegratineerd witloof/chicons gratinées,* Flemish *karbonaden/carbonnades à la flamande,* and *kroketen* (potato croquettes). The watercress in Belgian salads, also used widely for garnishes, is a tender, delicate sprout bearing no resemblance to the thick-stemmed cow fodder of the same name in American markets. Green eels are a big deal here too, but the fisherperson of us once caught one by mistake, and cannot bear to even think about these vile, nasty, slimy creatures. And of course, there are *musseln/moules,* a million different ways—the most common being a simple *moules-frites* (steamed mussels, with fries), and one of the best being *moules à l'escargot* (mussels done like escargots).

A tiny old restaurant/café that does the latter very well is **A Bruges Beertje,** squeezed in between two larger restaurants on Eiermarkt (the Egg Market square, just north of the Grote Markt).

The best seafood waterzooi we had in Belgium was at **De Visscherie** (on the Fish Market square, at Vismarkt 8), where it's easy for a couple to spend well over $100. But it's worth it. The fish and produce are all fresh, seasonal market stuff, and the nouvelle yet rich preparation, as in the light-as-sea-foam appetizer mousse served with a buttery puff pastry "fish" is perfect.

A currently hot place for innovative Belgian nouvelle cuisine, like warm foie gras or oysters topped with caviar, is **Den Gouden Harynck** (Groeninge 25; tel. 33 76 37, as reservations are a good idea). The atmosphere here is a mixture of elegant-colonial and rustic; it's also quite romantic—no cramped table spacing. One can eat à la carte, but people come for the menu deal: a gargantuan six-course dinner for about $65 per person, or the same for $85 or so with three different wines.

If you're feeling either stuffed or broke, take a break and picnic in your room or in the **Minnewater** (Lake of Love) **Park** just south of the beguinage, for roughly $2–$5. And we don't mean backpacker supermarket coldcuts, either. **Selfi** (58 Steenstraat) has a variety of the mouthwatering little sandwiches called *broodjes; filet américain,* mussel salad, smoked salmon, tiny shrimp, and Ardennes ham are just a few possibilities. Fish fans should try **Vishandel Ameloot** (Vismarkt 11) for take-out salads and smoked fish, or the even better **Geldhof Dolfin** next door (Vismarkt 12), which also has salads, plus outstanding take-out *koude schotel* (cold plates) laid out like Japanese art-food. One selection has smoked fish, crab, both gray and rose shrimp, scallops, five julienned salad veggies, and sliced hard-boiled egg; another features poached salmon and béarnaise sauce. **Delicatessen Deldijcke** (23 Wollestraat. Open 9 A.M. to 7 P.M., closed Sunday; takes all credit cards) has charcuterie meats, inexpensive sandwiches, and souvenir breads in elaborate shapes like chickens, or scrolled hearts with baked-in inspirational homilies. But most impressive are their Belgian-style "TV dinners," featuring stuff like braised veal and mushroom stew with tomato salad, broccoli, and cauliflower; waterzooi; and poached salmon in spinach cream, with salad and fluted *real* mashed potatoes.

While we eat very little fast food in America, we eat lots of it in Belgium. Foremost are *frieten/frites,* the world's best French fries, served with mayonnaise, béarnaise, spicy andalouse, or other sauces. *Frites* stands are all over the place, but one that's super tasty—especially when you have the between-bar munchies at 3 A.M.—is the portable *frites* wagon in front of the Belfry and Halles in the Grote Markt square. As well as fries with your choice of eight sauces, they have marinated *moules vinaigrette,* and about half a dozen types of Indonesian satays.

Belgian chocolates are also the world's best, and a quarter to half the price they are in the United States. Chocolatiers in Bruges that we particularly like: **Vendôme** (corner of Waalsestraat and Jozef Suveestraat), a small, homey place featuring pralines that are all homemade in the back room (you can smell them!), and other typical local specialties like Bruges *dentelles,* lace cookies. Some of the chocolates here are merely good, but the milk and white chocolate *crème fraîche* acorns are outstanding—a tissue-thin shell and buttery filling so light you can hardly feel it on your tongue. At **Verheecke** (Steenstraat 30), right off the Grote Markt, the pralines with coffee and vanilla *crème fraîche* fillings are especially terrific.

Unlike Chinese chop suey, Belgian waffles really are Belgian. These eggy *gaufres* with a crunchy caramelized coating (or sometimes butter, whipped cream, confectioners' sugar, or fruit) are sold everywhere, and even the ones from the most low-rent stands are good.

And then there's beer. This little country brews a beer for almost every day of the year, 355, so most people are sure to find one to their taste. Soft-drink lovers who don't like beer, for instance, should try the very nonbeerlike Peche-Bier (beer with peach extract) or cherry Kriek. Our favorite local bottled beer was heavy-duty Bruges Tripel (re-fermented in the bottle), which you will easily recognize at 50 paces by the quaint medieval Bruges scene on the label—picturesque peasants, canal, etc. Corsendonck is a nice blond beer. But in Belgium, even the no-alcohol beer *(alcoholvribier)* is good. One especially tasty kind is Tourtel.

In general we particularly like the Trappist beers, historically brewed in Cistercian monasteries. When drinking one of these, one should check the bottom of the bottle; if it's concave, leave the last quarter-inch or so on the bottom. This innocent-looking layer is natural sediment, and will give you diarrhea. Another bit of Belgian beer wisdom, learned through experience: Do not be fooled into thinking that darker, more flavorful beers are necessarily higher in alcohol. One good amber beer, Vieux Temps, is only 5.2 percent alcohol, while the excellent lighter Hoegarden Grand Cru is an 8.7 percent *tripel*.

To toast in Belgium, one says, *"Santé!"* (Even in Flanders.)

WHERE TO GET THE LATEST DIRT (INFORMATION RESOURCES)

For special gay events in Bruges, GOCA [see listing under "Where to Go (Night)"] publishes a dozen-page *GOCA Nieuws Brief,* in Flemish, but with a calendar of events that is decipherable.

There are gay bars, restaurants, organizations, etc., in almost three dozen other Belgian cities not listed below, including a few beguinage locales we didn't personally check out.

For the most complete and recent gay address lists for all Belgian cities, there are three periodicals published in nearby Brussels. *Tels Quels' Gay Guide de Bruxelles-Wallonie* covers, in French, Brussels and all of francophone Belgium —and gay info on Wallonia isn't otherwise easy to come by. The guide costs about a dollar. It is published by **Antenne Rose** (rue Marché au Charbon 81, 8000 Bruxelles, or B.P. 888, 1000 Bruxelles 1; tel. 02/512 45 87), which also publishes the monthly *Tels Quels* magazine; no listings per se in this one, but useful ads and current-events calendars as well as articles (all in French, naturally). *Regard* (published, in French, by l'A.S.B.L. Infor Homosexualités Belgique, B.P. 215, 1040 Bruxelles 4; tel. 648 77 41, or, in Liège, 041/23 07 60) is mostly useful for its calendar of special events, Brussels venue ads, lists of some Wallonian bookstores and newsstands carrying gay press, and AIDS-info phone helplines. Get it free in bars and other gay venues, plus some magazine stores.

De Gay Krant (see "Practical Information, Amsterdam" for international mail-order address) also has complete, if not descriptive, gay name-and-address listings for all Belgium.

In Brussels
telephone code 02

WHERE TO STAY

If you'd rather stay in Brussels than in Bruges, there is now a lovely, lovely gay hotel (the only one in town), half a block from Place du Béguinage, where the now-defunct Brussels beguinage used to be. **Residence Rouleau** (Rolstraat 15;

tel. 219 36 57), a town house with 11 rooms, all with double bed and all with shared W.C., though three have private showers. The decor is "typical stupid, bourgeois Belgian," to quote owner Justin Theuiessen, a former actor who is obviously still something of a comedian. "We try to personalize so you know you're in Belgium, not in a room that could be anywhere." Each is different: ours had a skylight, nice old furniture, mirrors around the huge bed, and pix from late-eighteenth-century French ladies' fashion magazines. There's a handy push-pinned gay map of Brussels in the front hall, and an elegant chandeliered breakfast room/lounge. The beefcake Tom of Finland pictures in the stairwell are the only jarringly cheap note, but some will adore them anyway, we realize. *Moderate.*

WHERE TO GO (DAY)

Watersports chickenhawks as well as the merely trashy will no doubt want to rush right over to see the famous **Manneken-Pis** statue of a little boy taking a leak, on the corner of rue de l'Etuve and rue du Chêne. People have been attempting to clothe this naked kid for years; the costume collection, if you'd also like to see the kid dolled up as a Buckingham Palace guard or an American Indian chief, is at the Museum of the City of Brussels, Maison du Roi, Grand' Place. More exciting, we feel, are the peeing wine corks and other exciting gift possibilities, to be found at the souvenir shops across and down rue de l'Etuve from the statue. And don't miss the anatomically correct white and dark chocolate Manneken replicas at **Lady Praline** (34 rue de l'Etuve), a small shop between Daskalides and Au Bon Chocolat.

Since June 1987, Brussels has also had **Jeanneke-Pis,** the Manneken's female equivalent. You'll find her squatting and doing her stuff at the end of Impasse de la Fidelité, a tiny dead-end off Beenhouwers Strasse, two blocks from the Grand' Place. All donations thrown in her fountain/W.C. go to fight cancer and AIDS.

We actually have quite a file on peeing and squirting-boob statues all over Europe. Some you might have missed are, for example, the small boy in Pescia, Italy (12 miles east of Lucca, at the train station), or in Duisburg, Germany (left of the train station's rear doors); and surely you wouldn't want to miss the female four-squirter in Nuremberg's Fountain of Virtues (Lorenzerplatz, adjacent to St. Lorenz church).

WHERE TO GO (NIGHT)

There are approximately 40 gay and lesbian bars in this town, most in central Brussels (1000 Bruxelles), within a leisurely 5–10 minute walk from Bruxelles Centrale train station. Most of these establishments are open until 5, 6, or 7 A.M.

When we were there, the most popular, and virtually only, lesbian bars were **L'Evenement** (rue des Pierres 20; tel. 514 04 69. Closed Mondays and Tuesdays), owned by a lesbian couple but featuring male *travesti* shows; disco **Capricorne** (Anderlectstraat 8; tel. 514 33 36. Open Fridays, Saturdays, Sundays from

11 P.M.); and **Le Feminin** (rue Borgval 9; tel. 511 17 09. Closed Wednesdays). Men are allowed at all of these mainly women's places.

We loved the look of the **Reserve,** on Petit Rue au Beurre. Near the Grand' Place, it draws both gay men and women, mostly age 28-plus, with its inviting, outstandingly atmospheric typical old Belgian-tapestried decor.

Men would have a difficult time *not* finding a gay bar on rue Marché au Charbon/Kornmarkt. An especially good bet for meeting people who know the latest local bar info is **Tels Quels** (rue Marché au Charbon 81; tel. 512 45 87; open Sunday through Thursday from 5 P.M. to 2 A.M., Friday and Saturday from 5 P.M. to 4 A.M.), associated with Antenne Rose, publisher of *Tels Quels* gay guide. The look here is basically held-together-by-spit, concrete block–scuzzy— a "Hey, kids, let's put on a show!" kind of place. Avoid **Big Noise** (rue Marché au Charbon 44), where the owner is very adamant about no women. Other features are earsplitting dated disco (hence the name, we suppose); and appallingly tacky fake-brick bar covering, like that Xmas fireplace shelf paper we all remember from childhood—perhaps here the result of an international garage sale?

Rue des Pierres is another multi-gay-bar street. Check out tasteful pink and gray **L'Evidence** (no. 57); woman-owned **Or Noir** (no. 45), with snacks and weekend *spectacle de travesti;* and **Can Can** (no. 55). Rue Duquesnoy, spitting distance from the train station and Artemys lesbian bookstore, also has several gay bars; but the dance bar **Duquesnoy** (no. 12) is men-only, and not very popular, and the disco **Garage** (nos. 16–18, upstairs) has become perhaps too trendy for some gay folk—meaning packed with aspiring-to-be-with-it hetero sightseers. **Le Petit Rouge,** however (on the corner, at no. 45) is cute, sunny, and perfectly cordial to women though mostly male-frequented. As well as drinks, this place serves light food and a few more substantial daily specials.

For cabaret lovers, the **Black Bottom** (rue du Lombard 1; tel. 511 06 08; closed Sundays) is a relatively inexpensive club owned by two gay guys who've been together 40 years—their *travesti* show spoofs their own relationship. Women as well as men are also welcome at cabaret **Coucou** (rue Jardin des Olives 8; tel. 511 33 36. Open 9 P.M., closed Thursdays; *grand spectacle de travesti* Fridays and Saturdays at approximately 1 or 2 A.M.) To enter, however, you must assure the doorpeople you're not straight!

For a complete, currently accurate name-and-address bar listing, see one of the "Info Resources" in the section below.

Springtime visitors to Brussels might also want to investigate the annual (separate) **lesbian and gay film festivals.** For info: FWH/Antenne Rose, tel. 233 33 02.

WHERE (AND WHAT) TO EAT

There are at least two dozen restaurants in Brussels that are gay-oriented and/or gay-popular. If you only have time to try one, we recommend **Taverne/Restaurant Falstaff** (rue Henri Maus 25–27; tel. 511 98 77 and 511 87 89). It's certainly not exclusively gay, but one look at the patrons will convince you of its gay-popularity. And one look at the Belle Epoque decor will tell you why:

elaborate murals of the Falstaff story, the mirrors and lamps all with those fantastical twisty frames—a queen's paradise. Sometimes there's a live accordion player. Most times in places that look this great, the food isn't—but here that is decidely not true; if you like good bistro-type fare, you'll love the *waterzooi,* the scampi, and lots more, including the beer. A few mugs of 11.3 per cent alcohol Trappiste Rochefort, and food as well as the rest of life becomes irrelevant, anyway. An also very gay eatery is **Gardian** (rue Marché au Charbon 45; tel. 511 84 77), which features rustic, reasonably priced, hearty, typical Belgian food: *moules,* fish, steaks.

However, gay people in Brussels constantly warned us that, with Brussels food being as fabulous as it is, no gay local would be fool enough to stick to just gay restaurants. Two places we adored, which were recommended to us by gay Belgians as gay-friendly places with food to die for: **Jacques** (quai aux Briques 44, at the newly trendy fish market; tel. 513 27 62; closed Sundays), one of those brownish places—a homey and very locally-popular bistro featuring nothing but perfectly fresh, perfectly cooked fish, with choice of sauce (though the dominatrix/hostess strongly suggests which sauce you should have); and **Serge and Anne** (rue de Peuplier 23; tel. 218 16 62; closed Wednesdays), which has a trendy new-wave red neon "canopy" outside; an old wave pink-and-gold mirrored elegance inside; an effusive, motherly hostess (Anne) who loves us queers, and gives a free aperitif to guests staying at the Rouleau, and astoundingly reasonable prices for nice versions of Belgian standards like chicken croquettes —here, quite mousselike—as well as considerably more ambitious nouvelle-y stuff.

Now look, this gay stuff is all well and good, but let's talk a little more about the real essentials of life, chocolate . . . and chocolate. All in central 1000 Brussels unless noted: **Corné de la Toison d'Or** (Galerie du Roi 24–26), where the light, meltingly buttery, not-overly-sweet white chocolate–covered coffee, *crème fraîche* pralines seduced even the virulent white-chocolate hater; **Mary's** (rue Royale 73, an address you fans of Art Nouveau architecture will conveniently pass on your way to the famous De Ultieme Hallucinatie bar/restaurant, at no. 316), where the purist proprietor, a successor to the real Mary and her partner, uses no white chocolate (plus only about 25 percent milk chocolate) and a bit less sugar; **Le Chocolatier Manon** (Chaussée de Louvain 9A, 1030 Brussels), with the town's biggest and, many feel, best-flavored, selection (60–80 varieties —try the walnut with coffee *crème fraîche* "Manon," too delicate to ship outside Brussels); **Wittamer** (Place du Grand-Sablon 12–13), which old-timers say is the most authentically Belgian chocolatier; and might as well try **Godiva,** too, if only to get your bowels in a righteous uproar about how much cheaper and better this brand is in Belgium, where you can get it everywhere—one store is right on the Grand' Place—than in America. (The Godiva chocolates we get aren't even imported. They're made in Pennsylvania.)

WHERE TO GET THE LATEST DIRT
(INFORMATION RESOURCES)

For lesbians, *the* place is **Artemys Vrouwenboekhandel,** a feminist bookstore. Men are allowed, albeit reluctantly, on the first floor; the second floor, where all the lesbian books are kept and which doubles as a very interesting art gallery, is for women only. Proprietor Marian Lens (who we'd love to have in our back pockets to drag out and flaunt whenever any jerk insists lesbian separatists are dogs with no sense of humor) keeps track of the best current lesbian establishments in Brussels, and throughout Flemish Belgium, and is happy to help female travelers with info. The women's book selection is also pretty irresistible.

An info line for women is **Sapphone:** tel. 346 28 12.

For both gay men and lesbians, A.S.B.L., which publishes *Regard,* has an info service, **Infor-Homosexualités-Belgique** (tel. 648 77 41; or write B.P. 215, 1040 Bruxelles 4). The group meets Monday evenings at chaussée d'Ixelles 281, 1050 Bruxelles. Information is also available from **Antenne Rose,** which publishes *Tels Quels* magazine and runs a "Gay Meeting Point" Mondays and Tuesdays 5 P.M.–7 P.M. and Fridays 7 P.M.–10 P.M. at the Tels Quels bar, whose address is listed in the Brussels night life section above. (An alternative mailing address for Antenne Rose is: B.P. 888, 1000 Bruxelles 1.)

The **AIDS help line** is 511 45 29. The **Ligue Entr'Aides SIDA** group running the line is located at rue Duquesnoy 45, 1000 Bruxelles.

A very handy place to buy, or obtain free, *De Gay Krant* and all local gay publications is librairie **Bon Secours** (100 rue Marché au Charbon). The gay mags are in the second room, to the right of the door.

Following is some gay info for other beguinage cities:

In Ghent
telephone code 091

Gay Organizations/Info Resources: Ghent's chief gay and lesbian group is **'T Gehoor** (care of Volkshogeschool Elcer-Ik, Hoogstraat 9, 9000 Gent), which holds a mixed male and female gay social night on Friday and a women's night on Saturday. The Volkshogeschool's address will be changing, but should be listed in the phone book. The area's lesbian organization is **Lesbisch Doefront** (Postbus 621, 9000 Gent).

Gay Bars and Restaurants: **De Grote Avond** (Huidvetterskaai 40) is a beautiful curio- and plant-filled traditional "brown café" that is gay-owned, very lesbian and gay friendly, and very popular with "all of us," as they say in Flanders code. Outside tables and snacks are available. At a location unbelievable for a gay-friendly place (because of being a major tourist area) is lesbian-owned **'t Ogenblik,** on the Vrijdagsmarkt, which has a terrace and snacks like spaghetti, omelettes, and grilled sandwiches. On tiny nearby Meerseniersstraat is **Cherry Lane,** for both gay women and men. **Paradox** (Vlaanderenstraat 22), a long-existing bar formerly on Kortemeer, has now moved center-city. It's open

Friday, Saturday and Sunday from 8 P.M. to 5 A.M.; Thursday is "women's night," but men are allowed. **Lady Inn** (Haaltebruggeesraat 31) is a long-established women's bar, very cozy and nice although the patrons are prone to butch-femme dress. A friendly lesbian-owned but mixed-clientele fish and vegetarian restaurant is **Warempel,** on the corner of the Zandberg and Onderstraat. Gay-owned but also mixed in clientele is the atmospheric "brown coffee-shop" **Ludwig** (Hoogpoort 37A).

In Leuven
telephone code 016

Gay Organizations/Info Resources: **De Roze Drempel** (Amerikaln 3; tel. 22 85 82) provides info and runs sporadic social events for both gay men and women. *Tels Quels* magazine is sold in Leuven–La Neuve, at **Aimer à Louvain–La Neuve** (31 cour des Trois Fontaines).

Gay Bars: We can't recommend highly enough *Lesbisch* café **Labyrint** (Visserstraat 2). Although it's intentionally almost all women, except for special party nights hosted by De Roze Drempel for the past five years, the café policy is that men *can* come *with* women. "We've had a lot of difficulties around that. There are still discussions." The main space here is a tiny bar/café room, where marathon card parties take place on many slower nights. But despite the place's size, the management still serves 15 Belgian beers (including one alcohol-free one), plus fruit juice, *wijn* (wine), coffee, tea, and chips. Up several steps, off the hall, is a larger high-tech neon-lit dance room with a terrific sound system and modern sculpture–decorated tables, for their weekend discos. The club also publishes a little newsletter/magazine, in Flemish, with a calendar of events. Labyrint is open from 8 P.M. to 2 A.M., except Fridays and Saturdays 8 P.M.–4 A.M., and Sundays 8 P.M.–midnight.

For men, the friendliest place for meeting and talking to people is the Wednesday café run by De Roze Drempel. Also in Leuven: **Pieter Coutereel** (Vaarstraat 16; open 4 P.M. to 2 A.M., except Wednesdays 7 P.M.–2 A.M. and Saturdays 9 P.M.–2 A.M.) is central, right near town hall, and a bit more leathery than **De Schrabbel** (Craenendonck 21; open 9 P.M.–1 A.M.).

In Kortrijk
telephone code 056

Gay Organizations/Info Resources: **Vrouwenhuis** (Plein 52, 8500 Kortrijk; tel. 20 07 13) holds **De Nymfen** café for women on Friday and Saturday, currently from 8 P.M., but best call about times.

Gay bars: De Gay Krant lists half a dozen.

Gay organizations/info resources: **FWH (Federatie Werkgroepen Homosex-ualiteit)** is at Dambruggestraat 204, B-2008 Antwerpen; tel. 233 25 02. **Roze Aktiefront** is at Helmstraat 5; tel. 236 64 80. The lesbian group **Atthis** (Verbondstraat 53, 2000 Antwerpen; tel. 216 37 37) has social evenings Fridays and Saturdays from 8:30 P.M.

Gay Bars: Antwerp is second only to Brussels in sheer number of gay venues, and while not outstanding for lesbians or any of us vanilla sort of vacationers, is second to none for gay men seeking hot action. Most bars are conveniently close to the railroad station. The big gay street is Van Schoohovenstraat, and you cannot miss the bars; but check *De Gay Krant* for specific addresses, if you're feeling insecure. For women, the best bar bet is **Shakespeare** (Oude Kornmarkt 26), where men are also allowed.

WHAT TO READ

Among the books in English that give some background on the beguines are *A Small Sound of the Trumpet: Women in Medieval Life,* by Margaret Wade Labarge (Beacon); *The Fourth Estate: A History of Women in the Middle Ages,* by Shulamith Shahar (University Paperbacks); and *A History of Their Own: Women in Europe, Volume 1,* by Bonnie S. Anderson and Judith P. Zinsser (Harper & Row).

WHAT TO BRING (WOMEN ONLY)

For info on the **wonderful peeing devices,** the manufacturer is Sani-fem Corporation (Box 4117, Downey, CA 90241; tel. 213/928-3435). The Freshette is also available retail for roughly $16, from Campmor (810 Route 17 North, Box 997-B, Paramus, NJ 07653-0997; orders 800/526-4784, or 201/445-9868 in NJ).

$\mathscr{P}$ARIS

Love, Literature . . .
and Lunch

$\mathscr{F}$or gay people—especially Americans, and most especially literary lesbians—Paris from the Gay Nineties through the roaring Twenties was one big publishing party, and everyone came.

If the party had been written up in a gossip column of the day (as it often was, if you count Janet Flanner's Paris letters, which she wrote for *The New Yorker* for half a century under the pen name "Genêt"), the gay-expatriate guest list would have included Gertrude Stein and Alice B. Toklas, bookseller–den mother Sylvia Beach of the legendary Shakespeare and Company, *Little Review* publishers Jane Heap and Margaret Anderson, Oscar Wilde, Djuna Barnes, Paul Bowles, composer Virgil Thomson, Cole Porter, fashion designer Erté, poet Renée Vivien, painter Romaine Brooks, and steely-eyed, golden-haired charisma queen Natalie Barney, informal commander in chief and fairy godmother of the lesbian community, who claimed that her life was her work, her writing merely a result of it. Among our French brothers and sisters of the time were André Gide, Marcel Proust, Jean Cocteau, bookseller (and Beach's lover) Adrienne Monnier, writer-actress Colette, and the great French poet Anna de Noailles, who was sometimes called the French Sappho.

Why Paris, instead of some other city, was such a gay—and especially a lesbian—mecca is difficult to pinpoint. No doubt the fact that the Napoleonic Code made no provision to punish homosexuality contributed to the city's development as a center of the arts and salon culture. And surely the reputation of Paris as the world's pleasure capital—and yet also a place where talent rather than money was the main passport to pleasure—attracted foreigners who wouldn't have dreamed of shedding their inhibitions or indulging their propensities at home, even had they been able to afford to. After all, do you think in 1901 America one could, at any price, have seen an opera like Xavier Leroux's *Astarté*—which climaxes with its lesbian cult high-priestess heroine happily setting sail for Lesbos with her new girlfriend, after turning her would-be suitor, Hercules, into a flaming shish kebab by means of the enchanted shirt of Nessus?

Although it was the era of the suffragist in the United States and Britain, the explosion of lesbian culture in Paris seems to have had little connection with feminism. Nor, with the possible exceptions of Barney and Gide, did the partyers of old seem to have had the glimmerings of what we would call a gay consciousness. The open, indulgent air that attracted so many had far more to do with a general cult of decadence that swept Paris in the mid-nineteenth century. Notorious artsy types like painter Rosa Bonheur and journalist Rachilde had been cross-dressing for decades, as had lesbian prostitutes of the 1880s. And the *L* word had no woman-centered political connotations: In artistic and aristocratic circles alike, lesbian eroticism was widely established as harmless fun for women and a source of voyeuristic jollies for men. "You women can do anything," declares male chauvinist *cochon* Renaud while encouraging his wife to have an affair with a female friend in Colette's 1902 *Claudine en Ménage*. "It's charming, and it doesn't matter at all."

Today Paris remains a prime destination for gay tourists, less for its gay life (although there's still plenty of that) than for the city's eternally undisputed claim as the world capital of romance, sensuality, and charm. It's still a place to reinvent yourself as a romantic, too, just as the Indiana-born Flanner transformed herself into the debonair Genêt; and you can do it simply by strolling along the Seine at dusk, watching the city lights blaze up like votive candles as the skies over Notre Dame slip from lavender to velvet black. Paris is a stage set, and if you've seen a million photos of the scenery and heard a million songs explicitly detailing your predecessors' romantic plot turns before you go, that only makes it easier to play your part—no matter how many times you return.

We'll let the other guidebooks tell you about the famous boulevards and monuments. The essentials of our personal Paris all just happen to be *L* words. Lesbians, of course. But also literature, love . . . and lunch.

France, like the rest of the Latin world, was slow to develop a post-Stonewall political culture. The French lesbian-feminist movement didn't gather much steam until after a gay-straight split in the late 1970s, during which Simone de Beauvoir declared lesbianism a bedroom issue not of concern to real feminists (who, after all, had such *poissons* to fry as arguing interminably over whether the pronoun *"je"* should be part of the Feminist Discourse, or whether it implied a male "I"). Today Paris has a lesbian organization, a chapter of ACT UP, a religion-based organization that serves all sexual minorities, plus a handful of other tiny political groups—a pittance compared to what's available anywhere in North America, Britain, or Northern Europe.

There are, however, nearly ninety gay-oriented restaurants in Paris.

"In France, the homosexual people are not so good at organizing gay centers, demonstrations, and these other political things," one of Paris's few activists told us, philosophically. "What we do very well here is getting together to make a feast."

A 1986–1987 survey conducted by the lesbian organization, MIEL (Mouvement d'Information et d'Expression des Lesbiennes) backs this up. Fewer than 30 percent of several hundred women questioned expressed a need for political groups. Nearly 54 percent found gay restaurants essential. Not surprisingly, MIEL itself runs a weekly lesbian dinner cafeteria.

Gay people hardly have a monopoly on eating in Paris. But we do find it amusing that so many French slang words concerning gayness are food-derived: *"gousse"* and *"gousse d'ail"* (clove of garlic) mean lesbian, and *"se gousser"* is the verb for lovemaking between women; *"mangeuse de lentilles"* (eater of lentils, meaning clitorises); *"prendre de l'oignon,"* to take some onion (anus); *"tuyau de poêle"* (stovepipe), the homosexual world; *"papa gâteau"* (papa cake), an older man supporting a younger one in exchange for sexual favors—in other words, a sugar daddy.

And there certainly are tons of famous food connections throughout gay Parisian history. Perhaps the most notorious is the *Alice B. Toklas Cookbook,* which we children of the sixties once pored through for the famous hashish-brownie recipe, only to realize that our 1960 U.S.-printed editions were expurgated. Our favorite Alice and Gertrude story, though, concerns their deliberations about whether to flee Europe for America, as so many expatriates did, during World War II. "Well, I don't know," Ms. Stein reportedly fretted to Ms. Toklas. "I *am* fussy about my food. Let's not leave."

And what about Marcel Proust's madeleines, those little scallop-shaped pastry memory-catalysts from *A la récherche du temps perdu:* Could any but a gay sensibility discover the entire universe of the subconscious mind, in a cookie? Throughout his short life, Proust was famous for throwing spectacular dinners, particularly at the Ritz; this hotel became so much his second home that he was known as Proust of the Ritz. The last thing he consumed before dying, actually, was a take-out order from the hotel, at ten A.M., of iced beer.

Who could forget Toulouse-Lautrec's paintings, symbolizing the whole era of the Decadents, of the Moulin Rouge cancan dancer La Goulue, who lived openly with another dancing girl, La Môme Fromage (Kid Cheese), and whose own nickname means "the Glutton"? Who ever wrote more sensually about food than Colette, whose story "Le Sémiramis-Bar," based on a real turn-of-the-century lesbian hangout on the place Blanche, lovingly describes women's voluptuous waltzes together between courses of *soupe de choux* and *boeuf bourguignon?*

As Hemingway and straight expatriates had their favorite hangouts in Paris's café society, so did gay writers. Djuna Barnes followed mostly-gay Robert McAlmon's ex–Greenwich village crowd to the popular boulevard Montparnasse joints like the Dôme, Coupole, and Rotonde (and once had a not entirely successful fistfight with Hemingway in the Select, when he began pawing Djuna and her girlfriend, artist Thelma Wood), but preferred the less Americanized Café de Flore on boulevard Saint-Germain, as did Janet Flanner and Solita Solano. Gide dined at the Deux Magots and La Closerie des Lilas, Cocteau at Le Jockey, Diaghilev at La Coupole. While Edna St. Vincent Millay's mother was visiting her, they frequented La Rotonde, which Millay once called a "famous sink of corruption." Rad-clyffe "John" Hall thought the best food in Paris was to be had at gorgeously Belle Epoque Lapérouse, where the decor is still hard to beat, although the food, in our opinion, is not. All of these places are still there for your dining pleasure, as is the most notorious gay restaurant hangout, the Pré-Catelan in the Bois de Boulogne. The area around the wooded park where Proust used to cruise is still a major spot for male *drague* (outdoor cruising) today.

Lesbians, after cruising each other from their horse carriages in the Bois de Boulogne (which is how Natalie Barney met both Renée Vivien and Liane de Pougy), preferred liquid refreshment at the Pavilion Chinois. It was here in 1895, on her first visit to Paris, that Barney's later lover Romaine Brooks was drinking lemonade when a beautiful woman abruptly sat down at her table without invitation, ordered and tossed off in one gulp an aperitif, and asked Brooks into her waiting carriage—all without removing her eyes from the young American's. The next night, as a couple, they returned to the Pavilion for a "honeymoon" dinner, the elegance of which was only slightly marred by the full carafe of water Brooks got in the face from one of her seductress's ex-girlfriends.

No way did we encounter anything nearly so exciting in human-drama terms, in any of today's gay-oriented Parisian restaurants. Surprisingly, though, in gastronomic-excitement terms, we ate very well.

Why "surprisingly?" Because we're one hundred percent total food snobs. Both of us are excellent amateur cooks, and what we look for when we eat out is a meal we could not possibly duplicate or surpass ourselves. Remember the famous story of the night in the place de la Concorde when the young Cocteau, trying to network with Diaghilev, was commanded, "Astonish me!"? That's what we want. And, although it has become distressingly easier in the last decade to encounter mediocre meals here, France is one of the few places one can still find astonishing quality.

So as much as we enjoy queer company, we've always tended to follow the recommendations of other serious foodies rather than gay or otherwise socially oriented sources. These recommendations have led us to a number of absolute temples of gastronomy, where we're certain that any gay couple who behave no more outrageously over lunch than we do would feel quite comfortable. And while we don't know about *your* outrageousness capabilities, an eighty-dollar bottle or two of Condrieu certainly has *us* at our best.

Jacques Cagna's eponymous restaurant is one personal favorite, for several reasons. Since we find most restaurant food discouragingly predictable, we adore the fact that we've always been completely unable to figure out even the "traditional," "simple" recipes the menu attributes to the chef's mom. As a gay couple, we've always been treated, despite our East Village clothes and hand-holding across the table, as just as good as any other paying customers. ("Ah, New York!" was the chef's most judgmental comment last time we lunched there. "You are 212 area code or 718?") And the sixteenth-century Relais Louis XIII—which, we rather feel, counts as a partly gay restaurant, since the king, who was crowned there, was bisexual—not only had two-star food, but an absolute stitch of a headwaiter. Noticing our interest in the building's history, he escorted us down to the old cellars after dinner for a look at a few even rarer relics: a combination throne and toilet, and a medieval iron chastity belt—for men. (To make certain we understood the workings, *le* maître d' personally modeled this clanking monstrosity for us.)

We do feel it would be a big mistake to ignore sublime dining experiences like these simply because they're not gay-oriented. Our own big mistake in the dozen or so trips we took to Paris before doing research for this book was assuming that we'd be paying the "gay tax" in Parisian gay restaurants; that is, accepting food inferior to the high Paris average, for the privilege of dining with our own. We were wrong.

For instance, on our earlier trips we missed Far Ouest in Montparnasse (the neighborhood where Hemingway KO'd Barnes), which serves dinner until the perfect disco-queen hour of five A.M. This is the sort of classic Paris bistro you always read about, but can't find anymore. In fact it's the kind of place Georges Simenon's detective Maigret always complained you couldn't find anymore even thirty years ago; one that serves, for dirt-cheap prices, impeccable *cuisine de mère* (Ma's cooking, roughly speaking, assuming Ma is Julia Child): crispy/creamy braised endives *gratinées;* a rich, almost beefy, turkey fricassee; ethereally light *oeufs à la neige* (meringues floating in custard); crackly-glazed, whipped cream–light *crème caramel* pie. The atmosphere is dark and smoky; the decor, spaghetti western—rifles and buffalo hides on the walls. The clientele is mixed straight and gay, New Wave fashionable but neighborhood friendly. So are the bar games, like the quote of the day, which earns you a free meal if you guess who said it. And the proprietor, Françoise, is hot. Sorry we can't tell you if she otherwise is or isn't. Lindsy assumed she was an obvious yes; Pam assumed she was a stylish no—so we didn't ask. Next time.

Then there was Le Petit Prince in the Latin Quarter, a tiny candlelit bistro with a bargain prix fixe dinner. At the table next to us were two guys speaking American English. Both sets of gay-dar went off, and after we'd leaned over to recommend the quenelles, we ended up pushing our table next to theirs and being regaled for hours with their European travel stories —like a recent gaffe in Amsterdam, where they'd worn their Miami pastels into one of the town's toughest leather bars. Dark-haired Mark had just spent the afternoon at one of the gay baths in Paris, where, he insisted, he had only wanted a massage, but ended up with what his masseur termed *le supplement*. Since several of the fancier dishes on the restaurant's menu also carried a small *"supplement,"* his blond boyfriend, Dennis, could not stop teasing. "We're in true love because we're both trash," they explained, beaming.

Most gay restaurants actually have at least one prix fixe menu, offering a full three-course dinner for about the price of one drink at some of Paris's glamorous gay discos. And the restaurants are a better deal than the bars in more ways than financially. Interestingly, they are, in our opinion, a much better way to meet other gay people, at least for couples. For starters, your high-school French is going to be severely challenged in a noisy bar or disco, and unlike Copenhagen or Amsterdam, Paris isn't a place where it's polite to assume people want to speak English. But even the French them-selves don't find their bars especially accessible: the news weekly *Gai Pied* recently complained that compared to the gay spaces of other lands, the Paris bars suffer from *"la prétention."*

We went barhopping one night with Daniel Placenti, whom we had met the previous month at London's Gay and Lesbian Centre, and a bunch of his friends—six of us packed Marx Brothers–style into a car which, like many French autos, was smaller than some handbags we have owned. Evidently, it had been a busy month: Daniel had already met, and broken up with, a new lover. "I think my heart is now entirely broken," he ex-plained, casting his long-lashed eyes to the ceiling of Le Swing, the casually trendy James Dean–clone men's bar where we'd arranged to rendezvous.

He flung himself dramatically into a chair. "It is nothing, really. Just that perhaps my life is over."

Daniel grew up in a small town in Burgundy where gay life consisted of men and boys furtively meeting for sex in the shadows of a bridge. He came out to his family the day his father, as an insult, called him a fairy. "Yes, that's what I am," Daniel agreed. Soon afterward he left home to pursue an advanced degree in Russian studies at the prestigious Ecole National de Commerce. Like gay people everywhere who've made the great escape from the provinces, Daniel is a much happier homo in Paris, even when he's temporarily desolate.

Daniel's friend François had also recently ended a relationship, and the two of them spent much of the evening in a living tableau of the cliché about hot-blooded, emotional Latin men, debating the depths of love and pain right down to the details of various types of tears, while we discussed stuff like the inferior exhaust systems on Eastern European cars with a straight Russian exchange student who was crashing at Daniel's apartment for the week. In any case, even though Daniel and François were too miserable to do much cruising, we recommend Le Swing to those of you who adamantly desire to mingle with models.

Like much of gay Paris, Le Swing is in the Les Halles/Marais area on the Right Bank, in one of the oldest parts of the city. In the same neighborhood is the men's hangout (women welcome) we personally enjoyed the most: the festive and friendly Le Zinc, a narrow three-level bar. The bottom floor looks like an old catacomb; the middle floor, painted with a mural of Fred Astaire and Rita Hayworth dancing, turns into a sing-along piano bar after ten, featuring gorgeous high-cheekboned actor types belting out mostly French-language cabaret songs with a smattering of Broadway-baby stuff.

For women, we liked Le Champmeslé, which has an informal neighborhood-hangout air that's a welcome rarity in glamour-conscious Parisian gay nightclubs. In the rustically decorated front room, a countercultureish mixed male and female crowd chats; through a big, arched, open doorway, there's a small but comfortable all-female table area. The night we were there, someone had brought in her pet kitten, much to the delighted ooh-la-las and ahs of the crowd.

More typically awash in *la prétention* was Katmandu. For well over a decade, until it closed in 1990, this place was invariably described by gay guides as the most glamorous women's bar in the world. Everyone in this mirror-walled place was terrifically cool and preoccupied-looking, carefully avoiding eye contact; there were packs of Marlboros everywhere, and palpable nerves in the air. It is not easy to get relaxed at nearly a hundred francs per beer. One dancer, an every-hair-in-place blonde in a tailored pantsuit, moved to the music (which was supposed to be simulating an orgasm, but actually sounded, as does all French rock'n'roll, like a Pepsi commercial) with such careful control that we suspected she still had the coat hanger in her jacket. The night's entertainment, *le spectacle*, was a tacky self-conscious drag queen in a gown the colors of a raspberry-orange Popsicle, lip-synching badly to "I Am What I Am." But worst of all was that once our eyes finally became accustomed to the darkness and strobe lights, we realized that the perimeter of the club was lined with GROSS, POP-EYED STRAIGHT GUYS: Adam's apples bobbing, expensive business suits sweating, the whole voyeuristic-thrill number. The real *spectacle*, obviously, was us.

Compare this with a night we spent at the Gai Moulin, a tiny but enormously popular restaurant in Les Halles. The food here is reasonable and perfectly okay, though nothing to write home about, but the clientele —mostly gay male with a sprinkling of lesbians and straights—was, as the French say, *super*. (Except that they pronounce it Soup Pear.) Our waiter's standard method of service was to fling plates at the table with a dramatic Zorro-like flourish, and say (in English), *"Take it, dahling."* Our neighboring male tablemates' standard method of getting our waiter's attention was to goose him.

We were having a conversation about other gay restaurants we should try, when we couldn't help but notice that the two guys at the table to our left, which was about two inches from our ears, were politely eavesdropping. Before long, they were, with intense concern, throwing in their two cents' worth of restaurant recommendations, as were the two tables to our right. The table across the aisle called loudly to the bartender for a copy of *Gai Pied*'s annual guide, and soon everyone from the nearest five tables was busy underlining favorite spots, arguing the merits of this place, pooh-poohing that place.

Now that we were friends, the guys at the table to our left firmly insisted that we try their red wine instead of our white, which they obviously felt was a sissy choice for dykes. Lindsy, who is a confirmed computer nut, ended up having a long discussion with one of them about gay life in the age of telecommunications. Apparently there are vast numbers of Frenchmen having safe sex with each other while typing with one hand on their Minitel, the ubiquitous home computer. Not just men, either: this fellow swore that two straight female secretaries in his office log on to the service pretending to be gay men, just because the sex is so torrid.

Before the night was over, forty-one-year-old Guy and twenty-three-year-old Noël had also told us the whole story of their relationship, which was mighty long, especially considering that they'd only met three days before. "He wants to get married!" explained Guy, looking terrified.

As enjoyable as all these restaurants are, though, we'd like to urge you to try a few alfresco picnics in Paris. Even if budget were not a consideration, we'd do this, for reasons both gastronomic and aesthetic. Either lunch or dinner is fine; during the summer, the sun doesn't set until about eleven P.M.

Buy your supplies at any charcuterie near your hotel. A charcuterie is the equivalent of an American neighborhood deli . . . except instead of counters full of gelatinous turkey roll and soggy potato salad and cole slaw, the average charcuterie stocks genuine Parma, Bayonne, and other regional hams; unpasteurized Brie, Camembert, and maybe a dozen or two other farm-fresh cheeses; several solid shelves of homemade specialty tidbits like *poireaux* (leeks) or *haricots verts* (delicate matchstick-thin stringbeans) vinaigrette, *céleri rémoulade,* crabmeat—real, not those hideous little "Sea Legs"—stuffed in an avocado and topped with a piping of rich *aïoli* mayonnaise, *oeufs en gelée,* and elegant salads of tiny shrimp or fresh salmon *garni* in large scallop shells; and perhaps half a dozen rich pastry desserts, like the mocha-whipped-cream-filled Paris-Brest.

There is not a single lowly neighborhood charcuterie in Paris that does not, in our opinion, blow America's most highly touted delis right out of the water. But for a special treat, if you don't mind schlepping over to the nontouristed out-of-the-way Tenth Arrondissement, try a gay charcuterie, or at any rate one that advertises heavily in the French gay media: Au Bon Porc, one of the few places left in Paris that carries, aside from an astoundingly large ham selection and fresh unprocessed caviars, fresh *foie gras* (goose liver)—a buttery piece of heaven which the meat-eater of us considers, generically, to be the second-best thing she has ever had in her mouth.

At any of these shops, order *une petite barquette* (a small container) *de* half a dozen fabulous things you point to. Then take them to some gay nostalgia spot: the Bois de Boulogne, perhaps. Or the Jardin du Luxembourg, where Gertrude and Alice spent their first afternoon alone together, strolling past the still-existing statues of all France's historic queens (female), while Gertrude gradually got over her annoyance at Alice's lateness: Toklas evidently ran on gay people's time. Or Lindsy's favorite gay picnic destination: Père Lachaise cemetery in the east end of the Right Bank, final reclining place of stars from Edith Piaf to Jim Morrison, and of many of our own.

There is a popular modern *drague* in Père Lachaise—at the south end, near the tomb of "French Sappho" Anna de Noailles. Proust rests in Père Lachaise, under a typically piss-elegant black-and-gold marble rectangle. Oscar Wilde is here, too. The modernistic-archaic sphinx-like flying angel, with a crown of men, that graces his tomb has had its genitals broken off by souvenir hunters, but is obviously much visited and decorated by graffiti from modern admirers. (Although we must say that scrawled messages like "You died not in vain for the love that dare not speak its name" cannot, however touching, begin to compare with hundreds of Wilde's own epigrams—like "Niagara Falls is only the second biggest disappointment of the standard honeymoon.")

While Wilde's grave is overflowing with gay tributes, Gertrude's and Alice's mutual single-stoned bathtub-shaped burial place is sadly bare. Happily, we did bring them a little something, though not without some to-do. Lindsy suggested flowers. Pam felt a roast chicken would be more appropriate. Finally, we settled on a leek, inscribed, "Bon appetit!"

We did not leave them even a crumb of the Paris-Brest. But we're certain that Gertrude and Alice understood, entirely.

If the number of Paris literary-walking-tour guides published is any indication, tourists can't get enough of this stuff. Unfortunately, with few exceptions, most of Paris's famous fag and dyke dwellings are not marked with those little historical plaques one sees everywhere else, and most of the guidebooks are distressingly weak on gay gossip. Nonetheless, historic gay sites are there to be found, and not just by us latter-day gay-American-expatriate wannabes. According to Catherine Gonnard, editor of *Lesbia*, the magazine born of the de Beauvoir purge, French lesbians also make dutiful pilgrimages to the places where Barney, Stein, and the rest held court.

We'll start our tour of queer Paris on the Right Bank, where Marcel Proust, the aristocratic invalid writer of *A la récherche du temps perdu*, lived—never more than a few hundred yards from his parents' first home at 8 rue Roy—for most of the nearly fifty years of his life. For almost thirty of those years, Proust lived at number 9 on the chestnut-tree-lined boulevard Malesherbes, a seven-story, double-doored, iron-balconied house that was a wing of the Hôtel de Maillé. At 6 rue du Cirque was the stone-fireplaced room of twenty-three-year-old Proust's first real (nontransitory) male lover, the nineteen-year-old Venezuelan pianist and composer Reynaldo Hahn. Their affair was passionate for only two years, but for Proust, many other younger and lower-class "friends" followed.

In 1900, a problem with the lease forced Proust and his mother, with whom he lived until her death, to move to 45 rue de Courcelles. It was at 69 rue de Courcelles that Proust first met his lifelong friend Prince Antoine Bibesco, who attempted to give him handshake lessons, advising a powerful grip rather than the limp-fish style Proust favored. "People would take me for an invert," the effete closet queen demurred. Oscar Wilde once visited and, much to Proust's annoyance, made disparaging comments about the furniture.

Following his mother's death, Proust moved to the first floor of 102 boulevard Haussmann. But much of Proust's second-best furniture found a home in the entrance hall of the Hôtel Marigny, at 11 rue de l'Arcade, opposite the Gare St. Lazare. Proust fans who wish to wallow a bit deeper in his mind and life will be intrigued to know that the Marigny, which was the model for Jupien's brothel in *A la récherche*, is today a regular hotel, where gay visitors are welcome. In 1917, though, the Marigny was also a real-life male whorehouse, opened with Proust's financial help.

Proust was not exactly a model happy homo. (He once wrote a fifteen-hundred-word *sentence* on homosexuality, beginning: "A race upon which a curse is laid . . ." and continuing in the same vein.) And at the point in his life when he frequented the Marigny, he was not perhaps at his best. To reach orgasm, he would quiz bogus "butcher boys"—actually just procured hirelings—on the bloody details of their day's animal-slaughtering. He also required the young men to beat live rats with sticks, or, alternatively, impale the rats with hatpins.

Finally, after sixteen years, Proust moved briefly to a series of places nearer the Bois de Boulogne, and then died. Meanwhile, the notorious Bois area had also become the home of another tortured artsy sort, the delicate young poet Renée Vivien. Unfortunately, the street she lived on no longer exists, but you wouldn't have been able to do much of a Peeping Tom number even back in 1900; all the apartment's windows were nailed shut and hung with heavy Oriental-tapestry curtains. One of the two most important lovers of the very twentieth-century Natalie Barney, Vivien was much the nineteenth-century Baudelairian hothouse flower, wandering through her dark, exotically-scented abode dressed entirely in black and purple. Here, Vivien threw dinner parties where she served nothing but overspiced hors d'oeuvres, herself only drinking champagne—and frequently deserting her guests in mid-meal, after receiving mysterious summonses from a baroness she referred to only as "the Master."

Barney tried repeatedly to lure Vivien back from the baroness. Once she inveigled an opera-star friend to sing outside Vivien's window, while Barney threw a poem tied to a bouquet of flowers through the gate. On another occasion, it is rumored, Barney had herself delivered to morbidly romantic Vivien in a coffin lined with white satin. But to no avail. Vivien was terrified of the baroness, and even gave her neighbor Colette a very sexually explicit four-word explanation of exactly how the Master would kill her, if not obeyed. In actuality, Vivien died—in a manner far more physiologically predictable, especially given her dining habits—of anorexia and tuberculosis.

Most of gay literary Paris hung out on the Left Bank, particularly in the Sixth Arrondissement. One headquarters was Sylvia Beach's bookstore–lending library–post office–rendezvous, Shakespeare and Company, first located at 8 rue Dupuytren and then, from 1921 to 1941, a block away at 12 rue de l'Odéon. (Neither is any relation to today's Shakespeare and Company, on the rue de la Bûcherie.) While you're on rue de l'Odéon, notice also number 7, home of La Maison des Amis des Livres, which was run by Beach's French lover, Adrienne Monnier; and number 18, where

Beach lived with Monnier on the top floor from 1921 to 1932. Beach moved out after Monnier took a new girlfriend, the photographer and sociologist Gisèle Freund, but, in typical incestuous lesbian-community style, continued dining here with them every night.

The most important gathering places of the period, however, were the salons. And the two most important were run by lesbians: Gertrude Stein and Natalie Barney.

Certainly the more celebrated was that of Stein, who did not fail to underestimate her own importance: Sculptor Jacques Lipchitz described Her Imperiousness as "a Buddha with a topknot." While Stein talked with the important folks at their Saturday soirées, Toklas, to whom Stein sometimes referred as her wife, entertained the other wives with talk of fashion and shopping. It is not difficult to see why Stein had few close women friends. However, the large, comfortable apartment at 27 rue de Fleurus where Stein and Toklas lived for thirty-five years is one of the few gay landmarks honored by an official plaque.

Personally, we prefer, although they did not, the location of Steins's and Toklas's later apartment. It is situated in narrow old one-block-long rue Christine, conveniently near Relais Louis XIII and Jacques Cagna, the two-star restaurants we mentioned earlier. In the seventeenth century, this flat at number 5 was the abode of Queen Christina of Sweden, a somewhat horsy-looking individual, who, many of us feel, was done better, sartorially at least, by Greta Garbo than by herself. Christina was known in Rome, where she spent her last years, as the Queen of Sodom, and in Sweden as Her Majesty the King.

While living in rue Christine, Toklas patronized the same rue de Seine market as former Cincinnati girl Natalie Clifford Barney, who lived in a two-story eighteenth-century pavilion off a courtyard in back of 20 rue Jacob. Barney, however, arrived to grocery-shop in a glass coach, complete with footmen. This is indicative of why it would have been our preference to wangle an invitation to one of Barney's do's—though not her Friday afternoon ones. These were mixed affairs, like Stein's salons, and somewhat staid. Poetry readings were the main fare, and tea the strongest drink.

Barney's all-lesbian gatherings at the Temple à l'Amitié, an early nineteenth century "Doric" shrine buried in her overgrown rue Jacob garden, were another story. Among the usual guests one might find Liane de Pougy and Emilienne d'Alençon, famous courtesans of the day who preferred women on their off hours; married ladies with the same off-hours preferences, like British feminist Anna Wickham; poet Lucie Delarue-Mardrus; Duchess Elisabeth de Clermont-Tonnerre, a French aristocrat; the Princesse de Polignac, formerly Winnaretta Singer, American sewing-machine-heiress-turned-French-aristocrat; and Barney's main lover for over forty years, the painter Romaine Brooks. Brooks finally left Barney, who was, on principle, both noncloseted and nonmonogamous, when the latter took up with another woman—at age eighty-plus. (Actually, most of the above guest list were also Barney exes.)

Drifting through the crowd dressed like her famous uncle might be Dolly Wilde, whose nickname was Oscaria, or Janet Flanner, outfitted in top hat and tails. At some soirées, guests came as Greek goddesses: as well as happily celebrating female sexuality, the strongly feminist Barney was committed to creating our own women's mythology, or rediscovering it from ancient models. For entertainment, Mata Hari rode into one of Barney's parties nude on a white horse. Colette once reportedly danced naked.

It was a bit farther down the block, in a dark third-floor flat at number 28 (corner of rue Jacob and rue Visconti) that Colette first lived with Henri "Willy" Gauthier-Villars; and here that the naïve young provincial bride began the sensational bestselling "Claudine" novels that her opportunistic writer-reviewer husband, for a time, passed off as his own. Though bisexual Colette later returned to men, she left Willy in 1906 to live and work as a female-"male" acting team for five years with the Marquise "Missy" de Belbeuf. Missy was a rather notorious transvestite. In fact, the disgruntled Willy is said to have consoled himself for the loss of his wife to a woman by traveling in "Ladies Only" compartments on trains and replying indignantly, when challenged, "But I am the Marquise de Belbeuf!"

Since we're big "Let's Pretend" players, one of the things that most excited us about Paris was discovering how many of our literary lesbian hero-worship objects lived in hotels that still exist—and whose managements, like that of the Martigny, have assured us that gay travelers are perfectly welcome. Anyone who wants to play at being Natalie Barney, for instance, couldn't do better these days than the Hôtel des Marronniers, almost right across the street from Barney, at 21 rue Jacob. The hotel is located in a beautiful garden courtyard, which ensures much the same private feel as Barney's own pavilion. In addition, the rooms are furnished with period furniture, and the heavy-beamed top floors have a great view over the Left Bank rooftops to the towers of St-Germain-des-Prés.

Down the block at 44 rue Jacob is the Hôtel d'Angleterre, where Djuna Barnes settled upon first arriving in Paris in 1920. Along with Janet Flanner, the flamboyantly caped Barnes was one of only a few of the Paris expatriates without an independent income, who had to work to support herself as well as for personal fulfillment. She did this sitting on her bed at the Angleterre, most mornings, after spending most nights chasing around the bars after her self-destructive and alcoholic but awfully good-looking girlfriend, sculptress Thelma Wood. Given the difficulty of writing on this sort of schedule, it is perhaps fortunate that in the 1920s a room at the Angleterre was seventy-five cents a day.

Around the corner at 36 rue Bonaparte, more upscale journalist couple Janet Flanner and Solita Solano were paying, in 1923, nearly a dollar for a large room on the fourth floor of the eighteenth-century Hôtel Saint-Germain-des-Prés. Roast-beef dinners at a nearby bistro cost the equivalent of ten cents. Later, Solano and Flanner ended up renting three additional rooms, remaining together at the hotel for sixteen years—seven years after both had taken up with other women. Flanner's girlfriend, as another understandably perplexed expatriate noted in a letter to Stephen Vincent Benét, even had an additional girlfriend. It is clear, ladies, that some things never change. Hopefully, an army of ex-lovers cannot fail.

Both Willa Cather and Oscar Wilde stayed for a time at the antique-furnished Hôtel Quai Voltaire, located at number 19 on this busy street right across the river from the Louvre. Both also left, but Wilde, after his imprisonment in England on sodomy charges, returned to Paris until his death. His last residence was the former Hôtel d'Alsace at 13 rue des Beaux-Arts, where the bill he'd run up caused Wilde to note, "I am dying beyond my means." The place is now a four-star decorator palace known simply as L'Hôtel; reportedly, a few pieces of Wilde's furniture are still in his room, number 16.

Gertrude and Alice used to put up their guests at the Hôtel Recamier, at 3 *bis* place Saint-Sulpice. But that isn't why we stayed at this intimate, florally decorated corner building. We were actually more intrigued by Thelma Wood, the love of Barnes's life, who was living here at the time they met. (According to Barnes's biographer Andrew Field, Edna St. Vincent Millay also found the Bugatti-driving wildwoman Wood irresistible, for a brief Parisian Sapphic interlude before her marriage.)

After they broke up, Wood was the model for the mysterious Robin Vote character in Barnes's best known (and gayest) novel, *Nightwood*. It wasn't actually until we'd unpacked all our clothes and books, though, and read the description in *Nightwood* of the second-floor abode with its two narrow windows overlooking the cathedral, that we realized we'd accidentally ended up in Robin Vote's very room.

We've saved love until last, since it's what everyone thinks of first when they think of Paris.

But enough about everyone; let's talk about us. Because we got "married" in Paris. By a Baptist minister, no less. And we'd recommend it as a dynamite alternative to any couple who have considered a gay wedding in America, but have not been able to find a truly decent caterer here.

A little background: We have never, ever been even remotely tempted to have a Metropolitan Community Church–type gay wedding ceremony at home. Although we expect to be together for the duration, and though we like gifts of cookware as well as the next person does, what we really want are the *legal* benefits of marriage. No ceremony in the world is going to change the fact that we spend thousands of dollars a year in taxes and health-insurance costs that we wouldn't have to shell out if we were straight.

Hence "gay weddings" had always struck us as a bit of a sop. We wanted a real wedding. And when we first heard that Denmark was close to passing registered-partnership legislation in 1989, we decided that as soon as it happened, we'd catch the next flight out, get married in Denmark, and then turn ourselves over to whatever U.S. gay organizations wanted a legal test case. By the time it became clear that the Danish law is only for Danes—at least one partner must be a citizen—we were already pretty far gone into the romantic, as well as legal, excitement of a European wedding.

Meanwhile we had signed a contract to write this guide and had begun writing to gay groups all over Europe asking for information. By chance one of our respondents was Pasteur Joseph Doucé, a Belgian Baptist Minister and head of the Centre du Christ Libérateur in Paris. As far as openly gay clergy in France go, the pastor later told us, "I am it." So great was his notoriety that his Tahitian-raised boyfriend Guy, who only became religious after moving to Paris, couldn't even find an established Protestant church that would baptize him.

Less a gay-rights group than what its letterhead describes as a "pastoral and psychological information and help center for sexual minorities in France," the CCL is the largest gay organization in the country. It has about a thousand official members, and many other people use the facility on a more casual, occasional basis. Affinity groups that meet more or less regularly at the center range from transsexuals and transvestites, to pedophiles, to sadomasochists, to gays and lesbians interested in artificial insemination, to gay birdwatchers. Needless to say, this being France, what many of these groups meet for is communal meals.

What we ourselves immediately noticed, however, in the CCL informational pamphlet that the pastor sent us, was a "celebration of a benediction of love and friendship for a homo or lesbian couple." The leaflet went on to note that "Although the Centre du Christ Libérateur is inspired by the Christian Evangelical Faith, non-Christians, *even atheists* [italics ours], are equally welcome . . . We are not a church or a sect but a social service open to everyone, on the sole condition that they are at least 18 years old."

That sounded pretty flexible to us. Although we were both baptized Protestant, one of us is now a nonchurchgoing Unitarian with vaguely Quaker leanings; the other, who is of half-Jewish ancestry to boot, is even further out of the fold. We both have a soft spot for the early Christians, whose struggles as a minority group are something that any gay activist can probably identify with. But like most politically aware gay-history buffs, we far more experience latter-day Christianity as oppressive rather than supportive of our kind. Nonetheless, we suddenly found ourselves emotionally psyched for a church wedding in Paris. We wrote the pastor back, detailing our theological quibbles and asking if he'd still bless our union.

Let us just summarize the ensuing negotiations by saying that numerous letters were exchanged, splitting hairs over such fine points as whether having a "Christian motivation" for the service meant that we had to start going to church regularly. But the bottom-line answer was yes: Despite our refusal to attend church services, we could have a ceremony as long as our commitment to each other was well thought out and sincere. We were told to show up at eleven A.M. on September sixteenth, with two rings and, if possible, two witnesses.

The cast of characters that morning could not have been better chosen by Fellini, or Almodóvar, or even Walt Disney. Since we'd been unable to convince any of our old American friends to fly over, we actually expected a pretty lonely ceremony. But it didn't turn out that way, thanks to the odd, Byzantine, magical connections of the international gay community.

Showing up behind a bouquet of flowers almost as large as our New York apartment were Mark Steinberg and Dennis Edwards, the Miami couple we'd met at the next table at Le Petit Prince.

Another guest, who also brought flowers, was a gay American student to whom we'd spoken for only a few minutes in the pastor's office when we'd confirmed our arrangements for the ceremony a few days earlier. Arriving straight off the train with full backpack, this cheerful young fellow clutching the CCL's address had materialized in the pastor's study in search of social and housing information. He'd arrived almost simultaneously with another American from Spokane, who was wondering, um, would a shower be possible? "As you see, it can get very busy here," the pastor had smiled, shuttling these total strangers upstairs to a tub while urging them to attend our wedding, with all the unflappable aplomb one would expect from God's PR man.

Then there was Erica, a darling Englishwoman topping six feet tall, who knew the pastor through the CCL's transsexual group.

Finally, there was our friend Daniel, whom we'd recruited as a witness, along with his Franco-Afro-Carribbean friend and roommate, Marie-Hélène, with whom we'd bar-hopped earlier in the week, and her fifteen-year-old little sister. Daniel and the young women, all raised Catholic, found being at a Protestant ceremony nearly as exotic as being at a gay one.

Anyway, we personally were resplendent in brand-new Belgian-lace shawls that were dripping wet. It had rained. Daniel gallantly assured us that, according to an old French proverb, it was lucky to have rain on one's wedding day. But by the time we all filed into the upstairs "chapel" (which also serves the CCL as a kitchen and dining area and general meeting room), the two of us were wrecks. Having already gotten to the point of arguing between ourselves whether "God, She . . ." would be okay or we should hold out for "God, It . . ." we had convinced ourselves that this was all going to be awful, some sort of conversion attempt, maybe; a definite "God, He . . ." experience; a dreadful mistake.

But Pasteur Doucé came through like a real mensch. Obviously having reread our letters, he started his dedication sermon by drawing parallels between early Christians and gay people today. Incorporating the Jewish roots we'd mentioned, he threw in a real zinger by informing us all that this very room in which we were celebrating a gay union had been a Gestapo headquarters during World War II, and musing on how things could change with a little faith, hope, charity, and love—especially love. He then swung into David and Jonathan, charmingly apologizing for the wrong gender even as we protested that the Song of Solomon was our Old Testament fave, and wound up with the story of Ruth and Naomi. We'd actually never thought of this one as a lesbian tale before. But you must hear the pastor's version.

By the time we put the traditional gold bands on each other's left pinkies and broke out the champagne and had everyone sign their names in our new French Bible, Lindsy was quite teary. Erica was heavily hitting the Kleenex, too. Dennis was astonished. *"Well!* I certainly never knew the Bible had those sorts of stories . . . Did he make them up?"

Several months later, we received envelopes in the mail from Erica and from Mark and Dennis. They contained wedding pictures. Everyone looks barely awake—and very, very sweet. "Hopefully one day, events such as your wedding will be widely accepted by most communities, and judged to be equal to other revered unions by all," Erica wrote, "just as it was in our eyes on that Saturday morning."

Believe us, we know that our "wedding" was no substitute for full, or near-full, rights like those granted by Denmark's registration. But for any who have considered celebrating their union publicly in the interim, we highly recommend doing it as we did. Because you have no idea how spiritually satisfying it is to look at American newlyweds, filing out of their frumpy neighborhood wedding halls en route to their tedious heart-shaped honeymoon tubs in the Poconos, and to think: "Hey—*you* may get health insurance, and tax breaks, and hospital visitation, and inheritance rights, and all that other stuff.

"But *we* got married in *Paris!*"

PRACTICAL INFORMATION

PARIS—NUMBER KEY

Organizations
1. Centre du Christ Libérateur (lesbian/gay; 3 bis rue Clairaut)
2. MIEL (women's; 8 cité Prost)

Bars and Discos
3. Le Swing (bar; 42 rue Vieille-du-Temple)
4. Le Quetzal (bar; 10 rue de la Verrerie)
5. Le Piano Zinc (bar; 49 rue des Blancs-Manteaux)
6. Broad-Café (bar; 13 rue de la Ferronnerie)
7. Le Transfert (bar; 3 rue de la Sourdière)
8. The Trap (bar; 10 rue Jacob)
9. Key Largo—Scorpion (disco; 50 rue de la Chaussée-d'Antin)
10. Le Boy (disco; 6 rue Caumartin)
11. La Champmeslé (bar, mainly women; 4 rue Chabanais)

Coffee Shops and Restaurants
12. Coffee-shop Central (3 rue Sainte-Croix-de-la-Bretonnerie)
13. Le Petit Prince (12, rue de Lanneau)
14. Au Petit Cabanon (7 rue Ste Apolline)
15. Le Gai Moulin (4 rue Saint-Merri)
16. L'Hydromel (48 rue Amelot)
17. Joel's (22 rue de Cotte)
18. Far-Ouest (101 rue de l'Ouest)

Bookstores
19. Les Mots à la Bouche (6 rue Sainte-Croix-de-la-Bretonnerie)
20. Autres-Cultures (46 rue Sauffroy)

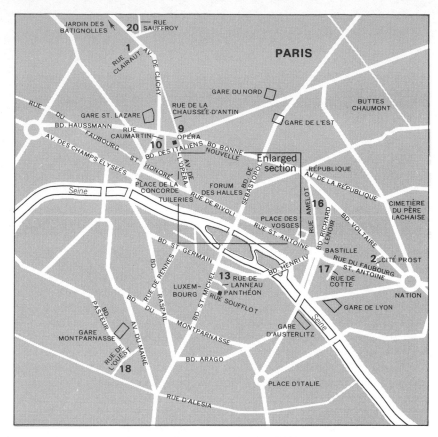

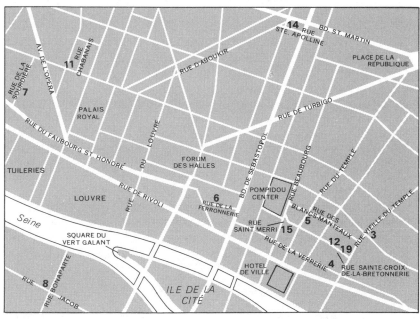

In general, blasé, seen-it-all-know-it-all Paris is not a place one has to fear much in the way of outright rude homophobia. It is helpful to remember that Parisians are not hostile because you are gay. They're just hostile.

Lesbians should not be at all surprised to be subject to extremely persistent pickup attempts, especially at night, but it's not because you're gay. It's because you're "alone"—even if you're in a couple, and point this out politely, and impolitely, in several languages. The up side is, these jerks don't seem to escalate automatically from persistence to physical violence, no matter how obnoxious you get. In fact, they don't even seem to notice your obnoxiousness: "Are you Danish?" "No, Lesbian." "You are Italian?" "We wish to be left alone." "English?" "Go jump in the Seine." "American?" "If you are not gone in ten seconds, I will begin to slowly and painfully disembowel you with the harpoon in my girlfriend's backpack." "Canadian?"

If arrondissement is not mentioned in a listing, you can figure it out by the last two numbers of the postal code—e.g., "75006" is in the sixth.

Clubgoers relying on public transportation should know that the *métro* stops running for the night between 12:30 and 1:15 A.M. and doesn't start again until 5 or 5:30 A.M. We've generally found it safe to walk back to our hotel after the métro shuts down, despite an increased percentage of street creeps. But there are also all-night buses, one of which stops right in gay-central Les Halles.

Best map: Regular full-size folding maps that try to fit everything on one big page are really not practical in Paris—too many tiny streets. So buy a book-form street-by-street map arranged by arrondissement. The *Cartes Taride plan-guide Paris, par arrondissement* is one good map-guide of this sort that has métro and bus routes, too.

Telephone code: 1
Currency unit: the franc (F)

WHERE TO STAY

There are no gay hotels as such in Paris, although one of the establishments listed below advertises in several gay guides. Nevertheless, a number of absolutely wonderful mixed hotels in all price ranges—some of them former homes and hangouts of our early twentieth century expatriate literary heroes—have assured us that gay guests are welcome.

Stars are French government ratings, not ours, included for your information. All prices are for double rooms, but availability of more expensive suites is indicated, if relevant. All hotels have elevators. The first five hotels listed below have, in addition to the direct Paris addresses given for reservations, a U.S. booking representative: Jacques de Larsay, 622 Broadway, New York, NY 10012; 212/477-1600 or 800/366-1510.

Prices: *Inexpensive* = under 230F; *inex./mod.* = 230–380F; *moderate* = 380–570F; *mod./exp.* = 570–700F; *expensive* = 700–850F; *very exp.* = 850–1,500F.

Hôtel des Marroniers ★★★, 21 rue Jacob, 75006 Paris; tel. 43 25 30 69; fax 40 46 88 56. No famous queers we know stayed here, but it's sure the place we'd pick to play Natalie Barney—and it's practically right across the street from her house. The rooms have modern amenities like direct-dial telephones and private bathrooms, yet are charmingly atmospheric. Public facilities include a lovely private garden. The breakfast room off the garden has curly white wrought-iron furniture and exotic drapery that makes it seem one is breakfasting with the Sheik (Rudolph Valentino, not a gross real-life one). *Moderate (suite exp.).*

L'Hôtel ★★★★ L, 13 rue des Beaux-Arts, 75006 Paris; tel. 43 25 27 22; telex 270 870. This is the place where Oscar Wilde died beyond his means, nevertheless complaining about the wallpaper. The wallpaper has unquestionably been fixed. It is still, pricewise, beyond the average couple's means, but has absolutely outstanding decor, atmosphere, and luxury, if you can afford it. Some rooms have balconies; some have semicircular and/or raised bed alcoves that make the beds look like throne rooms . . . pretty fabulous, kids. Downstairs is a "winter garden" piano bar and restaurant, and vaulted-ceiling cellar breakfast room. Métro: Odéon. *Very exp. (suites more).*

Hôtel du Quai Voltaire ★★, 19 quai Voltaire, 75007 Paris; tel. 42 61 50 91; fax (1) 42 61 62 26. Willa Cather and Oscar Wilde, among others, stayed in some of these 33 rooms, antique-furnished for an impression of salonlike dignity, many with panoramic views of the Seine. This nineteenth-century hotel has a modern café-bar, and is located directly across from the Louvre and Tuileries. Métro: Bac, Invalides, or Louvre. *Moderate–mod./exp.*

Hôtel Saint-Germain-des-Prés ★★★, 36 rue Bonaparte, 75006 Paris; tel. 326 00 19. American expatriate journalists and lovers Janet Flanner ("Genêt") and Solita Solano lived in this eighteenth-century hotel from 1925 until World War II. All 30 rooms have private bath, TV, radio, direct-dial phone, and minibar, plus brass beds and other similar festive, decorative touches. Métro: St-Germain-des-Prés. *Mod./exp.–expensive (suites very exp.).*

Hôtel d'Angleterre ★★★, 44 rue Jacob, 75006 Paris; tel. 42 60 34 72; fax 42 60 16 93. This was probably the most popular hotel among 1920s American literary expatriates, among them Djuna Barnes. All rooms have private bathrooms and direct-dial phones. Métro: St-Germain-des-Prés. *Mod./exp.–expensive (suites expensive and very exp.).*

Hôtel Rêcamier ★★, 3 *bis* place St. Sulpice, 75006 Paris; tel. 43 26 04 89. Gertrude and Alice put up guests here. It was also the hotel of *Nightwood*'s "Robin Vote" (and of her real-life model, Djuna Barnes's girlfriend Thelma Wood). Festive, extremely floral decor and some balconies overlooking beautiful St. Sulpice church. While most of the 30 rooms have private bathrooms, there are a few inexpensive bathless doubles. Métro: St. Sulpice. *Inex./mod.–moderate.*

Hôtel Marigny ★★, 11 rue de l'Arcade, 75008 Paris; tel. 42 66 42 71; fax 40 46 83 63. This is the model for Marcel Proust's fictional "Jupien's"—and in real life, the neighborhood male brothel the author frequented. Now it's a respectable middle-class hotel (rooms both with and without private bath), but you can pretend. Métro: Madeleine or St. Augustin. *Inex./mod.–moderate.*

Regent's Hotel ★★, 44 rue Madame, 75006 Paris; tel. 45 48 02 81. This comfortable hotel of 36 rooms (all with phone and private bath) has a cute back terrace for breakfasting, and is right down the street from Gertrude's and Alice's favorite promenade spot, the Jardin de Luxembourg. Métro: St Sulpice. *Moderate.*

Hôtel Plaisant ★★, 50 rue des Bernardins, 75005 Paris; tel. 43 54 74 57. In a quiet cul-de-sac by rue Monge and rue des Ecoles, this 24-room hotel is indeed pleasant, and the quaint decor has a particularly French feel. Rooms come both with and without bath, with the bathless doubles a real bargain. Métro: Maubert. *Inexpensive–inex./mod.*

Grand Hôtel Malher ★, 5 rue Malher, 75004 Paris; tel. 42 72 60 92. Lace curtains downstairs, 36 large rooms upstairs (many with private bath, but some budget rooms with only sink or sink plus shower). It's a simple hotel, but homey and friendly, and the Marais location can't be beat for proximity to gay nightlife. Métro: St.-Paul. *Inexpensive–inex./mod.*

Hôtel Louxor ★, 4 rue Taylor, 75010 Paris; tel. 42 08 23 91. This place advertises in gay media. On a quiet street close to place de la République, the hotel is newly renovated—tasteful modern with a few froufrou touches like gilt mirrors. Some rooms have charmingly old-fashioned balconies: all have bathrooms and telephones. Métro: République. *Inex./mod.*

Hôtel des Grandes Ecoles ★★, 75 rue du Cardinal-Lemoine, Paris 75005; tel. 43 28 79 23. No literary associations—just our favorite Paris hotel, near the Sorbonne and the Mouffetard walking street. From the street, it looks like nothing, a stucco wall. But through the gate and up the cobblestoned walk is a gorgeous and enormous private garden, with the hotel on both sides. Many rooms (which come both with and without bath, and vary dramatically in size) have full-length windows with garden views. The charmingly old-fashioned interior decor is also replete with flower-and-garden patterns. At least minimal French is a good idea here, unless you're a professional-quality mime. Métro: Cardinal-Lemoine. *Inexpensive, inex./mod., and moderate.*

WHERE TO GO (DAY)

We've already sent you off, in the essay section, on quite a literary walking tour, or two or three. But if you happen to have some spare minutes during the day, Paris has a few unusual museums that might particularly appeal to gay sensibilities: **Musée Edith Piaf** (5 rue Crespin-du-Gast, 75011 Paris; tel. 43 55 52 72; open Monday–Thursday 3 P.M.–6 P.M., by appointment only) features memorabilia from the old Parisian Streisand's life and career; **Musée du Cinéma** (Palais de Chaillot, 75016 Paris; tel. 45 53 74 39; open daily except Tuesday) has guided world film–history lecture tours at 10 and 11 A.M. and 2, 3, and 4 P.M.; **Musée des Arts Décoratifs et des Arts de la Mode** (107–109 rue de Rivoli, 75001 Paris; tel. 42 60 32 14; two museums featuring all sorts of different trendy design themes—furniture designs, French court costumes—handily located in the gay Marais, open Wednesday through Sunday; **Musée de la Femme et Des Automates** (12 rue du Centre, Neuilly; tel. 47 45 29 40; open 2 P.M.–5 P.M. daily) is a museum of women and automation, right in one of Natalie Barney's old neighborhoods. So who needs the Louvre?

If you're up for some real exercise, while meeting French gay people in a relaxed nonbar setting, the outdoors club **Rando's** (B.P. 30, 75642 Paris Cédex 10; tel. 47 70 44 45) sponsors a variety of walking and cycling trips for different athletic levels every month. They run tea dances and similar more conventional social stuff, too.

Maps of the grave locations at **Père Lachaise** cemetery are sold at numerous stationery and souvenir stores in the area. Really, you can't miss them. An alternative guide to *all* Paris's cemeteries is *Permanent Parisians* (see the "What to Read" section). The cemetery's main entrance is off boulevard de Ménilmontant near avenue Gambetta (Métro: Gambetta or Philippe-Auguste). It's open 9 A.M.–6 P.M. in the summer; 7:30 A.M.–6 P.M., in the spring and fall; and 8:30 A.M.–5 P.M. in the winter.

A final hint: *Les Miz* fans who loved the book and loved the show should not feel that they are also, therefore, certain to love the "Egouts de Paris" (Sewers of Paris) tour (pont de l'Alma, corner of quai d'Orsay). We were eagerly anticipating something bizarre. But in truth, the tour's not literary, it's not theatrical; it's just a lot of plumbing facts.

WHERE TO GO (NIGHT)

Nightspots mentioned in the text are: the always-packed **Le Swing** (42 rue Vieille-du-Temple, Fourth Arrondissement), open daily from noon (Sunday from 2 P.M.); **Le Piano Zinc** (49 rue des Blancs-Manteaux, First Arrondissement), a cabaret open (except Monday) from 6 P.M., but don't go until at least 10 or 11, to allow both singers and audience time to warm up; and for women, **Le Champmeslé** (4 rue Chabanais, Second Arrondissement), a rustic, comfortable bar with cabaret entertainment on Thursday, open from 6 P.M. Monday through Saturday—guys perfectly welcome in the front room.

For lesbians, the hottest dance ticket is *Lesbia* magazine's once-monthly **Péniche le Chaland** (Port de Suffern, 75015 Paris; Métro: Bir-Haleim; RER [the suburban train line]: Champ-de-Mars). This is a women-only disco on a barge. For info on the date each month, call *Lesbia* (see "Information Resources," below).

For gay men, probably the best all-around dance club is **Le Boy** (6 rue Caumartin, Ninth Arrondissement), which has no cover charge except Friday and Saturday, and popular theme nights early in the week. A young, exuberant crowd.

Gay men who are staying at one of the rue Jacob or rue Bonaparte hotels couldn't be in a more convenient location if they get a sudden late-night urge to cruise: **The Trap** (10 rue Jacob) is known as an hot pickup spot. Other popular cruisy places for guys are **Le Quetzal** (10 rue de la Verrerie, Fourth Arrondissement), and, for the leather crowd, **Le Transfert** (3 rue de la Sourdière, First Arrondissement). **The Broad Café** (13 rue de la Ferronerie, First Arrondissement) is better.

WHERE TO EAT

Gay-popular (-owned -oriented, -friendly) restaurants mentioned in the text are: romantic **Le Petit Prince** (12 rue de Lanneau, Fifth Arrondissement; tel. 43 54 77 26); **Far Ouest** (101 rue de l'Ouest, Fourteenth Arrondissement; tel. 45 42 28 33), the bistro that bistros used to be, and serving food until 4 or 5 A.M.; and friendly, festive **Gai Moulin** (4 rue Saint Merri, Fourth Arrondissement; tel. 42 77 60 60). Others we highly recommend are **Joel's** (22 rue de Cotte, Twelfth Arrondissement; tel. 43 43 88 20), which has bright—extremely bright—trendy decor, and a dynamite Sunday buffet brunch featuring regional charcuterie products from the Tarn; and very stylish, women-owned **L'Hydromel** (48 rue Amelot, Eleventh Arrondissement; tel. 43 38 35 52), which specializes in succulent wood-grilled meats, but cheerfully accommodates veggie people, too. (Don't confuse the latter with the women's center MIEL's **Hydromel** cafeteria, a totally different eatery open Friday nights from 7 P.M. [see "Information Resources" for address].)

Reverse-chic practitioners will understand at a glance why **Coffeeshop Central** (3 rue Sainte-Croix-de-la-Bretonnerie, Fourth Arrondissement) is currently *the* place to go for daytime *petite restauration* (a snack that satisfies). Mostly men patronize this small, very casual, deliberately downscale place, but it's comfy for all. They serve brunch and full lunch specials, or you can just have a coffee or beer.

A restaurant/disco much à la mode at the moment for fags and fagettes with show-biz flair, and a sincere love for lots of houseplants, is **Key Largo** (50 rue de la Chaussée d'Antin, Ninth Arrondissement; tel. 42 80 69 49). One of our Parisian gay male friends claims he and some lesbian buddies had the most fun of practically their whole lives here. Of course, they're young.

A place we couldn't find due to an insufficiently detailed map (object lesson here), but which several women recommended as very lesbian-popular, so we feel we should mention, is **Au Petit Cabanon** (7 rue Sainte Appolline, Third Arrondissement; tel. 48 87 66 53), which has traditional French cooking.

Avoid the inexplicably popular Chez Max—of all the restaurants we tried that actively solicit gay business, the only gross disappointment. Although if a salad with overcooked *foie de volaille*, limp pasta à la Chef Boyardee, beef ordered *bleu* that arrives medium-well done, and attitudinous waiters is just your cup of *thé*, do hurry right over, and say we sent you.

Nongay cafés mentioned in the text because of gay historical connections include: **Les Deux Magots** (6 place St.-Germain-des-Prés); **La Flore** (172 blvd. St. Germain); **Le Select** (99 blvd. du Montparnasse); **La Coupole** (102 blvd. du Montparnasse); and **Le Jockey** (127 blvd. du Montparnasse). All are in the Sixth Arrondissement. Restaurants mentioned are: **Lapérouse** (51 quai des Grands-Augustins, Sixth Arrondissement; tel. 43 26 68 04), which Radclyffe Hall loved (but she was British—so stick to the basic stuff like fresh oysters and enjoy the great decor); Proust's second-fave, after the Ritz, the classy **Pré-Catelan** (routes de Suresnes, Bois de Boulogne, Sixteenth Arrondissement; tel. 45 24 55 58); and the atmospheric and amusing old **Relais Louis XIII** (8 rue des Grands-Augustins, Sixth Arrondissement; tel. 43 26 75 96)—too bad Louis, being a bit of a Spartan foodwise, never ate this well himself. **Jacques Cagna** is at 14 rue des Grands-Augustins; tel. 43 26 49 39.

A restaurant that is not a bit known as gay-oriented, but we feel would be right up all your alleys, is **Restaurant A** (5 rue de Poissy, Fifth Arrondissement); tel. 46 33 85 54. The specialty here is described as "eighteenth-century Chinese cuisine." Tastewise, this translates as sophisticated haute cuisine Chinese: crispy-skinned lacquered duck with mangoes, spiced mushrooms stuffed with shrimp. But it's the food's look that really distinguishes it. Originally designed to stimulate a bored emperor's failing appetite, every dish is an artwork: Just try to imagine your usual nightly cartons of Szechuan take-out formed and decorated to imitate a fantasy fish, molded into a multicolored dragon, or served in a melon carved with a herd of galloping horses. Everything is garnished with rice-paste animal creatures; and the chef comes around and does personal demonstrations at each table. You get to take the custom-made creatures-of-your-choice home, too. *Big* fun.

For picnic supplies, it is impossible to find a better price on melt-in-your-mouth-buttery fresh foie gras of both *oie* (goose) and *canard* (duck) than at J. Divay's gay-friendly charcuterie **Au Bon Porc** (50–52 rue du Faubourg–St. Denis, 75010 Paris; tel. 770 06 86). They carry terrines, smoked salmon, roasted meats, and other traditional specialty products, too. There's a new branch at 4 rue Bayen in the Seventeenth.

For a one-stop picnic area, take a morning stroll past the open-air market stands and specialty food stores along the rue Mouffetard, on the Left Bank (Métro: Censier-Daubenton). Many of the produce stands are closed on Monday, though the great little cheese shops, charcuteries, and bakeries are always there.

No doubt your hotel will serve you better bread for breakfast than you're used to getting anywhere in America. But you won't really understand the fuss about French bread until you try the best. Paris's most famous wonderful bread is that of Lionel Poilâne (8 rue du Cherche-Midi, Sixth Arrondissement; closed Sunday). The classic is his *pain Poilâne au levain naturel* (just a perfectly flavored round sourdough loaf). Less well known and inconveniently located—but well worth the trip for those in the know—are the wood-fired ovens of **Ganachaud** (150 rue Ménilmontant, Twentieth Arrondissement; closed Monday; Métro: Pelleport); try the *flûte Ganachaud*.

WHERE TO GET THE LATEST DIRT
(INFORMATION RESOURCES)

We are truly sorry to report that Pasteur Joseph Doucé, the man who performed our "wedding," was taken from his home one night in July 1990 by two men who claimed to be police officers. Three months later, the pastor's body was found in a forest outside Paris. As we go to press, no one has yet been officially charged in his murder, but the circumstances surrounding his disappearance have mushroomed into a front-page national scandal, and a top-level investigation is under way.

Although the gay **Centre du Christ Libérateur** was largely a one-man show, it had many supporters. In faith and hope, therefore, that Pasteur Doucé's labor of love will somehow be carried on, we provide the following information:

Centre du Christ Libérateur, 3 bis rue Clairaux, 75017 Paris; tel. 46 27 49 36. This phone number doubles as the **SOS Homo helpline** (Wednesday and Friday, 6 P.M.–midnight). The center's Lesbian helpline, **Permanence Lesbiennes,** is 42 26 61 07 (Saturday 3 P.M.–7 P.M.).

Les Mots à la Bouche (6 rue St. Croix de la Bretonnerie, 75004 Paris; tel. 278 88 39) is the established gay bookstore. A newly opened gay bookshop/ meeting place is **Librairie Autres Cultures** (46 rue Sauffroy, 75017 Paris; tel. 42 20 70 48); it's associated with an organization of the same name which aids sexual minorities. A newsstand known as the **gay news kiosk** because of its quantity of gay-related periodicals is at 29 blvd. des Italiens, 75002 Paris; open Monday–Saturday, 8 A.M.–midnight.

Gai Pied Hebdo (mail order available from: 45 rue Sedaine, 75011 Paris; tel. 43 57 52 05) is Paris's gay weekly newsmagazine; each issue features a brief roundup in English of the important stories—and on the average, though no complete listings, at least half a dozen ads (surest sign that the place is still in business!) for gay-oriented restaurants. The paper's over-350-page *Gai Pied Gai Guide,* a French-language annual obtainable from the same address, is the best all-France info source available, even though it is mighty slim on women's stuff. *Paris Scene* is the gay guide just for the city, in English.

The monthly *Lesbia* (B.P. 539, 75529 Paris Cédex 11; tel. 43 48 89 54) is entirely in French and does not have listings per se, but does have an "Infos" column on current special events—plus they generally run at least four to six easily comprehensible display ads for women's restaurants and bars.

Oddly enough, there is also an entire (albeit small) "Gay Listings" section in the major English-language Parisian equivalent of *New York* magazine, *Paris Passion* (Time Out Ltd., 23 rue Yves Toudic, 75010 Paris). This monthly, which stays fairly well on top of changes in the club world, is available at most Parisian magazine kiosks; the American subscription address is: *Paris Passion,* c/o World-wide Media Services, 115 E. 23rd St., New York, NY 10010.

A valuable information source for women is **MIEL** (Mouvement d'information et d'expression des lesbiennes; address: Maison des Femmes, 8 cité Prost, 75011 Paris; tel. 43 48 24 91. Métro: Charonne or Faidherbe-Chaligny). This women's house is located on an out-of-the-way, sort of creepy little street where one must run a gauntlet of auto mechanics; evidently there have been some incidents of verbal homophobic harassment, though we experienced none. But the space itself, once you get upstairs, is homey. The bulletin board has lots of notices posted about Paris events, and also hard-to-find info about things like women's resorts throughout France. There's been a Friday night dinner here, too, since 1983. Their **Canal MIEL information line** is 43 79 61 91. (That's for listening; for leaving info, it's 43 79 66 07.)

AIDS hotline: 47 70 98 99. **Gay physicians:** Association des Médecins Gais, 45 rue Sedaine, 75011 Paris.

The local branch of **Act Up** is at 45 rue Rebeval, 75019 Paris; tel. 42 63 44 78.

We've always had remarkably good luck with female chefs in France, which is why we were pleased to hear about **ARC**, the Association Internationale des

Restauratrices-Cuisinières (International Association of Women Chefs). For ARC's directory of restaurants, in Paris and throughout France, with female chefs, contact the group's U.S. rep, Sylvi C. Brown (1230 24th St, Santa Monica, CA 90404; tel. 213/453-2850. For European correspondents, the association's headquarters is 11 rue Barbet-de-Jouy, 75007 Paris; tel. 45 55 15 29). Enclose a buck, or an envelope with 80 cents' postage on it.

With what we hope you're eating, you will no doubt be relieved to know that Paris has a hotline number offering help to those afflicted by thigh ripples: **SOS Cellulite** (tel. 42 61 23 32, Monday–Friday 10 A.M.–6 P.M.).

WHAT TO READ

Bohemian Paris: Culture, Politics and the Boundaries of Bourgeois Life, 1830–1930, by Jerrold Seigel (Penguin). We own a great many social histories of France, and most of them toss the homos into chapters on absinthe abusers, shit-eaters, and similar weirdos. Not this one. Its section on the tortured love affair of Verlaine and Rimbaud is especially well done.

Marcel Proust, by George Painter (Penguin). Our gay male and occasional lesbian friends who admire Proust don't want bios that treat him like a drawing-room dilettante; and this one takes him seriously. Very.

Walks in Gertrude Stein's Paris, by Mary Ellen Jordan Haight (Peregrine Smith). Exactly what it sounds like: literary walking tours of 1900–1940 Paris.

Permanent Parisians: An Illustrated Guide to the Cemeteries of Paris, by Judi Culbertson and Tom Randall (Chelsea Green). Precise instructions on how you can, at last, visit the great Salons in the Sky of Gertrude, Alice, Wilde, Proust, and many more.

Women of the Left Bank: Paris 1900–1940, by Shari Benstock (University of Texas). Mini-bios, about half of them portraits of lesbians and bisexuals: Stein, Flanner, H.D., Barney, Barnes, Beach, et al. One comes away from the book with the impression that even the lesbian women who ruined their lives did it with more panache than their straight sisters.

Lot's Wife: Lesbian Paris, 1890–1914, by Catherine van Casselaer (Janus). The bohemian period before and the twenties after are well known. This meticulously researched book, introducing many fascinating characters you probably never heard of, fills in the blanks.

The Amazon and the Page, by Karla Jay (Indiana). The only lesbian-feminist book in English that we know of on the topic of the love affair between Natalie Barney and Renée Vivien.

Sylvia Beach and the Lost Generation: A History of Literary Paris in the Twenties and Thirties, by Noel Riley Fitch (Norton). An interesting evocation of the milieu that nurtured so many lesbians. Unfortunately, there's very little insight into Beach's long affair with Adrienne Monnier.

Genêt, by Brenda Wineapple (Ticknor & Fields). A biography of Janet Flanner, detailing—with no homophobia, but also without much curiosity, dish, or other gay sensibility—the lifelong multiple relationships of the writer.

Darlinghissima: Letters to a Friend, ed. Natalia Danesi Murray (Random House). Flanner's letters to Murray, the last of her three overlapping lovers.

Janet Flanner's World: Uncollected Writings 1932–1975, ed. Irving Drutman (HBJ). Probably the best collection of this, one of our greatest gay journalists. Her Hitler profile is a classic and establishes her as a practitioner of New Journalism decades ahead of Tom Wolfe and Clay Felker.

Djuna: The Formidable Miss Barnes, by Andrew Field (University of Texas). It isn't easy to write a competent, detailed bio of someone who largely avoided talking to anyone at all for the last 40 years or so of her life. This is the best.

The Complete Claudine, by Colette (Averil). The first two books are okay and the fourth a throwaway from a gayness standpoint (there ain't none). However, the trash connoisseur of us feels that the fiercely protective lesbian-sex anticipation scenes in *Claudine en Ménage* are absolutely *à point.* Even if said connoisseur would just as soon shred the book's suck-up last pages.

The Pure and the Impure, by Colette (Farrar, Straus & Giroux). Snarky, amusing essays about everyone—and a fascinating study of contradictions and double roles in and outside the supposedly daring lesbian community of the time.

For a listing of works on French slang, see "Practical Information, Loire Valley."

440 RMS/RIV VU

The Stately Homos
of the Loire Valley

*U*nderneath that flannel shirt of yours does there beat the elegant heart of a would-be interior decorator? Do you find Princess Di or any other member of her family intrinsically interesting? Is your idea of a good time in West Hollywood taking the guided tour of the Homes of the Stars? Would you (if you're a woman) rather watch reruns of *Lifestyles of the Rich and Famous* than the motel scene from *Desert Hearts*? Do you (if you're a man) think *Architectural Digest* makes better bedside reading than *Blueboy*?

You know who you are. And you're going to adore the châteaux of the Loire.

We managed to have fun there, too, even though our actual personal home is decorated in what *AD* might call Early Lesbian-Feminist—i.e., various tasteful shades of cat hair. The valley of the Loire, where the rich and famous of the ancien régime would have built scepter-shaped swimming pools if only they'd thought of them, has something for everyone.

Although it's less than 150 miles southwest of Paris, the countryside around this middle stretch of the 635-mile-long Loire is as idyllic as a watercolor. Wide, pale-blue skies watch over somnambulant riverside towns with dusty streets and slate roofs—probably the same slate, possibly even the same dust, that has been there for hundreds of years. The region's color is golden, like the fertile alluvial sands which have long made this valley the market garden of kings; golden like the languorous summer sun reflecting from white chalk hills.

Vineyards and orchards slope down embankments to meandering waterways—not only the banks of the Loire proper, but of its many tributaries, also liberally dotted with the picturesque old homes of royalty and royal favorites: the deep Indre, where one finds the châteaux of Renaissance Azay-le-Rideau and medieval Loches; the branching Maine, river of the feudal fortress-château of Angers; the Cher, straddled by the lovely "chateau of six women," Chenonceaux; the wide, green Vienne, mirroring the ruined towers of the Plantagenets' Chinon. The famous wine is young and fresh, the history old and intricate. The *beurre blanc* sauce that's dribbled over the local river fish is probably rock-solid cholesterol, but in the spirit of the region, it too tastes as if it were made from something infinitely delicate—possibly the clouds overhead.

Even the less agriculturally fertile plateau areas of the valley temper their harshness with bounty: the dense brushwood forests covering them are full of game, which the kings of France used to hunt. It's hard to imagine dying here in anything but slo-mo. Few places on earth are more graceful. Nowhere on earth is more French.

One does not come here for gay life, although pockets of it do exist: a few bars, restaurants, and discos in the "big cities" like Tours; in the sticks, a gay-owned château hotel. Even among hipper French straights, the center of the country is known as *La France profonde:* "deep France," as in Deep South, with all the loveliness, and also all the sluggish provincialism that the American phrase implies. It is not unusual here for smaller hotels to close down altogether on Sunday. (Tough *merde:* You'll either have to move on, or, if they do let you stay, settle for not having your bed or breakfast made.) Shopkeepers may frown if you say *"bonjour"* instead of *"bonsoir,"* or if you forget to add "Monsieur/dame" at the end of either one. Even in the touristed towns of central France, we sometimes feel strangely conspicuous—although it's a nice change of pace to have the locals stare at you for your accent or your clothes instead of your sexual preference.

The Loire Valley is also the part of France where the purest French is supposedly spoken. Among the expressions you may need, and which you probably weren't taught at Berlitz, is *"tata,"* literally "auntie," which means a fairy, or at least a queen. (A stretch of the Tuileries park in Paris, where gay men have cruised since at least the time of Louis XIV, is known as Tata Beach.) *"Tapette"* is a synonym. *"Pédé"* is short for "pedophile," but it no longer has the explicit connotation of man-boy sex. It really translates as "faggot," since it's one of those words we use *entre nous* but which sounds hostile coming out of the mouth of a straight stranger. *"Gai"* and, surprisingly, *"homo"* are far milder, nicer words. In-the-closet *homos* in France are "in the cabinet": *au placard*. A bisexual, meanwhile, is said to be *"à voile et à vapeur"*—someone who goes by sail and by steamboat.

For guys, the operative anatomical terms are *"bite"* (cock), *"couilles"* (balls), and *"fesses"* (buns); the items you use in *le safer-sex* to prevent *SIDA* are *preservatifs,* or more slangily, *capotes*—short for *"capotes anglaises,"* or English raincoats. (Who knows why? A "French kiss," incidentally, is nothing of the sort in France: It's a *baiser profond*.)

If you want to call a woman a dyke, either as an accusation or a compliment, the word is *"gouine."* (A francophone lesbian we met in Brussels told us that a favorite graffiti slogan among the fagettes of her fair city is "God save the *gouine.*") *"Goudou"* and *"gousse"* are friendlier terms, as is *"lesbienne."* The most peculiar term of all we've ever heard for a gay woman is *"trieuse des lentilles,"* or bean picker; our slang dictionary explains that the imagery comes from "the finger-flicking action of someone sorting lentils prior to cooking." Tits are *nichons* (little nests), and a clitoris, quite wonderfully, is a *praline,* after the yummy sugared almond.

"Drague" sounds like it refers to the fellows from *La Cage aux Folles,* but it actually means "cruising"; the guys in the dresses are *en travesti.* Another one nonfrancophones will mishear is *"cuir,"* pronounced "queer." It's really leather. The title of the leading gay newsmagazine in France is *Gai Pied,* or "Gay Foot," a reference to the phrase *"prendre son pied,"* to have an orgasm. It's short for one of the most delicious sexual expressions in French or any other language: *"avoir les doigts de pied en bouquet de violettes,"* i.e., to be so transported by ecstasy that it feels like your toes are wiggling about in a bouquet of violets.

It'll all be on the final, kids, so do your homework.

The majority of the châteaux were constructed between 1415, when the English seized Paris during the Hundred Years' War, forcing the French crown to relocate, and 1682, when Louis XIV began consolidating court life around Versailles. There are dozens of châteaux, of which the most important are the Five C's—Chambord, Chenonceaux, Cheverny, Chaumont, and Chinon—plus Blois, Amboise, Villandry, Langeais, Azay-le-Rideau, Ussé, Angers, Saumur, Beaugency and Loches.

Most of them are accessible by public transportation, although it's frustrating if you're trying to hit more than one or two castles a day. Unless you're a hard-core history or architecture groupie, though, *don't* over-château in any case. Rent a bike, bring a picnic and a book, and soak up the pastoral atmosphere that the châteaux were, in fact, designed to exploit. Commune with the ghosts—who at Blois and Chinon, as we will relate, are definitely your kind of (former) people.

When you step out of the train station at Blois, you're assaulted with the delightful but completely disconcerting aroma of warm chocolate. The Poulain chocolate factory is only a few blocks away, and for your entire stay in Blois, you'll have the recurring sense that you're walking around in the middle of a soufflé. Blois is a typical medium-sized provincial town with some nice old half-timbered houses and an interesting medieval church, but the star of the show is the Château de Blois, smack in the center of town.

Like a great many other châteaux, Blois was built and added onto over a period of centuries. It consists of four wings in four wildly different styles all more or less Frankensteined together on a hill around a central court-yard: the core of the original fortress of the counts of Blois, the Louis XII wing, the François I wing, and the wing built by Louis XIII's brother, Gaston d'Orléans. Although each of the four eras drip with history, if there's one personality whose shade hangs over the whole château, it's that of Henri III, king of France from 1574 to 1589.

Henri wasn't the greatest of gay role models. To be fair, though, his straight relatives were no prizes, either.

His parents were the original distant father and close-binding mother beloved of homophobic shrinks. Henri II spent most of his time off fighting or with his beautiful mistress, Diane de Poitiers. As soon as Henri died in a jousting accident, his widow Catherine de Medici's first move was to have Diane evicted from *her* château at Chenonceaux. Always an intriguer (she had a "flying squad" of beautiful women who gathered information for her from straight male courtiers), Catherine then devoted her energies to prop-ping up her effete and probably hemophiliac sons on the throne of France, one after another.

The first, François II, died of an earache at the age of sixteen. Next came the tubercular and hallucination-prone Charles IX, who at his moth-er's urgings ordered the St. Bartholomew's Massacre, in which thousands of French Protestants were murdered in their beds. Charles managed to live to the age of twenty-three. Although both he and his older brother were by all accounts heterosexual (François was devoted to his wife, Mary Queen of Scots), neither one produced an heir.

A younger son, the Duke of Alençon, who died of consumption, was notoriously gay, as was Henri III, "the last of the Valois." One of the few women he was ever rumored to have had sex with of his own accord—this happened in his younger days—was his sister Margot. In the custom of the day, Henri had an arranged marriage. The nuptial mass was reportedly delayed for hours while he personally arranged the bride's hairdo.

In theory, homosexuality was punishable by death, but the divine right of kings is one hell of a gay-rights law. Henri III's boyfriends, the *mignons* (darlings), the actor/waiters of their day, were court fixtures. Henri loved nothing better than to arrange court balls where he and his buddies could dress in drag. The Venetian ambassador to the court wrote home in perplexity that it was hard to take Henri seriously, given his wardrobe and, especially, his earrings: *two* giant jewels on each pierced ear.

One of Henri's contemporaries summed him up with a snotty little ditty: *"Si bien qu'en le voyant chacun était en peine / S'il voyait un roi-femme ou bien un homme-reine."* (Which we would roughly translate as: "When people first laid eyes on him, they were torn between / Deciding if he were a lady king or perhaps a gentleman queen.")

If Henri had lived in a more peaceful time, he could have devoted himself to ever more high-tech curling irons and ever more elaborate pearl chokers and ostrich-plumed hats. But he had the misfortune to reign during the Wars of Religion. Henri, a nominal Catholic, ultimately decided that his ally, the duke of Guise, was his greatest threat, since as leader of the popular Catholic contingent at court, Guise (who, incidentally, was also an ex-lover of Margot's) was a contender for the unstable French throne. Henri betrayed Guise and secretly threw his support to the Protestant minority. The duke was lured to Blois. On the king's orders—and with Henri watching the dirty deed from behind a curtain—he was murdered in cold blood en route to the royal bedroom. This particular political move didn't play in Paris, Pau, or Poitiers; the outrage that followed resulted in Henri's own assassination six months later. With no son to succeed him, his throne passed to his Bourbon cousin, Henri IV—as it happens, Margot's husband.

At Blois today, the galleries are full of portraits commemorating the grisly assault on Guise. In one, Henri strokes his goatee, Snidely Whiplash–style, while standing with his foot on the duke's chest, like a big-game hunter. There are also portraits galore of the *mignons*, who like their patron, apparently favored earrings. The most homoerotic painting, however, is called "Ball at the Court of Henri III," showing dashing cavaliers and their ladies whirling about doing *la volta,* an Italian dance introduced by Catherine de Medici. Off to the side, wearing starched lace collars and holding in their joined hands a bunch of cherries, are two noblewomen, or, possibly, two very femme transvestites. They're paying no attention to the dancers because they're too busy gazing into each other's eyes.

In the François I wing, where Henri lived, you can visit room after room of Flemish tapestries, high-backed thrones, fleur-de-lis wallpaper, baronial fireplaces and carved coats-of-arms. You can also see the king's boudoir and his elaborate gold-brocade canopied bed; if the mattress seems a trifle on the short side, that's because it was the custom in Henri's day to sleep sitting up, as a precaution against catching cold. Among the most interesting of the other chambers is the "working cabinet room," whose walls consist of hundreds of gold-painted carved-wood panels of fat angels, pineapples, dragons, and dolphins; a trick pedal in the floorboards operates the spring that opens several of the panels, revealing numerous secret cupboards.

There Catherine de Medici supposedly hid a supply of poison which was sometimes pressed into service to slowly knock off the odd guest whose politics she found inconvenient. (In a plot worthy of Joan Crawford and Bette Davis, one of Catherine's alleged victims was her Protestant kinswoman-in-law, the mother of Henry IV.) Catherine herself died at Blois a few weeks after Guise's murder. According to a historian of the times, she left this world "to the total indifference of those around her. No more notice was taken than of a dead goat."

At Blois, unlike some of the other furnished châteaux, you can tour at your own pace, without a guide. You can also come back after dark for that peculiarly French institution, the *son et lumière*—a hokey PG-rated sound-and-light spectacular (one per night in English) featuring floodlit views of the castle's exterior, and a historical playlet over loud speakers. At Blois, the theme of the spiel is, inexplicably, the stories of the *women* who played a part in the history of the château: Catherine, several other wives of kings, and Joan of Arc, who bivouacked at Blois for a single night on her way to Orléans. (Why do we suspect the emphasis had less to do with feminism than with avoiding Henri and his *mignons*?)

One woman who didn't make the *son-et-lumière* lineup, to our chagrin, was Marie de Medici, a relative of Catherine's who was trucked into France to become Henri IV's second wife. (His first marriage was annulled after Queen Margot, in the by-now tedious Valois family tradition, had failed to produce an heir.) When Marie arrived at the French court, she made an immediate splash, thanks to her habit of walking about with a female dwarf, whom she described as her "foster sister," under her voluminous skirt.

The dwarf was removed long enough for Marie and Henri to duly produce Louis XIII. Henri was assassinated when Louis was only eight; it was Marie who, as regent, ruled France for many years, aided by an unpopular claque of Italians. Louis ultimately had to seize power from his mother and her entourage, and literally imprison her at Blois. One winter night in 1619, the queen mother—described as "stout" even in an era when Weight Watchers would have gone out of business—managed to escape by climbing out a window and lowering herself into the moat below on a ladder precariously perched by her supporters against the château's steep outer wall. History didn't record whether she had the good sense to leave her skirt upstairs.

Louis was himself bisexual. His most notorious gay affair was with the young marquis de Cinq-Mars, who used his position as favorite to peddle influence at court and ultimately to conspire against Louis with the king's

scheming brother, Gaston d'Orléans. Cinq-Mars was found out and beheaded. The ruins of *his* château are a few miles away, near Langeais.
Louis's second son, Philippe d'Orléans, was also as queer as a three-franc
bill . . . But we digress.

After the Valois-Bourbon-Medici gang, the Plantagenets seem like the
Brady Bunch. Their "château" at Chinon is actually the ruins of a rather
grim fortress dating from the Middle Ages. Looming high over the river
Vienne and the narrow medieval streets of the pretty town of Chinon, the
castle makes a nice change of pace from the region's stock parade of gra-
cious Renaissance palaces.

The first Plantagenet to hang his helmet at Chinon was Henry II, a
notoriously flaunting-type heterosexual, as was his wife, Eleanor of Aquitaine. Henry's inherited lands included all of England and a chunk of the
Loire region; Eleanor's included most of what is today the southwestern
quadrant of France. When the two met, Eleanor was also queen of France,
having married the boring Louis VII. Louis had become king by a fluke,
when his older brother died, but he'd spent his life preparing for a career in
the church. Eleanor referred to him disparagingly as "the monk."

Eleanor hated Paris, which was then a far more dour place than the
Aquitaine, a land of poetry and troubadours, where women enjoyed high
status and nobody let religion get in the way of a good time. Early on
Eleanor made an enemy of the future St. Bernard, who thought her clothes
were too flashy. (His own favorite fashion was the hair shirt.) At one point
the royal marriage was in such trouble that the pope himself made up a bed
for Louis and Eleanor to get it on in. Eleanor ultimately persuaded her
husband to let her and her ladies-in-waiting tag along on a Crusade; according to legend, they rode across Europe bare-breasted, pretending to be
Amazons.

Before managing to get her marriage annulled and hooking up with
Henry, Eleanor is rumored to have passed the time having an affair with
her uncle, the prince of Antioch, and also, possibly, with Henry's own
father, the count of Anjou. Despite it all, Louis never would have let her go
if he'd had a clue that she was plotting to link up with his major political
rival. The marriage of Eleanor and Henry in 1152 so upset the balance of
power in Europe that it is blamed for setting in motion the events that
eventually led to the Hundred Years' War.

Although Henry ultimately treated her badly, Eleanor had a strong
conviction that heterosexual relationships should be more equal. She and
her female entourage ruled over a remarkable "Court of Love" at Poitiers,
where gentlemen were encouraged to come before a panel of ladies and
submit questions about the proper treatment of women. The code of the
Court was the blueprint for what we know today as chivalry: woman as

venerated ideal and setter of the relationship's pace, man as obedient vassal. Chivalry had its downside (and applied only to the noble classes, even as far as it went), but it was still the most progressive trend to happen for European women for centuries.

Eleanor had ten children. The one who interests us is her favorite, the man who later became Richard I of England, a.k.a. Richard the Lion-Heart. Yep: the very same fellow in front of whom Robin Hood was endlessly falling down on his knees in worship. Maid Marian may have simply been a beard.

Richard was the prototypical butch gay man—famous for his fighting skills, at home and on the Crusades, and regarded as better kingly material than any of his brothers. According to one of his contemporaries, "He was tall in stature, graceful in figure, his hair between red and auburn, his limbs were straight and flexible, his arms rather long, and not to be matched for wielding the sword or for striking with it, and his long legs suited the rest of his frame." Richard lived an openly gay life, although his homosexuality bothered him enough that he at least twice made public confessions of it and vowed to repent . . . with the usual results. He avoided marriage until his mid-thirties, when his anxious, aging mother picked out a bride and personally schlepped her across Europe to Sicily, where Richard was off fighting.

Among Richard's male lovers was Philip Augustus, who was not only the king of France but also the son of Richard's own mother's first husband's second marriage. They were definitely strange bedfellows: Richard had teamed up with Philip militarily as well, in a squeeze play for land and power against Richard's father and brothers. (The brothers took their turns allying with Philip against Richard, or with Richard against each other. In fact, the entire Plantagenet history is a sort of murderous medieval musical chairs.)

Richard died at Chinon in 1199, of gangrene from an arrow wound. He was brought to the town from a nearby fort his troops were defending after he carelessly showed himself to the enemy. According to legend, Richard's troops captured the young marksman who'd fired the fatal arrow and brought him to Richard, who forgave him—after which the king died. His troops flayed the French boy alive anyway. Richard is buried a few miles from Chinon at the abbey of Fontevrault, next to his mother. For a peekaboo look at Chinon castle, a sense of the people and issues involved, and an astonishingly sympathetic pre-Stonewall portrayal of Richard's gayness, rent the movie The Lion in Winter. It's worth watching just for Katharine Hepburn's portrayal of Eleanor of Aquitaine in an elegantly lockjawed style that can only be described as Eleanor of Philadelphia.

Although the tourist office does put out a booklet in English, called "In Search of the Plantagenets," you could easily spend hours tromping around the town and castle of Chinon, occupied by Richard's family for more than a hundred and fifty years, and not get a whiff of them. The P's are upstaged, to put it mildly, by Chinon's favorite guest celebrity, who wasn't even a hometown girl: Joan of Arc. It was here in the castle, in a room that's now open to the sky and has very little left but a chimney, that Joan first met and unerringly identified the dauphin of France, a nasty little wimp who'd tried to "test" her here by switching clothes with a courtier.

We've always had a soft spot for Joan, especially after we read that she made a point of having a woman sleep in her quarters whenever possible—for the sake of modest appearances, of course. Vita Sackville-West, who ought to have known, also noted in her biography of Joan that the Maid's best friend, a girl named Hauviette, was more distraught than a mere best friend ought to be when Joan left Domrémy on her mission to put the Dauphin on the throne of France. Joan's sexuality is an unknown quantity, but even the one absolutely certifiable aspect of what we would today class as sexual rebellion—her cross-dressing—has been fudged over in her elevation to sainthood. Despite Joan's refusal to put on women's clothes or wear women's hairstyles, even off the battlefield, and even when it was clear that her refusal was infuriating her captors at Rouen, the statues one finds of her in churches and squares all over northern France often show her as Mademoiselle Superfemme, in a skirt.

In Chinon, the Joan hype is predictably plastic, and it gets tiresome fast. Although she spent only a few weeks in the town, in the spring of 1429, most of the rooms of the castle that aren't in ruins have been made into a museum of Joaniana. (We especially keeled over laughing at the room full of department-store mannequins dressed up as Joan, the dauphin, and his court.) You can also follow in her pointy-shoed footsteps for virtually every moment of her visit: the place she drove into town, the spot where she dismounted from her horse, the path she walked to the castle, the room where she slept, the chapel where she prayed. There's even a bell whose claim to fame is that Joan *listened* to it.

Another Chinon visitor of more than passing gay interest was Jacques de Molay, head honcho of the Knights Templar, a very rich order of ex-Crusaders. In 1307, King Philip the Fair arrested thousands of knights, at least in part to get his hands on their treasury. One of the pretexts for dissolving the order was that sodomy was rife, and even ritualized as part of the Templars' initiation ceremonies. The Templars' emblem—two men riding on the same horse—was suddenly discovered to be not a depiction of brotherhood in battle, but an obscene rubbing of the second rider's crotch against the first rider's butt. Historians have argued for centuries about the "guilt" of the knights, who were also accused of such sins as worshiping idols and ritually spitting and peeing on crucifixes, which, long before the likes of Robert Mapplethorpe and Andres Serrano, were the worst acts the late-medieval mind could imagine. The gay historian John Boswell sees the Templars' trial as something of a turning point, since barely more than a century earlier, in Richard the Lion-Heart's day, gay sex was a relatively minor sin, hardly more serious than heterosexual adultery or fornication.

De Molay and some of his men were kept prisoners at Chinon in the Coudray Keep, a crumbly round stone tower at the center of the castle grounds. You can still see traces of the hearts, crosses, maps, and other graffiti they carved into the walls during their captivity. De Molay was burned at the stake in Paris in 1314. He did at least get in the last word; as he went up in flames, he put a curse on Philip the Fair. The king died a few months later in a hunting accident. Nyah, nyah!

Do not assume for a minute that the spirit of gay nobility is as dead as the knights and kings of old. *Au contraire,* it's the basis of a small, controversial political movement. At its center are the magazine *Gaie France* and its editor, a thirty-five-year-old professional French-to-German translator named Michel Caignet. Interspersed between photos of naked adolescent boys are articles about gay men who have wielded power throughout history—people like the Templars, Yukio Mishima, the leaders of the Wandervogel movement in Nazi Germany, Gilles de Rais (Joan of Arc's gay lieutenant, who went down in history as Bluebeard after his conviction for killing scores of children), and the boy-lovers of the ancient world.

"I hate tolerance," Michel told us when we tracked him down in Paris. "I want true acceptance. The complete acceptance of pederasty, in particular, is well documented in many societies throughout history. This is why we are educating homosexuals to have a consciousness of the links with their own culture. Homosexuality does not need to be outside society."

Michel was active for many years on the French extreme right, but broke away when he couldn't cope with his peers' homophobia. He remains ideologically in synch with his former confrères, however, especially on the subject of nationalism: "What makes me right-wing, perhaps, is that I'm interested in preserving old cultures. We have too great a number of immigrants in France now. They are poorly educated. They commit crimes. Yes, it's true that they come from France's former colonies, but that is not my fault, and I do not feel guilt about it. If there was a small number of immigrants, perhaps they could assimilate and become French. But with this great number there are problems of integration. They are not French! And I am worried that because of them, French culture will disappear."

But Michel, we argue, how can you condone anti-Arab and anti-black bigotry when you know the bigots say exactly the same thing about gay people: that if *we're* treated equally, it's going to destroy the traditions of society?

Michel looks at us as if we're very slow. "But there's a big difference," he explains patiently. "That's what we're saying: gay people are *already* a part of French history."

We leave this scrupulously polite man, realizing that in some harsher future, fate could put him and us across enemy barricades . . . or side by side in the same camp.

LOIRE VALLEY

PRACTICAL INFORMATION

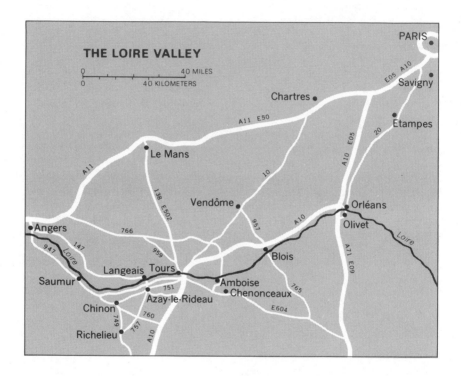

GENERAL HINTS / INFO

The Loire Valley is a historical rather than a hot gay-nightlife trip. Those who want the latter should definitely day-trip from Paris rather than settling in. Nevertheless, with a couple of gay hiking clubs and a gay château-hotel added to a scattering of the usual bars and discos, gay life is quite pleasant.

Orientation: France is divided into nearly 100 named and numbered official *départements*. The region we're dealing with when we refer to the Loire Valley is generally referred to as Touraine-Anjou-Orléanais. Just south of Ile-de-France (the region encircling Paris), it is composed, from north to southwest, of the *départements* Loiret, Loir-et-Cher, and Indre-et-Loire, and contains the towns of

Blois, Chinon, Amboise, and Tours. A few listed gay facilities are located in the bordering *départements* of Indre (just south) and Maine-et-Loire (just west). We mention all this just so you won't get confused if you look at a big map of France and notice there are about a zillion other *départements* with the word "Loire" in them. It's a long river.

If you stay at the recommended château below, the town of Richelieu, built to order by the cardinal, is handily located for gay-historical château visits. It's linked by steam train to Chinon, 13 miles north. And if you have a car, it's an easy 30- to 45-minute drive northwest to the Abbey of Fontevrault, where Richard the Lion-Heart is buried (Eleanor of Aquitaine, too); roughly one and a half hours northeast through Tours is Amboise, where brother Leonardo da Vinci worked during his last years and is buried; and only about half an hour farther along the Tours/Amboise road is Blois.

A rental car is not a bad idea in this area, even though the French drive as imaginatively as they cook, and with far less commendable results.

Currency unit: the franc (F)

WHERE TO STAY

Prices: Inexpensive = under 140F; *inex./mod.* = 140–230F; *moderate* = 230–350F; *mod./exp.* = 350–470F; *expensive* = over 470F.

The place to stay in the château country is in a gay château: **Château de la Vrillaye** (Chaveignes, 37120 Richelieu, France; tel. 47 95 32 25; fax 47 95 31 91; if you're not driving by the autoroute A10 from Paris, the château is reachable by train from Paris's Gare Austerlitz to Châteauroux, where, by prior arrangement, your train can be met). One look at this regal, turreted nineteenth-century white stone castle, set in 24 acres of gardens, park, and woodland, and you're gonna think you died and went to heaven with Henri and Richard. For over half a dozen years, British John Hadman has "received paying guests in what is not a hotel but very much my home," though Vrillaye is hardly humble. The clientele is mixed, but there are some "exclusively gay" weeks, as well as special week-long painting, music playing and appreciation, and architecture seminars, with ballooning and interior-decoration themes planned. The 33 bedrooms have either double or twin beds, writing tables, and easy chairs; all have at least handbasins, and luxury rooms have private bathrooms. There's a sitting room, a library with an extensive Oriental ceramics collection, and a large dining room where guests eat together, like a royal dinner party, at a banquet table. Both dinner and lunch (or a packed picnic lunch, for château-crawlers) are available, with vegetarian food possible; and you can luxuriate here on a bed-and-breakfast basis for less than you could in most regular old middle-class Paris hotels. *Inex./mod.–moderate* and *mod./exp.*

Hôtel Rive Droite (8 rue Ledru-Rollin, 36200 Argenton-sur-Creuse; tel. 54 24 01 06) is in the Indre, just south of the Loire-et-Cher region, where Blois is located. The Rive Droite is a seven-room exclusively gay hotel, run by a gay male couple who have been together more than 10 years. All rooms have private bathrooms. The establishment also has a restaurant where wood-grilled meat and fish are the specialty, as well as a pizzeria/bar, open until midnight. *Inexpensive—inex./mod.*

If you wish to stay in Blois itself, our favorite restaurant in town, located right on the river, is in a comfortable 17-room hotel, nongay but amenable to our business: **Hostellerie de la Loire** (8 blvd. de Lattre-de-Tassigny; tel. 54 74 26 60). *Inex./mod.—moderate.*

WHERE TO GO

The **château at Blois** is open from 9 A.M. to 6:30 P.M. in summer, with, of course, the usual civilized French two-hour lunch break between noon and 2 P.M. The regular guided tours at **Fontevrault Abbey** have the same hours as Blois, with more detailed lecture tours at 10:30 A.M. and 3:30 P.M. The **château at Chinon** is open, with the same lunch break, from 9 A.M. to 7 P.M. The **château at Amboise** has the same hours as Chinon.

In Blois, chocoholics who do not want to be disappointed should stop in or phone for advance reservations (don't just show up!), for the very popular Monday—Thursday factory tours at the excellent-smelling **Poulain chocolate factory** (6 avenue Gambetta, 41007 Blois; tel. 54 78 39 21). Hint: If actual consumption of quality chocolate is your priority, rather than seeing the stuff made, you might be happier going to **Pâtisserie Carré** (29 rue des Trois-Marchands), **Dubois,** or **Noël** (74 and 20 rue du Commerce, respectively) for some*patelins,* fine chocolates with hazelnuts, a local specialty.

Fags and dykes who like to hike are not alone in this area. In Angers, located in the Maine-et-Loire region just west of Loire-et-Cher, contact **Association Paroles** (B.P. 2404, 49024 Angers Cédex 02; tel. 16/41 88 47 56). This organization, which is proud to be equally lesbian and gay, organizes gay parties and car rallies, plus Sunday excursions to various destinations in the country. Everyone is invited and welcome; the ability to speak just a little French is advised. (Currently, the group's enthusiastic secretary, Hélène Sarrazin, is the only English-speaker.)

For semiserious nightlife, the nearest major regional city with the most gay stuff (a couple of bars, a couple of discos, and a sauna) is Tours. There are also gay facilities in Nantes and Le Mans. For truly serious nightlife, stay in Paris. Couch *pommes-de-terres* like ourselves will just hoist a few at our nice gay hotel and/or simply eat ourselves silly on the Loire regional specialties discussed below. (See the "Information Resources" section for sources listing current nearby gay bars, etc.)

In Blois at night, gay guys interested in *la drague* (outdoor cruising) could, after the grandiose and silly *son-et-lumière* (sound and light) show at the château, swing by place Victor-Hugo, between the northwest (non-Loire) side of the château and the Eglise St. Vincent. The park/garden overlook by Cathédrale St.-Louis is often also promising cruising ground.

WHERE (AND WHAT) TO EAT

Not surprisingly, freshwater fish is a specialty in the Loire region. Look for *brochet* (pike), especially in mousse form, *saumon sauvage* (wild river salmon), *alose* (shad), *carpe, brème* (bream), and *sandre* (river perch). The fisherperson of us, who is one of the world's foremost bream-and-perch-family specialists—these being all she ever catches, even in stocked trout streams—insists that you *must* try these plebeian species here, as they are prepared nothing like dime-a-dozen American sunnies and perch. Coq au vin (chicken stewed in wine sauce) is also big. Winewise, you already know Vouvray comes from this area, and Sancerre from nearby. But if you're dining in a Chinon restaurant, do also try the local specialty aperitif, the *cardinal*—red wine with crème de cassis—before your meal.

For picnics in the polite, gently rolling Loire countryside, a few interesting regional cheeses you might not be familiar with are *Olivet bleu* and *cendré d'Olivet* (a blue cheese, and one rolled in ash), and the rich, creamy *crémets d'Anjou*. The region is a big strawberry-growing area, so if you see a box of tiny *frais des bois* (wild strawberries), don't pass them up. But since they're delicate as well as perfectly ripe, don't expect them to last more than a couple of hours in a hot picnic knapsack, no matter how carefully you pack them. Bring along, too, a bottle of the full-bodied local Chinon red wine, which you wouldn't believe was dry if we described it as pungently floral with a hint of prune-plum and raspberry . . . so we won't. It's very pleasant and obviously unique, so you should spring for a bottle.

In Blois we tried several restaurants, but recommend the one we simply *had* to try twice: **Hostellerie de la Loire** (see "Where to Stay" section above for address). The cooking here is classical French with inventive, original touches. The house specialty is fresh local fish; the *paupiette de sandre au beurre rouge* and the *beurre blanc* are perfect. But the *magret au canard* (breast of duck, here cooked rare, as it should be but often is not), and the salad with fresh foie gras are just as irresistible as were the snails and champagne sorbet, and the several specially priced menus are great deals.

The recognized serious-foodie place among Chinon restaurants, if you're up for an elegant, more expensive meal of classical but light dishes, is the very pretty eighteenth-century **Le Plaisir Gourmand** (2 rue Parmentier). For tasty, inexpensive bistro-type food, we were very happy with **Les Années 30**, right around the corner at 78 rue Voltaire, Chinon's main medieval-building street—to reach the restaurant, you'll walk right past the house where Richard the Lion-Heart died.

If you go hiking in Angers, a very gay-friendly restaurant is **La Refuge de la Soulane** in rue St.-Martin (right in the center of town), whose specialties are foods from the Savoie—fondue, raclette, and all sorts of other melted-cheese items.

WHERE TO GET THE LATEST DIRT
(INFORMATION RESOURCES)

Gai Pied's annual *Gai Guide* is the most comprehensive and up-to-date source of French regional information on gay bars, etc.; see "Practical Information, Paris" for mail-order address. And see this chapter's "Where to Go" section for the address, in Angers, of **Association Paroles.**

In Nantes, a collective gay help and info group for the whole Loire-Atlantique region is **CHAILA** (c/o Homosaïque, B.P. 358, 44012 Nantes, Cédex 01; hikers: They can put you in touch with Les Gais Randonneurs Nantais, a gay hiking group).

Given the particular sparsity of lesbian facilities in this area, women might want to check *Lesbia* and **the bulletin board at La Maison des Femmes,** in Paris (see "Practical Information, Paris," for both), and the French listings in *Ma'dam* magazine (see "Practical Information, Amsterdam").

The address for *Gaie France* magazine is 8 rue Nicolet, 75018 Paris; tel. 1/42 54 78 96.

WHAT TO READ

Eleanor of Aquitaine and the Four Kings, by Amy Kelly (Harvard University Press). There are several flashier biographies of the Plantagenet family, but this one remains the best.

St. Joan of Arc, by V. Sackville-West (G. K. Hall). An exhaustive study of a woman who dared to follow her dreams, by one who mostly didn't.

Gilles and Jeanne, by Michel Tournier (Grove Weidenfeld). A novel about real-life Gilles de Rais, "Bluebeard," exploring how Joan of Arc supposedly turned his whole life around. Meaning that, in a twist as unlikely as it is yucky, the book somehow connects Joan's pure heroism to Gilles' ritual sexual molestation/mutilation/murder of hundreds of children, mostly boys, after her death—one of those Byzantinely introspective pseudopsychological pseudophilosophical bones French authors love to worry. Proust fans might find all this right up their alley.

The Dark Pageant, by Edward Lucie-Smith (GMP). Gilles de Rais fictionalized again. This take, less psychologically convoluted and reading more like an adventure novel, is told from the point of view of a lifetime friend and comrade-at-arms.

Young Henry of Navarre and *Henry, King of France,* by Heinrich Mann (Tusk). A huge, two-volume novelized account of the doings of the Medici-Valois-Bourbon gang. Heinrich was brother of Thomas, uncle of Klaus and Erika.

The King's Minion: Richelieu, Louis XIII and the Affair of Cinq-Mars, by Philippe Erlanger (Prentice-Hall). One of those rare historic accounts that's also a fabulous read.

Mignon, by Chris Hunt (GMP). Deliciously trashy fake historical "memoirs" of a French cutie (male) who becomes one of chicken hawk Henri III's many, many boy favorites. An affair with English poet Christopher Marlowe, too!

Books on French slang: *Street French* and *More Street French,* by David Burke (Wiley); *Merde!* and *Merde Encore,* by Geneviève (Angus and Robertson); *Dictionary of Modern Colloquial French,* by René James Hérail and Edwin A. Lovatt (Routledge).

$\mathscr{S}$ITGES

Provincetown
with Paella

$\mathscr{I}$t's a warm fall evening in Sitges, a tiny, traditional two-thousand-year-old fishing village in Spanish Catalonia, and we are sipping parasol-packed purple potions at the outdoor café of tropical Parrot's Pub, on Plaça Industria. This "plaza," really little more than an intersection of two cobblestoned pedestrian streets, is full of small local children playing happily under the fond surveillance of parents who operate the surrounding restaurants and fast-food wagons.

Suddenly from an adjacent street, an absolute vision prances into the square: an approximately twenty-five-year-old Spanish fellow done up as Dolly Parton would look, if only her wig included a waist-length ponytail and she were wearing a Day-Glo neon pink-green-and-yellow-striped muumuu. From the other side of the plaza strides a shirtless leather man, in Levis with strategically placed heart-shaped cutouts on the ass. Mutual shrieks of delight. They meet center square, clinch, and start nuzzling each other.

In the United States and much of the rest of the universe, this would naturally be the cue for cries of outrage from all available parents, as they converged to drag off their innocent children, who would themselves, no doubt, be jeering and throwing Popsicles. But in Sitges, no one bats an eye. Apparently noticing nothing amiss, the fond parents keep selling soft drinks, and the kids keep happily wheeling their bikes around the couple, until the two finally stroll off hand in hand.

The town that the French gay men's magazine *Gai Pied* not long ago named the premier gay resort destination in all of Europe strikes one at first glance as quite nice, but nothing to leave one's mouth hanging open.

Sitges (which rhymes with "bitches," with a touch of "beaches") has a Mediterranean setting, including a long crescent of sand seafront and even some bordering cliffs—but nothing as toe-curlingly spectacular as the Amalfi coast. It has waving, beachfront palm trees and other tropical flora—but nothing like Capri's luxuriant vegetation. The surrounding inland hills are not desert-arid; the land does support agriculture, and is in fact a big grape-growing region. The region's feel is hot and dry, however, rather than lush and balmy.

Sitges has some villas, but none as glamorous as in St.-Jean-Cap-Ferrat, or indeed most of the French Riviera. It has a good many medieval cobble-stoned streets—many, thankfully, even zoned pedestrian-only—but nothing as conducive to time-tripping as Taormina's gaslight-atmospheric walled old town. Sitges has lots of typical quaint southern-European-sea-side white stucco buildings, too, garnished with wrought-iron froufrou. And almost no typical Spanish–New Jersey coast high-rise crapola! But nothing as uniformly and purely blinding-white dramatic as Greek island architecture, either. Nothing even as uniformly cutesy-poo as Carmel, California. Sitges does have a bit of the Moorish flavor one expects of Spain, particularly in the ornate ceramic tiles on the walls and floors of many Sitgean houses. But these are a drop in the bucket compared to the Eastern exoticism one finds in almost any Andalusian town large enough to have indoor plumbing.

Although Arabs, Carthaginians, Romans, Visigoths, and Charlemagne's Franks all frequented this ancient trading port, Sitges does not feel partic-ularly exotic. It doesn't even feel particularly foreign, despite the fact that the signs in the fast-food stands and clothing stores on tourist-packed carrer Parrellada, the old town's main commercial and pedestrian street, are in English, French, Spanish, Catalan, and occasionally Italian, Swedish, Dutch, and German. The much-vaunted new post-1992 united Europe has been old-sombrero in Sitges for some time.

There are, however, in the perfectly nice though unspectacular buildings of Sitges, approximately two dozen gay bars. This village of 11,500 people has as many exclusively gay bars as cosmopolitan Barcelona, thirty-five kilometers away (population two million)—and more than New York City.

It also has several gay clothing boutiques, almost half a dozen gay hotels and an equal number of gay-owned or gay-oriented restaurants, and *two* gay beaches: one right in the thick of things, surrounded by "family"-type beaches, and one on the outskirts of town, for gay nudists.

But what makes Sitges so seductive isn't simply the vast quantity of gay facilities. It's the unbelievably open and matter-of-fact way gayness meshes with the very traditional family–oriented culture of this town—which, one can't help but remember, was ruled until 1975, along with the rest of Franco's Spain, by a right-wing fascist dictatorship that was not only anti-gay but antisexuality, period. Although homosexuality is now legal, gay life in much of Spain is still closeted: unmarked bars, the kind of furtive cama-raderie that characterized New York gay life pre-Stonewall. But not in Catalunya, a.k.a. Catalonia, a border region historically receptive to new ideas rather than dreamily insular like the conservative interior of Spain; a region which really considers itself more European than Spanish. And es-pecially not in Sitges.

Max, a gay Genevan we met in an all-queer car of Spain's finest and fastest train, the Talgo, is one of the many regulars who come back year after year. (No, unfortunately you can't reserve an all-queer car. This was just another Catalan surprise.) Max is drawn to Sitges precisely by the relaxed, integrated quality of its gay life. After eight vacation seasons, he had become so confident about the general town tolerance level that he'd decided to pass on the crowded gay beaches for something with a bit more elbow room, maybe even a little scenery. You know. The factors regular folks get to base their decisions on, rather than, "Will they kill me here?" A local female restaurant-owner recommended a little-known cove just over the hill past Platja de Sant Sebastià.

"It's a lovely small sandy spot at the base of some cliffs at the east end, a family beach," Max explains, "but some gays are there, like everywhere in Sitges. One day, I saw a young man about twenty start talking with another fellow. The conversation became more and more intimate. And then, they started kissing, necking. It went on for at least half an hour, surrounded by nuclear families who were playing beach tennis or reading. People would notice, and look. But nobody said anything, or seemed to care.

"Now, these guys kept this up every day for a week. I thought it was incredible. So I said to this restaurant woman—who's straight and has two adolescent sons, so I figured if anyone is going to be threatened . . . I said, 'What must you and all these other local families think of carryings-on like this, all over your town?'

"She just looked at me with the most puzzled expression, and said, 'But of course, it is no matter. To be gay is perfectly normal.' "

To put things in perspective, outrageous public sexual displays like the above are not the all-day, every day norm in Sitges. But everywhere in town, one does see, constantly, the kind of casual "Yes, we're a couple" same-sex gestures—like two men holding hands—that one virtually never sees in even the most liberal European places with the most progay attitudes and laws, like Copenhagen and Amsterdam.

This, like Sitges' physical appearance, may strike you as merely very nice rather than spectacular. But as gay people know, it's often little things that mean the most: the small pleasant surprises, like being treated as *boringly normal* when exchanging romantic glances over a restaurant table; the lack of small unpleasant surprises, like being gay-baited on the streets. After all, why should our vacations be any different from the rest of our lives, where even the big gay issues are ultimately about little things? (Let's take a vote: How many of us really see coming out as a window of opportunity to DO IT IN THE ROAD, or otherwise "flaunt" what we do in bed; and how many would just like to, say, casually discuss weekend plans with office colleagues without changing pronoun genders—without fear, without lying, without feeling like it's a big deal?)

The bottom line is this: There are many more spectacular places. But Sitges may well be the most spectacularly *comfortable* place you'll ever visit as a gay couple. It simply feels good to be at a family resort where, for a change, gay families count.

Sitgean gay tolerance is a fact. The reasons for it are harder to pinpoint. The most common answer from locals is a shrug and the explanation "It has always been that way here."

As an aside: One of the few difficult things about Sitges is getting anyone, gay or straight, to put *anything* in a sociopolitical context. Says Richard, a young, gay architecture-preservationist-turned English-tutor from Boston, who's one of the area's many expatriates: "There's more gay *visibility* here than in Boston; the sexuality in the streets is incredible. But I've found it almost impossible to sustain a relationship here because most people, especially young gay men, are sadly apolitical. Guys I otherwise find interesting literally ridicule me for things I find important, like public demonstrations for women's or gay rights. The last Barcelona gay-pride parade I went to was about three hundred people, in a city of two million. In the baths of Barcelona, there's not a condom to be seen. The AIDS rate in Spain is low so far, but that's not it. The thing is, there's such a strong emphasis on youth here, no one thinks about later. I think, having only been a democracy since '75, they're too confident about it. It's like, 'We have democracy, there isn't anything to worry about.' "

Long-haired hunk Carlos, a co-owner of Bourbon's bar, doesn't even understand our question about putting Sitgean gay acceptance in a historical and political context. We have to repeat it four times, defining "political" differently. "To tell the truth, I am not too politic," he finally replies.

"In Sitges, there is so many gays, we don't need to think like this. We have no trouble of acceptance, but if I do, I go to the mayor directly. And he listens."

There is something to be said for the "if it ain't broke, don't fix it" theory. It just doesn't make getting answers about the town's gay background easy.

When pressed to the wall, though, most townies will trace Sitges' history as a gay paradise to "the artists," who discovered the town just before the turn of the century. The most influential was Santiago Rusiñol, one of the pioneers of Catalan Art Nouveau (called, in Catalonia, *el modernisme*). Wild modernist parties were held at Rusiñol's dramatically cliff-perched seaside workshop-home, now the Cap Ferrat museum; and meetings of his artists' group, held at the still-existing restaurant Els Quatre Gats, attracted budding Catalonian art luminaries. "Picasso come here? Of course!" exclaims our waiter. "He had his first exposition right on that wall. Was *full* of his paintings. You could buy then for very small money, two pesetas. . . . Utrillo ate here, too! Dali! All!"

This initial artsy group was hetero, "but naturally, where artists go, gay people soon follow," chuckles Gonçal Sobrer, owner of the Hotel Romàntic. With its upper-class villa setting, high ceilings, huge individual balconies, ceramic tile floors and walls, ornate antique furniture, rampant wrought-iron, outdoor *and* indoor fountains, and extensive walled-in tropical garden complete with artificial grotto, the Romàntic is *muy gay* and itself something of an artwork—which figures, as Gonçal himself is gay, and was an artist, prehotel. "Though not famous," he smiles, "so I decide to put my art into my hotel."

Initial famous gay artist visitors included G. K. Chesterton, Federico García-Lorca, Nijinsky and Diaghilev. "The first moment the fashionable gays came was World War I, when Spain was neutral," says Gonçal. The 1930s Spanish Civil War wiped out Sitges' golden age as a city of culture. "But there was a second moment at the end of the 1950s, when Spain became very cheap. So it was then that the many *regular* gay people came, with the tour operators."

At that time, homosexuality was illegal. "But Sitges was better, because we are Catalan," insists Gonçal, who moved to Sitges from Barcelona in 1958. "And Catalonia is not really Spain." Like the Basque country, the province of Catalonia has always been independence-minded. In 1980, in fact, the Spanish government approved statutes of autonomy for both regions, and in Catalonia today, all street signs and other official communications are bilingual in Catalan / Spanish—with Catalan first. Pre-1975, how Catalonia's rebellious spirit worked for Sitges' gay life was a bit different, but effective.

For example, *Carnaval* (Mardi Gras—Europe's primo gay holiday) was prohibited under Franco. But every year, Gonçal explains, Sitges celebrated anyway. "I remember once in the early '60s Franco's police came and took twelve or fifteen people, boys dressed as women, to prison. They were taking them to Vilanova through the streets, with the police in back and the boys in front, like the boys were condemned to death. Their wigs were gone, their make-up was all running. . . . They were a *disaster*! This was a very hard police, you know—the Civil Guard. But as they pass, the people of Sitges all line up, and applaud for the boys—and hiss the police! The same afternoon, they let the boys go home."

Gonçal has a few ideas of his own about why gay people are so accepted in Sitges. "For one thing, we have always had the influence of many strange cultures, because Catalonia is historically the Path Hispánica." The region is in northeast Spain, on the French border—as inevitably a corridor between Northern Europe and Arab Africa as the New Jersey Turnpike is between New York City and Philadelphia. "So the Carolingians come down, the Arabs go back up. . . . Everybody passes by here, everybody comes and goes. And eventually everybody is accepted. Except people who are not behaving. Especially those who are not behaving, how to say it, economically. People who avoid to pay their bills.

"Here, you know, the Spanish people call the Catalans the Jews of Spain," Gonçal laughs. "And gay people are good for business. So gays is no serious problem."

He does remember a massive town meeting the previous year, when hoteliers were addressing something that *is* considered a serious problem in Sitges: very salty tap water. "The first question I got from a man in the audience was, 'Why you never mention in Sitges is too many homosexuals?' I was shocked! Because I never thought anyone would ask *that* about sanitation. So I make a speech. I say a person is a person and a visitor is a visitor, and if you treat them well, they remember you with love, which is good for everyone.

"But then I hear the room start going '*rrrrrRRRR*.' And I think, 'Oh no, what is happening? They know of me and my hotel. How is this going to end today?'

It ended with the entire room exploding—against the bigot. "Everybody is yelling at once, 'No, no, gay people is good, they are so clean, we are so happy, they drink so much gins and tonics.' And it closes with applause— for the gay people!"

It's embarrassing to admit, but the first time we two trooped around Sitges, on a very brief day trip from Barcelona, we somehow managed to miss not only every gay establishment, but virtually every gay person in town. It's hard to imagine how.

"Perhaps I think you don't open the eyes?" suggests an unbelieving Carlos.

What really happened is that we visited in the morning, leaving town by about one thirty P.M. In Sitges, at that hour, most gay people barely have their eyelids pried open. There's a definite gay timetable here, and like most things in Spain, it both starts and ends very late. If you reverse what we did that first time—and it really does make for a much more relaxing, luxuriant-feeling vacation to stay in Sitges and day-trip to Barcelona—you'll have no trouble discovering and falling into the rhythm.

Our first morning, we fail to drag ourselves up until after noon; for inexplicable reasons even the gay hotels, whose management must know that much of their clientele was out dancing till sunrise, seem to serve breakfast only until eleven. That is no doubt why Elsa's tiny coffee shop, run by an expatriate Dutch lesbian who's lived in Sitges for thirty years, is *the* gay brunch hangout in town. Elsa's personality is doubtless part of the attraction, too: She's kind of a crusty yet kindly mother/dominatrix combo. As we walk in, she has just *ordered* a table of gay men to have the home-made piña colada pie. "It will positively melt on your tongue," she guarantees, with a steely brook-no-opposition firmness and a brief, faintly lascivious smile. The guys are thrilled by this approach. We're thrilled by the pie, which is as promised.

You can also get real breakfasts of all nations (the "American" one is with hamburger) until seven P.M. But twelve thirty is the prime coffee hour: just early enough to rouse yourself and get down to the gay beach by one or so. If you're considering beating the crowds by catching morning rays, don't. One morning at eleven at Elsa's, we ran into a local lesbian who runs the gay-beach concession, and she hadn't even started setting up the deck chairs yet.

This woman, by the way, is married. "She married young," Elsa confides.

"But if she's gay, why doesn't she get divorced?" we whisper back, eyeballing the lady—who would have to be described, in any language, as an obvious killer dyke (complete with killer miniature poodle).

"In Spain, they don't do that," Elsa shrugs. "He has his women, she has her women, they both have their beach chairs, and it all works out fine."

If Elsa's four or five tables are already full of half the people you probably did something scandalous with the previous night, you'll find the other half brunching at Money's, on easy-to-remember (from a gay point of view) Carrer/Calle San Francisco—the word for "street," by the way, normally abbreviated "c." or "c/" in both Catalan and Spanish. At noon one day our waiter there, much to our surprise, is an English lad named Kerry, whom we'd parted from only several hours before, at Trailers' disco. Kerry had earlier been introduced to us as "my toy boy" by a retired American Southern gent whose business cards read "Consultant to the Confederacy in Exile." (This at a bar where we also met a nice woman described to us in whispers as "the biggest madam in Hamburg," and her son, "the porno king.") But we'd already encountered Kerry moonlighting as a waiter at the gay-owned Flamboyant restaurant, as well as sunlighting at Money's, and "entertaining" all night. As he pours us coffee, his hands shake. We all laugh.

Outside the window, another companion of the night before, "Fabiola de Paris," a macho, cossack-moustached Parisian gay-bar owner here on the classic busman's holiday, glances in and waves. When you know where to go, there is no easier place on earth to make gay friends than Sitges. We've been in town less than twenty-four hours, and already have partners in crime whom we're running into, quite by accident, right and left.

By twelve-thirty or one, we are settled, with most of the other early birds, on blue-and-white cushioned lounge chairs on the gay beach, directly in front of the ugly high-rise Calípolis Hotel, at the foot of Avenguda de Sofía, which more or less marks the end of Sitges' old town. Other gay beach–location landmarks are a breakwater with a first-aid station and a lavender flag. Actually, the beach does have a name: Ribera. But the name is never used. Most everyone just navigates by the Calípolis, because its white Miami modernity stands out on the skyline. Having been a planned tourist town since the turn of the century, Sitges blessedly escaped the worst of the 1970s' building boom that ruined the beachfronts of most other Spanish coastal resorts.

This is the gay non-nudist beach, although many of the bathing suits could better be called posing straps. In addition to the beautiful bodies, there are plenty of unself-consciously slightly out-of-shape bodies, and even a few bodies that can only be described as great street theater—like that of the queen who descends onto the beach in four-inch heels, which he kicks off with a flourish when he hits the sand. His three hundred–plus parading pounds are clad in a 1940s flying saucer–sized, fuschia, broad-brimmed Hollywood hat, a women's designer swimsuit in purple (with trim on the bosom to match the hat), and, over it all, a major Rosemary Clooney–style caftan, held up like a royal train by two scantily clad local-boy attendants. We have no idea how he/she made out him/herself, but his/her appearance is such a fabulous icebreaker for the hundred or so other folks on the beach that we wouldn't have been at all surprised to find out he/she had been hired by the chamber of commerce.

The gay nudist beach, l'Home Mort, is in a cove, one cove past the straight nudist beach, at the far west end of town. "Is really more for single guys who want, how do you say, the hot action," warns a nice salesguy who is customizing the gay map of Sitges and Barcelona we picked up at the trendy T-shirt boutique–cum–informal gay info center, Dream Boys, on c. San Francisco. The beach is about a forty-five minute walk from town —too far away to be on the map. Actually, the action takes place in the pine woods on the other side of the railroad tracks from the beach. This series of wooded terraces is where two thirds of the beach patrons can be found at any given time. And a good thing, too: If they all really wanted to catch rays, the beach itself would be far too small to hold them, even packed shoulder to shoulder, or crotch to crotch. Not to mention that you gotta lie on *rocks.*

So most gays use the midtown gay beach, which has actual sand and friendly, talkative actual sunbathers; comfy loungers you can rent for something like fifty cents per day (including the services of a couple of muscular beachboys who, at the appropriate time, come around and *turn the chair* for you, to follow the sun); an old guy with a raspy getcher-cold-beer voice, who circulates with a cooler yelling, *"Agua! Cerveza!* Fanta! Coca-Cola!"; and the usual comfortably reminiscent shore smells of salt and suntan lotion —but with the intriguing addition, carried on the breeze from nearby establishments, of sautéed garlic.

If two and a half hours of intense sun are enough for you, you'll be happy to know that three thirty P.M. is pretty much the height of lunch period in Sitges. Spain eats late. But with the sun not setting until after nine in the evening, even in September, serious beach bunnies hold out until five or seven thirty P.M., gay cocktail hour.

The scene at this point shifts to c. Primer de Maig, also referred to (and in fact labeled with dueling street signs) as "Calle *Dos* de Mayo." The "first of May street" Catalan designation was in honor of a liberal victory over right-wingers who attacked Sitges on May 1, 1938. The "second of May street" (Spanish) designation was Franco's typically arrogant rewriting of history (in the language he tried to impose uniformly over all Spain, despite strong and ancient local linguistic loyalties). The confusion about the names today, decades later, is basically because, hey, a street sign is a street sign. It's a lotta work to replace those things, you know? Maybe *mañana.*

Anyway, the signs make little difference, because everybody, including the official town tourist-office promo brochure, gleefully recognizes this wide pedestrian stretch near the west end of the old town as c. del Pecado, "Sin Street." The brochure claims the name originated with some Swedish women, whose doings were not really sinful, merely stylishly fun, like the late afternoon–early evening promenade of gay people today. This is where you'll find Parrot's (Plaça Industria is the street's main intersection), as well as numerous other outdoor cafés where one watches the passing parade, sips silly tropical drinks, listens to the old Peggy Lee and fifties American rock tapes that seem to be the favored afternoon gay-bar music (one never hears what we think of as "Latin" music in this town), and perhaps munches on tapas. These little plates of garlicky sautéed shrimp, thin slices of delicate country hams like *jamón serrano* or darker and richer *jamón de Jambugo,* sections of cold rolled omelette *(tortilla)* with a filling either savory or sweet, and numerous other hot and cold hors d'oeuvres–sized appetite appeasers are available in bars all over Spain.

For the benefit of those who've never visited Spain, we should explain that tapas are something bars have to do, like keeping a first-aid kit, just to keep Americans from becoming comatose and dying in the streets before dinnertime. Dinner in Spain is very, very late. And honestly, we're not rubes about this. Although we *are* both members of Adult Children of Parents from Suburban New Jersey, we have been in recovery from the six P.M. supper hour for years. Nine-ish is great with us. It's a little surprising, though, to walk into restaurants at nine thirty P.M., and find the room empty and the waiters barely finished clearing the lunch dishes.

As far as the food itself goes, in Catalonia in general as well as Sitges specifically, our feeling is that its strength is its simplicity. What's done best here is fresh fish and shellfish, commonly served smothered in a generic Catalan sauce of tomatoes, peppers, and onions: light, healthy, and perfectly okay, although eventually a bit tedious. Alternatively, at its best, the fish may be wood-grilled and served with *alioli* (a garlic mayonnaise) or *romesco* (a sauce of tomato, sweet peppers, hazelnuts, and almonds, from the nearby ancient Roman town of Tarragona); or it may be stewed, hopefully in one of the traditional Sitgean specialty dishes some restaurants are reviving: *arroz de Sitges,* a more complex local version of paella; *suquet de peix,* a sometimes brandied fish-and-shellfish bouillabaisse, flavored with a garlic-pepper-almond-herb *picada* sauce; *almejas con alcachofas,* clams and artichokes; or perhaps *fideuà,* golden-fried thin noodles and fish chunks, simmered in a tomato-almond-garlic fish stock, served with *alioli*—sort of your basic Catalan lo mein.

Sitges is part of the El Penedés region, known for its *cava,* sparkling wine (you can visit the wineries at Sant Sadurni d'Anoia, only a few kilometers away), so with dinner you'll want to drink either one of the neighborhood bubblies, or a local white like the now rare Sitges Malvasía, or Bodegas Torres' Vina Esmeralda, whose unusually complex, light fruitiness perfectly counterbalances the spiced Manzanilla olives many restaurants serve premeal.

With the emphasis on freshness rather than complexity of preparation, it is just as easy to find credible versions of most of the above dishes in inexpensive restaurants as in the more pricy beachfront places. So we concentrate instead, as most gay visitors to Sitges quickly learn to do, on finding major atmosphere—the traditional stucco arches at cavelike, candlelit El Trull; the myriad tiny white lights festooning the trees at the extensive outdoor garden of the Flamboyant (owned by an ex-American male couple, and featuring food that's sort of nouvelle-Catalan *Joy of Cooking*).

The postdinner gay scene (roughly eleven P.M. to two A.M., though *nobody* would really *dream* of showing up until midnight) moves to c. San Buenaventura, in central old-town Sitges, off c. San Francisco. This one short narrow block holds the largest single concentration of gay bars in town: seven, during our last visit. Personally, we're big fans of major picture windows in gay bars; the "knock three times and ask for José" closety feel is not our style. So we wander down San Buenaventura trying to pinpoint the most indiscreet-looking place, and end up at Bourbon's.

Behind the mirror-walled front bar (and flashwise, we must explain that we're talking about not one but five revolving disco balls . . . above the front bar alone) is Carlos's lover Eric, a fortyish Bavarian Peter Pan. In still life Eric has exactly the kind of ice-blond, square-jawed, eternal Hitler-youth poster-boy looks that normally set our teeth on edge, but the minute he starts moving—prancing about in his Bette Davis T-shirt, vogueing while shaking drinks, blowing the disco whistle chained to his neck, a constant blur of action—we are fascinated. He has a rapid ball-bearing way of swiveling around, hips first, that one normally does not see except in high-fashion models on a runway. "I have *never* in my life seen a *guy* walk that way," Lindsy marvels.

"Oh yes, all the *lesbianas* like Eric," Carlos laughs. He seems to like lesbians, too, although evidently not enough to put toilet paper in the ladies' room. (The ladies' room at Bourbon's is where people of both sexes go to use the toilet, the men's room being largely for liaisons.) But there definitely were a number of lesbians hanging out at the club, which is nice, because we're all too rare in Sitges. Although two other bars on San Buenaventura —Azul and Reflejos—do draw a small female crowd, there are no gay women's bars in town or even in Barcelona—and few gay female visitors, period.

"Oh, living here are many gay women," says Elsa. "But is like everywhere. The young girls go to the bars, but in a few years they have a relationship and then you don't ever see them again!"

The dearth of lesbian *tourists* is, for us, harder to figure. Admittedly, with no organized women's community, a single woman might have a tough time meeting someone. But most lesbian couples we know would be perfectly happy with atmosphere, art, sun and sand, decent food, virtually no male street harassment or homophobia, and prices that don't break the bank of a sixty-one-cents-on-the-dollar female DINK twosome. Sitges, while not as inexpensive as Greece, beats most other gay destinations on all these scores. A full-bath room at the most romantic, atmospheric hotel we've ever stayed at in our lives cost far less than your typical Holiday Inn offering. And the straight men basically keep to themselves, with the exception of one awfully strange tic: They seem to find it intriguing to *shake hands* with lesbians. Just shaking—no funny business.

"He says he'd like to shake your hands," translates one gay bartender who'd just introduced us as *tortilleras* (slang, like plain *tortillas*, for gay women) to an older straight restaurateur. This is at least the fifth or sixth time this has happened in twenty-four hours. In fact, we've been dodging the clerk at the straight hotel we had to check into when we couldn't immediately get a double-bedded room at the Romàntic, and who has insisted on elaborately formal palm-pressing every time we get the key. Anyway, we shake the straight restaurateur's hand. He looks puzzled, and says something we can't follow in Pam's C −/ D + level college Spanish.

"He is unbelieving you are lesbian," the bartender explains, "because he says one of you has the force of life in your handshake." We've heard plenty of stereotypes about lesbians in our day, but pulsing pinkies is a new one on us.

Luckily, it's now two A.M., time to move, along with much of the rest of gay Sitges, to bars nearer the beachfront, itself a major public-sex area until streetlights were installed several years ago. One concentration of bars is in the oldest medieval streets of town, near the town hall, which was the town castle until its last lord sold it in the 1300s to pay for his daughter's wedding. Evidently Sitgeans have always put a premium upon throwing a good party.

Here, we check out a couple of the most popular spots: hi-tech gray-and-neon El Candil and traditionally Spanish-looking El Comodin, locally famed for friendliness as well as for bartender Juan's occasional lip-synch of "Hello, Dolly." Combining hairy, moustached muscularity with full-length evening gown, this rendition pretty well defines genderfuck.

But it is in the other late-late-night gay area, on the side streets off of Primer de Maig, that we catch one of the few genuinely hysterical drag troupes we've ever seen (apart from Britain's Bloolips, whose political conscience, not to mention their Volkswagen-sized Carmen Miranda hats, sets them apart from the misogynistic norm). This show is a once-or-twice-weekly homegrown effort by the staff at Planta Baja, a bar whose rep is leather but whose looks are downtown New York City New Wave psychedelic. The drag has a New-Wave feel, too, instead of the usual tired old bitchiness, and an ironic sense of performing satire intended to poke fun at female stereotypes, rather than at females.

Under his/her wig, the revue's star, "Carmela," also the bar's owner, has a punk-style shaved head, but with a natural long mahogany ponytail. The backstage crew delights in sabotaging Carmela's act at every possible opportunity, in the totally obnoxious way only real friends would do: dropping the curtain abruptly atop his/her head mid-song, for instance. And you know how it is when flamenco femme fatales stomp around haughtily, with the ruffled layers swirling just so, and you always wonder: Why the heck don't those flashing high heels get caught, like any regular woman's would, and leave six feet of trailing petticoat strips? At this show, they do.

The finale—lip-synched to a tune about Barcelona we've never heard before and can't catch the words of, but just know in our guts is the Catalan equivalent of "New York, New York"—is a "boy/girl duet" between a costar señorita and Carmela, who is by now in reverse drag, posing as a man. This proves not only funny, but unexpectedly jarring. You *know* Carmela is a guy, so this is reality, or should be. But what you *feel* while you're watching his/her Romeo routine is, "Wait a minute—this guy is a lesbian, *impersonating* a man."

It's hard to explain. You wanna trust us on this one?

The late-late-late-night dancing scene is easy. Trailer's, a strobe-lighted vapor-clouded hotspot which is virtually empty until four A.M., is the only disco any self-respecting gay barfly would dream of frequenting the week we're in town. We must add that, gay fashion being what it is, the place probably folded five minutes after we staggered out its doors, at five thirty A.M. We were certainly in no condition to know.

One thing we did manage to notice, though. There's a certain relaxing confidence in realizing that, unless one has picked an August weekend night (which is when the beer-swilling young day-trippers descend) to visit Sitges the biggest hazard you'll face while staggering back to your hotel is, for women, the lack of public ladies' rooms; and, for the more formally attired men, that persistent Olde Europe problem of getting your spike heels caught between two cobblestones.

One thing that most gay tourists we spoke with did find terribly hard to deal with is that the unaccustomed lack of the self-protective paranoia and self-consciousness we're so used to as constants of life takes quite a toll on one's metabolism. Namely, it totally stops.

For us two urban-energetic, compulsive culture vultures, a planned three or four days in Sitges stretched to eight, and we still hadn't managed to drift through more than one of the town's three small local museums, much less get ourselves into Barcelona, a daunting twenty minutes away and a city we'd come to love on a previous trip to Spain. If you're interested, Sitges' Cau Ferrat museum was worth the energy expenditure, not so much for Rusiñol's own paintings, or even for two eye-popping El Grecos (Rusiñol championed the late-Renaissance artist at a time when his paintings were largely lying forgotten in the storerooms of Madrid's Prado Museum), as for the house itself. You like ornate? In the solidly tiled downstairs, we counted fourteen completely different Spanish and Moorish patterns—on one wall alone.

Many do manage a day trip to Barcelona, Spain's oldest, yet newest-feeling, city. Go for the gay scene, of course, which is relatively dead on weekdays, very festive on Fridays and Saturdays. But go also for the equally festive architecture of Antonio Gaudí, especially Guëll Park in the northern part of town—a Mediterranean Munchkinland. Our two favorite Gaudí buildings are the undulating Casa Milà apartments, whose exterior looks as if it was grown from giant mushroom spores or hatched from a dragon's egg, rather than built; and Casa Batlló, with its sparkly "first I'll blow the fairy dust on you!" lobby.

Both of these are on Passeig de Gràcia, a northward continuation of the scuzzy-stylish-sexy Rambles (pronounced "RAHM-blehs"), a wide tree-shaded pedestrian corridor that attracts the gay and the straight, the Gucci-bagged and the bag ladies, and every other imaginable opposite. Though a generalized sexuality seems to humidify the very air on this boulevard, women seem basically safe from aggressive male harassment; the only approach we encountered was from a female hooker suggesting a threesome. No one here is safe from pickpockets. And no one should get so caught up in watching the passing parade that they miss La Boquería, a 150-year-old covered market packed with stalls where you can pick up some of the best snack food in Barcelona.

Naturally, there is also Gaudí's still-under-construction Temple de la Sagrada Familia, a fantastical carved, surreal circus of a church, which you'd want to see even if the *plaça* on its western side did not happen to be one of the city's main outdoor gay cruising areas. But it does.

The other hotspot is the Jardins Montjuïc, about a half hour's walk due northwest of Barcelona's friendly gay sex shop–information center, Sextienda. The gardens share a formerly fortified mountain slope with a few places of more general interest that you might want to check out, as long as you're in the neighborhood: the 1992 Olympics stadium, Mies van der Rohe's landmark bauhaus German Pavilion, the Miró Foundation, the Museum of Catalan Art in the grandiose Palau Nacional, and the Poble Espanyol, an open-air museum—like a Spanish "Colonial Williamsburg"—originally assembled for the 1929 World's Fair.

At this point you should find, as we did, that you've filled fifty hours of each twenty-four-hour day. But with the Roman ruins in ancient, walled Tarragona less than an hour's drive away, possibly you could find the time to squeeze in just one more day trip.

Unless, that is, you run into a Sitgean festival.

One mid-September morning, about an hour after we've rolled home for the night, we're awakened by a growing din under our window. It sounds like a herd of accordions blowing their noses. Or perhaps like an eighty-piece orchestra composed entirely of musicians playing combs-and-tissue-paper.

It's actually just the opening parade of the festival of Santa Tecla, one of Sitges' patron saints.

Down the street marches a six-foot-long dragon with yellow, red, and kelly-green scales. It is breathing fire. Well, okay: It is breathing little sparks —shitting them, too. There are holes in the dragon's nostrils and tail, designed to hold Roman candle–type spouting firecrackers. These are kept lit and replenished by a claque of attendants wearing pants that match the dragon's scales.

In back of the dragon are the nose-blowing accordions, which turn out to be some sort of native Catalan woodwind instruments we've never seen or heard before or since, but hear an awful lot of during the three days the fest lasts. They are accompanied by a drum corps wearing headbands of cabbage-sized crepe-paper flowers, who play the same primitive Excedrin-headache rhythm endlessly: DAH-duh-duh, DAH-duh-duh, DAH duh duh duh.

Behind the musical sinus conditions are more flaming dragons, scores of them, all different variations on dragon physiology. One has a flopsing crocodile tail. One has wings. One has huge tits. There are also giant kings and queens (all with some bizarrely funny facial deformity, like a banana nose) and cavorting devils galore. Union Congregational Church in Upper Montclair, New Jersey, certainly never had this sort of religious celebration.

Punctuating the procession of giant papier-mâché pagans are more drummers, and quite a few all-boy "majorette" squads performing—with little polish, but with enormous, brow-wrinkling sincerity—precision stick-dancing routines. The parade has gone on for over an hour before we finally give up the idea of sleeping (for most of the duration of the festival, as it turns out), make our way down to the street, and discover that *all* the participants are children.

"Oh yes, they must work on their costumes for many months. But this is nothing compared to the Festa of San Bartolemé, in August," a local viewer assures us. "Santa Tecla is only the secondary saint. And to tell you the truth, the people of Sitges are a little pissed at her." It seems Tecla tends to ruin her own festival with surprise flash floods and other amusing weather tricks, so she only gets a kiddie tribute. At the Festa Mejor, the twirler boys and silly-suit wearers are the Santa Tecla dragons' *parents.*

But that's not to say the grown-ups don't participate at all. Most of the dragon contingents are accompanied by adult coaches; in Sitges, festivals are serious business.

The Saturday-night fireworks (which do indeed get postponed forty-eight hours, due to Ms. Tecla's customary surprise hurricane) are obviously an adult effort, too, and well worth the wait. Instead of the usual American-style slow buildup to a grand finale, this display, in keeping with Mediterranean exuberance, is more a whopping fifteen-minute orgasm.

Perhaps the most thought-provoking feature of the festa are the daily all-ages demonstrations, held throughout town with accompaniment by live nose-flute orchestra, of Catalonia's best-known folk dance, the Sardana. These demos last way into the night.

The Sardana is more or less a hora on downers. Max from Geneva insists that it's the true key to understanding Catalan gay-tolerance. "The song starts. It plays for five minutes before anyone does anything. Then all these people who were just standing around—on the dance stage, mind you, but having conversations about their laundry or something—shuffle into circles. They go slowly up and down. They go a few steps to one side. They come right back. They don't move! They're completely impassive. That's the Catalan nature. So when they see all this gay stuff going on, they just say, 'Well, we'll see what happens.' "

To carry the Sardana metaphor a bit further, we could also point out that it is danced to a rhythm with no discernible connection to the beat (actually, many juxtaposed and shifting beats) of the music. And this, too, fits, considering the pride Catalans take in being out of synch with the rest of their nation, in synch only with each other.

Personally, though, the festival gave us a different insight altogether into Sitgean gay-tolerance. Our theory is not only more positive, but delightfully shallow, and we like it much better.

It's simply this: The complete degree of acceptance gay travelers will find in Sitges is indeed astonishing.

But would it not be even *more* surprising for gays to find anything less in a town where baton twirling is considered a serious, necessary life skill for little boys, and getting dressed up in silly clothes is considered valid work for grown men?

PRACTICAL INFORMATION

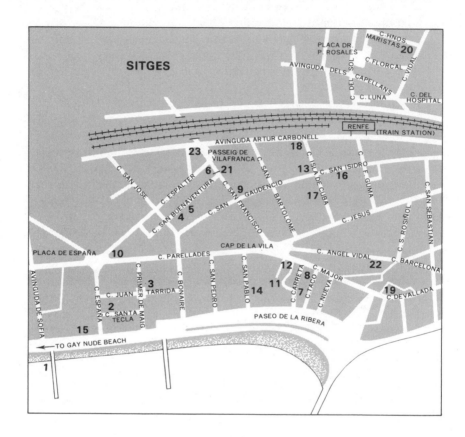

SITGES—NUMBER KEY

1. gay beach

Bars

2. Planta Baja (c. Santa Tecla)
3. Parrot's Pub (c. Juan Tarrida)
4. Reflejos (c. San Buenaventura)

5. Bourbon's (c. San Buenaventura)
6. Money's (c. San Francisco)
7. El Candil (c. Carreta)
8. El Comodin (c. Taco)
9. Company (corner of c. San Francisco and c. San Gaudencio)

Restaurants

10. Elsa's coffee shop (c. Parellades)
11. Flamboyant (off c. Carreta)
12. El Trull (off c. Major near Cap de la Vila)
13. El Xalet (corner of c. Isla de Cuba and c. San Gaudencio)
14. Els 4 Gats (c. San Pablo)
15. Mare Nostrum (Paseo de la Ribera)

Hotels

16. Hotel Romàntic (c. San Isidro)
17. Hostal La Renaixença (c. Isla de Cuba)
18. Hostal Liberty (c. Isla de Cuba)
19. Hostal Tropicana (c. Devallada)
20. Hostal Incógnito (c. Hnos. Maristas)

21. Dream Boys (boutique) (c. San Francisco)
22. Trailer (disco) (c. Angel Vidal)
23. main tourist information office (Avinguda Artur Carbonell)

GENERAL INFO / HINTS

With an average of 300 sunny days per year, Sitges is pleasant to visit at any season. Even *Carnaval*, the town's gayest festival (roughly the two weeks before Ash Wednesday, usually in February or early March), is sometimes sunbathing weather. As far as hotel reservations and rates go, high season runs approximately from the beginning of July through the beginning of September. At other times, rates are lower and it is usually possible for walk-ins without reservations to get a room at even the best gay hotels. Personally, we'd prefer to avoid the most tourist-packed month, August, even though it is also the month of the fabulous Festa Mejor of San Bartolemé. We must admit, though, that the quality-of-life contrast between high versus low season in Sitges is not nearly the life-and-death proposition it is in many other more well-known gay beach resorts, like Mykonos, which we would never dream of visiting in August. From mid-October until mid-May, tourism is minimal—even *Carnaval* does not draw the international hordes that Venice's does—and some establishments keep reduced hours. June and September are perfect in all ways: fabulous beach weather, high gay presence, lower hotel rates.

While at least a little English is spoken at many establishments, we did encounter a fair number of people at markets, charcuteries, drugstores, clothing stores, tourist and post offices, and even one gay hotelkeeper who spoke only the official languages, Catalá and Spanish. So a few hours with a Spanish-language tape will make you much happier. To help you in deciphering the only Catalan-language problem you're likely to encounter with no interpreter in sight —namely posted signs, or guidebook listings, for gay bar and restaurant opening and closing hours and days: "open" is *obert;* "closed" is *tancat;* and the days, Monday through Sunday, are *Dilluns, Dimarts, Dimecres, Dijous, Divendres, Dissabte,* and *Diumenge.* French is widely spoken in Catalunya.

If, like us, you find inhaling exhaust fumes and dodging cars particularly jarring on otherwise quaint European city streets, you'll also be happy to know that most of Sitges' cobbled old-town streets from c. Parelladas down to the beach road, paseo de la Ribera, are pedestrian-zoned.

Barwise, **gay central** is c. Buenaventura. But the areas on and surrounding Primer de Maig/Dos de Mayo/"Sin Street," as well as the oldest old-town section between c. Major and paseo de la Ribera, have a heavy concentration of gay facilities, also.

Banks, on a strict schedule, are normally open from 9 A.M. to 2 P.M. (9 A.M.–1 P.M. on Saturday). **Post offices** operate from 9 A.M. to 1 P.M. and from 5 P.M. to 7 P.M.; the central office is on c. Joan Llopis, just west of Plaça Espanya on the western edge of the old town.

Incidentally, any of you on prescription drugs might be interested to know that antibiotics, much stronger than the average U.S. doctor-prescribed dosages, are over-the-counter in Spain.

Postal code: 08870.

Telephone code: 34-3.

Currency unit: the peseta (pta)

WHERE TO STAY

All rates are for a double room during the high season. All hotels also have single rooms at lower rates, unless noted. At all establishments except the Ròmantic and La Renaixença, where prices are the same year round, off-season rates are cut by about half. There are no beachfront gay-oriented hotels.

Prices: *Inexpensive* = under 4,000 ptas; *moderate* = 4,000–5,000 ptas; *mod./exp.* = 5,000–6,000 ptas; *expensive* = over 6,000 ptas.

Hotel Ròmantic, c. de Sant Isidre, 33; tel. 894 06 43 or 894 2 53; fax 34 3 894 0643; telex. 52962 SITH E. Possibly our favorite hotel of all time: 60 romantically period bedrooms, all with bathroom and many with enormous terraces, in three joined nineteenth-century town houses. The hotel is decorated with antiques, spouting fountains, and other ceramic kitsch, plus many varieties of colorfully patterned traditional Spanish glazed tiles and original murals, by artist-owner Gonçal Sobrer. A generous buffet breakfast (juice, cheese, cold cuts, tomatoes, breads and jams, coffee/tea), included in the rates, is served in several festive dining rooms. Or even better, you can breakfast in the hotel's huge enclosed private tropical garden, which is open all day and night for sunning and drinking. Drinks at the hotel's wicker-furnished bar/lounge are more reason-able than in any gay bar in town, and though the hotel is mixed gay and straight, the owner and staff actively welcome more gay patrons. Special features include revolving art exhibits, gay choir practices and concerts, and an informal lending-and-exchange library with some English-language books. *Mod./exp.*

Hostal La Renaixença Isla de Cuba, 13; tel. 894 06 43. With the same management and prices as the Romàntic, this smaller 1890s town house with similar elegant/exotic decor is mostly booked by gay male block-tours and agencies like Uranian (England), Mantours (Germany) and Odysseus (USA). Non–tour-affiliated singles and couples can stay here, if they wish. However, since there's no garden (guests have to walk a half block over to share the Romàntic's), we feel the Renaixeça is only preferable to the Romàntic if you want all-male halls to cruise. *Mod./exp.*

Hostal Tropicana, c. Devallada, 7; tel. 894 18 41. Although this town house is in the heart of oldest old town and is the closest gay-oriented hotel to the sea, some of the 13 rooms (both with and without private shower and toilet) are pretty basic. That is, they are absolutely clean, but lack niceties like antique furniture, tiled walls, carpets, and views. However, proprietors Roberto and Frank are awfully friendly, and there are some less college-dormlike rooms; one even has a pretty terrific ocean-view terrace. There's also a third-floor solarium leading to a large common terrace, with bar, for all guests. *Inexpensive–moderate.*

Hostal Incognito, c. Hnos. Maristas, 3; tel. 894 26 98. This newly renovated hotel has extremely cordial Dutch gay male owners, generous-sized modern rooms (one with a terrace that could easily accommodate a party of 30, as the management helpfully suggested), and what must be Spain's most modern plumbing: American-style toilets, instead of the usual deafening Niagara Falls models. There's one studio apartment/suite, too. The big drawback, aside from the total absence of old-style Spanish charm, is location. The hotel is on the wrong side of the tracks—not unsafe, but not atmospheric—and across from a motorcycle garage, to boot. *Moderate.*

Hostal Liberty, c. Isla de Cuba, 45; tel. 894 46 50. Personally, we find establishments that only allow women in the off season offensive; but if that policy doesn't bother you, this place has a back garden and the nicest typical Catalan interior and room decor of the non-Gonçal gay hotels. The management speaks Catalan and Spanish only. *Mod./exp.*

A last tip: Some gay men who are staying a minimum of three nights prefer to rent apartments in segregated complexes. We haven't the vaguest clue why anyone except the sort of straight all-Americans who put catsup on their paella would prefer these generally generic modern wonders to the Romàntic, anyway; but gay men who don't mind staying in places where gay women aren't welcome can book through **Mantours** (Motzstraße 70, D-1000, Berlin, Germany; tel. 030/213 8090).

WHERE TO GO (DAY)

The **gay beach** section of the town beach is directly across the Passeig Maritim/paseo de la Ribera from the large, modern Hotel Calípolis on the corner of Avinguda (or avenida) de Sofía. Walking southwest from the heart of old town, look also for the lavender beach umbrella and the first-aid station on the break-water bordering the gay beach's near side.

To find the **gay nude beach,** L'Home Mort, continue walking southwest in the direction of Vilanova for about one and a half miles, past the hideous humongous hotel, the golf course and bridge, and the parking lot. From the first (straight) nude beach, just follow the railroad tracks, to the next cove.

WHERE TO GO (NIGHT)

Although there are no women's bars in Sitges, we felt perfectly welcome in all the places listed—which are not all the bars in town, just our faves. The "Night" and "Late Night" categories are fluid, reflecting the hours that we found most exciting in various places rather than actual opening and closing hours. Most bars open at 11 P.M. and don't close till you drop, but the more midtown joints heat up earlier than the beachier ones.

Cocktail Hour (Mid-Afternoon to Evening) Bars
Parrot's Pub, Plaça Industria (intersection of c. Primer de Maig and c. Juan Tarrida). Go between 3 P.M. and 6 P.M. and grab an outdoor table to watch the gay beach-bunny parade.
Money's, c. San Francisco, 39.
Company, c. San Francisco, 36. No English spoken, but good French; light food available.

Night (11:30 p.m.–2 a.m. Hottest) Bars
Bourbon's, San Buenaventura, 9. Popular with women . . . at least six of us. Mirrored madness.
Reflejos, San Buenaventura, 19. Also popular with women.

Late Night (1 a.m.–3:30 a.m. Hottest) Bars
El Candil, c. Carreta, 9. Multiroom hi-tech spot popular with women.
El Comodin, c. Taco, 14. Very male crowd, perfectly friendly to us. Traditional decor.
Planta Baja, c. Santa Tecla, 4. Everyone goes for the hysterical drag show, approximately 1:30 A.M. several nights weekly; the rest of the time, the Planta Baja draws a more leather-y crowd.

Disco (3:30 a.m. On)
Trailers, Angel Vidal, 36.
Additionally, tub queens who go into Barcelona for some action might want to know that **Thermas** (c. Diputación, 46) is the most popular sauna, certainly drawing a younger crowd than **Condal** (c. Condal, 18). However, most of the local under-thirties are not giving it away for free, and safe sex is not at a premium. Personally, we'd go to Amsterdam if international sauna-ing were our thing. At any rate, we're told you should absolutely avoid the Thermas's tired restaurant offerings.

Golden-fried/simmered *fideuà* noodles, *arroz de Sitges, xato* fish salad, *zarzuela de mariscos* and *suquet de peix* fish stews, traditional chicken-sausage-shellfish or all-seafood paella, the cold ratatouille *escalivada,* and other traditional local specialties are most reliably found on the menus of restaurants belonging to the Club de Tast de Sitges, an association dedicated to keeping old Sitgean recipes alive and well. **Mare Nostrum** (paseo de la Ribera, 60, on the seafront near the gay beach), which serves a lovely *muselina de sanfaina* vegetable mousse plus nicely grilled, though relatively expensive, seafood, is a Club de Tast member. So is Rusiñol and Picasso's old hangout **Els 4 Gats** (c. San Pablo, 13), which offers great period atmosphere, okay food, and good lunch deals. The town tourist office can best advise you on the latest complete Club de Tast membership list.

Otherwise, in terms of haute cuisine, Sitges is regrettably not Barcelona. What most restaurants in town do best is fresh local fish and shellfish; particularly good types to look for are *lubina* (sea bass), *rape* (anglerfish), *sardina, langosta* (tiny lobsters), *langostinos* (prawns), *dátites* (date mussels), *almejas* (clams), and *berberechos* (cockles). The ubiquitous *merluza* (hake), which Lindsy likes and Pam considers boring junk fish, is hard to avoid. But the upside of Sitges' having no gastronomic standouts is that you can patronize gay-oriented restaurants without feeling torn between your stomach and your aesthetic sense.

Inexpensive and tasty homemade diner-type food and a location only a couple of blocks from the gay beach make **Elsa's** (c. Parelladas, 86; open 9 A.M.– 7 P.M.) the absolutely primo breakfast and brunch hangout. If you don't try her melting piña colada pie, we guarantee you will be sorry for your whole life. **Money's, Company** [see "Where to Go (Night)," above], or any of their neighboring c. San Francisco "tapas" bars, are also amusing brunch and afternoon snack spots, as the whole street is closed to traffic during the day—turning the area into one big happy street café.

Unless copatron Santa Tecla is doing one of her bitchy weather tricks, our evening (that's 9:30 P.M. on) dinner favorite is the twinkling fairyland outdoor garden of the extremely gay, gay-owned **Flamboyant** (c. Pau Barrabeig, 16), where the Catalan–*Joy of Cooking* hybrid food is a welcome change from the town's tomato/pepper/onion sauce–heavy norm. Another extraordinarily lovely and gay-friendly garden restaurant, only half a block from the Romàntic, is **El Xalet** (Isla de Cuba, 31). For romantic indoor dining in a classic, arched, stucco old-town interior—and French plus French-influenced-Catalan dishes a few cuts up in elegance, complexity, and sophistication from the food in most Sitgean restaurants—we liked the very gay-popular **El Trull** (c. M. Fèlix Clarà, 3).

For beach snacking, our favorite one-stop specialty food shop was **La Estrella** (c. Major, 52; also spelled c. Mayor). The pastry casings for their meat and fish pies are flakier than the town norm; the sandwich *vegetal* (tuna plus veggies) is tasty; and if you are not entirely conversant with all 500 varieties of Spanish cheese they are happy to recommend a few local cheeses from their selection. (For starters: *manchego,* which comes fresh, semicured, and cured, is most popular; *idiazabal* is a good Basque cheese; *cabrales,* from Asturias, is a respectable blue.) And a mere two-block walk from the beach, up c. Primer de Maig, on the corner of c. Parelladas, is one of the world's outstanding *frites* stands; try an order with their garlic *alioli* sauce.

As for wine, Sitges was historically famed for its Malmsey, the vines for which supposedly arrived with raiding soldiers in the fourteenth century. However, there is scant production now. Modern Catalonia, specifically Penedés, is best known for its inexpensive sparkling whites, from firms like Freixenet, Codorniu, Castellblanch, Juve, Segura Vidas, and Marqués de Monistrol—all from Sant Sadurni d'Anoia, two sneezes down the road from Sitges. A number of young and two- or three-year-old native still white wines are also excellent, like Blanc Pescador, Californian Jean Leon's Chardonnay, Alella Vinicola's Alella Marfil, and the Marqués de Alella of Atalella S.A. An exceptional and unusual white that might normally be too fruity for dry-wine tastes, but which perfectly complements garlicky Catalan sauces and the salty richness of the Spanish olives you'll usually find on your restaurant table, is Viña Esmeralda of Bodegas Torres. Catalan reds are definitely iffier: Like Italian wines, they are most drinkable but forgettable. Still, there are few new gems, like Miguel Torres's snazziest offering, Gran Coronas Etiqueta Negra. Some wine experts even consider this one of the world's greatest reds—one Paris jury termed it better than Château Latour.

WHERE TO GET THE LATEST DIRT (INFO RESOURCES)

In Sitges, the main town tourist-information office is located to the west of the train station, on Passeig de Vilafranca; and there's an auxiliary office near the seafront, almost directly across from the Museu Cau Ferrat/Maricel de Mar; tel. 894 4700 or 894 1230.

Although Barcelona has several politically oriented gay organizations, the best information sources for tourists to Sitges and Barcelona are gay businesses. Several shops even have ". . . and gay information center" in their names—and they mean it.

Dream Boys (c. San Francisco, 39), Sitges' first and only "exclusively gay boutique," distributes a free, invaluable, annually revised gay map to Sitges and Barcelona.

In Barcelona, you can get the same map at **Zeus Gay Shop,** c. Riera Alta, 20, a short street that branches to the right off Carmen, which in turn is a right off the Rambles. Even closer to the Rambles, in a particularly gay part of the medieval Barri Gótic (Gothic quarter) is **Sextienda** (c. Raurich, 11), the first gay "sex shop" in Spain (opened in 1981). Here you can buy gay magazines, cards, and toys—or pick up the store's own free gay map—while the extremely helpful and friendly proprietor, Jorge, tells you anything you want to know about gay bars, hotels, restaurants, and special events like Barcelona's annual gay film festival or periodic trips and parties organized by gay groups.

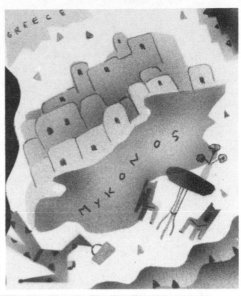

MYKONOS

Partying in the
Lap of the Gods

*P*ierro's Bar might be reason enough to go to Mykonos, and maybe even to Greece—especially if you can manage to be there on a night when Evangelina Sirianou, the most famous gay person on the island, does her equally famous belly dance on top of the bar.

Not that Pierro's doesn't seem, at first glance, like a million other gay bars. You have your basic semicheesy disco lighting: tubes of flashing, pulsating color, snaking around the room like the bulbs on a movie marquee. Confetti dangles from the ceiling in permanent Perpetual Party motif. The music is mostly brain-cell-deadening Europop, with a soupçon of traditional Greek melodies, American rap, and South American lambada, *the* sound enjoying its fifteen minutes of hipness this particular season. At least once a night the disco features a percussion-enhanced sound track of an endless and patently faked female orgasm. In time-honored gay-bar custom, the drinks at Pierro's are overpriced. To be fair, Evangelina, who is bartendrix and bouncer as well as resident living legend, probably makes the best Bloody Mary east of Fire Island.

Pierro's is not Mykonos's only gay night spot. In fact, the three most popular others are conveniently located in the same building off Matoyanni Street, on a little plaza that also hosts an Irish bar with outdoor tables and, believe it or not, a Catholic church. Mantos, a straighter but still substantially gay coffee-and-liquor bar, is next door to Pierro's. Icaros, up the stairs, is a small, sleek, cruise disco, featuring self-consciously artsy attempted new-wave decor and mostly wannabe-trendy gay male patrons. The giddily tropical Nefeli's Hollywood Bar, upstairs next to Icaros, is decorated like a piña colada, and has perhaps the most exclusively gay clientele of any of the four joints. In addition, many gay Mykonian night owls run over at one A.M. to the City disco for the nightly drag show. This may consist of a dead ringer for Marilyn Monroe doing "Diamonds Are a Girl's Best Friend," followed by a native Greek musical extravaganza by the (also male) "Little Gypsy Girl," who is at least sixty and weighs at least two-forty. Quite obviously, Mykonos is not lacking in unique gay nightlife opportunities. But most gay people agree Pierro's is *the* place in town, and everybody eventually ends up here.

Evangelina calls it a "bisexual bar," meaning that it's open to everybody. But most of the people who patronize Pierro's, male and female, of whatever nationality, are gay. On some evenings—especially as the sound effects spilling out onto the square start hitting tribal-celebration level—you'll see straight couples wistfully hanging about the perimeter of Pierro's porch, trying to dredge up the nerve to enter. (For the record, we personally have no objection to well-behaved straights in gay space, although ideally we wish there were a way to restrict entry to those who'd bother to fight for *our* rights to occupy the rest of the universe. *(Okay, you with the beer belly . . . whadaya done for domestic-partnership legislation lately?)*

One night an entire crew of straights charged in with the rest of us porch potatoes after a howl went up from inside the bar that Evangelina was dancing on the counter. Many of the patrons were in various states of undress, with the exception of those—like the German guy in an authentic striped Turkish prison uniform—whose ensembles would have been spoiled by even partial removal. And there was Evangelina, amid a sea of raised fists, slithering and bumping to the bouzouki music in her skintight black leather pants, a cigarette pack scrunched into the top of her cowboy boots. She is, you must understand, a true dyke heatthrob, a woman who somehow manages to combine the appeal of Anna Magnani, Sharon Gless, and the young Marlon Brando. Her eyes were closed like those of someone in a trance. On her head she balanced, perfectly, a glass of vodka.

One straight fellow was so excited that he grabbed one of our hands by mistake, thinking it was his girlfriend's. When he realized his error, he looked terrified and whimpered profuse apologies. Poor baby. He probably thought he'd just stumbled into the bar from *Star Wars*.

Greece doesn't have an especially active gay movement of its own today, but from its history to its myths, it probably offers more cultural resonance for gay foreigners than any other country. This is, after all, the place that gave its name not only to those Greek active/passive references in the personals, but to all lesbians. And it is, of course, the spawning ground of the ancient world's great gay love affairs: Zeus and Ganymede, Apollo and Hyacinthus, Achilles and Patroclus, Hercules and Iolaus, Hercules and Hylas, Hercules and Nestor, Hercules and Admetus, Hercules and Jason, Hercules and . . . Well, let's just go with Plutarch's assessment (which your high-school English teacher no doubt forgot to mention) of Herc's homosexual relationships: To wit, this prototype Nautilus queen was unquestionably *quite* the little slut.

In modern-day reality, Mykonos is probably the gayest locale in Greece. It is unquestionably the gayest island in the Aegean, and has been ever since 1955, when the Greek tourist ship *Semiramis* discharged its first group of, you'll pardon the expression, cruisers. Passé gay? You'll hear it. But don't you believe it. Like Greta Garbo, Mykonos—no matter how old it is or how many eyes have seen it—is eternally glamourous and exotically, if stagily, elusive.

Getting there, however, definitely isn't half the fun. If you want to go, do consider an all-Greece vacation rather than combining Mykonos with other destinations in Europe. The problem is that a commercial flight to Greece from anywhere else on the Continent costs nearly as much as a transatlantic ticket.

Hence for us, as for many North Americans, the trip to Mykonos began in Brindisi, Italy, point of departure for numerous overnight ships to western Greece, including several lines that honor the Eurailpass. We wound up on the Hellenic Mediterranean Lines' *Poseidonia.* We certainly hope you don't, unless your idea of intellectual stimulation is vigilantly watching out for the bar staff's canny efforts to shortchange you. Then there was our "cabin," which, along with most of our deck, had no fresh air and a serious mildew problem. Dozing off to sleep felt like curling up inside an overused kitchen sponge.

The Greek transportation schedules are cleverly arranged so that once you finally disembark from the *S.S. Brillo Pad,* you need to spend several hours in Patras—a town with all the sparkle of Gary, Indiana—before boarding an impossibly crowded train to Athens. We ended up in a screaming fight with a dentist's wife from Minnesota, who bounded into the first-class car ahead of us and then tried to "save" seats for her entire tour group, à la junior high school.

Even if your train doesn't break down, which ours did (and we'll bet yours will too), it won't arrive in Athens until around midnight, at a station in the ass end of town and light-years away from the nearest subway stop. At this hour the buses have stopped running, and the station's waiting room is closed until morning. One glance outside quickly establishes that you are smack in the middle of the South Bronx section of Athens. And at that point, you'll discover that the local taxi drivers won't take you anywhere except certain expensive hotels which pay them commissions for delivering guests.

We walked.

Depending upon your gender, this tale of woe will now start sounding a whole lot better or else infinitely worse. The streets of Athens are buzzingly lively in the pre-dawn hours, and all you see are men, men, men. You could be on the corner of Castro and 18th, circa 1980. A gay American guy we later met in Mykonos swore to us that a lot of these men were definitely sexually available, but they sure could have fooled us. Or else maybe they were trying to fool each other. Our favorites were the automobile wolf packs, who followed us down the street, yelling propositions in English, French, and German out their car windows. In fact, hetero male street harassment in Athens is so much an institution that its practitioners even have a name: *kalamaki*.

Like most women who travel sans male "protection," we have, of course, had our share of *kalamaki* the world over. One of our smuggest memories was of the hot summer day we were walking down the street in Dijon, France, guzzling from a just-opened bottle of mineral water. From out between two parked cars popped a flasher, delightedly beating *le* meat at us. We promptly poured two liters of Perrier directly on his crotch.

Unfortunately, we found no equally sure-fire ways to discourage Athenian street jerks. There did not even appear to be a readily available Greek sparkling mineral water. What seemed to work best was to flash our palms —an insult in Greece, akin to giving someone the finger. Simply pretend that you're declaring a runner safe at home plate, and that the guys in the cars are the plate.

For sheer classiness, though, nothing we ever did could beat the response tossed to a chest-ogling rube by the spunky middle-aged New Zealand backpackerette who was trudging the two A.M. Athenian gauntlet with us. "Great pair of knockers!" he yelled. Unbeknownst to him, she'd had a mastectomy. "Oh, you like them?" she replied sweetly, reaching into her blouse. "Then 'ere, 'ave one"—and hit him square in the kisser with her prosthesis.

While Athens-bashing is too easy to be truly sporting, we must also mention that it is one of the most polluted cities in Europe, and the dirtiest. Our middle-range hotel in a "nice" section of town had roaches, dirty water-glasses, and a vague whiff of sewage. Only a water-sports queen would love Greek plumbing: Everywhere we went we encountered toilets that simply didn't work, next to multilingual signs urging patrons not to flush their used toilet paper. You deposit it instead in a fetid little wastebasket.

Our coping skills, meanwhile, were at a distinct disadvantage, thanks to caffeine withdrawal. In Greece, you have a choice of Exxon-quality "Greek Coffee," or "Nescafé," generic weak instant served with evaporated milk. Don't be fooled by places that claim to serve "French coffee." This term only means they boil the evaporated milk. "Cappuccino" means they steam it.

Our advice about Athens: See the Acropolis, pay your tribute to Athena Nike (goddess of sneakers), and then split.

From the minute you spot the island from the ferry, it's obvious that Mykonos is as beautiful as any Greek tale, mythical or real, gay or otherwise, has ever led you to believe. Brilliant-white hills drop to a blindingly blue sea. Medieval windmills dot the hills in all the places where resorts in most parts of the world have plopped sore-thumb high-rises.

True, the beauty of Mykonos is not the sort that appeals to everyone. "It's too dry" is the most usual complaint. This is, of course, the case with most Greek islands. For those who are used to, and insist upon the gentle, moistly-perfumed Caribbean rain-forest lushness, Mykonos's sun-bleached, dramatic aridity will not satisfy. The ground, including the pebbly beaches, is too rocky. The scrub grass is too sparse. (Cattle think so, too, which is why Greek cuisine features so much lamb.) But those whose souls exult in the powerful, joyful simplicity of ruggedly landscaped but well-used earth —and ruggedly landscaped but well-lived-in human faces—will find the look of Mykonos very simpatico.

From an aesthetic standpoint, there are other big pluses here, too. The coffee is no better in Mykonos than anywhere else in Greece, but the place is squeaky clean. In season, the gleaming white streets of Mykonos town, the island's main (really only) center of nightlife and shopping, are actually relimewashed into a Colgate brightness twice a week. Women seem to be in charge of all sorts of things, from moped rentals to travel agencies to hotels. And unlike Athenians, most Mykonian straight men are at least housebroken.

To get there is naturally a hassle. One of the Cyclades (a group of several dozen islands including Paros, Naxos, Andros, Ios, Syros and Santorini), Mykonos is a good six hours south of Athens by boat. Olympic has cheap flights, but even in the off season planes are often booked far in advance. We took the ferry from Athens' scuzzy seaport Piraeus and, after passing through a mini-typhoon at sea, arrived in Mykonos late afternoon.

We would later realize that, like Sitges, Mykonos has a "schedule," and that we had hit town smack in between eastern standard gay beach time and the hour when one descends on the waterfront Kastro Bar to display one's tan and watch the sunset. Every self-respecting faggot or dyke for miles around was probably in the shower. To us, however, the whole town looked like Hetero Heaven, with nuclear families parading their 2.2 kids up and down the harbor. Like Rick, who'd come to Casablanca for the waters, we began to wonder if we'd been grievously misinformed.

On the dock we'd seen a chorus line of Mykonos landladies in black housedresses, all brandishing glossies of their spare rooms. We'd passed them by, since we'd planned to phone a couple of hotels that supposedly had a gay clientele. Ha. We soon discovered that pay phones in Mykonos are few and far between, that any number you dial will connect at random to any other number, and that in any case the mini-typhoon had temporarily knocked out most phone service. So we tromped around Mykonos town a bit, hoping that we'd simply blunder into the right places.

Dumb move: The narrow, winding streets, originally designed to confound invading pirates, either have no names, or else transliterated names that change every block or so, never coming close to matching the names in your guidebooks. No one we stopped on the street had ever heard of the hotels we were looking for. Some, in fact, we never did locate, they having apparently been swallowed up in some gay Hellenic Brigadoon.

After about an hour of this, we were doing the usual thing that couples do in frustrating situations: snarling at each other. Pam stomped off to find a room, any room, while Lindsy sulked in the harbor with the luggage.

Every cloud has a lavender lining; ours led us to Vaso, landlady extraordinaire. Pam eventually flung herself on the mercy of a travel agent who, upon hearing that we were writing a gay travel book, gave her the name of a woman whose hotel, he circumspectly noted, might prove to have a "conducive" atmosphere. Alas, when Pam arrived, the woman wasn't there. Worse, the elderly housekeeper who was staffing the desk showed her only rooms with twin beds. "We really wanted a double bed," Pam explained.

"Ah," The housekeeper shrugged philosophically. "So you push together."

"No, no really," Pam struggled. "We're just . . . not twin-bed sort of people."

Big smile. "Ah. Then you stay at *my* house," she announced. "I have very nice room, quiet, you will like, only two minutes from here." It turned out to be cute, spotlessly clean, dirt cheap, genuinely double-bedded, private-bath'ed, and perfect.

"So now you bring husband?" asked Vaso.

"Husband? Oh no. No husband. My friend is another woman."

"So . . . is two womans?" Vaso asked slowly.

"Well, yes. We are both women."

Vaso knitted her brow. "Two womans . . . in one bed?"

"That's right," sighed Pam, waiting for the whole deal to fall through.

Vaso suddenly let out a loud snort and jabbed her elbow into Pam's ribs. "Two womans in one bed? Hey, no problem!" She began cackling. "You see? *Hah, hah, hah!* Here, is *nooooooo problem!*"

We sensed that we had come to the right place after all.

Later that afternoon, at a café, we spied four guys who definitely set off our gay-dar. We maneuvered a table next to theirs, introduced ourselves, and asked them if they by some remote chance could tell us if there was gay life in Mykonos. All of them obligingly began groping each other.

They turned out to be a Dutch couple, Marcel and Arnd, and a French couple, Serge and Olivier. Serge offered to take the two of us on a little tour of Mykonos town, past all the gay hot spots.

On our walk, he told us in a melange of French and English that he was a student in Paris, and that this was his first trip to Mykonos. His boyfriend, an Air France steward, had been here once before, with straight friends, and promised himself that he'd come back some day when he had a lover. Their new Dutch friend Marcel was a flight attendant for KLM, and *his* boyfriend got to fly free to Greece as a spouse-equivalent. Serge had now been urging Oliver to go to work for KLM. This discussion had in turn made Serge begin to think about coming out.

He and Olivier had been together for a year; before that Serge had a girlfriend. The two lived together, but their parents had no idea that they were lovers. "One thing I love about Mykonos is that if I want to hold Olivier's hand or even kiss him, it is possible," Serge exclaimed in wonderment. He dreaded going back to a place where being openly gay was harder. "But I think maybe we will tell our parents now."

Nobody could tell us exactly why Mykonos is so receptive to gays. The straight young Greek woman behind the desk in the local tourist office laughed and explained, "Maybe it's because Mykonians don't really like anybody but other Mykonians," so all tourists are considered equal. But were there any *problems* with gay tourists? Anything that our readers should be aware of?

The tourist-office woman put on her thinking cap. Finally she acknowledged that while it was important that everyone feel welcome everywhere on the island, in her capacity as official meeter and greeter she personally wished there were at least one bar catering especially to lesbians.

Other Mykonians were equally straightforward. For that matter, gays seem to be preferred to the other major tourist group: Italian families who come to Mykonos for a cheap vacation. "They're a disaster!" one local businesswoman complained. "They have a souvlaki, boom, the napkins in the street."

"Gays, of course, it is fine," said the manager of the hotel where Serge and Olivier stayed. "What we do *not* like is people who make much noise all the time." If anything, gay stereotypes seem to work in our favor. As another hotel manager burbled, "Gay people we like very well; because I can tell you, the gay women are so nice, and the men are such gentlemen. And so clean!"

Our own landlady seemed thrilled with us. One night we came home and found that she'd left a huge bouquet of fresh daisies in our room. She insisted on making chamomile tea one morning when Lindsy was clearly in major misery from the excesses at Pierro's the night before. The day we left she gave us each a big hug and told us. "Send more people just like you."

If anything, on Mykonos we felt less like gay aliens than like members of any of a number of outlander groups that float like so much seaweed on the surface of the local culture. You see the fishermen with their oh-so-fashionable sweaters, the farmers selling herbs from the packs of their donkeys—but this could be Zorba-Land at Epcot. We've been to places, like Scandinavia, where virtually the entire population speaks a little English; but in Mykonos English is so widely agreed upon as the lingua franca that more signs are in English than in Greek.

Nonetheless, we happily found ourselves in total disagreement with the conventional glib guidebook wisdom that one must really get oneself to a less well known island. That Mykonos is "spoiled." That rampant gay (and student) tourism has left no true indigenous culture for heterosexual travelers to experience, and rampant hetero tourism has left no gay life for the rest of us. This is donkey poop, with one important caveat: Unless you are the sort of gay person who'd rather be in New Orleans for Super Bowl Sunday than for Mardi Gras, *do not visit Mykonos during July or August*. If that's the "Greek" experience you crave, save yourself a bundle and book a week at the local Phi Delt house. Off season, though, both gay and Mykonian culture are alive and well, if largely separate.

Occasionally the two worlds do collide. One day we were having lunch at an outdoor restaurant next to one of the larger chapels in town. There were dozens of us, gay and straight, in our trendy Day-Glo windbreakers and high-tech running shoes. Suddenly the church doors opened, and out streamed a huge human inkblot: scores of Mykonians in black shoes, black hose, black skirts, black pants, black sweaters and fishermen's caps and babushkas. It was like the scene in *The Wizard of Oz* where Dorothy steps out into Technicolor, but run in reverse. First came a procession of priests in long, Father Time beards. Then a thick-bodied, bowlegged old woman, wailing inconsolably on the arms of two friends. Several people carried wreaths made out of basil. Just outside the door, a clump of men stood stiffly holding what looked like a tall black wooden shield with the year, 1989, lettered on it in gold. When pallbearers filed out carrying a chalk-white old man in a coffin, we realized the black shield was the lid. As the entire group set off on foot, presumably for the cemetery, the tourists discreetly returned their attention to their taramasalata.

The one person who easily straddles both worlds is Evangelina, who was born on Mykonos in 1951. Or at least we think she was; the dates and details in all of her stories tend to change at every telling, in a way that suggests not so much that she's manipulating the facts as that she's above them. Evangelina, after all, has her image to consider. "In every magazine story about Mykonos," bitched a woman who is married to one of Evangelina's many, many cousins, "there is her face. I don't know how she does it."

By the time we finally met Evangelina, we'd been treated to numerous rapturous accounts from gay men about her prowess in ejecting disruptive assholes from Pierro's by the scruffs of their necks, like kittens. We were expecting the Incredible She-Hulk, at least. Sure enough, the night we first ventured into Pierro's, Evangelina was greeting favored male patrons with a hearty "Hey, maw-thare-fuck-air," in a voice that made Lauren Bacall sound like a soprano. But she was smaller than we had imagined, and softer —although the tomboy vulnerability she projects is probably invisible to anyone but another lesbian. She was also far more conventionally good-looking than anyone had mentioned: long black hair veeing from a widow's peak that draws attention to enormous blue eyes, and a body that could be an ad for barbells.

The next afternoon, we met Evangelina at the bar for an interview. She was exhausted; after closing the bar at dawn, she'd gone out with the professional fishermen on their daily haul of mullet and calamari, an activity she adores. But she was also in a state of near-murderous rage, and threatening to quit her job. (We did not know that Evangelina threatens at least four times per week to leave Pierro's, which is owned by yet another cousin.) Today's crisis involved a would-be drug pusher who had tried to ply his trade in Pierro's the previous night. "I swear on my cousin's death, that if that cunt [pronounced kont] comes in here tonight and does it again, I will cut out his throat," she hissed. "Not his teeth. His *throat!*"

Outside some church bells rang, and Evangelina crossed herself. "I love it here," she explained. "These are my roots." Nonetheless, she acknowledges that she was always different. "They used to call me the little boy with tits. I used to play only with the boys. With the girls, they had dolls and these stupidities. With the boys I would play policeman, climbing trees, ringing the bells of the church." She was a square peg in another way, as well: "I always said when I'm older I'll travel. They laughed at me. Traveling is unusual for the Greeks. But at eighteen, I did it. I left."

She had never known any gay women on Mykonos, and it was in

Montreal in the mid-seventies that she came out. "You know the bar Baby Face? The owner was a fighter in the boxing, and I tell you the honest truth, I was frightened to go in, to see all the dykes. Women dressed up with a tie, a man's suit, the hair. *Trockdrivers!* And you go up to the bar, and they say"—here Evangelina improbably lowers her voice and goes into her trockdriver impersonation—*"Hey you! You wanna go wit' me?'"*

She lived in New York and in Paris (where she still has a lover), but eventually felt the need to come back home. "I'm one hundred percent Mykonian—*not* Greek. If you ask the local people, everyone will say the same thing. The Mykonians are different. A different mentality. How can I say to help you understand? They don't criticize, they don't have the gossip. They don't give a damn shit what you do in your private life. Nobody insults me, nobody tells me what I do it's not right. They like me the way I am." Outside the family, anyway. Although Evangelina's father and brothers have been accepting of her lesbianism, her mother and sister have not. "My sister keeps saying to me, 'Find a husband! Pay him!'" Evangelina sneers. "I said, 'If I *want* a man, I can get one just like that! I don't hate men—but I *don't* want one!'"

When we ask her whether she's ever been active in feminism or the gay movement, she responds with obvious distaste: "No, I don't want to have to do with the politics." She is, she adds, a royalist, like most Mykonians. And a good Christian.

With three other gay and mixed bars in the very same building as Pierro's, there were certainly no tough decisions about where to spend our nights. There was really only one daily dilemma on Mykonos: what to do between eleven A.M., when we had our wake-up beer (our solution to the coffee problem) in one of the harbor-front outdoor cafés where all gay breakfasters wake up, and eleven P.M., when the bars opened. Fortunately, there is only one answer in Mykonos: Hit the beach. Or try to.

As a rule of thumb on Mykonos, the closer a beach is to civilization, the less likely it is to be gay. Or rather "alternative," since gays, including those who wouldn't dream of doffing their Speedos in public, tend to share their beaches with straight nudists. Most out-of-the-way beaches are in coves at the end of dirt roads, accessible only by rented jeep or moped, or by boat. What most people do is take a city bus to Plati Yialos, a beach a few miles southeast of Mykonos town. When the bus stops, the nuclear families troop off to the beach on the left, while the gays and a few straight nudists file to the right and wait for the boat to two of the most popular destinations, Paradise and Super Paradise Beaches.

One day we waited. And waited. Soon we were awash in Clones of All Nations. Eventually it dawned on us that indeed the boat wasn't coming. Rather than stay at the straight beach, the Clones of All Nations took off one by one on a ridge high above the sea, in the general direction of Paradise. We bought a few cold beers, packed them in our always handy Thinsulate-insulated collapsible lunchboxes (we *were* Brownie Scouts), and followed.

We do concede it was useful information to find that Super Paradise is accessible by foot. No map shows this. According to the average maps one finds in guidebooks, Mykonos has one road between Mykonos town and the airport, one additional major road running inland through Anó Merá (the island's only other real town), a few other secondary vehicle roads, and half a dozen dirt donkey paths, none going anywhere near most of the desirable remote beaches. I.e., it looks like ya can't get there from here.

Actually, you can. That said, we wouldn't recommend the hike. Unless, of course, tromping over rock piles, goat turds, and Mojave Desert–type thistles for an hour and a half is your thing. It wasn't quite like wearing the Crown of Thorns. It *was* like walking on it.

Once you get there, Super Paradise is an oasis. It was obvious, from the two restaurant/bars located just off the secluded beach cove, that we hadn't really needed to bring our own cool drinks—just a hot book would've sufficed. There are both hot and cool meals here: homemade yogurt with fresh fruit, pungent moussaka and other less known but equally tasty lamb-and-eggplant and pasta casseroles, fresh local curd cheeses. There are bathrooms. There are showers. There are rentable lounge chairs. There are even thoughtful bamboo windbreaks on the beach, to cut Mykonos' eternal, *very* strong winds.

Much later we would learn that while Mykonos was drenched in sunshine, the mini-typhoon we'd passed through on our way to the island was still raging intermittently out at sea, wreaking havoc with the tides. In fact, we were soon to find out that no boats were moving either around Mykonos or between the island and the rest of the universe, and wouldn't for several more days. This was in October, and unreliable weather is the price one sometimes pays in the far fringes of the tourist season. For both hetero-to-homo and sun-to-typhoon ratios, May and the end of September are the ideal times for gay travelers.

But in any season, even when boats are running, the best way to beach it, as far as we're concerned, is by moped. On Mykonos, renting mopeds is both cheap and fun for even novice riders, since most of the island's narrow dirt roads are virtually inaccessible to cars. Just you and a whole lot of donkeys. As we discovered, the tiniest, wimpiest six-dollar-per-day mopeds will easily enable you to try, in one afternoon, not only Super Paradise but other gay-popular beaches like Paradise, Elia, and even remote Panormos, on the north coast. Since the island is so small (only thirty-three square miles), the most secluded beaches are only about half an hours' ride apart at most, even when one does have to help one's somewhat less than Harley-powered bikes up a few hills with one's feet.

Mykonos: Partying in the Lap of the Gods / 285

The only problem is that aside from the beaches, there's virtually no-where to go on your moped. Geographically, the island is barren, with no natural springs, so the variety of scenery is limited. And historically, My-konos was not a place of significance in antiquity. Although the island has been home since the third millennium B.C. to everyone from Egyptians to Cretans to Venetians to godlings (a rather thin local legend identifies the island's massive boulders as giants slain by Hercules), Mykonos has none of the snazzy crumbling temples one drools over on Crete and numerous other Greek islands; actually Mykonos town's small archaeological mu-seum mostly features objects excavated from the nearby islet of Rineia. There are a couple of visitable old monasteries: Agios Panteleimon, looming above Mykonos town, and Tourlianí, six miles east in Anó Merá. But even the tourist office can't manage to get overly enthusiastic about them.

Shopping? Well, all you lezzies will find Mykonos the best place on earth for buying a labyris to sport at the next wimmin's music festival. The silver and gold jewelry here is not only nicely crafted, but oddly (for such a popular resort area) much less expensive than in Athens, without the push-iness and bargaining. Aside from jewelry, though, Mykonian stores are largely limited to such authentic Greek items as pizza, T-shirts and aerobics classes.

A more exciting spot for some of you guys—one that you women should avoid at all costs—is the three wells in the center of town. According to legend, if you drink the water of all three, you'll find a husband.

Otherwise, what most gay visitors to Mykonos do every single day post-beach and pre-Pierro's is have a drink at one of the already-mentioned "sunset bars" overlooking the ocean—and then eat.

This sort of lazy schedule may not seem ideal to hardcore "if this is Tuesday, it must be Belgium" types, to whom no vacation day is complete without whirlwind do's of at least fifteen awfully important museums. But for compulsively energetic types who can't, even when we should, resist seeing everything there is to see, being in a place where there is absolutely nothing to do but hit gorgeous beaches by day and fabulous bars by night —and eat in between—soon feels like the most pampered, indulgent (albeit enforced) kind of luxury there is. And really—the food in Mykonos isn't Parisian in terms of sophistication, but it's fine. Just fine.

Don't leave Greece without trying the taramasalata. Even at worst, meaning the way one normally finds it in the United States, this concoction is like a great, though heavy, cream-cheese-and-lox spread. At best, as at Philippi's (a Mykonian restaurant that's very gay-popular, thanks to its very romantic outdoor garden as well as its food), tarama is a cross between caviar and a cloud. Vegetarians will want to know that the word for "greens" is *horiatiki;* and if you do dairy, a tangy local specialty cheese is *kopanisti. Yiaourti me meli,* an impossibly thick and rich sour-creamlike homemade yogurt with honey that one would kill for in America, is available at virtually any fast-food stand in Mykonos. And the fast-food souv-laki here is packed with succulently grilled thin slices of real lamb, as opposed to the usual American souvlaki we're used to. You know, that nasty pressed mystery meat, highly yet badly spiced to disguise the fact that the sheep (or rat or kangaroo) in question died when our country was young.

We are not going to single out lots of specific Mykonian restaurants, because, quite frankly, the island has few standouts. Aside from atmo-spheric Philippi's, gay people appear to favor the inexpensive, largely veg-etarian Sesame Kitchen and the expensive fish grill Katrin's, both in Mykonos town; and we heard that Jackie O. and whoever else is left of the Beautiful People drive a few miles away to Mathew's in Tourlos Beach. If you like something with your breakfast beer, the homemade apple fritters and fresh yogurt at the Donut Factory, right across from Sesame Kitchen, are scrumptious. But the rule here, as in most of Greece, is that since the cuisine's strength is impeccably fresh raw ingredients simply yet perfectly prepared, one follows one's hungry nose and picks from what the various restaurants have on view, rather than relying slavishly on the printed menus or anyone else's recommendations.

One quite reliable Mykonian culinary tip we're happy to pass on, though, is this: Judge the quality of food by how picky the restaurant's cats are. Being typical feline-fetishist lesbians, we were delighted to discover that most Mykonian restaurants have not just one but many semiresident cats. The actual statistic is that Mykonos has three thousand year-round inhab-itants, two thousand churches, and five thousand cats. People told us the cats were originally brought to the island to save the grain from the rats—remember those windmills?—and that the Mykonians take care of the strays. Most of them do appear to be healthy compared, say, with the pathetic strays who live in the ruins of Rome. At any rate, since so much dining on the island is outdoors, on terraces or in gardens, odds are that some kitty will be in your lap by the end of the meal, and you, being the emotional sucker most of us gay folk are, will shamelessly encourage them, as we did. This turns out to be an especially expensive indulgence if you order fish, whose price we calculated at twenty dollars a pound, including head, tail, and bones. (A fish shortage may seem mind-blowingly illogical on a small island. But everyone on Mykonos wants to be a waiter, not a fisherperson.)

Most tourists also manage to spend inordinate amounts of time dogging the webbed heels of the island's official mascots: Petros II and Irini, male and female pelicans who hang around the harbor giving photo opportunity. True to form, the male is pink, perfectly groomed, and fabulously outgoing, while the female is a butch little number with scraggly gray feathers. Irini was brought in as a companion for the original Petros, who arrived in a storm in the fifties, saw a good thing, and never left. "An actual wedding ceremony was held on her arrival, complete with crowns and priests," according to a brochure handed out free to tourists. "One might have called it a marriage of convenience, for Petros totally ignored her after the ceremony." Irini in turn had zero interest in sucking up to anyone, pelican or human.

Petros I died in 1985 under mysterious circumstances. The official story is that he was hit by a car. We had heard rumors before we came to Mykonos that he died of internal injuries sustained during a rape by a drunken gay tourist. What on earth could possibly be a worse advertisement for Our Crowd? But when we asked the woman in the tourist office point-blank about the incident, she firmly responded that no one knew who raped Petros I—that it could just as easily have been a straight man.

Evangelina claimed indignantly that the incident hadn't even happened on Mykonos. "A pelican was raped by an Arab in *Tinos*. An hour and a half away! If it happened in Mykonos," she added ominously, "we would shoot the one who did it in the harbor and make him into souvlaki." We never found out what really happened. But even if the worst-case-scenario rumor is true, Mykonians haven't used it to judge the rest of us.

Perhaps part of Mykonians' tolerance of our particular difference is that its central maritime position has accustomed residents to a bridge mix of peoples for millennia. And while Mykonos itself has virtually no significant history for culture vultures to wallow in, tiny nearby Delos was in fact the main Aegean commercial port from the fourth to the first century B.C. At one time, Delos simultaneously supported, on its 1.4 square miles, the domestic settlements (*including* the different gods) of four nations: Italy, Egypt, Syria, and Greece.

Most tourists do take a one-day excursion to Delos, whose extensive cosmopolitan ruins, excavated from 1872 onward by various French teams, make it one of the most important archaeological sites in Greece. Legendary birthplace of the twin godlets Apollo and Artemis, Delos ("Illustrious") was home to an Apollonian sanctuary which, by the seventh or sixth century B.C., had made the island a religious center equal to Delphi. And the Artemis-cult buildings, while less prestigious, were even older, traceable back to the pre-Greek cult of the Great Goddess (Gaia or Ge). That's 1500 or 2000, maybe even third millennium, B.C. At any rate, definitely predating even Judy Garland, as cult heroines go.

But what you boys musn't miss is the section known as the Sanctuary of Dionysus. It features the sculptural shreds of a phallus-worship cult, a row of stone penises that have all seen better days—what we called the Boulevard of Broken Dicks.

The story behind this, which you will not find in any of the official guidebooks, is that Dionysus needed desperately to visit Hades, but didn't know the way. Fortunately a human named Prosymnus did, so they made a deal: Dionysus would get a map to the underworld, and, upon the god's return, Prosymnus would get Dionysus. Erotic bartering with a deity may appear a bit cheeky from a Judeo-Christian standpoint, but you have to remember that back then, running into one or another of these Greek gods on the street was pretty commonplace, sort of like running into Woody Allen at Elaine's.

Anyway, by the time Dionysus got back, poor Prosymnus had died. But the god was no piker. He cut down an olive tree, carved a giant penis, set it up on Prosymnus' tomb, and sat on it—thus fulfilling his end of the bargain. Giant memorial phalli were set up at various other sites, as well as on Delos, to commemorate the event.

As well as day-tripping, most tourists on a Greek vacation island-hop. Greece has more than fourteen hundred islands, after all, so it seems to make sense to see more than just one while you're there. It makes somewhat less sense once you realize that although the whole of Greece covers only fifty thousand square miles, the territory is so chopped up and widely dispersed into various seas that for many hops, especially those encompassing different island groups, returning to Athens is far more efficient than trying to make boat connections between islands. Often, in fact, it is the only option. Then there are the boat schedules, which, depending as they do on Greek weather as well as Greek temperament, are, well, iffy. What it comes down to is that if a given ferry is scheduled to leave Mykonos for Santorini at ten A.M. Monday, it will depart at ten or eleven A.M., maybe two or six P.M. and if not on Monday, in all probability on Tuesday or Wednesday, or perhaps some other time that week, if not the next.

Having only a couple of vacation weeks to play with, we stayed on Mykonos.

We've heard, however, that there is a bit of semi-organized gay life on other islands; specifically Rhodes, Crete, Hydra, Paros, and a few other smaller islands. Not much in the way of actually gay-oriented facilities, mind you, but some native receptiveness to gay tourism. This does not seem to be true, surprisingly, on Lesbos. We hear that the locals, who prefer to call their island Mytilene after its largest town (which should be your first clue), actively discourage small-*l* lesbian pilgrims. Evidently the citizens of the village where Sappho was born have even posted a none-too-subtle sign for the small-*l*'s who sometimes camp on the beach nearby: "WELCOME TO ERESOS. IT WILL BE A PLEASURE TO SEE YOU ENJOYING AND FOLLOWING OUR TRADITIONAL WAY OF LIFE."

After hearing, as well, of several instances of outright harassment, we decided to skip Lesbos. This is too bad, because we were definitely intrigued by the post-card possibilities, not to mention the hilarity factor of using the usually invisible L-word in everyday conversation. ("Waiter, do you have any lezz-bee-yan wine? Lezz-bee-yan cheese? What's that? Sorry, but I'm just not attracted to lesbian men.")

It's our last night on Mykonos. The storms at sea have continued to sabotage all transportation in and out of the island. Mykonos is one big ship of fools, minus the ship; we've been marooned for days, with nothing to do but drink and go to the beach. Naturally, we're in Pierro's.

When we first come in, Evangelina is standing behind the bar, holding hands across the counter with a customer named Piera, staring deeply into her eyes, and muttering sweet *riens* in French. She doesn't appreciate it when we make snide references to her girlfriend in Paris. But Evangelina is in a good mood, and when we ask her if she's quit her job today she appears stunned. "This bar is like my heart," she insists.

Piera, who is actually Italian, explains in rapid-fire French that she knows Evangelina from a previous trip and has come back for her vacation this year with two gay male friends. The previous night, Piera and a Greek guy did a chair-top strip to the ever-popular orgasm tape. Tonight she appears subdued—at least until a strange man walks in, gooses Evangelina, and kisses her. The man turns out to be Evangelina's cousin, or maybe her brother—by now we realize that everyone on Mykonos is related. Piera is not amused.

The cast of characters tonight also includes two guys from L.A., Doug and George, old friends who've met up here. Doug has been approached by the Greek stripper boy, but he's busy eyeballing one of the Germans. George is drooling over one of Piera's friends, who speaks no English and is desperately (and with apparent success) passing off his loneliness as an air of mystery. George is also eloquent on the subject of the cousin of Evangelina's who actually owns Pierro's. This man is straight, but his tight American blue jeans—with a pair of artful rips on the ass, one on each bun —have made a deep impression on George.

Then there's a wiry little Italian elf, dressed all in black, with multiple earrings. Doug and George have dubbed him Topo Gigio. We've noticed him before: While he dances mostly with other men, he's accompanied every night by an apparently straight female companion.

Meanwhile virtually the whole male population of the bar is intensely focused on a man who's a dead ringer for Clive, the closety upper-class Brit who breaks the hero's heart in *Maurice*. The illusion holds until "Clive" opens his mouth, and out comes a Dutch accent as thick as pea soup. Before long he's passionately making out with a Mexican guy from San Francisco.

Later we find Evangelina out on the porch, smooching with Topo Gigio's date. Topo Gigio, who has been boogying his ass off with one Northern European guy after another, wrings his hands and lamely protests, "No! Please! That's my *wife*."

Evangelina elaborately surveys his crotch, and with a withering sneer holds up her thumb and forefinger as if she's measuring a fish so tiny that only an amateur wouldn't throw it back in the water. Topo Giogio reaches over, feels her arm muscle, and does the same. Just as we're all wondering if it's the beginning of another brawl, they both burst out laughing and embrace.

The music starts again, and everybody dances. Another night in Mykonos lurches toward the morning.

PRACTICAL INFORMATION

MYKONOS ISLAND—NUMBER KEY

1. Hotel Tagu
2. Hotel Petroulas
3. Hotel Madalena
4. Mykonos Bay Hotel and Mykonos Beach Hotel (at Megali Ammos)

MYKONOS TOWN—NUMBER KEY

Bars
1. Montparnasse (sunset bar, on the "Little Venice")
2. Kastro (sunset bar, on the "Little Venice")
3. Pierro's, Mantos's, Icaros, and Nefeli's Hollywood Bar (all in the same building on Adronikou-Matoyanni)
4. Anchor (Adronikou-Matoyanni)
5. Vengera (Adronikou-Matoyanni)
6. City disco (end of Mitropoleos)

Restaurants
7. Katrin's (Ag. Gerasimos)
8. Sesame Kitchen (off Enoplon Dynameon)
9. Philippi's (off Kalogera)

10. post office
11. telephones and tourist office

Hotel
12. Hotel Elena

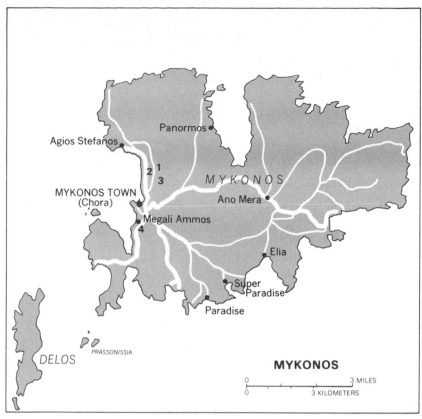

Agios Stefanos

Panormos

MYKONOS

2 1
3

MYKONOS TOWN
(Chora)

Megali Ammos

Ano Mera

4

Elia

Super
Paradise

Paradise

DELOS

PRASSONISSIA

MYKONOS

0   3 MILES
0   3 KILOMETERS

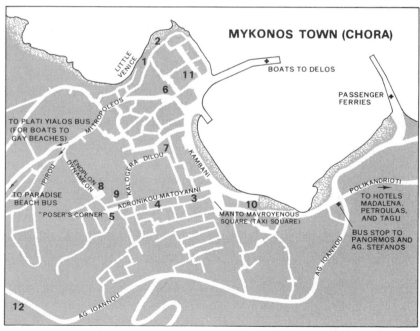

MYKONOS TOWN (CHORA)

LITTLE
VENICE

2
1
11
6

BOATS TO DELOS

PASSENGER
FERRIES

TO PLATI YIALOS BUS
(FOR BOATS TO
GAY BEACHES)

MTROPOLEOS

7

ENOPLON
DYNAMEON

8

KALOGERA DILOU

KAMBANI

POLIKANDRIOTI

TO PARADISE
BEACH BUS

IPIROU

9

ADRONIKOU-MATOYANNI

3

10

TO HOTELS
MADALENA,
PETROULAS,
AND TAGU

"POSER'S CORNER"

5

4

MANTO MAVROYENOUS
SQUARE (TAXI SQUARE)

BUS STOP TO
PANORMOS AND
AG. STEFANOS

AG. IOANNOU

12

AG. IOANNOU

Every *place* in Mykonos is or will be described by locals as, only two minutes away. Every *price* in Mykonos is both whimsical and negotiable. Every *street* in Mykonos is spelled at least four different ways, none of them matching any spelling on any map you own. And every *one* in Mykonos is a cousin.

Orientation: A good central reference point is Manto Mavroyenous (Mavrogenous, etc.) Square, also called Taxi Square. Locate this by its statue of the Mykonian heroine on the harbor. Matoyanni Street, for example, starts here, and the square that is Mykonos's main gay meeting place (on which Pierro's and three other gay/mixed bars are located) is about 45 seconds' walk along Matoyanni Street from Manto's statue.

To locate the only **pay phone booths** in town, first find the **tourist office,** by walking around the harbor from the Piraeus boat side to the Delos boat side, and hanging a left just as you're about to fall into the water. As you face the office, the phone booths are uphill to the left. If lost, ask a native to direct you to the place the pelicans sleep at night.

To change money, the National Bank of Greece, on the harbor, north of Taxi Square, is open from about 8 A.M.–2 P.M., Mon.–Fri.; an additional exchange window is open Mon.–Fri. 6–8 P.M. and 6–8 P.M. & Sat.–Sun. 9:30 A.M.–1 P.M. Better hours and virtually identical rates are to be found at the **post office,** on the harbor east of Taxi Square. It's the first white building north of the beach; hours are 8:30 A.M.–8:30 P.M.

Postal code: 846 00.

Telephone code: 0289.

Best town map: Toubi's (blue and red, with Delos map and history on flip side).

Currency unit: the drachma (dr).

WHERE TO STAY

There is currently only one exclusively gay hotel in Mykonos (possibly two; no one on the island had ever heard of the second one, but this means nothing). As usual, though, all mixed gay/straight hotels were put through the Drill—with one possible exception. At the Karboni-Matogianni, the two extremely jovial women in charge spoke no English whatsoever, and since our Greek lacks totally 100 percent complete polish . . . Well, what it boils down to is, we either came to an agreement that gays were absolutely welcome, or else that Africa and Hawaii were absolutely great places for a vacation. We're not sure which. They did offer us orange juice, and invite us to stay and converse in sign language forever.

Sadly, double beds are almost unheard-of in Mykonos. Happily, we found most of them.

The A-B-C-D classes mentioned are Greek government ratings, not ours, but included for your information.

Prices: *Inexpensive* = under 3,500 dr. double; *moderate* = 3,500–4,800 dr.; *mod./exp.* = 4,800–6,500 dr.; *expensive* = above 6,500 dr. All prices are for the civilized season, which other books call the off season (April, May, and the end of September through October). This is when you should go to Mykonos. We especially recommend May. Prices during June and the beginning of September are up approximately 50 percent from those quoted; in July and August many prices are doubled.

Hotel Elena, Rohari St. (by Mykonos Theatre); tel. 23457/23458, or home tel. 22361. Class D. On a quiet hillside two minutes from the town center, this hotel with charming female proprietor has been well known for years as gay-friendly. All 24 rooms are with bath, and some have balconies. Only two rooms have double beds, and these are technically singles, but Elena will let them to couples. The large lobby, which opens onto an oleander-drenched front porch, includes a bar/snackbar, and living-room lounge. After dark there's an extremely romantic look and feel to this place—amber lighting, much wrought iron, ocean view—which is only slightly marred by a location within earshot of a nightlit public basketball court. Breakfast included. *Moderate to mod./exp.*

Pension Giovani, Ag. Ioanou-Giovani (but write: Costas and Rania Cosmas, Poste Restante, Mykonos 846 00); tel. 22485. Class C. This friendly pension is situated on a not-quite-so-scenic hillside, two minutes from the bus stop to Plati Yialos. The 12 large, immaculate rooms, all with bath, are walled in chalet-golden knotty pine—the whole place smells wonderfully of new wood. Some rooms have private balconies, but there's also a large common terrace with sea view. Breakfast is 300 dr. extra off-season (included in the high season). *Inexpensive.*

Mykonos Beach Hotel and **Mykonos Bay Hotel,** Megali Ammos town beach; tel. 22572/22573. Class C and Class B. These two hotels, facing each other across the seafront road to Plati Yialos, share the same management. The Mykonos Bay is more luxurious, with pool, bar, inner courtyard, and garden, as well as genuine marble floors, stereos, and phones in its 35 *en suite* rooms (many with balconies). The 27-room Mykonos Beach, built as individual super-cute Cycladic-style white bungalows (all with bath), is more private, which manager Statis Koysathanas says makes it more popular with gay women and men. The Beach shares the Bay's pool and bar/snack bar. Breakfast is included. Mykonos Beach: *Moderate.* Mykonos Bay: *Mod./exp.*

Hotel Maria, 18 N. Kalogera St. (proprietor: Petros E. Koussathanas); tel.: 24212-24213, or alternatively 22317 and 22480. Class D. Sixteen beamed-ceiling rooms (four with bath) in a quiet central location, near the end of a tiny road off one of Mykonos's main pedestrian streets. Many rooms overlook a lush, little-used walled public garden. *Inexpensive.*

Hotel Matogianni-Karboni, Matoyanni St; tel. 22217/23264/23448, or home tel. 22475. Class C. Located in the town center, this hotel has 14 good-sized rooms, all with bath, phone, and stereo; three with double bed. Unlike some rooms in town, these have little atmosphere (only basic white-linoleum floors rather than marble or tile, for instance), but some do have small balconies overlooking the hotel's pleasantly overgrown garden. On the ground floor is a bar/snack bar decorated in homey fashion with personal vacation souvenirs of the family who run the place. Most of the proprietors speak no English, but seem to greatly enjoy lame American attempts at Greek. Breakfast included. *Inexpensive.*

Hotel Madalena or Mantalena, P.O. Box 94; tel. 24283/22954. Class C. Blue-and-white hillside hotel with typical many-leveled Mykonian architecture, located approx. 300 meters outside of Mykonos town on the *upper* road to Agios Stefanos Beach. Has 27 rooms, all with bath, balcony, telephone, stereo, and panoramic view of town and sea; 3 single, 20 double (4 with double bed), 4 triple; 5 additional double rooms in adjoining building, with shared bath. Spare, beachy room decor. Buffet breakfast included. *Mod./exp. if you mention this book when reserving.* (We didn't ask for special rates, but for some reason proprietor Nikos Kabouroglou insisted on giving you all 1000–3000 dr. off.)

Hotel Petroulas or Petrula; tel. 23328. Class D. About 100 meters farther along the same road as the Madalena, this gay hotel has virtually no walk-in traffic, as it's booked exclusively and pretty solidly by Mantours (Motzstraße 70, D-1000 Berlin, Germany; tel. 30/213-8090; telex: 181 524 atlas d.) But occasional straights and strays do get rooms. A pretty, very large, common terrace overlooks the sea and town, compensating for the hotel's rather basic little bar and plain lobby. The 11 rooms, all with bath and 5 with double bed, have nice blue tile floors and most have a sea view. Unfortunately, some also have stained walls; according to the management, "We are having a few plumbing problems." A German-style buffet breakfast, with ham and cheese added to the usual Continental breads, is included. *Expensive.*

Hotel Tagu or Tagou or Tangou; tel. 22611. Class E. Yet another 100 meters along, this is the most luxurious hotel of the three on this road. Formerly all-gay, the Tagu is now mixed but still very popular with our crowd; comanager Anna explains, "We try to have everything here, and every night's a party!" This multilevel hillside structure, which has been written up in several architecture magazines, counts among its features a 24-hour bar/snack bar, a large pool, a separate quiet outdoor area for reading, and a lovely arched stucco breakfast room. The 20 rooms, all with bath and telephone, are like cottages in that each has its own door to the outside world—always a plus for gay folk who don't enjoy running the hotel-lobby gauntlet. The rooms' drawback is that all beds are twins. Free airport transfers and a German-style buffet breakfast, with champagne on Sunday, are all included in rates. *Moderate to mod./exp.*

And finally, our sentimental favorite: **Vaso's house**, tel. 13998. This is one of blue-and-white Mykonos's only red-and-white houses. But don't even think of trying to find it on your own. Just find Vaso herself, at the Hotel Apollon right on the harbor, where she works every day from about 9 A.M. to 9 P.M. Her one, and only one, large white stucco room has dark wood trim, a dark wood queen-sized bed, a composite tile floor, a private bath, and a balcony. It is full of flowers and weird, adorable little Mykonian knicknacks. It has a great landlady. And the central location can't be beat. You can *roll* home from Pierro's. *Inexpensive (actually, Dirt Cheap).*

WHERE TO GO (DAY)

The beach most popular among lesbians and gay men is **Super Paradise**, a long hill and cliff-bordered crescent of sand with two resident bar/restaurants and varying degrees of beach attire, including none, the option many gay men seem to favor. Don't be misled by references in other guides to "Super Super Paradise." This is not a separate beach. It's actually just the most scandalous and least-clothed part of Super Paradise, on the far left as the boat lands. You really can't miss it . . . though lesbians and monogamous males might prefer to. Bathing suits are also optional at **Paradise,** one cove nearer to Mykonos town, which is more mixed gay/straight but perfectly nice—no macho drunken yahoos, etc. Paradise has a lovely campground, plus a restaurant/bar/cafeteria with great homemade yogurt, great cats, and frequent live music and dancing at night. **Elia** (or Elios), one cove farther than Super Paradise, is popular with gays who prefer a less populated strand; it also has a bar/restaurant. And we hear that **Panormos,** on the opposite side of Mykonos, is the newest gay find. Unfortunately, it's virutally inaccessible. There are no scheduled boats, no one we met had ever been there, and we got totally lost trying to find it for ourselves on mopeds. So you'll have to fend for yourselves on this one, kids.

Most people reach the above beaches by bus from the west side of Mykonos town to Plati Yialos beach, and from there by small boat. Total price round-trip to Paradise is about 350 dr; to Super Paradise, 450 dr.; to Elios, 550 dr. We recommend renting small mopeds instead, for about 800–1000 dr. per 24 hours. It's freer; it makes sense financially, if you want to hit several beaches (all the above-mentioned ones are accessible by moped, though not by car); and after all, it's only $6–$7 we're talking about. For well-maintained bikes, try **Anna Hajidakis** (tel. 23484), on the upper road to Agios Stefanos beach, second rental shop on the right, or **"Ping Panthir"** rentals, next to Pension Giovani.

To buy your labyris: **Elisa's Gallerie** (Mavrogeni St., tel. 24481).

WHERE TO GO (NIGHT)

Afternoon/early evening
Piano Bar, at the back end of Mavroyenous Square, has been open over 10 years, though gay visitors who knew it when complain it's recently become somewhat straight-infested during high season.

From 5 P.M. to 8 P.M.
Park yourself in front of a wall-wide picture window at one of the waterfront "sunset bars" in Mykonos's oldest Kastro section, next to "Little Venice." The favorite is **Kastro Bar,** where you can render yourself semicomatose drinking smoothly lethal "Kastro Coffee." Also popular is **Montparnasse.**

From 8 P.M. to 11 P.M.
Vengera Bar and **Anchor Bar** are both expensive, style-oriented, and popular with the gay preppie and yacht crowd. (At this hour, gay nonposeurs are eating rather than drinking their dinner.)

From 11 P.M. to 4 A.M.

Conveniently sharing the same Matoyianni St. building are **Pierro's, Mantos, Icaros,** and **Nefeli's Hollywood Bar.** And at 1 A.M. do follow the crowd over to the drag show at **City** disco, on the phone booth/pelican square.

WHERE (AND WHAT) TO EAT

There are no gay restaurants per se in Mykonos. But perhaps not uncoincidentally, our own personal favorite eateries did all have a sizeable gay clientele (after 8:30 P.M., naturally). **Sesame Kitchen** (in the cul-de-sac off Enoplon Dynameon), currently Mykonos's hottest bargain joint, has a cozy, informal, early-1970s San Francisco ambiance, sincere service, and tasty veggie-oriented food. Don't miss the garlic-and-bread dip or vegetarian moussaka. **Philippi's** (Matoyianni St.; tel. 22295) has a seductive tropical dining garden and equally seductive taramasalata. **Katrin**'s (Ag. Gerasimos; tel. 22169) intimate, candlelit, white stone-arched rooms are backdrop to a very limited and very expensive but very good fresh-fish menu. For breakfast, try the homemade apple fritters and rich yogurt with fresh fruit at the **Donut Factory,** across from Sesame Kitchen at the intersection of Mitropoleos and Enoplon Dynamion Sts.

By the way, if you ignore our wise advice to avoid the ferry from Italy to Greece, we do have a little restaurant in Brindisi, where the boats embark, that possibly even makes the whole hideous voyage worthwhile: **L'Angoletto** (via Pergola; tel: 25029), right off the main corso Garibaldi. The place looks like a Brooklyn pizza parlor, but Mama's house special pasta is as simple yet elusive to describe as a great orgasm.

WHERE TO GET THE LATEST DIRT
(INFO RESOURCES)

Unfortunately, Mykonos has no gay bookstores, organizations, or periodicals. But we found the tourist office totally nonhomophobic and quite helpful in locating gay stuff.

For those who will be passing through Athens, there is a lesbian-feminist organization headquartered at 20 Massalias, Kolonaki, Athens, 10680; tel. 361 142 23), and a feminist bookstore at the same address. The mixed Athenian gay group is **AKOE,** 21 Patission, in Omonia (Athens); they publish a newsmagazine, *Amphi.*

WHAT TO READ

Homosexuality in Greek Myth, by Bernard Sergent (Beacon). Explores the mythological roots of institutionalized pederasty—i.e., once you wade through the tedious pedagogy, what gods were sleeping with whom.

Down There on a Visit, by Christopher Isherwood (Methuen). Fictionalized memoirs of the author's stay "roughing it" on a Greek island owned by an eccentric fellow Englishman, pre–World War II.

Memoirs of Hadrian, by Marguerite Yourcenar (Farrar, Straus & Giroux). A novelized biography of the great emperor and his boy lover.

And naturally any of Mary Renault's ancient world boy-king tales, especially *The Persian Boy, The King Must Die,* and *The Last of the Wine* . . . assuming you don't begin frothing at the mouth at too many exchanges like the following: "Tell me, Lypsis; where do you think the soul goes, when we die?" "Into a philosopher if we have deserved it, or a woman if we were weak."

OTHER-ISLAND ODDS AND ENDS
MENTIONED IN THE TEXT

If you do go to **Lesbos,** we hear you shouldn't miss the Petrified Forest, west, between Sigri, Andissa and Eressos (hike in only; no cars). Most women camp on the beach near Eressos, Sappho's birthplace. We're told the most sympathetic bars for women are the Blue Bar and the Yellow Bar. However, Greek lesbians and female travelers alike have told us that local homophobia grows worse every year, as more and more lesbians make the pilgrimage.

On small, vehicle-free **Hydra,** a strongly gay/lesbian–oriented 10-room guesthouse (multilingual, including English) is Pension Kamini (P.O. Box 51, Hydra, 180-40, Greece; tel. 0298/523 35).

CAPRI

The First Gay Resort

*I*n the category of "Categories That Will Never Make the Guinness (or Any Other) Book of World Records," Capri has a good claim to the title of First Gay Mega-Resort.

The first superstar from our crowd to fall willing victim to the charms of this glamorous little island off the tip of the Amalfi coast, about an hour and a half's boatride from Naples, was the Roman emperor Tiberius, way back in A.D. 26.

First, that is, if you don't count the Sirens. Many literary historians over the centuries have identified Capri, once a Greek possession, as the beautiful rock-islet to which these mythical sharp-clawed birdwomen would lure passing sailors, whom they'd then rip to shreds. Given the nasty mother-raping baby-eating habits of those Homeric types, we feel this certainly makes the Sirens our kind of gals. More authoritative authorities tracing the legend's real-life roots have, however, suggested that piracy, rather than righteous sisterhood, was probably the Sirens' motive. And, given the prices on Capri today, they have a point.

So back to Tiberius, who discovered Capri more or less by chance: His predecessor, Augustus, liked the place, and made the Greeks, who then controlled the whole Neapolitan region, a deal they couldn't refuse.

Tiberius wasn't the only Roman emperor with gay inclinations. There had been, and were to be, many others, Caligula and Hadrian being among the best known. Neither was Tiberius Rome's most queeny king. Even in the reams of scandalized accounts of Tiberius' reign, there is nothing to match Elagabalus, who ruled from A.D. 218 to A.D. 222. This former teen temple dancer met with the Roman senate in full drag; failed to produce offspring despite six or seven arranged marriages, perhaps due to his one official and scores of unofficial male consorts; and was given to blatantly swish gestures: He sent servants to collect all the cobwebs in Rome, for instance, and once killed several dinner guests through a slight special-effects miscalculation, when tons of violets falling through hidden panels in the dining-room ceiling proved a bit heavier than anticipated. Elagabalus was also given to outrageous bons mots, our own favorite being "Don't call me Caesar; I'm a lady."

What makes Tiberius unique as well as relevant is that for most of his reign, he was a model of decorum—more British than Italian, really. He was a sixty-eight-year-old self-controlled stick by the time he moved permanently to Capri, where he built twelve villas in favorite scenic spots. Then suddenly, as the second-century historian Tacitus wrote, "Tiberius, once much absorbed in the cares of State, now relaxed with equal application into secret indulgences and immoral pastimes." He'd heard the song of the Sirens—who'd evidently learned, during their years on Capri, the skill of adapting one's act for the sake of commerce.

As chronicled by Tacitus' contemporary Suetonius, Tiberius established secret vice parlors called *sellaria* in various caves and grottos throughout the island, where young *spintriae* (the ancient equivalent of Chippendale's dancers) dressed as Pans and wood nymphs put on live sex shows and performed other services for the still very healthy emperor. One of the *spintriae* was the future emperor Vitellius.

Other, younger *capresi* youths, who performed between Tiberius' legs, were known as his *pisciculi* ("tiddlers"). The term, we hope, is self-explanatory. Even trash, as we proudly consider ourselves, has limits . . . Which Tiberius, apparently, had not. During one religious ceremony, the emperor was reportedly so overcome by the boy who was offering the incense that he could barely wait for the sacrifice's conclusion to ravish the fellow—and, immediately afterward, his brother.

Capri has always had this effect on people. In fact, the island's instant transformation of staid sticks into walking erogenous zones is perhaps the most noteworthy constant throughout Capri's two millennia of foreign rule (Greek, Roman, Norman, Anjou, Hapsburg, Spanish, Bourbon, British, French again—you name it). In the seventeenth century, Parisian tourist Jean-Jacques Bouchard reported that both the women and the boys of Capri were beautiful and willing. And in the stuffy climate of the rest of nineteenth-century Europe, Capri had an open reputation for sexual permissiveness of all kinds. It was this otherworldly lotus-land rep—that here was a place where proper folk from proper nations like England could turn into instant party animals, with no one the wiser—that was responsible for the beginning of Capri's modern boom as a perv paradise, in the late 1800s.

The trend was started by Germans, among them the artist Christian Wilhelm Allers. Like photographer Wilhelm von Gloeden in Taormina, Allers specialized in depictions of young boys; one of his most famous engravings is of a middle-aged German professor bargaining with a Capri youth to accompany him to the Blue Grotto—not, presumably, to check out the water color. Roman remains found inside the Grotto indicate that it might even have been one of Tiberius' bathhouses.

Allers's first boyfriend, by the way, was a Marina Grande sailor, whose nickname, Meza Recchia, is derived from *orecchione,* ("big ear"), slang for "homosexual." To call someone a homo, you flip your ear. Why? Probably for the same reason *finocchio,* fennel, is a hugely insulting word for "gay man." Which is the same reason why, despite Italy's sexism, the slang word for "penis," *cazzo,* is something you say when you want to be mildly negative—roughly, "oh, shit"—while words derived from the equivalent for vagina, *figa,* are positive; *figata,* though not an expression you'd use on your mom, conveys to peers "something wonderously cool." In other words, we don't know why. It's just another Italian peculiarity. If anything about Italy ever started making sense to us, we'd be at the shrink's within minutes.

At any rate, Allers's liaisons with local boys eventually attracted the attention of the Neapolitan police force. He escaped, however, thanks to Donna Lucia Morgano, unofficial den mother to the foreign gay community and proprietor of Morgano's bar, now long gone, but the place where anyone who was anyone hung out in turn of the century Capri.

Probably the most famous German victim of the Sirens' song was industrialist Fritz Krupp, whose story nearly duplicates that of Tiberius, seventeen centuries earlier. Married and the father of two daughters, this upright forty-four-year-old armaments manufacturer came to Capri on business in 1898, checked into a suite at the newly-built Quisisana (still the island's most luxurious hotel)—and totally lost it.

Krupp's four seasons in Capri began with a modest liaison with an eighteen-year-old local barber. By 1902, he was filling Berlin hotel suites with imported *capresi* rent boys; and his exploits at Capri's Grotta di Fra' Felice, a two-room cave halfway down the steep cliffside from Capri town to Marina Piccolo, where Krupp docked his yachts, were local legend. The fat, formerly placid German transformed the cave into a sort of all-male Playboy club. Members dressed as monks, in keeping with the grotto's name, carried on with local boys to the accompaniment of three violinists. Orgasms were saluted with skyrockets.

Unfortunately for Krupp, the lovemaking was sometimes photographed, and the results sold by local porn vendors. A scandal ensued that did Krupp no harm in Capri, but ruined him in Germany. In 1902, he died from what could have been a stroke or could have been suicide. Meanwhile, though, he had contributed to Capri both the public park officially named the Giardini di Augusto (but which everyone calls the Villa Krupp) and the via Krupp, which scales the cliffs between Capri town and the Marina Piccolo beach and boat basin. This precipitous winding path is still to this day one of the major outdoor hangouts for young *capresi* male hookers.

Reclining in a lounge chair on the terrace of one of Capri's many small, luxurious, hillside hotels, it's easy to understand instinctively what it is about this island that has always seemed to bring out people's most hidden sexual natures. Whether one chooses to stay in glamorous mountaintop Capri town, where international Beautiful People haunt the famous Piazza, or even farther uphill in quieter Anacapri, the island is physically a very seductive place. It may not be a kind of seduction familiar to gay American island bunnies used to the flat sandbar aphrodisia of Fire Island or Key West; like many southern European islands, Capri is geologically little more than a hunk of limestone, evident in the famous white spine that juts dramatically down the center of all island photos and has been likened to a giant sleeping hedgehog. Unlike so many mountainous Greek isles, though, Capri is not a sun-bleached rock pile but a verdant garden. Except for the hedgehog and a number of smaller but also artistically effective wind-sculpted bare-rock outcroppings, Capri's mountains are carpeted wall to wall with trees, flowers, and tropical houseplants. Approached from the sea, the island looked to us like a floating cupcake. Startling. Intriguing. Humpy. Delicious.

It is locally popular to attribute visitors' relaxed sexual attitudes to the famous *aria di Capri;* residents of rivalrous Capri and Anacapri go so far as to blame each other's faults on differences between the lower and upper air. In a novelized account of the doings on the Capri colony circa 1919, the British writer Compton Mackenzie related the explanation of a distressed expatriate Englishwoman on Capri (fictionalized as the isle of Sirene), who found it necessary to outfit her dogs with chastity belts: "Must do it. Must do it. Dogs in Sirene most immoral dogs in the world. Everybody immoral in Sirene. It's the air. Dogs. People. Can't help it, poor dears."

It is a bit harder to understand why Capriot natives have always, save for a brief attempt at cleanup during Mussolini's reign, been so receptive to foreign homosexuals, when so many of the guys were pedophiles. Doubtless the Greek background helped. It is likely, for example, that the *erastes-eromenos* tradition (adult educator/sexual initiator–adolescent *ephebe*) long persisted in Capri because, until acquired by Tiberius' predecessor Augustus, the island had belonged to Naples, which retained its Greek customs and language.

But probably the main reason for Capri's tolerance is simply money. Since the island's prosperity depends entirely on the exploitation of foreigners, Capri's most noted historian, James Money, explains, "everything is geared to this end and the characters of most of the islanders are moulded accordingly." This is plainly illustrated by the way local opinion divided in the Krupp case: pro-Krupp were all the locals he'd done business with; the antis were all barbers, restaurateurs, hotel owners, and artists he hadn't patronized. As for a little dallying with local youth . . . Well, a former mayor of Capri once remarked, according to Money, that many of the island's best families, "if not actually launched on the road to success, at least benefited substantially from [the financial donations of foreign homosexual men] to their willing young ancestors."

At the beginning of this century, though, the price for Capri's pleasures was still very small, so eager potential wild-and-crazy guys from Britain, America, and other uptight nations soon followed the Germans. Gay artists and writers were particularly drawn, among them Mackenzie and his wife Faith (both apparently bisexual with a leaning towards men), John Ellingham Brooks (husband of Romaine), E. F. Benson, Norman Douglas, Oscar Wilde and Lord Alfred Douglas, and W. Somerset Maugham (who had inscribed on his gate, in place of the usual CAVE CANEM, a sign reading CAVE HOMINEM).

For gay-history groupies like ourselves, a chance to time-travel in the footsteps of all the above luminaries while enjoying the island's physical charms, would be more than enough reason to visit Capri.

But for us, the most irresistible Siren song of all was one two-year period that was probably the silliest of Capri's whole gay history, and one *very* silly book that describes them.

The years were 1918 and 1919, the final year and immediate aftermath of World War I. (Other European vacation spots waited for the end. Capri anticipated it.) The book is Compton Mackenzie's *Extraordinary Women*. And the event was a two-season-long women's party that reads like a lesbian *Who's Who in Expatriate Arts, Royalty, and Catfights*.

Extraordinary Women was published in 1928, several months after Radclyffe Hall's *The Well of Loneliness*. Initially, it was scheduled for publication before *The Well*, but Hall and her publisher, seeing Mackenzie as competition in the novelty-book field, busted their butts to hit the stores first.

Hall's book was banned and went through years of court cases. Mackenzie's did have initial difficulties in getting published. It was rejected by the first two publishers to which it was submitted, including his regular house, Cassell's—and when you consider that his previous novel, *Vestal Fire*, centered around the Capri adventures of Count Jacques d'Adelsward-

Fersen, a dishonest, social-climbing drug addict and pederast convicted in France of corrupting minors, you can see what a hot topic the *L* word was back then. But once published, *E.W.* was not suppressed.

Why? Perhaps because the author was a man. Perhaps because being first wasn't such a hot idea after all. Or else for the same reason many people still get upset about *The Well* vs. *E.W.*: one is a "Serious" book, obligatory tragic ending and all, about female "inverts"; the other satirically views Capri's summer-long Sapphic swap meet as a period drawing-room comedy, and nobody gets run over by a truck in the end, physically or psychologically. (We could also point out that in the "Serious" book, the gay girl does end up with a guy, which doesn't happen in the shallow book.)

Both books initially sold well, but Hall's has lived in reputation as *the* lesbo classic, while Mackenzie's is largely unknown today even to fans of his other works. We only found the book by chance, in a secondhand bin, although we're thrilled to report that it's recently been reprinted by London's Hogarth Press. We can't help but wonder what difference it would have made for us if Mackenzie's book, rather than Hall's, had been the standard we encountered in those first, young, intense times of wondering what a redefinition of our sexuality would mean to our lives.

Reviews of *The Well* make it clear that the book's literary and legal opponents considered lesbianism a disease transmittable to young people. Actually, Hall's book makes no suggestion of contagion, much less recruitment, merely presenting our condition as terminal. The plot revolves around Stephen Gordon, so christened by her dad. Dad wanted a boy, but also, no doubt, couldn't fail to notice that his sweetie snookums had been born with (ta-dah!) linebacker shoulders (a sure sign, as we all know) and a fashion sense that is, unfortunately, more New York Rangers than Sloane Rangers. After many trials and tribulations, including an exile in Paris— pretty tough, by any standard—Stephen gets a great-looking girlfriend, Mary, who is incredibly devoted to her. So, realizing what a hopeless, depraved life she is dooming her girlfriend to (this was 1920s Paris— lesbians had to hang out with Gertrude Stein, Natalie Barney, Janet Flanner, and other similar losers), the anguished Stephen drives Mary into the arms of a sympathetically presented swinish wannabe ex-boyfriend of Stephen's own, though, not first without a macho/machette "may the best man win the Real Woman" contest first. Which Stephen wins, of course.

This book, we realize, might have been groundbreaking in its time, and meaningful to certain women. But we can't believe it didn't also have the same effect on many others as it did on Pam, who read it during a period of first doubts in college, and regretfully concluded, "Not me. No way. Guess I was mistaken." Really: Many lesbian friends swear this book postponed their coming-out for years. Women who love other women are one thing. Depressed losers who compulsively wear expensive yet exceedingly dull men's suits, and can't find a single amusing thing to do in Paris, are another.

The plot of *Extraordinary Women* is harder to summarize, because, as usual in Mackenzie's books, nothing really happens. But "nothing" happens so festively.

Exactly why a lesbian scene suddenly flowered in Capri during 1918 and 1919 can't be pinpointed, but it doubtless had to do with the early-twentieth-century lesbian explosion in Paris, as many of the cast of characters were the same. For these women with discretionary incomes, who worked for personal fulfillment rather than need, wintering in northern climes and summering in Italy was the norm. Mackenzie just chronicled, accurately though amusingly, their real-life goings-on. Every character but one, he claimed, was an exact portrait.

The leading extraordinary women were beautiful, self-absorbed ne'er-do-well Rosalba Donsante (in real life Mimi Franchetti, daughter of Italian opera composer Alberto Franchetti) and Rory Freemantle, the book's only composite character. With her monocle, her bulldog kennel, and her penchant for full white-tie male evening dress over an inconveniently female-shaped bosom, Rory suggests a combination of Hall and Hall's lover, Lady Una Troubridge. The book's events, though, indicate that Rory was also modeled on a rich Australian, Checca Lloyd. The plot, such as it is, centers on the loyal Rory's dogged pursuit of Rosalba, as Rosalba flirts her way through shallow romantic liaisons with most of the gay, and straight, women on Capri. At times, the fictional characters' interactions seem impossibly melodramatic and public. In real life, however, some older Capri locals can still recall Mimi and Checca throwing bottles at each other in their abode at the Quisisana (called the Hotel Augusto in *E.W.*).

Supporting characters include pianist Cléo Gazay, whose crushes tend toward unattainable women, and the Countess Hermina de Randan. In actuality these characters were pianist Renata Borgatti, daughter of the famous Wagnerian opera star Giuseppe Borgatti, and Russian-princess-in-exile Helène Soldatenkov. In real life as well as fictionally, the monocled Principessa Soldatenkov was a revolutionarily zealous lesbian, whose entire household staff, from gardeners to grooms, was female. Hermina has come to "Sirene" to remove her lovely but essentially Jell-O–brained teenaged daughter, Lulu, from the clutches of a young male Neapolitan barber Lulu has taken a fancy to. Once on Sirene, to the principessa's delight, Lulu succumbs to Rosalba's charms.

Into this seething stewpot of passion sails coolly charismatic composer Olimpia Leigh. This fictional dragon-lady was in reality the glamorous fortyish American painter Romaine Brooks, longtime, though not live-in or monogamous, lover of Natalie Barney. And the cauldron boils over.

———

Faith Mackenzie, in her 1940 memoir *More Than I Should,* describes the effect of Romaine's arrival at Capri's Villa Eolia (actually the Villa Cercola, which Brooks's *mariage blanc* husband John had shared with Benson and Maugham): "To be loved by Romaine for even five minutes gave any young woman who cared about it a cachet not obtainable since the days when young women could boast of being loved by the mighty Sappho herself. . . . Feverish bouquets of exhausted blooms lay about [Romaine's] big studio, letters and invitations strewed her desk, ignored for the most part, while she, wrapped in her cloak, would wander down to the town as the evening cooled and sit in the darkest corner of Morgano's terrace ["Zampone's", in *E.W.*], maddeningly remote and provocative."

E.W.'s climax is a long-delayed housewarming party at Rory's Villa Leucadia, located at exactly the point on the road to Anacapri where the Hotel Caesar Augustus is today. The real party, at Lloyd's Cà del Sole/Villa Alba in Via Castello, was attended by the entire Mytilene crowd including Rosalba/Mimi, whose summer-long efforts had resulted in seductions of numerous of Olimpia/Romaine's conquests, but not of the dragon lady herself. This night of nights, which is still remembered in real-life Capri, is highlighted by a "classical dance" performed by an Englishwoman named Hewetson (actually a Dutchman named Van Decker), who is dressed in nothing but a pink silk handkerchief and a paper rose. Shortly after, Olimpia steams away for good, accompanied by the Principessa Bébé Buonograzia. In real life, Romaine Brooks was accompanied by Faith Mackenzie. There's more, but we wouldn't want to confuse you.

For us, three things make *E.W.* irresistibly charming. One is Mackenzie's mastery of dialect. Most authors' broken English sounds generic. Mackenzie's Italians fracture English in a uniquely Italian way, different from the way his French mangle the language; his Brits sound brusquely English; his Americans sound oh-you-kid 1920s midwestern; and his only marginally multilingual—but totally pretentious—"international set" phonies, like Rosalba, sound like Miss Piggy speaking *franglais* to Kermit.

There's also *E.W.*'s upbeat, routine acceptance of lesbianism. These ladies may be trashy and shallow, but their orientation is a nonissue; there is even some bozo precurser of gay pride in them. Contrast Stephen Gordon's breast-beating about our terrible, unavoidable condition—the assumption being that we'd certainly avoid it if we could—to the indignant response of Rosalba, upon being accused by Cléo Gazay of the unthinkable: heterosexuality. "A lie! A lie! I find you insufferably arrogant, *ma chère* Cléo. I do not admit that a complete lack of *chic* gives you the right to criticize my sincerity. I am quite as abnormal as you are."

Finally, we adore the romance. Many people, we realize, find humor incompatible with eroticism. We, on the other hand, feel that one of the most intimate things two lovers can do in bed is share laughter, even in the most intense moments. Hence our delight at the thrilling silliness of scenes like Rosalba's initial seduction of the slightly tipsy Lulu, whom she whisks from a suggestive public dancing lesson at the ballroom of the Hotel Augusto to a moonlit carriage ride.

It makes all the drivers waiting on the Piazza feel that this terrible war cannot go on much longer. Rosalba rushes up to one of the hopeful hacks with Lulu in hand, having momentarily evaded parents, governesses, lovers, and the other authority figures pursuing them—and obviously with nothing in mind save the usual eternal business of Capri in the midnight hour.

> *"Dove andare?"* he turned round on his box to enquire.
> *"Alla luna,"* Rosalba commanded.
> *"Si, signorina,"* he cried enthusiastically, urging his cob to greater speed.

And the young, romance-minded driver is off, with enthusiastic cries of "Bella! Bella!" to Anacapri. As Mackenzie notes, you can't with any degree of success tell a cabbie in England to take you to the moon, but in Capri, in those days at least, drivers had a less literal notion of direction.

To the moon!

There is a very brief answer as to whether it is possible to recapture those deliciously scandalous years between 1918 and 1920: No.

It is immediately apparent upon landing in Marina Grande that the days of gayla processions up the hill to Capri, accompanied by residents with your luggage on their heads, are long past. These days, if one doesn't use the funicular up to the Piazza in Capri town, one takes a taxi. Even if one is perfectly able and willing, as we are, to schlep our own luggage, the unrelenting onslaught of the careening cabs—as well as gas-belching tour buses—on all the islands's major access roads (between Marina Grande and Capri, and between Capri and Anacapri), makes walking the narrow old cliffside ways an exhaust-swamped, and exhausting, agoraphobic nightmare.

To the moon? Also in a taxi. There are no horse carriages left, even as tourist traps.

Let us disillusion you a bit further: The famous Piazza is really awfully small. During the afternoon, it's filled with international day-trippers, just out of the Blue Grotto and looking for glamour with a capital G in the two hours before their boat steams back to Naples. Since Glamour is still asleep at that hour in Capri, they are invariably disappointed. And at night, the Piazza is filled with small groups of thin, self-consciously attitudinous people wearing black clothes identical to those worn in New York's East Village, but three seasons ago.

As usual in Italy, there are no gay bars in town. Meeting other gay people in this country is more a matter of discreet eye contact than of anything as open as actually claiming some gay real estate. There is a basement disco positioned tantalizingly close to the once-upon-a-time location of the old Tip-Top (a 1920s all-night pub, opposite the Quisisana, frequented by Mackenzie and other English homos) that supposedly draws many gay people today. But to us, though there was some gay male presence, the disco's clientele mostly just looked like a sparse crowd of more Piazza poseurs checking out other poseurs, for a stiff cover charge.

Men looking for boys-for-hire can still do well. In fact, the town tourist office directed us to the right spot, though not without a bit of internal dissension. "They would not be interested in those gays," one official scolded another after we had introduced ourselves as travel-book writers. "Those are just locals, nobody famous." The same folks also bristled when we suggested that, perhaps, Capri wasn't quite the gay destination it had once been. Yes, they acknowledged, there had been a brief falling off, but lately *molti, molti* gays were rediscovering the place.

At any rate, if you're interested, night cruising is on the Piazza, and day cruising is along via Krupp. The road is offically closed, due to avalanches of falling boulders, which are alarmingly obvious blocking the path on the way down. But it's easy to just ignore the warning signs and climb the fence; and by and by, past Krupp's Grotto di Fra' Felice, you can't fail to miss some great young bods sunning on the larger of the fallen rocks. Bring your bike helmet.

Capri is also not terribly far from one of the most spectacular Greek ruins anywhere, including Greece: the ancient colony of Paestum on the mainland south of Salerno. Aside from its two state-of-the-art temples— one, the "Basilica," the best-preserved sixth-century Doric temple anywhere —Paestum has an on-site museum that boasts one of the most moving pieces of gay male art we've ever seen. This painted slab, originally found in the baths-like ruin known as the Tomb of the Divers, shows two laurel-crowned men, both naked to the waist with great bronze chests, sitting together on a divan. The older, bearded man has his fingers in the younger man's hair, and the younger man's fingers are grazing the older man's nipples. They are looking into each other's eyes with a gaze of absolute and totally concentrated delight.

You girls will have a harder time dredging up the ghosts of lesbians past —or, for that matter, any latter-day dykes besides yourselves. Of course, as we all know, this is a hard one. How can one really tell about two women, unless there are actual bottles flying from their window at the Quisisana, or something? We had so hoped for just a remnant of the stylish presence Faith Mackenzie describes: "They had but to walk on the Piazza or Funicular terrace, swinging military capes, or wearing feminine little frocks as the case might be, fingering interminable cigarette-holders, to be immediately the objects of popular interest." But no—not a monocle in sight.

Capri: The First Gay Resort / 309

Still, aside from believing that the chamber of commerce is missing a big moneymaker by not hiring a few Rosalbas and Romaines to vamp around for the season, we enjoyed Capri. And we strongly feel that for gay visitors, the key to avoiding the usual disappointments we often hear voiced about Capri is simply to do as historical gay visitors in fact did, and avoid the usual kind of visit.

The usual visit is a day trip from Naples or Sorrento, in *alta stagione* (high season), when people are packed chic-by-jowl and prices, as well as temperatures, are highest. The mobs arrive at Marina Grande late in the morning and hop immediately into a boat for the Blue Grotto, even though the color is really better (despite what the cheezy guidebook you bought at the souvenir stand says) later in the afternoon. They then have roughly two or three hours to rush up to the Capri Piazza for a grossly overpriced drink or mediocre snack and a little shopping at the designer boutiques along via Camerelle (higher priced than Milan, and duller), before the last steamer leaves, full of grouchy people feeling let down and ripped off.

How much more sensual sounds Somerset Maugham's schedule: "One does nothing from morning till night, yet the day is so short that it seems impossible to find a minute. All the morning I bathe; after luncheon I sleep till tea-time, then wander among the interminable vineyards, in the evening read or look at the moon."

Not being English in dietary preference, we'd personally skip tea-time and wait for dinner—especially after discovering the house special Caprese pasta, homemade fresh cheese, and *scaròla e fave in brodo* at La Capannina, on tiny via Botteghe about a block from the Piazza. (We know escarole and fava bean soup doesn't sound perfect, but it is.) We'd most often also skip the nap in favor of some sort of an adventure: exploring some Roman ruins, maybe—there are substantial remains of at least three of Tiberius' twelve villas, the most extensive and spectacularly situated being the mountaintop Villa Iovis, from which one can see the whole Amalfi coast.

Otherwise, Maugham's schedule strikes us as just about perfect. And what we would not change a bit is the day's pace. Capri is small, but it is really not the sort of place that can be rushed around in an afternoon. It is a place to be savored slowly, one ruin or beach per day, reached by a long, leisurely stroll (avoiding the few main auto roads in favor of the island's network of footpaths) interrupted by many rest stops . . . and preferably accompanied by a bottle of the excellent, light local Caprese white. (Do, by the way, look for "Denom. Origine Controlata" on the label. Much Capri Bianco is inferior stuff produced from shipped-in mainland grapes.)

Maugham had a villa, of course, and to discover a bit of Capri's magic, you too will have to settle in for a while. Doing so is an unavoidably expensive proposition these days, made more expensive and far more annoying by an island-wide practice we call the breakfast scam. In a nutshell:

It is clearly printed on the official town hotel-rate booklet (and we personally confirmed this with the Capri tourist office) that breakfasts are supposed to be optional and separately charged for. The hotels we talked to however, including our own, routinely ignore this rule, quoting inclusive rates from which they will not budge. Since the unconscionably inflated prices for these typically meager Continental repasts range from about twelve dollars to thirty dollars apiece, the breakfast scam can double the price of a double room. And aside from commiserating with you about how these darned hoteliers will indeed try to get away with this violation, the local Capri tourist office is no help. (Neither, incidentally, was MasterCard company.) We did finally get a refund from our hotel, but only after a heated written complaint to the cordial Italian Government Travel Office in New York—and nearly a year after our visit to Capri.

That said, though, we must admit that it was pretty idyllic to start the day snarfing our thirty-dollar rolls-and-coffee on our own floral-tiled terrace, overlooking the sea and Capri's wildly luxuriant vegetation. Fig, lemon, olive, pine, bay laurel, juniper, flowering ash, ilex, mimosa, and wild palm trees blanket the hillsides; red lilies, huge purple anemones, blue irises and anemones, silvery Egyptian squill, hyacinths, narcissi, wild daffodils, tulips, and twenty-eight species of orchid overflow villa walls and burst out of every cranny, releasing an exuberant wild perfume after every warm rain. According to author Norman Douglas, another northern European family man whose gay nature awakened on the Siren island around the turn of the century, Capri holds the record for variety of plants in a small space. And fortunately for those of us without the discretionary income of 1920s lesbians, the height of flora season is in late April and May, still *bassa stagione* (low season) on Capri: sunny, warm, but with dramatically reduced hotel rates.

As for Maugham's morning "bathing," the island has two scenic, if nonsandy, public beach areas, at Marina Grande and Marina Piccolo. But the whole coast is honeycombed with grottoes and coves, reachable by boat or steep climb, that seem deliberately designed by Mother Nature for private parties. Or perhaps the designers were Eros and Dionysus, if the priapic altar in prehistoric Grotto delle Felci and the Neolithic "cosmetic kits"—powdered colored rock, mixed with fat in seashell vanity cases—and pottery wine vessels found in some of the other caves are any indication.

Most visitors to Capri experience only the crowded tour-boat excursions and overpriced boutiques. But it's all the historical magic and scenic beauty that have given Capri its reputation as an earthly paradise.

As you can tell, we have mixed feelings about Capri. To be completely honest, if we personally were looking for a gay resort with no apparent gay people in it, we'd rather be in Taormina, which also has narrow old streets and Roman ruins, plus equally spectacular vistas, sandier beaches, some to-drool-for shopping bargains (like handmade lace/knit dress sweaters, for a third their New York price), and far more reasonable hotel prices.

Still, we have recently found ourselves thinking back more and more fondly on Capri.

Rereading *Vestal Fire*, for instance, got us thinking about Count Fersen, whom Mackenzie describes thus: "Carlisle once said that Herbert Spencer was the most unending ass in Christendom. He had not met the Count." This was a felon convicted of corrupting minors; his main contribution to *caprese* culture appears to have been notable orgies. There was, for example, an all-night, all-male, all-pink theme revel featuring a *couleur de rose* dinner of roast flamingo. The count also threw a by-invitation-only ceremonial flogging of his teenaged boyfriend Nino, in the Grotta Matermania, on the occasion of the lad's compulsory induction into the Italian military.

Yet during our stay, an official photo exhibit of Capri history prominently featured Fersen, and the tourist office as well as several hoteliers enthusiastically admonished us not to forget to mention the count in our book. To have these sorts of people touting Fersen's sort of person is really quite bent. It's a nice change of pace from the usual invisibility problem—and certainly beats Bath, England, where our guide snottily referred to the Emperor Hadrian as a "woman hater," among other homophobic references. In Capri, they have civic pride about even their most odious queers, assuming the latter were sufficiently rich and colorful.

We think occasionally about the Grotta Matermania, which we descended halfway to hell down a cliffside path to reach before dark—but not enough before: We could barely pick out the cave's Roman fortifications. We wouldn't mind trying again.

We've been wondering, too, whether the Red Grotto, White Grotto, and Green Grotto are as red, white, and green as the Blue is blue. No big deal, you understand. Just wondering.

We've also been thinking about all Tiberius' ruins we never had time to see. And about how special it felt and will always feel—since most of the island's out-of-the-way wonders are only accessible on foot—to have those ruins we did have time to see largely to ourselves. And how we sort of hope, for that reason, that the day-trippers *never* get their act together.

And quite honestly, a lot of what we've been thinking about is the bean and escarole soup.

Whether our attraction to Capri is more like that of the swallows annually migrating back to Capistrano, or like that of the buzzards returning to Hinckley, Ohio, we're not sure. And we certainly know now that on Capri, historically, we can't really go back. But we suspect we will return.

PRACTICAL INFORMATION

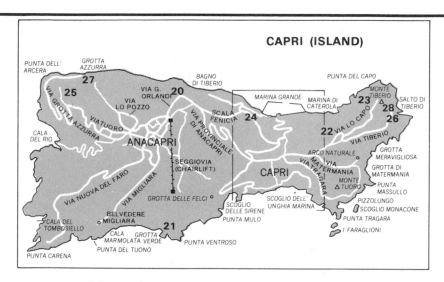

ISLE OF CAPRI—NUMBER KEY

Hotels

20. Hotel Caesar Augustus (fictional site of "Rory Freemantle's" "Villa Leuca-dia")

Historic Sites

21. Casa La Solitaria (home of authors Compton and Faith Mackenzie)
22. Villa Cesina (fictional "Villa San Giorgio")
23. Villa Fersen/Villa Lysis (fictional "Count Marsac's" "Villa Hylas")
24. Villa Torricella (fictional "Villa Amabile")
25. Damecuta
26. Torre del Faro
27. Villa di Gradola
28. Villa Iovis

CAPRI TOWN—NUMBER KEY

Historic and Scenic Sites

1. Ca Del Sole and Villa Alba (home of Checca Lloyd)
2. Giardini di Augusto
3. Grotta del Castiglione
4. Grotta dell'Arsenale
5. Pensione Esperia (fictional "Villa Botticelli")

6. Petrara (where Norman Douglas began a house)
7. Tiberio Palace (fictional "Hotel Grandioso")
8. Villa Blaesus (residence of Lica Riola, fictional "Olga Linati")
9. Villa Castello (fictional "Villa Parnassus")
10. Villa Cercola (residence of Somerset Maugham, E. F. Benson, and John Ellingham Brooks; later, home of Romaine Brooks, the fictional "Olimpia Leigh")
11. Villa Narcissus (fictional "Villa Adonis")
12. Villa Tragara (fictional "Villa Minerva")

Hotels

13. Quisisana (fictional "Hotel Augusto")
14. La Minerva
15. La Prora
16. Quattro Stagioni
17. Villa Palomba
18. Villa La Tosca
19. Villa Krupp
20. Caesar Augustus (see full island map)

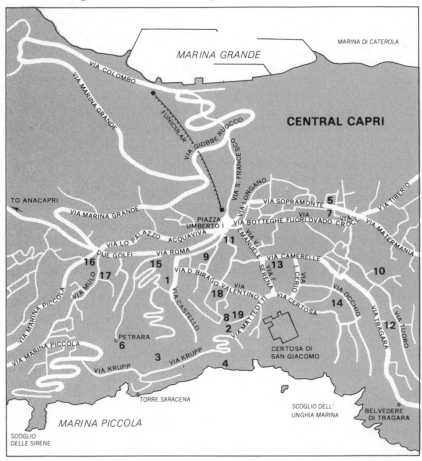

GENERAL HINTS / INFO

Capri is a very gay-popular resort with no gay bars, organizations, bookstores, restaurants, or other facilities. How Italian, eh?

To **orient** you, the isle of Capri has three towns: Marina Grande, at sea level, with several hotels and a restaurant or two, is mainly just where the ferries dock; Capri town, on the next level up, has the Piazza (also called the Piazzetta) as well as most of the glamorous hotels, restaurants, and shops; and smaller, quieter, somewhat cheaper, even higher-perched Anacapri to the east, hidden by Monte Solaro, the hedgehog spine of bare rock cliffs that run all the way down the island's center.

You probably won't listen to us, but don't day-trip to Capri. Settle in and relax for a few days. And *don't,* if you have a choice of vacation times, go during the midsummer high season. *Alta stagione* visits here are not the overcrowded disaster they are on Mykonos, but May, the height of flower-blooming time, is the ideal month on Capri. There are sunny beach days and balmy breezes at night—plus reduced hotel rates, which means a lot on this very expensive island. April and the first half of October are iffier, weather-wise, with possible sprinkles and frequent ocean choppiness, but still mostly beach-temperature sunny and cheaper than summer.

Traghetti (steamer ferries) and *aliscafi* (hydrofoils, twice as fast and nearly twice the price) run to Marina Grande from Naples and from Sorrento/Amalfi/ Positano on the closer Amalfi peninsula every hour or two. Trips start at about 7 A.M. or 8:30 A.M., depending upon the boat company, and return to the mainland at 6:30 or 7:00 P.M. at the latest.

Once on Capri, to get from Marina Grande up to the Piazza in Capri town, the steep *funicolare* is faster and more fun than the bus. The price is the same, about a buck.

The central **post office** on via Roma, two blocks from the Piazzetta, is open from about 8:30 A.M. to 6:30 P.M. Monday through Friday, and Saturday till noon; there's an Anacapri branch office at viale di Tommaso, 4. For **money changing,** there's a commission-free *cambio* (foreign-exchange bank) with good hours, 9 A.M. to 9 P.M. daily, across from the bus depot in Capri town. Several other banks are located right off the Piazza.

Postal code: 80073, Capri; 80071, Anacapri
Telephone code: 081
Currency unit: the lira (L)

WHERE TO STAY

There are no gay hotels on Capri. But all hotels listed below did respond to the Drill—*molto cordialmente,* in fact.

As you may notice, the hotel price ranges we've assigned are usually quite a bit higher than the "official" rates quoted in the Capri tourist office hotels booklet obtainable through the Italian Government Travel Office (630 Fifth Ave., New York, NY 10011) or the tourist office in Capri. However, ours are indeed the prices quoted to us by the hoteliers, for a double room room during high season (Easter, and June through September,) including what was in many cases supposed to be an optional, but is actually a nonoptional, $12–$30 pair of continental breakfasts. (To keep things in perspective, however, do notice that the rates of all except one hotel, though far more than we normally spend, still fall well below the average "budget" hotel prices listed in leading American travel periodicals.) Low-season prices are generally at least 15% to 20%, sometimes as much as a third, lower.

It is not too soon to make reservations for the high season two months in advance. During the low season, you can just walk into many hotels.

The stars—Italian government ratings, not ours—are included FYI.

Prices: *Inexpensive* = under L80,000; *moderate* = L80,000–130,000; *mod./exp.* = L130,000–200,000; *expensive* = L200,000–350,000; *very expensive* = L350,000–500,000.

Grand Hotel Quisisana★★★★★, via Camerelle 2, 80073 Capri; tel. 837 0788; fax 837 6080; telex 710.520 I. To reserve from the USA, tel. 800-223-6800, or in New York City 212-838-3110. Only about a block from the Piazzetta, the Quisi ("Augusto") was where lady-killer femme Rosalba and monocled butch Rory stayed (and threw bottles), along with all visiting royalty and anyone else who was "it" at the time of *Extraordinary Women*. This exotic neoclassical/Brit/ Oriental–style hotel is still it in Capri today. Fully air-conditioned, it has extensive landscaped private grounds, two restaurants, a piano bar, a theater, a swimming pool with poolside bar, tennis courts, a beauty parlor, sauna/massage/gym facilities, and every other conceivable luxury. The 150 rooms and suites have full bathrooms, whirlpool baths, minibars, color TVs, direct-dial phones, and numerous ocean/garden-view terraces. *Very expensive (even more for suites and apartments).*

Hotel Caesar Augustus ★★★, Via Orlandi 4, Anacapri, 80071 Capri; tel. 837 1444. The hotel is dramatically located on a peninsula 850 feet above the Bay of Naples at the final sharp turn of the mountain road between Capri and Anacapri. As far as we can figure, this is the exact location of Rory's "Villa Leucedia" in *Extraordinary Women*—the fictional site of the famous party where everyone who was anyone on Capri during the summer of 1920 disgraced him- or herself. The 58 rooms here vary in wonderfulness, the less wonderful being annex and interior no-view rooms. But all have private bathrooms, telephones, and color TVs; and those with separate, curtained bed-alcoves, chaise longues, and sea-view balconies are knockouts. There's also a garden, a solarium, Oriental-carpeted salons, and some large terraces open to all guests, plus a bar and open-air restaurant. *Moderate.*

La Minerva ★★★, via Occhio Marino; tel. 837 7067. Built on many levels in a floral garden setting spilling down the hillside, this lovely, luxurious smaller hotel is decorated with colorful, highly-glazed tile floors, Oriental carpets, antique and wicker furniture, and tropical plants everywhere. The romantic, tropical-feeling rooms have full bathrooms, phones, and large ocean-view terraces perfect for breakfasting and catching rays. *Moderate.*

Villa Krupp ★★, via Mateotti, tel. 837 0362. For guys whose sightseeing preferences lean towards young Caprese youths rather than old Caprese ruins, the comfortable Villa Krupp couldn't be better situated on a hillside overlooking crusty via Krupp and the Giardini di Augusto. *Moderate.*

Hotel La Prora ★, via Castello 6, tel. 837 0281. A small in-town lodging house only half a block off the Piazzetta, and just a few doors away from Villa Alba and Cà del Sole, where Checca Lloyd, on whom *Extraordinary Women*'s Rory was partly modeled, actually lived and threw the scandalous party in real life. The hotel has no garden or grounds, but does have an ocean view from the non-street side. Rooms, most with bath, are done in whites and earth tones, with tile and travertine floors and some brass beds; a couple (#11 and #20) have balconies. *Moderate.*

Pensione Quattro Stagioni★, via Marina Piccola; tel. 837 0041. Outstanding sea views from this guest house with garden terrace and restaurant (dinner only), whose very genial English-speaking owner assures us they've had many lesbian and gay guests. Rooms with and without bath. *Inexpensive.*

Pensione Villa Palomba ★, via Mulo 3; tel. 837 7322. In a perfect location for beach access, on the steep, narrow, ancient pedestrian road to Marina Piccola, this small white-stucco family-run pension has just undergone extensive renovations; rooms with bath are a good deal here. Owner Margaret Palomba is from England, so obviously no language barrier. *Inexpensive.*

Pensione Villa La Tosca ★, via D. Birago 5; tel. 837 0989. The Tosca overlooks the sea near the end of a narrow, grassy lane where one of Maugham's rented villas was located. Rooms are large, some with ocean view and bath. The management speaks some English—not fluently, but enough to explain what to see and do in Capri. *Inexpensive.*

Avoid the **Hotel Aida,** on via D. Birago, which responded to the Drill with a request not to be listed.

WHERE TO GO (DAY),
ASIDE FROM THE BLUE GROTTO

For action-seeking guys, the gayest sunning scene, minus sand, is **at the foot of via Krupp,** where you surely won't miss the young, nude, male bods on the giant ocean rocks. If you're nearsighted, just follow the disco thump of the cassette players. We should warn you that this spectacularly twisting road was officially closed when we were in Capri, due to rockslides and rock damage that showed no signs of being repaired anytime soon. But in actuality, the barrier at the top of the road was no deterrent to anyone with a halfway agile body and a philosophical attitude about possibly getting bonked with a boulder. Do notice, on the now unreachable cliff path off to the left about two thirds of the way down, Herr Krupp's gentrified hermit's cave–cum–gay den of iniquity, the **Grotta di Fra Felice.** The public **Giardini di Augusto** garden at the top of via Krupp is also well known for gay male cruising.

Personally, we liked the beaches at Marina Piccola, which are pebbled but have a great view of either the weirdo **Scoglio delle Sirene** (Siren Rocks) or the ancient **Torre Saracena** (Saracen Tower), depending upon which beach you pick. We'd advise hanging a right at the road's bottom and going to the next cove where it's less crowded. The pebbles are easily dealt with by bringing one of the cheap woven-straw mats you can buy in town, or renting chairs. Unlike via Krupp, Marina Piccola has restaurants and other comfort facilities, and lazy slobs like ourselves can take a bus back up. (The most scenic way down, although you can also ride, is to stroll along via Mulo.)

Shockingly few tourists even manage to make it out to the extensive ruins of Tiberius' most famous **Villa Iovis/Jovis,** much less to the remains of any of his other buildings, like **Damecuta** in Anacapri or the **Bagno di Tiberio.** It's true that the Iovis is at least 35–45 minutes from the Piazza, and quite uphill, but the trudge is well worth it. The Baths' site is only about 15 minutes' walk west of Marina Grande. We also had the **Grotta di Matermania** entirely to ourselves— probably because of the very long, steep, approximately three-heart-attack hike down, and then up from the overlook to the **Arco Naturale,** the rock formation you've seen on every Capri postcard that wasn't the Blue Grotto. We passed at least a dozen other tourists on the wooded path out to the Arco, but no others bothered to take the precipitous and overgrown little side trail down to this quite magical-feeling Roman-fortified cave, which was the site of Count Fersen's ceremonial flogging of his boyfriend, Nino.

If the day trip we recommended in the text, from Capri to the uncrowded and beautifully preserved Greek temple site in rural **Paestum,** interests you, you'll be relieved to know that it's not necessary to drag along your 45-pound art history textbook from America. Some of the books sold at the stands right on the site are much more informative than the average souvenir-quality crapola one usually finds. A particularly solid one is the rust-red *Paestum and Velia,* a bit more expensive than the other booklets on sale but worth it. On the Italian mainland, Paestum is only about a half hour by train from Salerno at the southern base of the Amalfi peninsula, or slightly over an hour from Naples farther to the north.

WHERE TO GO (NIGHT)

Naturally everyone spends a great many of the post-dinner hours hanging out, and checking everyone else out, on the **Piazzetta.** Although a great many of the would-be scene-makers just stand around in small, rather pathetically self-conscious groups, the cafés here all have outdoor tables where one can, and probably will, sit and buy overpriced drinks. For a far more glamorous nighttime outdoor-café experience, as long as you're committed to buying a relatively expensive drink anyway, we'd recommend **the front terrace café of the Quisisana.** There you can listen to live music wafting from the piano bar, while watching the BPs cruising from the Piazza down fashion central, via Camerelle.

For indoor scenes, there are no gay discos per se. But the two dance places most gay-popular are both on via Camerelle: **Atmosphere** (at no. 61b; call 837 6011 for their hours—they close for much of the low season), where the music is good and the people friendly; and the expensive, rather outré **Number Two** (at no. 2, surprise). A few hops off the Piazza in the other direction, on via Oratorio, is **Maxim,** a relaxed mixed bar with a sort of casual Italian nouvelle San Franciscan look. Maxim is popular with a younger crowd and non–glamour-impaired gay people, for light meals as well as hanging out over drinks.

WHERE (AND WHAT) TO EAT

Need we mention there are no "gay restaurants" on Capri? But we did meet a nice gay male couple one night at the next table of our favorite local restaurant, **La Capannina,** on via Botteghe (tel. 837 0732). We can hardly pretend that this place is an exclusive discovery; in fact, dinner reservations are not a bad idea even off-season, since La Capannina is generally recognized as the island's best, foodwise. Don't fail to try the unspectacular-sounding but divinely spectacular-tasting escarole and favas in broth, garnished with either fresh Parmesan or excellent olive oil. And we must say that between us and our two friendly neighboring tables, nobody had a pasta that he or she wasn't crazy about. Every restaurant in town makes a *ravioli alla caprese,* but this one, stuffed with ravishingly fresh local cheese, is the best we found.

Also on via La Botteghe, you'll find a cheese store, a butcher, and a small charcuterie/wine store (all on the left, walking from the Piazza), where you can buy picnic-lunch supplies for your jaunts to the ruins and beaches. Our idea of a perfect picnic would be a ball of the local mozzarella, great either alone or combined with green olive oil plus vine-ripened tomatoes and fresh oregano for a classic *insalata caprese;* a few slices of succulent *prosciutto di Parma;* some marinated fresh anchovies, entirely different from the snotoid salty lumps one picks off American pizzas; a bottle of the lovely local Capri Bianco wine (be sure to pay a bit extra for one that's appellation controlled, *Denom. Origine Controlata*), and, if you have a *very* sweet tooth, some *torta di Mandorla,* a local chocolate-almond confection that'll pull out every filling in your mouth. An alternate one-stop grocery with reasonable prices and tasty ready-made *panini,* like the mozzarella–tomato–fresh herb *panino caprese,* is the **Salumeria Capri** (via Roma 30), near the bus station on Capri town's main vehicle road.

Hikers to the Villa Iovis or the Villa Fersen who don't want to be bothered with picnics can follow the handwritten signs at the split of via Tiberio and via Lo Capo to **La Cantina del Marchese** (via Tiberio 7). This vineyard restaurant is a good 20-minute uphill walk from the Piazzetta, but the wine, cheese, and most everything else are homemade. And overlooking the Arco Naturale on the steep forest path to the Grotta di Matermania is the informal **Le Grotelle,** a scenic food-and-beverage stop which, built into the cliff, looks half grottolike itself.

For day-trippers to the Amalfi coast, we have a favorite restaurant in Ravello (where Wagner and lots of other celebs had villas, some still visitable) that even somehow, unbelievably, makes the absolutely hideous, careening, cliff-hugging bus ride up to this mountaintop village entirely worthwhile: **Cumpo Cosima.** If there's a street address, we don't know it, but it's a cinch to find: Face the church in the town's main piazza, and hang a left down the little alleyway. Cumpo Cosima is the first and only restaurant on the right, about half a block down. The genial, concerned proprietors will assure you that one each of the humungous assorted pasta-and-mixed-vegetable specialty platters is too much food for two, but you must get both anyway—especially if you're a pretty great amateur chef who's never really understood what people mean when they refer to food that's simple yet impossible to duplicate. Possibly you will need an extra order of the creamy, pillow-light, crepelike spinach *crespelle,* too.

WHERE TO GET THE LATEST DIRT
(INFORMATION RESOURCES)

The *Italia Gay* guide has very little Capri info, but it's better than the nothing you'll find in the other guides and gay periodicals (see "Practical Information, Venice" for address).

The **Capri Tourist Office** (open 8 A.M.–8 P.M. daily, except Sundays 8:30 A.M.–2:30 P.M.), right where the funicular stops up in Capri town, was quite nonhomophobic, and helpful in directing us not only to bars and establishments popular with gay people, but to the best gay cruising and rent-boy spots. If Capri town is not a handy location for your inquiries, there's also a tourist office branch at the end of the ferry dock in Marina Grande, and an info booth at via Orlandi 19 in Anacapri.

A bookstore with a good selection of books in English, some about Capri (including Compton Mackenzie's) is **La Conchiglia** on via Botteghe.

WHAT TO READ

Extraordinary Women and *Vestal Fire*, by Compton Mackenzie (Hogarth Press).

Capri: Island of Pleasure, by James Money (Hamish Hamilton). The definitive true story of Capri, from the mythological and Stone Ages and Tiberius through all the modern extraordinary women, gay men, and other weirdos. One especially nice feature is an index that matches real-life names and addresses to the pseudonyms Mackenzie used—exactly what hopeless, compulsive lit. addicts need.

Paestum and Velia by A. C. Carpiceci and L. Pennino (Matoni-Salerno). Though naturally intended for visitors in Paestum, the general Greek temple construction info is useful background for Capri's ruins as well.

OTHER GAY-POPULAR
ITALIAN BEACH RESORTS

Guys going to **Riccione** will want to know about the **Classic Club** in nearby Rimini (via Coriano 4; tel. 0541 73 11 13; less than half an hour by bus, car, or train from Riccione). When we describe this as a disco complex, we're talking not just nightclub, but outdoor pool with extensive sunbathing-and-lounging area, sauna, and more. A mixed beach hotel whose restaurant is popular with gay people is the **Granada** (via Gramisci 23, 47036 Riccione; tel. 0541 60 06 52). After the beach, many gay people head for the mixed **Bar della Lina** on the seafront, or to the enormous restaurant **Diane** on viale Ceccarini.

In **Taormina** there are no gay discos, but the most gay-popular disco/restaurant, situated on a mountainside with a panoramic ocean view to die for, is **Bella Blu** [via Pirandello 28 (via Guardola Vecchia); tel. 0942/24 23 9]. Another good bet for dancing is **Le Perroquet** (piazza S. Domenico 2; tel. 0942/24 80 8). In the evening, gay and other beautiful people sit at the several gorgeous open-air piano bars off **piazza IX Aprile.** At **spiaggia Spisone,** a long sand beach, there were a number of gay guys taking a sunbathing break at mixed **La Dolce Vita** on the beachfront, and there's gay male cruising action among the **Rocce Bianche.** You can't miss these giant white rocks dividing Spisone's free beach area. In fact, one of us, who was responsibly checking things out, actually slid down one boulder right onto the laps of a busy male couple. Personally, being more interested in scenery than cruising, we preferred **spiaggia Isolabella,** even though it's gravel; you can rent chairs, or buy cheap straw mats in town that make lying on the pebbled surface quite bearable.

There is a gay nude beach outside **Genoa,** in **Pieve Ligure,** right by the train station. **ARCI-Gay** in Genoa is at via Sottoripa 1/B; their info line is 010/28 14 30. Their dance hangout is **La Cage** (via Sanpierdarena 167 R; tel. 010/45 45 55).

For summertime visitors to the **Veneto** (the region including Venice and Verona), the most beautiful popular gay beach is **Grotte di Catullo,** in Sirmione. Nearer to Venice, try the **spiaggia degli Alberoni.** The Veneto's most famous gay disco is **l'Alcazar,** in Fontaniva, which has an extensive outdoor garden with love-seat swings.

In the Versilia coast of **Tuscany,** lesbians and gay men alike frequent **Frau Marleen,** an entertainment complex on the beach at Torre del Lago Puccini (Viareggio). In the area, a gay-popular mixed hotel near a gay beach (nudity allowed), is the **Dorian** (via Roma, 154, Lido di Camaiore, Lucca 51100: tel. 0584/64 60 8 or 67 10 0).

$\mathcal{M}$ASKS

Carnival in Venice and Beyond

$\mathcal{A}$ccording to our watches, it is two thirty on a dark February morning. According to our map, at which we are peering intently through the eyeholes of our fuschia-and-silver bird-beak masks and the shadowy veils of our Napoleon Bonaparte tricorne hats, we are standing in the middle of the enormous Rialto Bridge spanning Venice's Grand Canal. According to our keen sense of vision, however, this seems unlikely, since the bridge we are on is maybe ten feet long. But no matter. Getting lost in Venice is not like getting lost in other places. It's not really getting lost at all. It is an opportunity to experience something new, something magical. Especially at night. And especially during Venice *Carnevale*.

Carnevale is the pre-Lenten bacchanal we Americans know only as New Orleans's Mardi Gras, where drag queens flock to have straight drunks throw up on their ruby slippers; or as Rio's Carnival, where *Playboy*-centerfold types reign over glitzy Rose Bowl–esque spectacles. Here in Europe, carnival is something much older and far more serious.

Tonight, for example, as we squint through the fog trying to figure out exactly where in Venice's medieval maze we went wrong, a gondola silently materializes beneath our feet. Seated in the prow are two costumed figures. From their *tricorno* hats to their hooded cloaks, they are identically covered head to foot in black, with one eerie exception: Each sports a *bautta,* the stark white full-face mask dating from the Middle Ages. This most popular *Carnevale* mask was once worn by all—men and women, nobles and commoners—the idea being that *Carnevale* was a safety valve for the oppressed classes, and that the *bautta*'s complete disguise would eliminate at one go all visible social distinctions. Everyone was equal, if only for the few weeks *Carnevale* season lasted. And the *bautta* works: The gondola riders might be male, might be female, or might be one of each. It is impossible to tell.

As they pass under the bridge, whoever or whatever they are, they very slowly, very deliberately, very elegantly incline their heads to us in a synchronized bow that would put the Rockettes to shame. And we, who have not even thought of curtsying or similar formalities since involuntary fifth-grade incarceration at the New Jersey School of Ballroom Dancing, very naturally return the bow.

It's a courtly sort of exchange and an old one, older even than the masks. But neither the gestures nor the masks seem out of place, or out of their time, here in Venice.

What does seem out of place are the *usual* visitors we remember packing Venice's streets and bridges and gondolas all the other times we've been here, during the city's regular summer tourist season. The groups of chattering, camera-clicking Japanese tourists, in matching Bermuda shorts. The permanent-pressed Mr. and Mrs. Middle-of-the-Road, U.S.A., searching thousand-year-old stone streets for a Burger King. The backpacking hordes, either unwashed or stone-washed, with their ears glued to Walkmans. Anyone carrying a briefcase, even native Venetians. In fact, anyone at all born after 1500, give or take a couple of centuries.

Perhaps it's this sense that the Boring Normals have all been banished that makes *Carnevale* so appealing to the gay sensibility. Certainly it isn't Venice's gay bar scene that does the trick. There are no gay bars, not a one. No gay guest houses, discos, restaurants, saunas, organizations, or other year-round facilities, either, and no gay masked balls during the *Carnevale* season.

Nonetheless, Venice at any time of the year has a certain *je ne sais queer* quality, and Venice at *Carnevale* time—the three weeks or so prior to Ash Wednesday every year—is one of the great gay destinations of Europe. For starters, there are the sheer numbers of our own, including not only the expected Marie Antoinette drag-queen presence but, for a change, an enormous number of Louis XVI lesbians.

The gay presence in Venice goes back centuries, according to the travel writer Kate Simon. More than any other city in Europe, she writes in *A Renaissance Tapestry,* Venice was a particular haven for sodomy, for wandering among a generous bounty of pages in clinging hose joined at flowery codpieces, like the pretty boys of the supercilious stare as painted, for one, by Bronzino. The patrons of the boys were often older aristocrats, writers and artists who chose, with varying degrees of discretion, to follow "the Greek ideal," to side with Giovanni Antonio Bazzi de Vercelli, a painter and orator, who at public meetings and as signature to his paintings proclaimed himself "Il Sodoma."

But even more than the ghosts of Renaissance codpiece-niks or their twentieth-century gay kin, something about the setting itself makes Venice *Carnevale* the classic Mardi Gras, the perfect backdrop for a festival of illusion, the catalyst that compels one to look at the *bautte* versus the briefcases, burgers, and Bermuda shorts, and wonder: Which is real? And which the mask?

Venice is one of the slipperiest places in the world to describe. But that hasn't stopped every visiting diarist, journalist, and poet for the last five hundred years or so from trying. A slick souvenir booklet on sale in Piazza San Marco characterizes the town thusly: "Everything in Venice is paradoxical, upside-down and illusory." Got it?

We generally just advise our friends, "Like Disneyland? Then you'll love Venice." This works because most Americans can best relate, and some can only relate, to Venice as totally unreal. It's awfully cute, they argue, with its canals and medieval Eastern/Western architecture and automobile-free alleys, but it's not the "real Italy." Milan is the "real Italy." Even Rome is the "real Italy." Venice is a stage set.

To be quite frank, however, this is a crock, and so is our glib Disney analogy: clever, reasonable, and untrue. Venice may *feel* like Fantasyland to modern sensibilities—but fantasy is only half the story, because every Venetian "nonreality" has a root in hard practicality. Venice is real, but a city enchanted. It is a place where time did the impossible: stop.

It is "artificial" only in the sense that even the ground itself was built by people. The town, originally settled in A.D. 811 by refugees fleeing Attila the Hun, is supported by petrified-wood pilings built out into the marshy lagoon. These pilings are still sound.

It has always been different from the rest of Italy, but only in the sense that in an otherwise feudal, agriculture-based society, Venice was a republic —the world's oldest—and one based on trade. That accounts for the city's look: the picturesque palazzo façades adorned with marquetry of contrasting-colored marble, and groupings of loggia'ed windows as ornate as cutout doilies—indeed, quite exotically Eastern for a Western city. But back when the Orient, rather than America, was Europe's main trade destination, Venice was the traders' main gateway, so the Eastern influence is hardly phony. Besides, Venetians have always been canny bargain hunters. The Crusades may have been a religious mission for much of Europe (at least ostensibly), but for Venice, they were a major interior-decoration opportunity. Byzantine gold plate galore, plus rare relics like the pulpit of St. Mark, a nail from the True Cross, a thorn from the Crown, and other booty from Doge Dandolo's "conversion" of Constantinople in 1204 can still be seen in the treasury of San Marco.

It's also logical that in Venice both the water's reflective surface and the ground's inability to take weight would give Byzantine and Gothic surface decoration priority over the usual Italian Renaissance monumentality. Even had Venice's inhabitants been totally nonpreservationist and commercially minded, the ground's weight and space limitations would have made other "realistic" modern city developments—skyscrapers, for instance, and cars —impossible.

The air in Venice, too, contributes to a sense of timelessness and illusion: luminescent, iridescent, slightly misty-looking even on bright sunny days; the city's domes and turrets float weightless on it, softened around the edges, miragelike. It is not surprising that Venice's most important painters were either colorists—the Bellini family, Titian, Veronese, Tintoretto—or specialists in physical atmosphere—painters of the light like Canaletto, Guardi, and Tiepolo. What *was* a shock, the first time we visited Venice, was to realize that the fairylandish atmospheric haze in all those Venetian paintings, which one naturally assumes was artists' imagination and/or some fashionable stylistic device of the times, is realism. They were just painting what they saw, as you can still see for yourself.

Talk to the town's locals, and time and reality warp a little more. Venetians have a way of telling you about something that happened several hundred years ago as though it were their own memory—something they'd personally seen and participated in. In one of James (now Jan) Morris's wonderful books about Venice, the author's housekeeper, Emilia, explains how everyone in town gave money to Santa Maria della Salute as a celestial bribe to end the plague. This happened three hundred years before, Morris points out, but the sense of centuries in Venice is so compressed "that Emilia half believed she had contributed a few hundred lire herself." Perhaps when one lives a lifetime with—and in—remnants of history, there is not so much division between past and present.

Even the city's size seems to change daily. One day, Venice seems far too large and confusing to ever know. The next day, you're always turning a corner and ending up in the very same square you've just been in; in fact, it feels like you've been *everywhere* in this little burg at least three times that day. Until you look a little closer . . . and that same old square has a different church on it. Or that brand-new square has a church you've already visited. And this is not just the perception of rube foreigners who can't read a map. "Venice is not a city you can ever completely know," says tourist official Cesare Battisti. "Some nights, if I walk after work, even I can get lost, after living here a lifetime."

One cannot remain long here before everything feels, quite naturally, real and unreal at the same time. And this sense is heightened at night, because Venice has a darkness like no other place. There's a feel of danger in it, though not New York's kind of danger: There's virtually no violent crime here to speak of—just violent emotions, and fantasies, and the disturbing urge to vent them. Walk around in the surreal wee morning hours, and you realize it wasn't any accident that Thomas Mann set *Death in Venice* here. In a place whose mere physical weirdness so charges the psychological atmosphere that one honestly half expects to meet a vampire, what's so surprising about an upright, aging member of the German upper class suddenly feeling it appropriate to dye his hair *I Love Lucy* orange to impress an adolescent boy?

For gay people, of course, there is safety as well as danger in darkness, because it promises the anonymity so many of us sadly feel we need just to be ourselves. Perhaps this is why—especially in the lonely hours that further blur the already shaky Venetian line between reality and unreality—*Carnevale* here seems so much more compellingly, perfectly gay than other carnivals: Darkness is a disguise, a mask; *Carnevale* is a festival of masks; we are a people of masks. And Venice is the city of masks.

At five thirty A.M. on the Sunday before Shrove Tuesday, Venice's Santa Lucia central train station looks like a flophouse for homeless circus folk from other planets. It is almost impossible to find room to walk between the apparitions sacked out all over the not-overly-clean floor. Some are obviously gay. All are mighty queer.

Two guys, who are sleeping with their arms around each other, are decked out in matching ash-blond Let-Them-Eat-Cake wigs. Another twin-gowned male pair is having considerable difficulty getting comfy because of the huge angel wings sprouting out of their shoulder blades. Two identical female harlequins snooze in all-white suits and whiteface, beneath sparkling black sequined hats. There is a pink male bunny rabbit, in a woman's bathing suit. There is a female Santa Claus with a humongous beard. There are enough male nuns to open a convent, plus monks, clowns, fuzzy animals, and gondoliers galore, all sacked out on the station floor. The entire spectacle looks like a bloodless, bozo version of the famous crane's-eye-view Atlanta railroad station scene in *Gone With the Wind.*

The last Saturday before Lent begins is known as the biggest night of *Carnevale,* which is why people from all over Europe are in Venice. Why they're in the station at five thirty A.M. is because it's far too cold to walk the streets. Tomorrow and the next day, it will be shirt-sleeve sunny. During some past Carnivals, the problem has been melted snow; old postcards show costumed celebrants wading around Piazza San Marco under two feet of water. The Italian weather at this time of year, late winter, is as reliable as Italian trains are any time—which is why *we* are in the station at five thirty A.M. instead of having arrived at eleven the previous night, as scheduled.

Although it's an appropriately bizarre intro to *Carnevale,* we wouldn't recommend it. In fact, we'd recommend skipping this whole particular weekend. Even if one has remembered to make hotel reservations at least six months (and preferably a year) in advance, as one must to find a room that's either desirable or affordable, *Carnevale* on the Saturday night before Shrove Tuesday is a zoo; a prime example that bigger does not mean better, just more crowded with weekenders from neighboring cities and countries. Since we had been unable to obtain a schedule of events in advance (the Italian tourist authorities being as dependable as the weather and trains), we had naturally assumed that this biggest night of *Carnevale* would be the most glamorous, with height-of-elegance masked balls in every palazzo in town. In fact, there are official events fairly evenly distributed throughout the weeks before Shrove Tuesday.

We soon realized, though, that our biggest mistake was scheduling our stay around official events at all. Some were interesting enough, like a "Costumed Chess" game on Giudecca, a still nontouristy island right across the wide Giudecca Canal from the Doge's Palace and San Marco. The fact that the whole neighborhood is involved in this traditional *Carnevale* entertainment, in which the chessboard takes up a whole piazza and the chess pieces are elaborately costumed humans, is as charming as the fact that they haven't quite gotten the tourist polish all together: Overhead, laundry still hangs.

And there is indeed at least one major-glamour *gran ballo mascherato* (grand masked ball) open to the public each season. This particular season the theme is "Casanova in the Courts of Europe," and the ball is in Palazzo Pisano. It's all yours, for a mere $225 per ticket.

But more typical of the scheduled events is Teatro Scientifico di Verona's advertised "Stilt-Walking Procession and Entertainments": Sounds like a parade, looks like three people, only two of whom are even on stilts. Or the "Traditional Last-Night-of-Carnival Entertainment in the Water off St. Mark's," which never materialized at all. Truthfully, many of the official events are second-rate, and all are secondary. Even the tourist office, which schedules the *Carnevale* events, admits that the official stuff is really beside the point.

"In Venice, the Carnival is not mainly the spectacles, as it is in some other places with all the floats and big parades," explains Signore Battisti. "Here, *Carnevale* is more to participate than to see. It is the people, everyone who wants to get into another skin. You might feel like living in the eighteenth century. You might feel like becoming a teddy bear."

Masks: Carnival in Venice and Beyond / 327

For many celebrants, months of preparation have obviously gone into their fantasies—not just into the richly elegant costumes (which bear no relation at all to the plastic horror/humor/hero genres dominating American Halloween disguises), but into the stylized gestures that go with them. Previously, we'd always assumed that those theatrically ballet-posed *Carnevale* postcards that one sees reproduced in every coffee-table book ever written about Venice were carefully choreographed setups by some artsy-fartsy professional photographer artiste. Strolling around town, though, it becomes clear that these little set pieces are created by the costumed figures themselves: Last week's grocery checkers are today's stars. Anyone who walks from one square to the next cannot fail to encounter several frozen tableaux; anyone who can point an Instamatic cannot fail to go home with a few rolls of instant art.

In San Marco, cameras click as a ceramic-faced king, whose bejeweled crown is topped by a purple tulle headdress half again as tall as he, poises to "knight" a traditionally striped-suited *capitano* soldier. A caricature of a vain medieval lawyer—in ruffled Queen Elizabeth collar, wide-brimmed hat, and mask incorporating built-in false nose and oversized spectacles—freezes in mid-declamation, lawbook open, one toe pointed. The whole business is a cross between history and vogueing.

On a *campo* somewhere in Dorsoduro, a nontouristy neighborhood on the non–San Marco side of the Grand Canal, two Pierrots with half-black and half-white faces leap onto opposite sides of an old black wrought-iron streetlight, fling their arms out, and freeze like matching bookends. On Campo San Barnaba is a cocker spaniel–type mutt (a real dog, not a guy in a spaniel suit) wearing a full gondolier ensemble: striped shirt, flat beribboned hat, huge sunglasses. We run into this dog posing all over town, for days.

Some revelers have coordinated efforts with their friends. One couple has dressed as a chimney sweep and a chimney. There is a group that could be the entire population of a small hill town, dressed as a pack of playing cards. There is a sombrero'ed Mexican band (who, when they play, have a suspiciously Swiss rhythm). A "grocery wagon" spills, and a gang of living "oranges" roll around the street for a while, before piling back in to be wheeled to another square by the "grocer." By the front of an outdoor restaurant, on the other side of the door from the seafood-antipasto table, six costumed people freeze in a circle, as though on a giant plate: an order of a half dozen giant clams on the half shell.

The masquerade never lets up, even to eat. As we pig out on real clams (actually on spaghetti *alla vongole,* tiny Venetian cockles with shells decorated in geometric patterns that look like sepia pen-and-ink drawings) at one of our favorite restaurants, the Antica Locanda Montin, a flock of gold lamé butterflies bursts through the door, their six-foot gauze wings nearly upsetting our waiter's tray of wondrous Adriatic fish and shellfish.

It *is* amazing to discover how soon a mask can feel so much like one's real skin—or so much better—that one is reluctant to remove it. There are limitations, as we discover one day in the Trattoria Madonna, another personal fave, when we try to lunch without removing our foot-long lacquered bird beaks and end up with a distressing amount of the world's best seafood risotto, garlicky fresh *piselli* (tiny peas), and *granceola* (a special local crab) on the tablecloth. But once the mechanics get smoothed out, one becomes quite blasé about dining in a room that looks like a living Punch and Judy show.

Though one sees a certain number of modern designs, traditional Venetian masks like the *bautta* predominate. Our own bird noses are actually a very old design called the *medico della peste,* the plague doctor, meant to caricature the protective costumes medieval doctors wore to visit the sick without catching the disease. (In the Venetian Carnival's early years, during the Middle Ages, laughter was seen as a way to drive out the fear of contagion always present in a swampy malarial environment.) Others are characters popularized by the commedia dell'arte: the mischievous upturned-nose mask of the underworld spirit Harlequin; the hook-nosed poor peasant, Pulchinella.

Approaching us on the side of one small canal is a Pantalone, the theatrical merchant of Venice, traditionally costumed in a red velvet suit and beret, with a long feather-collared black cloak, hook-nosed black leather mask, and false beard. Although we have no cameras, he poses for us anyway, crouching slightly in an old man's stoop and gesturing toward the water, as though inviting us to inspect his invisible produce boat. He freezes for several seconds, for the invisible cameras in our heads. Click! Then we all continue on, bowing slightly to each other as we pass.

This elegant mini-bow we think of as the Nod is something else you'll run into throughout *Carnevale,* but only if you, too, are masked. The costumed figures will *pose* for anyone at all. The Nod is reserved for others who are fellow participants rather than mere spectators, a sort of secret handshake of recognition and appreciation that you are both, for these few days, living in a totally different world than that of the shutter-snappers. Although we have no idea who lurks behind any given Nod, we experience each encounter as somehow quintessentially gay.

Most people get into the spirit at least a little, if only to buy a *tricorno,* or to get their faces decorated in metallic gold and silver colors by street artisans. For those with more elaborate inclinations who haven't come prepared, there are *maschere* shops all over town. Needless to say many are mediocre, retailing schlocky machine-made reproductions. But others are artist-owned; a few even incorporate workshops where you can see the masks being made by hand. Part of the charm of Venice is that it seems to have more mask stores than, say, functioning post offices.

We've always been partial to Laura Scocco, who specializes in highly glazed nontraditional variations on traditional designs. For original trendy New Wave–type masks, there's La Mano, which features eyeglass-frame masks such as a two-faced woman (the eyeholes are their open mouths) and a pair of boxer shorts with a crab claw emerging from the fly, which is actually over the nosepiece.

And the most respected as Art with a capital *A* is *MondoNovo,* which in addition to selling masks designs an entire theme costume for each *Carnevale.* In 1986, the design team's best-known year, the theme was *Caccadura e Caccamola,* or Hard and Soft Turds. One of the artists dressed dark brown and lumpy; the other was light brown and runny, with a whipped point.

This year, the pair is wandering the streets as giant genitalia. We encountered Mister Penis and Mister Labia one night as they were closing up shop and heading out for a hard night of reveling. We wish we could remember more details of the penis suit, but we *are* lesbians, and research skills only go so far when you're riveted to the spot by a strutting, high-heeled, six-foot-tall pussy with red satin labia majora, pink satin labia minora and clitoris, and black ostrich-feather pubic hair. Meet your spouse at the front door in this getup, girls, and you'll perk up that sagging marriage in no time.

At *Carnevale,* as at Halloween or any other festival of disguise, what many men choose is drag. According to the exhibits at the International Carnival Museum in Binche, Belgium (we told you Europeans take this stuff seriously), drag is actually a midwinter festival tradition from way back. To ensure good crops and prosperity for the coming season, tribesmen in the Amazon basin wore fertility masks as part of anatomically correct female suits—bright, multicolored potholderlike numbers with built-in tits and even umbilical cords.

In the Middle Ages, boys in Hungary dolled up at Carnival time as housewives, complete with brooms and spoons. Bopping folks with these implements was also supposed to bring fertility and prosperity. Fellows at the Carnival of Ebensee, in Austria, dressed as old women, mostly in rags, but topped by hats decorated with everything but the kitchen sink: colored streamers, flowers, tree branches, baby dolls, giant fake chickens. Evidently, there was much secrecy here around the guys' annual new hats; if designs were duplicated, it meant major hat feuds.

Obviously modern gay men's urge to cross-dress is less agricultural but, we suspect, no less transcendent: to play games with cast-iron gender roles, and to express femininity, or at least the masculine concept of what is feminine. "Everything that is deep loves the mask," as Nietzsche put it, because the mask is an opportunity to reveal the deepest aspects of ourselves, the ones so disturbing we can't reveal them in the open.

For many straight people, being hidden behind a mask is the one time they can safely pretend to be *other* than their real selves. For many gay people, the opposite is true: Being hidden behind the mask is the one time we can safely drop pretense, and be our real selves.

Not that we're the kind of gals who would normally stoop to cheap tricks like overstretching a metaphor. But we cannot resist pointing out that if Venice is a city of masks, Italy, for gay people, seems like a whole country of chameleons in disguise. Although Capri has a more explicit gay past, and cities like Bologna have a more familiar gay present, Venice *Carnevale* may be the perfect introductory course to the real spirit of gay Italy.

A particularly poignant revelation, for us, of just how deep Italian closets go is a conversation we had not too long ago in Mykonos with a young vacationer from Rimini. Does his family know about his sexual orientation, we ask? He gasps at the very suggestion. Of course he could not come out, especially to his father and brothers! He does not plan to tell them, ever. But he has made a courageous decision that will let him live his life "honestly," without parting ways with his family. He will move as far away from them as possible. This way, he explains without a trace of irony, he will not have to do what most of his gay male friends will do: marry a woman.

The very good Milan-based gay publication *Babilonia* is a living example of the national schizophrenia; hard-hitting political articles alternate with personals ads from desperate GMs seeking marriage-minded GFs. Depictions of that hot Colt Model of the ancient world, St. Sebastian, also appear in the magazine with amazing frequency—martyrdom apparently being something that gay Italian men can relate to.

"It is easy in Italy to have gay *sex*," says Angelo Pezzana, whom we interviewed in Milan. "But it is difficult to have a gay *identity*, even in the closet. To marry and have children is expected." Angelo himself is one of Italy's few exceptions: owner of a gay/straight bookstore in Torino, founder of the Fondazione Sandro Penna (an official nonprofit cultural organization, which, since 1980, has researched, published, and otherwise disseminated information on homosexuality), and an openly gay executive of the Radical Party, one of Italy's most liberal.

An even bigger progay force in the country is the Communist Party, particularly its cultural arm, ARCI (Associazione Ricreativa Culturale Italiana), pronounced "Archie." To reassure any gay Republican readers who haven't yet burned this book, we should point out that in Italy, the Communist Party is very different from those in China or Cuba. As the major leaders in the historic fight against fascism, Italian communists are seen as pro-democracy, and they are, after the long-dominant Christian Democrats, the second-largest national political party in the country. In any case, the Red Menace began courting the Lavender Vote more than a decade ago, and at this point, ARCI-GAY, the party's official gay group, even operates a couple of gay discos. With the exception of a few lesbian-separatist groups, it is the *only* major gay-rights umbrella organization in Italy.

Angelo's party, the Radicals, is much smaller, and more of a libertarian group. The Radicals don't discriminate on the basis of sexual activity; in fact, the party is probably most famous for sending porn star Ilona "Cicciolina" Staller to Parliament. Our Milan rendezvous with Angelo is at one of the party's nongay conferences—a general sort of "Just Say No to Saying No to Anything At All" rally in a palace down the block from the church containing "The Last Supper." A roomful of people are arguing strenuously against proposals to toughen the Italian drug laws. Although we've never met him before, it's easy to pick out the gay leader in this counterculture crowd with its long sixties hair and long sixties skirts: in a gray business suit and a tie, Angelo is the straightest-looking person in the place.

In Angelo's case, the straight appearance is just another Italian paradox: He has been out for over twenty years. "I just didn't want to hide," he says. His younger friend and political colleague Enzo Cucco is out, too. "But by far it is more common for gay men here, even the young ones, to make a very different choice," says Enzo. "To accept a life of cruising for men at night, then joking at work the next day about all the girls they had."

In a nutshell, as Angelo and Enzo explain it, the problem for Italian gays is almost perfectly opposite to the situation in the United States. Here, straight-looking/acting gay men and lesbians are increasingly accepted as individuals with a gay *identity*. After all, even Ron and Nancy used to claim that some of their best friends . . . etc. But as for what we *do,* the sexual acts, in our puritanical nation—YUCK! In Italy, gay acts are not so bad— or, at least, they're seen as part of the spectrum of sexuality. And sexuality is accepted, in general. A gay *identity,* though, is a political concept— YUCKORINO!

"We live in a very nonserious country," sighs Angelo. "So it is difficult for us gays to think in these serious political terms. Latin countries seem more tolerant, but we are really more hypocritical, because none of this is open. Here, homosexuals can be very happy. But not gay. That is why, even under fascism, there were no laws against gay people: Mussolini's position was, 'If we have laws against homosexuals, we must admit we have homosexuals. We have none here.'

"In Italy, you see, we are used to living with the double morality. You can kill ten people now, and tomorrow say to the priest, 'You must forgive me.' And so it is."

Doubt the extent of these coexisting standards? Then obviously, when you visited Vatican City, you were overly preoccupied by the Michelangelo stuff, and did not pay proper attention to the souvenir shops ringing the square around St. Peter's. Virtually any item you buy here can be blessed by the pope: Buy it in the morning, pick it up at five P.M. Or they'll mail. Possibilities include toy guns, beer steins, corkscrews, Stars of David, ceramic ashtrays in the shape of a toilet, and switchblade knives. (And sisters: How could you have missed the papally blessed tarot decks?)

To American logic, all this makes about as much sense as the Moral Majority going into the business of manufacturing nipple clamps. But let's face it. To visit Italy because being gay in Italy makes sense, makes about as much sense as visiting Italy because the trains run on time. Does anything else in Italy make sense? And who cares? One loves Italy, in our opinion, because of something to do with emotional overload, something irresistible, something operatic—something that makes an end run around anything to do with being sensible. You accept the contradictions, and have a wonderful, warm time.

"In Denmark, they have the good laws. Here, we have the sun," Angelo beams. Even as a sometimes frustrated politico, it is obvious which alternative is in his blood.

To the extent to which traditional post-Stonewall gay life does exist in Italy, it's more prevalent in business and political centers like Turin, Milan, and Bologna than in tourist centers like Rome or Florence. Indeed, Bologna, the traditional heart of the Communist party (and the first Italian city to allocate public housing for gay couples), is probably the closest thing to the Italian gay capital. On the other hand, any given backwater town you've never heard of in England or Germany will probably have more specifically gay facilities. With the possible exception of the newly gayified Adriatic beach town of Riccione, the same lack of a strong gay cultural or commercial presence characterizes Italian resorts, including historic homo hangouts like Capri and Taormina.

"Everywhere in Italy," Enzo explains, "the gay scene is really not so much something you will find in a bar. It is *molto diffuso.*"

"It is like so," offers Angelo. He mimes strolling past a café, some enchanted evening. Suddenly: contact! He slows ever so slightly; his head tilts backward ever so slightly, over a coyly raised shoulder; his eyes swivel sideways to the imaginary prospect, and move deliberately up and down, up and down.

For single lesbian tourists, the gay Italian mask is even more of a practical problem; with few exceptions—an organization here, a women's campground there—women's hangouts don't exist. But the good news for female couples like ourselves—who certainly might enjoy meeting our foreign counterparts, but are more interested in simply relating to each other without hassles—is that a side effect of Italian feminist fervor and gains since the 1970s has been to substantially reduce street harassment problems for female travelers.

Before 1969, adultery by a woman bore greater penalties than rape, essentially because women were seen not as self-owned, but as property. How this affected the female tourist experience was that to guys on the street, a no from us was like a no from a Walkman they'd just bought: not possible, does not compute. Today, Italian women are legally on a par with men in essential fields like work, pay, rights over children, and property retention after marriage. With traditional female resignation and automatic male domination no longer assured, guys on the street, while no less likely to give street pickups a try, have become noticeably less persistent when discouraged.

This is not to promise miracles. But it made a huge difference to us that on our most recent trip to Italy, the guys weren't actually driving their Fiats up on the sidewalks before taking no—or actually, *va fa'n culo* (roughly, "Go fuck yourself in the butt")—for an answer.

The last night of *Carnevale,* on our way to San Marco for the traditional entertainments that weren't, we are doing some of our usual "World Of Women" fantasies. "Just imagine how safe you'd feel, walking down even this spooky old street, if everyone else coming up on you was female," muses Pam.

Lindsy is cracking up. Because it's not instantly apparent to someone in deep pseudo-philosophical mode—especially when it looks like you're sharing the cobblestones with two Harlequins, two fuzzy pink sheepdogs, two Thomas Jefferson look-alikes in male courtier suits complete with moles and powdered wigs, and a walking fruit cocktail (an apple and an orange, with linked arms)—that they *are* all female couples on this street. Even though it's kind of rude to squint under people's robes and gowns and fruit peels and all, you can always tell by the foot size. Either every straight woman in Europe came to *Carnevale* with her best friend, or there are more lesbian couples here in Venice than we've ever seen anywhere in Europe.

In a side alley, two boys tenderly apply makeup to each other's faces.

In the middle of Piazza San Marco, two men with painted faces writhe on the ground, having mock sex.

In the shadow of the Rialto bridge, two men with painted faces have real sex.

Over the bridges strides a queen in a black, purple, and gold gown that veritably glows in the dark, with two delicate faggots-in-waiting carrying his/her ten-foot satin-and-velvet train. All the straight tourists clap, cheer, and take photos.

Tomorrow the applauding photographers will probably just be part of the 75 percent of Italians who thought, according to a mid-1980s survey, that having a gay child would be a major tragedy. The queen will be back with the wife and kids. But tonight, he's a heroine.

VENICE

PRACTICAL INFORMATION

GENERAL HINTS/INFO

Carnevale di Venezia is officially the eighteen days before the beginning of Lent on Ash Wednesday, so the dates are different each year. To avoid overcrowding on peak days (Shrove Tuesday and the preceding few days, especially Saturday night) official events are spread out through *Carnevale* season, and held outside the tourist-central San Marco area.

The enchantment of Venice *Carnevale* is the street life rather than the official attractions; we really didn't need to go to Venice to see the Batmobile. But if you'd like to know what's going on in advance—in order to make reservations for certain theater productions, for example—write the **Azienda di Promozione Turistico di Venezia, "Carnevale di Venezia" Company,** and ask for their *Calendar of Official and Other Events,* in English. Depending on when Easter, hence Carnival, is, also pick up the February or March issue of the tourist office's monthly **Marco Polo** magazine.

As for timing, we do not personally recommend the jam-packed pre–*Martedi Grasso* weekend. Contrary to what one might think, these days have no especially spectacular special events or parties; they're just most popular because they're business and school holidays for European working people and students, who don't have Shrove Tuesday itself off. For real vacationers who do, we suggest arriving on Sunday or Monday and then staying for a day or two after *Carnevale,* when you'll have the city largely to yourselves—quite an unusual experience in Venice.

Transportation in the medieval maze that is Venice is by foot or boat. There are no cars. Parking, for those who arrive by car, is at Piazzale Roma, on the mainland just one boat stop up the Grand Canal from the Ferrovia (train station) Santa Lucia. Your primary motorized transport will be the efficient network of *vaporetti.* Oddly, *accelerati* are the slower locals; faster express boats are called *diretti.* (We suppose this labeling method is like the one they say you'd need for condoms: If they came in sizes small, medium, and large, guys wouldn't buy them; instead they'd have to be labeled "huge," "extra huge," and "super colossal.") Anyway, the main lines you'll use are the no.5 Motoscafi-Circolare *destra e sinestra* (right and left), which totally circle the perimeter of Venice, hitting both sides of the Giudecca Canal, as well as San Marco; and lines no.1 and no.2, which go down the Grand Canal to San Marco and finally on to the Lido.

Best map: In our opinion, there are two considerations. One, buy a map with

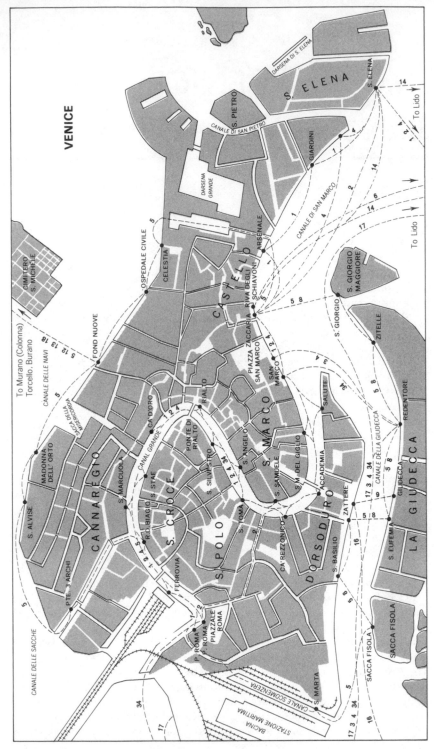

VENICE

all the canals and streets named. Despite the lure of having something portable, do not rely on any map that would fit into any book this size— or even four times bigger. Two, do not buy any map that does not have the *vaporetti* lines *and names of stops* marked on the *main* plan. Some maps, including most sold in front of the rail station when we last checked, name the stops inconveniently only on the reverse side. The *pianta della città*, Edizioni Ezio Tedesci, which has a rust-red cover with international flags superimposed on a view over the Giudecca Canal, is fine; the one by Rialto Edizioni is not.

Additional orientation tip: Once your map has gotten you into the correct *sestiere* (district, of which there are eight in tourist-central Venice: San Marco, Castello, and Cannaregio on one side of the Grand Canal; Dorsoduro, Santa Croce, and San Polo on the other; and Giudecca and Sacca Fisola across the Giudecca Canal) it is possible to find a place just by mailing address, even if one doesn't know the name of the street or can't find the street name on a map. This is because, for example, "Calle del Whatsis, San Marco 4813" refers to a *position* in the *sestiere* of San Marco, not, as most addresses anywhere else in the world do, to house number 4813 on two-block-long Whatsis Street. So what you do is simply try to follow the numbers up, down, left, and right—getting sometimes hotter and sometimes colder, as in "Huckle Buckle Beanstalk." This may just be confusing to some of you. But for puzzle lovers and would-be trackers, it's fun.

For those who don't wish to pay the always inflated hotel telephone-call charges, the most hassle-free **public phones** in town are to be found at the ASST public phone office, open 8 A.M.–8 P.M. daily, at San Marco 5551, next to the **main post office** (San Marco 5554, at Salizzade Fontego dei Tedeschi, off Campo San Bartolemeo at the eastern end of the Rialto bridge). What makes these phones better than most in town, or anywhere in Italy, is that you don't need endless L200 pieces or *gettoni* (phone tokens). Instead you just dial, and pay the adequately English-speaking desk personnel after the call ends. For **currency exchange**, banks (of which there are many near San Marco), travel agencies (when the banks are closed), and even American Express (San Marco 1471) all beat the long lines and not-great rates at the train station.

There are no gay and/or lesbian hotels, bars or restaurants. Just a lot of gay and lesbian tourists.

Telephone code: 041

Currency unit: the lira (L).

WHERE TO STAY

For the Saturday night preceding Ash Wednesday, many visitors make their reservations as they are leaving their hotels the year before. On Shrove Tuesday hotels are slightly less packed, but October is not too early to reserve. This is especially true of the most picturesque and popular inexpensive hotels, as a number of these smaller, family-run places still consider the period until mid-March low season, as it used to be before *Carnevale* was revived in 1979. Hence they are closed in February even if Carnival falls then. However, don't give up and decide to vacation in Omaha if you can't make plans that far in advance. We did manage, with only 140 zillion letters and international phone calls, to book a moderately priced room in early December and locate several other more expensive available possibilities.

Totally ignore budget guidebooks that advise you to stay in the mainland bedroom suburb and industrial center of Mestre. Sure, it's cheaper and easier to find a room there than in Venice. Secaucus, New Jersey, is cheaper and easier than Manhattan, too.

For the rundown on mosquito-zapping devices, see the hotel section for Bruges, in "Practical Information, Belgium." These little plug-in miracles are not necessary in Venice during the Carnival season, but we assume some of you will be summer visitors. And you know them canals.

All prices we quote are for double rooms in the high season unless otherwise noted. The stars, included FYI, are Italian government ratings, not ours.

Incidentally, as on Capri, official tourist-office policy is that breakfast is optional and is to be charged separately from room rates. In practice, however, you will most often be quoted a room price inclusive of mandatory breakfasts (Continental), especially during high-demand summer months and holidays like *Carnevale*, when your only practical option is to accept. But you can also complain, with written proof of overcharge, to: **Amministrazione Provinciale/Assessorato al Turismo, Ca' Corner, Venezia** (tel. 520 0911).

Prices: *Inexpensive* = under L55,000; *inex./mod.* = L55,000–70,000; *moderate* = L70,000–90,000; *mod./exp.* = L90,000–130,000; *expensive* = over L130,000.

Albergo Casa Verardo ★, Ruga Giuffa, Castello 4785, 30122 Venezia; tel. 528 61 27. This adorable little nine-room inn, next to Ponte Storto bridge, is a former fifteenth-century palazzo. Run by a very friendly English-and-a-million-other-languages-speaking woman and her mother, it is ideally located, on a small canal very close to San Marco but in quieter, less touristy Castello, which some locals consider the most truly Venetian part of Venice. Rooms come both with and without bath. *Inex./mod–moderate.*

Albergo Da Bepi ★, Fondamenta Minotto, Santa Croce 160; tel. 522 67 35. For those who hate luggage-lugging, relatives of the Verardo's management run this restaurant/hotel. The 12-room establishment is located only about three blocks from the Piazzale Roma car park, and even closer to the train station (but across the bridge on the less people-packed side of the Grand Canal). *Inex./mod.–moderate.*

Antica Locanda Montin ★, Fondamenta di Borgo, Dorsoduro 1147; tel, 522

71 51. Only seven rooms, conveniently located in the upper two floors of our favorite Venetian restaurant. Although rooms share bathrooms, they are grand and lovely old spaces, with the high ceilings, big furniture, and tall heavy doors that make one feel like Alice in Wonderland after eating the mushroom that made her shrink. We like best the canal-front room on the lower level, so don't take it—okay? *Inexpensive.*

Hotel Kette ★★★, Piscina San Moise, San Marco 2053, 30124 Venezia; tel. 522 27 30, 522 89 64, or 520 77 66; telex 311877; fax 5228964. Lovers of amenities should be most happy in one of this canal-side elevator hotel's 44 rooms, which have bathrooms, telephones, color TVs, refrigerators, hair dryers, and air-conditioning (rare for Venice, and unnecessary during *Carnevale* but welcome in this city's humid summers). Although near La Fenice theater in the city's most touristed district, this street is a quieter one. *Mod./exp.–expensive* (the lower rate for part of *Carnevale;* for some reason, only 12 days of *Carnevale* count as high season).

Pensione Smeraldo, Rio Terà S. Leonardo, Cannaregio 1333d 1333; tel. 71 78 38. These high-ceilinged rooms, full of festive faded grandeur, are in a former palazzo near the Ponte Guglie. The pension is located on the busy main walking street between the train station to San Marco, which makes for good effort-free costume-watching. Rooms come both with and without bath. *Inex./mod.*

Allogi Biasin, Fondamenta di Cannaregio 1252; tel. 71 72 31. Under the same management as the Smeraldo around the corner. These big, sunny, more modern rooms (with or without bath) are right over the bridge from Fondamenta Labia. How could you miss 'em? They also overlook the Canale di Cannaregio, a wide canal right off the Grand Canal, and the restored Palazzo Manfrin across the water. *Inex./mod.*

Casa Frollo ★★, Fondamenta Zitelle, Giudecca 50, 30123 Venezia; tel. 522 27 23. We first heard of this elegant seventeenth-century palazzo-hotel on quiet Giudecca island from two British lesbians who told us, with a delighted shiver, that the female proprietor was "formidable." It's across the canal from, and has the world's best view of, San Marco. The 26 bedrooms come both with and without bath; there are so many public baths that we've found the more inexpensive rooms no hardship—especially as this is one place where bathless rooms are no less huge or less luxurious than those with plumbing. Out back, there is a large private garden. Inside, the place is all grandeur: high beamed ceilings, tile and stone floors, dark polished wood, good antique furniture, chandeliers. *Moderate–mod./exp.*

Hotel Iris ★★, S. Tomà, San Polo 2910A, 31025 Venezia; tel. 522 28 82. We like the look of the old main building, but probably most people would prefer the airy rooms with new furniture in the new wing. And really, the whole hotel is awfully cute. The place is right on a small canal by a stone bridge, has an enclosed canalside garden restaurant, and is in a refreshingly nontouristy area across the Grand Canal from San Marco. Rooms come both with and without shower. The very sweet management says they're honored to be mentioned in our gay guide, and will treat you "special" readers with the maximum regard. *Moderate–mod./exp.*

WHERE TO GO (DAY AND NIGHT)

The usual official daytime events are strolling musical groups, mimes, jugglers, dancers, acrobats, and clowns, performing in various squares around the city—along with a few really silly things like the floating of a 25-meter-long bottle down the Grand Canal to San Marco, to "toast" the start of *Carnevale*. Lots of the larger fun fair-type events are around the via Garibaldi area in Castello.

As for after-dark events, the endless rounds of glamorous private costume parties, salons at local aristocrats' palazzos, and fancy-dress grand balls at the Fenice that characterized the first years of the revived *Carnevale,* are gone. Their loss has been compensated for by events geared more to visitors than to locals, like open-air dances and free festivals in various piazzas. But thus far there has still been, every year, one expensive *Gran Ballo Mascherato* dinner and dance open to the public. Although locale and sponsor vary, likely contacts for tickets are **Centro Organizzativo, Operativo E Panto Vendita Venezia Turismo SRL—Agenzia Viaggi Bucintoro** (San Marco 2568-30124, Venezia; tel. 521 06 32 telex 420658, fax (041)5223306; and **Venezia per Voi** (San Marco 3316, 30124 Venezia; tel. 522 60 88, fax (041)5222433). Or else try **Box Office Italia,** Via G. Verdi 34b, 37131 Venezia-Mestre; tel. 98 83 69, fax (041)950888.

As usual, Venice's interesting and beautiful old **theaters** operate during Carnival season; while we were there, Teatro a l'Avogaria in Dorsoduro even had a free production, though advance booking was required. And Teatro Toniolo, in Mestre, was doing an Italian comedy version of *Gone with the Wind*. For specific production info and schedules, see the official *Carnevale* program or other tourist-office handouts. Some numbers to call: for opera tix at Teatro la Fenice (they were doing *La Bohème* during our visit), 521 01 61; Teatro a l'Avogaria, 520 61 30; Teatro Carlo Goldoni, 52 05 422; Teatro Toniolo, 97 55 58; Teatro del Ridotto, 522 29 39. There are also nighttime events at the Casinò del Lido, on the Lido.

Late-night **gay male cruising** appears to center on bridges—under the Rialto, and also the Accademia (despite the closing of this locale's ever-popular toilets).

The best thing to do, day and night, is just to wander and watch the street theater. And, of course, buy a mask for yourself. Our all-around **fave mask shop:** Atelier Laura Scocco [Calle della Mandola 3654/A (corner of Calle Dei Assassini), 30124 Venezia; tel. 523 17 47 or 71 99 85]. The best glazes and decorations. Prices begin at about L35,000–40,000 for *naso* "bird noses," and go to L250,000–270,000 and beyond. **Best leather** (and okay cheap *bautta* spook faces): Ca'Macane [Calle Botteghe 3172 (corner of Fondamenta Rezzonico and canal)] has standouts like a super-heroic leather winged-head hawk person. The store also carries plain white—and more unusual for the price, plain painted black or red—*bautta* masks, and also velvet versions, in various colors, textures, and subtle patterns. **Most innovative/amusing** modern (nontraditional, new wave, trendy): La Mano (several branches: SS Giovanni e Paolo, Castello 6468-6469; tel. 70 02 04; Fondamenta Nove, Rio Terra dei Biri, Cannaregio 5415; tel. 70 86 43; wholesale, Calle Longa S.M. Formosa, Castello 5175; tel 29 995). Especially terrific are the eyeglass-frame masks. **Best hats:** Marzato (San Marco, Calle del Lovo 4813; tel. 522 64 54) has elephantine feathered tricornes, Venetian Carmen Miranda fruit-bowl extravaganzas, and even more elaborate creations—like a gold sequined skullcap decorated with lace net, gold lamé butterflies, and white roses. **Best complete costumes,** conceptually: MondoNovo Maschere [Dorsoduro 3036 (near Ponte dei Pugni, Rio Terra Canal), 30123 Venezia; tel. 528 73 44]. As illustrated on the official *Carnevale '86* poster *Caccadura e Caccamola* (Hard and Soft Turd), plus 1990's complete head-to-toe labia and penis suits, and other similarly original concepts.

WHERE (AND WHAT) TO EAT

The **Trattoria Madonna** (Calle della Madonna 594, near the Rialto bridge; tel. 522 38 24) is well known, but that doesn't make it any less wonderful. Don't miss the *granceola* (spider crab), the seafood risotto, or the fresh garlic-flavored *piselli* (peas) in olive oil. **Antica Locanda Montin** (for address, see hotels section) is an old inn with great atmosphere and food—especially anything done *alla griglia* (grilled), like the *coda di rospo* (angler fish), *triglia* (red mullet), or any veggies; as well as the Venetian specialty *fégato alla Venezia* (quickly-cooked calf's liver with lengthily-sautéed onions and grilled polenta). There's a large outdoor garden in a grape arbor, for nice-weather dining. **Al Graspo de Ua** (Calle dei Bombaseri 5094; tel. 522 36 47) is spoken of by many gourmets in the same breath as Harry's Bar, but Harry's bottom prices start where Al Graspo's top ones leave off. (Go to Harry's only for a Bellini—white peaches and sparkling wine—if it's peach season; the food's good, but not worth the inflated prices.) We particularly like, especially on nice days when one can sit in the beautiful outdoor court, **Restaurant Columbo** [San Marco 4619-20 (off Corte Teatro, half a block from Fond. del Carbon near the Rialto); tel. 522 26 27 or 523 74 98]. It's expensive but has the most flavorfully-sauced spaghetti *alle vongole* in town. For very good, crispy, thin-crusted wood-oven pizzas, with nouvelle-y toppings, and giant carafes of wine, though pretty lame main dishes: **Antica Capon,** on Piazza San Margherita.

With meals, it's generally just as well to drink *un litro* (or *mezzo litro* for Spartans) of house wine, as many wines from the region are fine but few outstanding. Several that it's worth spending a little extra to try are the rather intense 1988 Chardonnay from Maculan, in the Veneto just inland of Venice, which has an almond-and-clove-ish spiciness; and the underrated, but quite nicely dry, Prosecco Carpene-Malvoti sparkling wine which Harry's uses in its Bellinis.

For fast food, a *paninoteca* (ready-made sandwich joint) we particularly like for *tramezzini* (triangular half-sandwiches on white bread with the crusts cut off) is at 1186 Dorsoduro. The sautéed-mushroom models with sliced *uova* (eggs) or *prosciutto* (ham, cooked unless called *crudo*) are terrific, especially with a glass of this place's wines on tap. For great, greasy *porchetta* (roast suckling pig) *panini,* the meat-eater of us highly recommends the fabulous little hole-in-the-wall at 4186 Cannareggio, on the Strada Nova.

WHERE TO GET THE LATEST DIRT
(INFORMATION RESOURCES)

For Venice

Closest thing to a gay organization is Venice's **ARCI** (Associazione Ricreativa Culturale Italiana) branch, which has one fellow in charge of gay stuff. If you speak Italian, Giuseppe Tasca can be reached c/o ARCI's **Sede Provinciale,** 2 via Olivi, Mestre; tel. 9836 53; or after 6 P.M. (or sometimes 8 or 9 P.M., this being Italy) at his *consultorio* office in Venice, tel. 524 21 21.

Venice's tourist office, the **Azienda di Promozione Turistica Venezia** (APT), has an office under the arcade on the side opposite the cathedral; it's open Mon.–Sat. 9 A.M.–2 P.M. (tel. 522 63 56). Another office with accommodations-finding service, is open 8:30 A.M.–9 P.M. in the train station (tel. 71 50 16).

Summer visitors to Venice might be interested in the Veneto and other northern Italian regional information we've included under "Other Gay-Popular Italian Beach Resorts" in the "Practical Information, Capri" section.

For All Italy

Babilonia (via Ebro 11, 20141 Milano; or, for mail-order subscriptions and copies, P.O. Box 11224-20110 Milano; tel. 02/569 64 68 or 564 47 88; fax 02 55213419), the Italian gay magazine, is not English-language; nor does it carry gay listings. But a number of the ads it runs for gay establishments are easy for non–Italian speakers to understand. *Babilonia* is sold at most newsstands in Italy, except in the traditional and provincial "deep South," where there are difficulties with distribution.

Italia Gay is the best multilocale Italian guide. Bilingual Italian/English, it carries much the same name/address/two-word "description" info as *Spartacus,* down to the same typos in some cases, but is much less expensive and a whole lot smaller and easier to carry around. It also lists stuff like cruising/meeting places in many smaller towns and cities with no organized gay life, which the American-published gay guides don't.

Most of Italy's relatively small amount of organized and/or open, identifiable gay life is not in the resort areas and tourist-oriented towns (even those that attract many gay visitors), but in major cities. Contacts in these places are the most reliable sources for word-of-mouth info on the rest of this country of masks.

In Turin

Angelo Pezzana's bookstore is **Luxemburg Libreria Internationale,** via Cesare Battisti 7, 10123 Torino; tel. 011/53 20 07.

Fondazione Sandro Penna, via Accademia della Scienze 1, 10123 Torino; tel. 011/54 03 70. Not a bar hotline by any means! But in pursuit of their historical and cultural research on homosexuality they maintain contacts with, and therefore have addresses for, gay groups and individuals throughout Italy.

An Italian gay travel agency that, among its other services, books the snazzier classes of gay hotels in Italy and throughout Europe, is **Lion's Travel Club,** via dei Mercanti 18, Torino; tel. 011/54 07 90. Their service is essentially by telephone, not walk-in.

In Rome

A knockout-gorgeous hotel that advertises in gay press is **Hotel Scalinata di Spagna** (Piazza Trinità dei Monti 17, Roma 00187; tel. 06/679 30 06; fax 684 08 96), right at the top of the Spanish steps.

CLI (Collegamento Lesbiche Italiane, via San Francesca di Sales 1/A, 00165 Roma; tel. 06/656 42 01) is an autonomous lesbian-separatist group in Rome, which women travelers might want to contact for information on the scene there and elsewhere in Italy. (They have an "Agendonna" list of women's info sources throughout the country.)

For **gay info**, call Circolo Culturale Mario Mieli (tel. 06/73 32 27).

The **lesbian info line** is: 055/24 03 84, Wed. and Sat., 8:30 P.M.–10:30 P.M.

A friendly women's bookshop where you can get information on the local scene (from a bulletin board as well as orally) is **Al Tempo Ritrovato** (Piazza Farnese 103; tel. 654 37 49).

An elegant disco with mostly gay men, but a few lesbians, is **Easy Going** (via della Purificazione 9; tel. 06/474 55 78). Another mostly male disco/restaurant where lesbians are welcome is **L'Alibi** (via di Monte Testaccio 44; tel. 06/575 34 48).

In Milan

The **gay community center** is at via Torricelli 19; tel. 839 46 04. The center has a **gay guide to Milan** translated into English.

The well-known **Libreria Babele** gay bookshop is at via Sammartini 23, 21025 Milano; tel. 02/669 29 85.

In Florence

The **lesbian info line:** 055/24 03 84, Wed. and Sat., 8:00 P.M.–10:30 P.M.

For men only, good places to start your inquiries into the gay scene are the disco **Tabasco** (piazza S. Cecilia 3r) and the heavy-duty backroom **Crisco Club** (via s. Egidio 43r).

Other Cities

To contact the national office of **ARCI-Gay:** Direzione Nazionale, 40123 Bologna, P.O. Box 691, Bologna Centro Bo; tel. 051/43 67 00 or 43 33 95. In **Genoa, ARCI-Gay's info line** is: 010/28 14 30 (Tues. and Thurs., 4:30 P.M.–7 P.M.); the address is via Sottoripa 1/B.

WHAT TO READ

Death in Venice, by Thomas Mann (various editions). The classic: When vacationing in Venice causes a dignified middle-aged German fellow to discover his true nature, he makes a fool of himself over a pretty young boy, gets a silly hairdo, catches the plague, and dies.

The Passion, by Jeanette Winterson (Vintage). A fanciful, wonderful novel about a straight man who deserts his post as Napoleon's official chicken-plucker, the web-footed cross-dressing Venetian gondolier's daughter he loves, and the married lady *she* loves.

OTHER RECOMMENDED EUROPEAN
CARNIVALS

The Venice Carnival is the *bambino* of European Mardi Gras celebrations. Although its roots are medieval, eighteenth-century Venetian yuppies considered the whole thing a waste of good business hours, and discontinued it. It was only reinstituted in 1979, as a tourist draw. There are older festivals elsewhere in Italy, Spain, Portugal, Austria and Belgium; a famous winter Carnival in Nice, and huge seasonal celebrations throughout the Rhineland areas of southern Germany, where the event is known as *Fasching*, and western Switzerland, where it's called *Fastnacht*.

Sitges is probably Europe's gayest Carnival destination. Official town tourist literature actually brags with pride about our presence: "It is a celebration that welcomes people from all over the world, the most outstanding being the gay community." In Sitges, work begins the day after Christmas on Carnival gowns often costing several hundred dollars. This is serious gay business. In recent years, a Sitgean restaurant owner assured us, one fellow even ended up in the local hospital with a nervous breakdown, when his velour somehow got cut on an improper bias. Some gowns are so voluminous that their wearers are actually unable to fit through the doors of the town's gay bars.

For full particulars, see the "Practical Information" section of our Sitges chapter. We might add that Sitges is also a great destination for last-minute planners; according to gay hoteliers, a month in advance—sometimes less—is early enough for reservations.

In **Belgium** the address for the Carnival/mask museum is: Musée International du Carnival et du Masque, rue de l'Eglise 71, 7130 Binche; tel. 064/33 57 41. It's two blocks from Binche's Grand Place. Binche itself has a famous Carnival that's been celebrated without interruption since the fourteenth century. The biggest dress-up days for gay people are the "Carnival Sunday" before Shrove Tuesday, when there's a parade and many guys dress in drag, and Tuesday night after the all-day processions of Binche's "Gilles," who are too weird to explain. (Well, okay. They wear Emerald-City-of-Oz sunglasses and big fuzzy hats, and they throw oranges. Although the origins of this costume are unclear, some historians have speculated that the design, which dates back at least 400–500 years, is an attempted portrayal of American Indians. Got it?) Carnival is celebrated in other Belgian cities, too, **Ostend** being especially famous for its annual Carnival "Dead Rat Ball." None of these celebrations is especially gay. A number of **Brussels** gay bars, however, have Mardi Gras parties.

In **Germany** there is a particularly large celebration in **Cologne**, featuring savage parodies of politicians (finally! a place to break out our old Skijump-Nose Tricky Dick masks!), as well as a special Women's Carnival with clown processions on the Thursday before Shrove Tuesday. Cologne has lots of gay facilities, many of them pleasantly centered in the Old Town. For gay books and info, hit the English-speaking **Lavendelschwert Buchladen** at Bayardsgaße 3 (located behind the city library, near Neumarkt; tel. 0221/23 26 26).

Switzerland's three-day *Fastnacht*, celebrated in many of the country's major cities, is not particularly known as a gay holiday. But it's very amusing and more political than Southern European carnivals. As in Germany, there are lots of costumes satirizing people and events in the news over the past year; the Gorbachevs and the entire British royal family are favorites, as are more local politicians. Doubtless some travelers would also appreciate the ancient pagan-rooted Swiss festival's complete and deliberate nonassociation with any Christian rituals: Even the dates of *Fastnacht* (from the Monday after Ash Wednesday through way past midnight on Wednesday) are deliberately scheduled after the beginning of Lent. Plus, of course, "the thing for some gays always is to be costumed in the opposite sex for the three days!" according to P. Thommen, manager of **Basel's** wonderful **Arcados** gay bookstore (Rheingasse 63–69, CH 4002, Basel). **Basel's** *Fastnacht* is the country's most famous, and if you go there, Arcados can fill you in all the town's gay establishments. In fact, they publish a helpful, free monthly newsmagazine, *Come Out*—in German, but the plentiful bar/restaurant info is easily understood. As for Venice *Carnevale*, it's a good idea to make Swiss *Fastnacht* hotel reservations for your gay children now, before they're born. Well, the sooner the better. A quaint gay-owned (and "gay-minded" according to the charming owner, Claude) mixed hotel, with a nongay but gay-friendly bar downstairs, is the moderately priced 16-room **White Horse Hotel** (Webergasse 23, 4058 Basel, Switzerland; tel. 061/691 57 57).

Many other Swiss cities also have *Fastnacht* celebrations. The Zurich version, which one of us once attended, features rival identically-costumed affinity groups that march through the old town all night, belting out tunes like "Lady of Spain" on kazoos and washboards. The city also has a number of gay facilities. **SOH** (Schweizerische Organisation der Homosexuellen) (Postfach 4580, CH-8022 Zürich; tel. 01/271 70 11) has a Sunday brunch at the center at Sihlquai 67, to which gay and lesbian travelers are invited. SOH also sponsors other special events, and can give visitors info. **Frauenbuchladen** (Gerechtigkeitsgasse 6, CH-8002 Zürich; tel. 01/202 62 74) is a cordial, very well stocked feminist bookstore in an old town house, with a bulletin board and address file for women's vacation houses, helplines, and other lesbian services all over Europe. The name of the street the bookstore is on, by the way, means "justice."

And finally, Connie from Zurich's **Frauenzentrum** (Mattengasse 27, Zurich 8005; tel. 01/272 85 03) recommends, instead of her own city, smaller and far more Alpine-picturesque **Lucerne** for *Fastnacht*. "You can get into a trance dancing the whole night long to the drums!"

ABOUT THE AUTHORS

LINDSY VAN GELDER is a former newspaper reporter whose work has also appeared in *Ms., New York Woman, Town & Country, European Travel & Life, Connoisseur, PC, Omni, New York,* and numerous other magazines. She was a semifinalist in NASA's Journalist in Space competition and has been listed in *Who's Who of Emerging Leaders in America* and *Who's Who of American Women.*

PAMELA ROBIN BRANDT has written for *Rolling Stone, McCall's,* the *New York Daily News Magazine, Student Traveler,* and other publications. She also plays electric bass, was a member of the pioneering women's rock band Deadly Nightshade, and has appeared as both a performer and songwriter on *Sesame Street.*

They have been "together" since 1978.